*(Please turn the page
for more extraordinary acclaim . . .)*

JOHN HUBNER is a reporter for the *San Jose
Mercury News*.LINDSEY GRUSON is the El Sal-
vador bureau chief for *The New York Times*. They
have covered the Hare Krishna movement separately for their respective papers and jointly for
Rolling Stone.

"The progress from sanctity to savagery is traced meticulously and matter-of-factly, and the efforts of sincere members of ISKON to reform and cleanse their faith are presented with great sympathy."

—*Bookbeat*

"AN EXCITING STORY OF GOOD BECOMING EVIL."

—*Monterey Sunday Herald*

"FASCINATING . . . terrifying facts are presented to make anyone think more than twice about joining any type of cult."

—*Weekend*

MURDER, MADNESS, AND THE HARE KRISHNAS

John Hubner
and Lindsey Gruson

AN ONYX BOOK

*For Jill
and Jane*

Published by the Penguin Group
Penguin Books USA Inc., 375 Hudson Street,
New York, New York 10014, U.S.A.
Penguin Books Ltd, 27 Wrights Lane,
London W8 T5Z,England
Penguin Books Australia Ltd, Ringwood,
Victoria, Australia
Penguin Books Canada, 2801 John Street,
Markham, Ontario, Canada L3R 1B4
Penguin Books (N.Z.) Ltd , 182–190 Wairau Road,
Auckland 10, New Zealand

Penguin Books Ltd, Registered Offices:
Harmondsworth, Middlesex, England

First Onyx Printing, April, 1990
10 9 8 7 6 5 4 3 2 1

The accounts of the Chuck St. Denis murder in the chapter entitled "The
Planting Party" and the Steve Bryant murder in the chapter entitled "Monkey
on a Stick" appeared in the authors' article, "Dial Om for Murder,"
Rolling Stone, April 9, 1987.

Published by arrangement with Harcourt Brace Jovanovich, Publishers.

 REGISTERED TRADEMARK—MARCA REGISTRADA

PRINTED IN THE UNITED STATES OF AMERICA

Contents

Author's Note on Methodology   xi

Prologue   xiii

Krishna Names   xvii

1: BLOOD FEUD

The Planting Party   3

Dig a Hole   22

2: BLIND FAITH

The Messiah and the Mott Street Gang   47

Drop Out, Fall In, Sing Out   66

Ambitious Pupil   81

3: WINDS OF WAR

A Guru Defects, the Beatles Enlist   95

The Pretender's Throne   112

Clouds of Change   128

Stocking God's Treasury   149

4: THE PRIMROSE PATH

Marriage and Murder Made in Godhead   167
Conning for Krishna   185
Krishna's Mules   206
The Chosen   216

5: CHAOS

Plundering the Legacy   223
Hansadutta: Secretary for God   231
Krishna's Arsenal   248
Sex, Pigs, and Husbands   269

6: SHADOWS OF TERROR

Black and Blue   291
A Fork in the Path   302
A Messianic Mission   315
Jonestown in Moundsville   329

7: HOLY WAR

Monkey on a Stick   343
The Executioner's Trail   349
Revenge from the Grave   359

8: GHOSTS

Sex Is Sex   371
Expecting the Barbarians   379
Going Fishing   384
Epilogue   393

Notes   401
Acknowledgments   448
Index   451

Author's Note on Methodology

This book is based on hundreds of hours of taped interviews with present and former devotees, hundreds of newspaper stories and magazine articles, and thousands of pages of trial transcripts. For two years, the authors have had unprecedented access to the movement's internal documents and have benefited from the close cooperation of federal, state, and local law-enforcement officials.

Most of the scenes depicted in this book are taken directly from the recollections of eyewitnesses and participants as recounted in interviews and trial transcripts. In addition, while conducting interviews and going through documents, the authors strove to discover what players in the drama were thinking and feeling. Dialogue, thoughts, and feelings have been re-created based on this research in an attempt to establish the essence of what occurred. In a few instances, the authors have created dramatizations based on their analysis of the participants' personalities and on subsequent events. These instances are pointed out in the Notes.

Of the scores of people the reader will encounter in this book, five are portrayed with pseudonyms to protect their privacy, and two are composite characters. These are also pointed out in the Notes.

In general, the reader is encouraged to consult the supplementary information and documentation offered in the back of the book.

Prologue

In the sixties, all things seemed possible. Flower power was going to end the war in Vietnam; rock and roll was going to liberate our uptight culture. And a religious movement started by an obscure Hindu mendicant was going to fulfill an Arnold Toynbee prophecy: that centuries from now, historians would see the fusion of Eastern and Western religions—not the development of the atom bomb or the battle between capitalism and communism—as the critical event of the midtwentieth century.

The synthesis would begin when A.C. Bhaktivedanta Swami Prabhupada arrived in New York City in 1965 carrying seven dollars in rupees, the phone number of the son of a friend, and a few battered cooking utensils. When Prabhupada died in Vrindaban, India, in 1977, the International Society for Krishna Consciousness, or ISKCON, the movement he started in a New York storefront, had over two hundred temples and farms in sixty countries, tens of thousands of followers, and tens of millions of dollars. In the United States alone, ISKCON had fifty-seven temples and farms, more than five thousand devotees, and thousands of uninitiated believers.

Once grasped, the basic tenets of Krishna Consciousness are surprisingly simple. Man is not his body; he is an eternal spirit. The body goes through countless incarnations; the eternal spirit that is buried deep within us is unchanging and everpresent. Christians call it the soul; Krishna Consciousness calls it the *atman*.

The purpose of life is to become one with the atman. This is harder than it sounds and usually takes many, many lifetimes. To reach the atman, we must defeat the ego. The ego would have us think that life is about accumulating money, exercising power and satisfying the senses' unquenchable desires for sex, food, and countless luxuries. But the ego can be defeated and the atman uncovered by dedicating every action to God. "Whatever you do, make it an offering to me—the food you eat, the sacrifices you make, the help you give, even your suffering," Krishna tells Arjuna in Chapter Nine of the *Bhagavad-Gita*. To assure that every action is dedicated to God, devotees chant the names of the Lord. When they chant the Hare Krishna mantra ("Hare Krishna, Hare Krishna, Krishna, Krishna, Hare, Hare; Hare Rama, Hare Rama, Rama, Rama, Hare, Hare"), devotees believe that God is literally present on their lips.

Krishna is a personal God, like the Jewish Yahweh and the Christian God. But part of Krishna Consciousness' great appeal is that Krishna was a fun-loving, beautiful blue boy, not a wrathful Jehovah. And, in the sixties and seventies, Krishna Consciousness was exotic, it was new, it was fresh, it was from India, home of the Vedic scriptures, the world's oldest revealed scriptures.

It was also hard work. Many of the Catholics who joined the movement had decided the sin-confess-sin-confess cycle was meaningless; many of the Jews had decided that their synagogue was more of a social center than a holy place; many of the Protestants thought that the confirmation process in their churches was so easy, it was a joke. Krishna devotees were united by the belief that finding God is the hardest work you can do. They relished the opportunity to spread their new faith by chanting and begging for alms in public places.

Some of the new devotees were spiritual people, genuinely dedicated to serving Krishna. Others were stoned-out hippies from troubled homes who had never had much to believe in. Heirs to fortunes, M.D.'s, and M.B.A.'s joined street people who had dropped out of high school. They shaved their heads and put on robes; they handed out literature and solicited money on street corners and in airports; they opened vegetarian restaurants and temples in major cities. They became part of the American scene, a bridge between East and West.

"The fact that there is now in the West a vigorous,

disciplined, and seemingly well-organized [religious] movement—not merely a philosophical movement or a yoga or meditation movement . . . is a stunning accomplishment," said Harvey Cox, a Harvard divinity professor. "The more I came to know about the movement, the more I came to find out there was a striking similarity between what [Prabhupada] was saying and my understanding of the original core of Christianity: Live simply; do not try to accumulate worldly goods or profit; live with compassion toward all creatures; live joyfully. . . . When I say [Prabhupada was] 'one in a million,' I think that is in some ways an underestimate. Perhaps he was one in a hundred million."

In the beginning, the movement attracted thousands of people. For some, Krishna Consciousness provided an opportunity to leave competitive America and follow a spiritual path. For others, the movement offered a family far more stable than the ones they had been raised in, and a highly structured refuge from the hedonism of the sixties. Krishna Consciousness embodies the wisdom of Eastern religions; it has much to offer America. Even today, there are hundreds of sincere, gentle devotees who are chanting Hare Krishna in countries around the world.

The gurus who succeeded Prabhupada theoretically accepted the premise that to find God, the ego must be defeated. And yet with few exceptions they had huge egos. Religious scholars say that a crisis occurs when the charismatic leader of a new religious movement dies. The success or failure of the movement depends upon how the successors spread the teachings of the founder. To a large degree, Krishna Consciousness is in shambles because too many gurus did not want to spread Prabhupada's teachings; they wanted to *be* Prabhupada. Because of that, the Hare Krishna movement degenerated into a number of competing cults that have known murder, the abuse of women and children, drug dealing, and swindles that would impress a Mafia don.

Since 1987, reformers in the movement have worked to purge ISKCON of the horrors portrayed in this book.

They hope to restore the spiritually powerful principles on which the movement was founded.

But this is the story of how the destructive metamorphosis happened; of how good became evil; of how gurus claiming to embody Krishna's mercy behaved with no mercy. And no power, as we will discover, corrupts as absolutely as fanatical religious power.

Krishna Names

Advaita: Emile Sofsky, aka John Jenkins; allegedly established and supervised a smuggling ring that brought hash oil from India and Pakistan to the United States.

Ambudrara: Debra Gere; common-law wife of Charles St. Denis, the murdered New Vrindaban "fringie" and marijuana dealer.

Atreya Rishi: ISKCON GBC member who became locked in a struggle with Keith Ham (Kirtanananda) and Hans Kary (Hansadutta) for control of the Berkeley temple.

Bahudaka: Peter Chatterton, president of the Vancouver temple; Krishna reformist.

Balimardan: President of New York temple expelled by Prabhupada.

Bhagavan: William Ehrlichman, ISKCON guru overseeing the European temples, whose imperious governing style and fondness for luxury earned him the nickname "The Sun King."

Bhaktisiddhanta: The Indian guru who converted Prabhupada to Krishna Consciousness in 1922.

Bhavananda: Charles Backus, ISKCON guru overseeing the Australian temples, excommunicated for improprieties.

Brahmananda: Bruce Scharf, president of ISKCON's first temple, at 26 Second Avenue in New York City.

Chakradara: Charles St. Denis, New Vrindaban "fringie" and marijuana dealer murdered by Thomas Drescher and Dan Reid.

Chitta: Cynthia, second wife of Steven Hebel.

Darpada: Ronald Roy Walters, gunsmith and weapons procurer for the Berkeley temple; held three federal firearms licenses.

Daruka: Dan Reid, New Vrindaban devotee accomplice of Thomas Drescher (Tirtha) in the murder of Charles St. Denis (Chakradara).

Dharmaraja: Devin Wheeler, son of Howard Wheeler (Hayagriva); also known as Samba; as a child, the constant companion of Keith Ham (Kirtanananda).

Dharmatma: Dennis Gorrick, leader of the New Vrindaban women's sankirtan team.

Goverdhan: Michael Pugliese, aka Dino Bhandu, aka Lance Presley; Hansadutta's driver and personal servant in Berkeley.

Guru Kripa: Gregory Gottfried, president of the Tokyo temple; leader of sankirtan team operating in Japan.

Hansadutta: Hans Kary, ISKCON guru residing at the Berkeley temple, who mixed Krishna Consciousness with rock and roll, guns, and paranoia.

Harikesa: ISKCON guru; one of the eleven rtvik acharyas who succeeded Prabhupada.

Hayagriva: Howard Wheeler, close friend of Keith Ham (Kirtanananda) and early Krishna devotee; chronicler of the early years of the Krishna movement.

Himavati: Helena, wife of Hans Kary (Hansadutta).

Jadurani: Judy Koslofsky, the first brahmacharini (unmarried female) to join ISKCON; beaten up at New Vrindaban for questioning Kirtanananda's status as a guru.

Jamuna: Jane, wife of Steve Bryant (Sulocana); later married Ralph Seward.

Jayatirtha: James Immel, London guru who mixed LSD with chanting Hare Krishna; expelled from ISKCON; started his own movement under the name of Tirthapada; decapitated by one of his followers.

Jitendriya: Patrick Manning, New Vrindaban treasurer.

Jiva: James Underwood, ex-convict, head of Berkeley women's sankirtan team; supervised the "radio scam."

Kanka: Susan, first wife of Steven Hebel (Swarup); star member of the New Vrindaban women's sankirtan team before fleeing the commune with her children.

Kirtanananda: Keith Ham, His Divine Grace, Kirtanananda Swami Bhaktipada; early Krishna devotee, guru, founder of New Vrindaban temple.

Krishna Das: Rinnian, son of Jane Bryant and her former boyfriend John Morgan.

Kuladri: Arthur Villa, president of the New Vrindaban temple; Kirtanananda's right-hand man.

Mahaprabhu: Lord Chaitanya (1485–1533), founder of bhakti yoga and Krishna Consciousness.

Mahara: Mary St. John, wife of Thomas Meyers (Taru).

Mukunda: Michael Grant, former jazz musician and early devotee of Prabhupada, who opened the San Francisco temple; now ISKCON's director of public relations.

Naranayana: Nathan Zakheim, early ISKCON member; a carpenter who helped build temples across America.

Nataipada: Former ISKCON devotee who joined Jayatirtha-Tirthapada's splinter group in Nepal; allegedly murdered after threatening to expose the group's use of LSD.

Navaniticara: John Tierney, member of Jayatirtha-Tirthapada's splinter group accused of decapitating his spiritual master in London.

Nimai: Son of Steve Bryant (Sulocana); drowned in a man-made lake at New Vrindaban.

Nistrigunya: Steve Forbes, longtime friend of Steve Bryant (Sulocana).

Prabhupada: His Divine Grace A. C. Bhaktivedanta Swami Prabhupada, founder of the International Society for Krishna Consciousness, ISKCON.

Prithu: Peter Brinkmann, president of the Belfast temple.

Radheya: Son of Charles St. Denis; suffocated with Rohini in an abandoned refrigerator at New Vrindaban.

Ramesvara: Robert Grant, ISKCON guru residing at the Los Angeles temple; president of the Bhaktivedanta Book Trust (BBT).

Rashadeva: Roy Christopher Richard, president of the Laguna Beach Temple, and drug runner.

Ravindra Svarupa: William Deadwyler, president of the Philadelphia temple; leader of the ISKCON reform movement.

Rohini: Son of Dan and Brenda Reid; suffocated with Radheya in an abandoned refrigerator at New Vrindaban.

Samba: Devin Wheeler, son of Howard Wheeler (Hayagriva); also known as Dharmaraja.

Sarva Dharma: Son of Steve Bryant (Sulocana).

Satsvarupa: Former ISKCON guru; author of six-volume biography of Prabhupada.

Sri Galima: Larry Gardner, former headmaster of the boys' guru kula at New Vrindaban; wanted by police for sexually molesting his students.

Sulocana: Steve Bryant, a New Vrindaban devotee who challenged the authority of Keith Ham (Kirtanananda) and sought to expose illegal activities at New Vrindaban; murdered in 1986.

Swarup: Steven Hebel, an early ISKCON devotee, married to Susan (Kanka) then Cynthia (Chitta); later became a drug runner.

Syamasundara: One of six devotees Prabhupada sent to London in 1968 to open a temple; became friendly with George Harrison of the Beatles.

Tamal Krishna: Thomas Hertzog, GBC member; became one of the eleven rtvik acharyas after Prabhupada's death.

Tapahpunja: Terry Sheldon; succeeded Kuladri as Kirtanananda's right-hand man, and former president of the Cleveland temple.

Taru: Thomas Meyers, an intellectual New Vrindaban devotee, who disappeared during the winter of 1980 and has not been seen since.

Tirtha: Thomas Drescher, New Vrindaban's enforcer; convicted murderer and drug dealer.

Triyogi: Michael Shockman, a mentally disturbed devotee who in 1985 attacked Kirtanananda with a steel spike, fracturing his skull.

Vipra: Vladimir Vassilievich, aka Vladimir Panasenko; a Berkeley devotee who built guns for Hansadutta.

Blood Feud

The Planting Party

"Chakradara, you been diggin' like a woodchuck for days," said Dan Reid, a little man with a black goatee who was straddling a big Yamaha motorcycle. "What you need is a party. Wouldn't a taste of something clean and white go good after all that dirt?"

Chakradara, Chuck St. Denis, was digging a trench, searching for a break in a water line. It was early on the morning of June 9, 1983. The sun had already cleared the West Virginia hills in the east and St. Denis's T-shirt was soaked with sweat. He looked at Reid and thought, I'll be damned!

There are few secrets in a commune. St. Denis knew that for some weeks Reid had been running around New Vrindaban, the largest Hare Krishna community in America, telling devotees that St. Denis had raped his wife, Brenda.

It was true that St. Denis had gone through the commune's supply of available women with the same rapacity he devoured ice cream, which he liked to eat with his fingers a half gallon at a time. It was true he had fathered four children by three women. It was even true that he and Brenda had once had a little thing going. But that was all in the past, a long time ago. He had quit screwing around.

He'd been faithful to Debra Gere, the commune's nurse, for almost two years, ever since he had moved out of his trailer and into hers. Debra, or Ambudrara, was the best woman he'd ever had. She was smart and tough and pretty, with dark brown eyes, pale white skin covered with light freckles, and red hair that glistened in the sun. He'd fathered her six-month-old baby girl and was

3

now working with her fourteen hours a day, trying to open a plant nursery. They were going to call it Blue Boy Nursery, after Krishna, the blue lord.

Chuck had told Debra about his previous affair and it didn't bother her. She knew that Dan Reid treated his wife like some kind of bug that had infested his life. He was always flying into red-faced rages, screaming that Brenda was fat and ugly and couldn't do a damn thing right. Brenda would run out of the house and end up sitting at a neighbor's kitchen table, sobbing. Finally, Reid had left his wife and three kids and moved into a shack up in the hills above the commune, called the Artist's Studio. That was when St. Denis had moved in on Brenda.

Debra had been wondering why Reid was spreading the rape story around now. She knew that if Chuck had not been so busy, he'd have grabbed the little jerk by the throat and asked him just what the hell he thought he was doing, spreading all that garbage around. That was how Chuck handled a problem.

"White stuff?" St. Denis asked, flashing his toothy grin. "Come on, Daruka, you don't have no coke. You've never had no coke."

"But I do," Reid said. "And if you don't show up, I'll have to do it all by myself."

Reid gave the Yamaha's throttle a couple of quick, nervous twists as St. Denis walked over to the bike and slapped him on the back. St. Denis was twenty-nine years old, six foot two, and 220 pounds, with shoulder-length brown hair and hazel eyes. Strung around his seventeen-inch neck was a "Krishna's dog collar," as devotees call the sacred *kanthi* beads. The muscles in his arms were huge, pumped up from all the digging he had been doing.

"We can't have you getting coked up alone, Daruka." St. Denis said. "I mean, what are friends for? But the thing is, we're having a planting party tonight. I had the field behind the greenhouse plowed the other day. We've got twenty flats of Shasta daisies to get in the ground. If we don't get them in soon, they'll all be dead. Everybody is gonna help. Why don't you come? You ain't been around in weeks."

"All right, I will," Reid said. "We can go up to my place afterward. Hell, who cares how late it is when you're gonna get wired?"

St. Denis flashed his big grin. "Daruka, you know all my weaknesses," he said.

"Everybody knows your weaknesses," Reid replied. "You couldn't hide them if you tried."

St. Denis laughed. Reid shifted into first gear and turned the bike around.

"Just remember, don't tell anyone," Reid said. "There isn't enough to go around."

"There's never enough to go around," St. Denis yelled as Reid rode away.

St. Denis watched Reid work the bike through the six-inch ruts in the dirt road. So, Daruka wants to be friends again, he thought. Good. We'll do a few lines; he'll bring up the Brenda thing; then we'll work it out and everything will be cool.

He picked up his shovel and went back to the trench.

Chuck and Debra were "fringies," devotees who were on the New Vrindaban equivalent of an injured-reserve list. They believed in the religion, but had not been able to follow the strict vows they took at initiation. Chuck had not been able to give up drugs or alcohol, let alone milder stimulants like coffee and tea. His close relationship with Debra had made a joke out of the ban against illicit sex: Krishnas are supposed to have sex only once a month, and only for the purpose of producing Krishna-conscious children. He had long ago forgotten the ban against eating meat, fish, eggs, or onions.

Devout Krishnas are not supposed to eat onions because they reek of the world. They do not drink tea because it stimulates the mind and disturbs the tranquillity that comes with thinking always of Krishna. Spices are banned for the same reason. Food, drink, everything devotees consume, should remind them of Krishna, not of this world.

Like Chuck, Debra found the religion too demanding to practice on an everyday basis. She was expected to rise every day with the other devotees at four in the morning, take a cold shower, and attend *Mangalaratik*, the morning devotional service at four-thirty. She also had to attend classes on sacred Hindu texts and chant sixteen rounds of the Hare Krishna *maha* ("great") mantra every day. It took almost two hours to do 1,728 repetitions of *Hare Krishna, Hare Krishna, Krishna Krishna, Hare Hare, Hare Rama, Hare Rama, Rama Rama, Hare Hare.*

Debra just couldn't make the time. The commune's only nurse, she worked twelve hours a day, seven days a week. She also had two children. She could not be a good mother, a good nurse, and a good devotee too. Besides, she liked to sit in the kitchen of the rambling farmhouse they'd moved into, put up her feet, and relax with a beer. It was a good way to end the day.

One evening in the winter of 1982, a year and a half ago, Debra had been washing the dishes and looking forward to a cold beer. Chuck had been there with her, sitting at the table nursing a Molson's. The phone had rung, but Chuck didn't move. A little annoyed, Debra had grabbed the phone without stopping to dry her hands.

"Hi, Mom. I'm glad it's you," she said a moment later. "I was starting to get a little worried. It's been a while since you called."

St. Denis gazed into his green bottle of Molson ale, half-listening to the conversation. He glanced up when he noticed Debra had stopped talking. Her mouth was hanging open. She was staring at him, but looking right through him.

"You're kidding!" Debra said softly.

St. Denis got up and walked over to her. "What's up?" he whispered.

Debra ignored him. "All right, Mom. I'm kind of too stunned to talk about it right now, anyway. You go have a good cry and we'll talk in the morning."

She hung up and sat down at the table. St. Denis dropped into a chair facing her.

"Dad's will just cleared probate," Debra said. "I'm going to get fifty thousand dollars."

From that moment on, there was only one topic of conversation in the old farmhouse: "What are we going to do with the money?"

They knew what they should do if they were good devotees: surrender it to Kirtanananda Swami Bhaktipada, the guru who had built New Vrindaban. Kirtanananda was like a god on earth; devotees dropped to the ground to offer obeisances when they saw him. They carried him on a bejeweled palanquin during Krishna ceremonies. To live in New Vrindaban was to surrender everything, body, soul, family, and bankbook to Kirtanananda. Especially bankbook.

"Money is the honey," Kirtanananda liked to say, rubbing his hands.

But fifty thousand dollars? That ain't hay. And neither Chuck nor Debra had ever had much money.

Kirtanananda had started the commune in 1968 on a rundown 130-acre farm in West Virginia's beautiful northern panhandle. Neighboring farmers, born and raised in adjoining farms, shook their heads and told one another not to worry: Those "Hairy Critters" with their shaved heads and their orange bedsheets wouldn't make it through the first winter.

They didn't. But the Hare Krishnas came back in the spring, and this time they prospered. They sent around a straw man, a local fellow named Randall Gorby, to snap up land, often at thousands of dollars an acre above market value. The farmers on McCreary's Ridge talked themselves into believing they were selling to Gorby, not to the commune, and cashed out. By 1983, the original 130 acres had grown to 2,884.

Kirtanananda named the commune after the sacred town in India where Krishna appeared as a cowherd boy to slay demons, play his flute, sing, dance, and engage in other pastimes with the *gopis,* the milkmaids. He billed it as a farming community where devotees could practice the Hare Krishna philosophy of "simple living, high thinking." In time, the simple farm grew into a massive project no more simple and spiritual than the pyramids.

Its jewel, the first temple of a planned spiritual city, is Prabhupada's Palace of Gold, named after A.C. Bhaktivedanta Swami Prabhupada, the founder of the International Society for Krishna Consciousness, or

ISKCON. Kirtanananda bills it as America's Taj Mahal, the first of seven temples in a spiritual Disneyland that will propagate Krishna Consciousness. Actually, the palace is a monument to Kirtanananda's obsession with becoming Prabhupada's successor.

When Prabhupada died in 1977, the ISKCON world divided into eleven zones. Each zone was governed by a guru who ruled his devotees by divine right, the way medieval kings ruled serfs. Kirtanananda has always condemned the division as anathema and refused to share power with the ten other gurus. "Purity must come before unity," he is fond of saying.

Kirtanananda believes that he, and he alone, has realized the eternal truths Prabhupada brought to America. Only through him can devotees understand Prabhupada's message and reach Krishna. He built the Palace of Gold to attract the followers of other gurus. Seeing the gold-crested towers shimmering in the sun and climbing the swirling red marble steps, they would stop and think, Such splendor! No one else is doing such great service for Prabhupada. I'm going to leave my guru and surrender to Kirtanananda Swami.

The gold, silver, rare jewels, and tons of exotic marble imported to build the Palace of Gold cost a staggering sum of money. Kirtanananda had a dozen ways to get it.

The guru's deep conviction that he, and he alone, had fully realized Prabhupada's message deeply impressed Chuck St. Denis. He didn't think twice when he was told to deal marijuana and turn the profits over to the temple. He was honored to perform such important service. So were many others. Devotees with Ph.D.'s in religious studies joined the Krishnas, as did lawyers, artisans, Harvard M.B.A.'s, Henry Ford's grandson, and Walter Reuther's daughter. But by far the majority of the devotees were members of the lost sixties generation, flower children and street people—kids like Chuck St. Denis, who started dealing drugs when he was eleven years old.

St. Denis came from Arcadia, California. Home of the Santa Anita racetrack, Arcadia was a town whose identity was snuffed out long ago by the great sprawl of Los

Angeles. His parents were alcoholics. His father, a bartender, had abandoned the family early; neither Chuck, nor his older sister, Chrislyn, and certainly not his younger brother, Michael, remembered him. Their mother, a cocktail waitress, had remarried several times.

Chrislyn was the nearest thing to a mother the two boys had. Every day after school, she came straight home and started cooking dinner. She did her best, but she was no match for the harsh life of the streets. By the time she was eleven, all three kids were in trouble.

With Chuck, it was grass and LSD. Then downers, reds, and Seconals. All those drugs did nothing to stunt Chuck's physical growth. At age ten he was big enough to steal his stepfather's car without any help. At thirteen he was a veteran drug dealer and running with a black street gang, whose sworn enemies were Chicanos.

A juvenile court judge finally declared Chuck incorrigible and sent him to juvenile hall. The same court packed his younger brother, Michael, off to a boys' ranch in Oregon.

When they let him out of kiddie jail, Chuck went right back to the only thing he knew: drugs and dealing. He ate huge hits of LSD and began shooting Seconal. At sixteen, he was over six feet tall, and very angry. He got into terrible fights with his brother and sister. He stole from his mother and refused to speak to his stepfather.

His attitude was, You hurt me, you owe me—gimme, gimme, gimme.

Chuck drifted away from home to join the great hippie migration along the California coast. He settled, more or less, in Santa Cruz, a beautiful coastal town that was a hippie haven when St. Denis arrived in 1969. He hung around the Santa Cruz pier, dealing drugs, soaking his brain in LSD, rapping, and getting laid.

And then he met the Krishnas.

He went away a hippie and came back in a robe with his head shaved. Chrislyn thought he'd been brainwashed, especially the way he tried to cram that religion down the family's throats. When his siblings wouldn't go to the Sunday Krishna feasts, he would get mad.

But after a while, Chrislyn realized the Krishnas were

good for Chuck. He was doing a lot of chanting, but he wasn't doing drugs. His whole life, he'd never had a job and never wanted to work. But suddenly it seemed the Krishnas had changed all that. They gave him something to live for, maybe for the first time. In return Chuck worked hard for them.

The Krishnas were the family St. Denis had never had but always wanted. They ordered the world for him; they told him when to get up and what to do until he went to sleep. Even better, they made his poverty righteous. Since he had nothing to lose, it was easy to reject the material world and live a spiritual life. Discipline for people like St. Denis, who have no self-discipline, is an all-or-nothing thing. For almost six years he was a devout follower, chanting and following the regulative principles.

His life as a Krishna monk crumbled in the mid-1970s, when he moved into the Laguna Beach temple, south of Los Angeles. There, a group of devotees that included the temple president were smuggling hash oil into the U.S. from Pakistan and Afghanistan. Most of the money was turned over to ISKCON.

The smugglers recruited St. Denis. Before long, he had moved out of the temple and into an apartment with a girlfriend. He was soon sleeping through the morning service and smoking dope instead of chanting. He was only a bit player in the drug operation, however. When the cops broke up the ring, they did not even bother to question him. St. Denis moved to New Vrindaban and was soon running marijuana to raise money for Kirtanananda's temple. He took to the new role like an avid car salesman to a new dealership and made dozens of trips from West Virginia back to the West Coast, usually returning with five or ten pounds of marijuana at a time.

"You hypocrite!" Chrislyn screamed at him one night in Los Angeles, interrupting another one of his seemingly endless sermons. "I can't believe you're sitting in my house sucking on a joint, dealing, and preaching to me about that fucker Kirtanananda the whole time. Every dime you make goes right to that psycho!"

"It belongs to my family," St. Denis said. "We need

the money to build the temple. It's a shrine. We're doing good deeds with the money. The glory of Krishna makes everything clean."

"We've done service for Kirtanananda, lots of service," Chuck told Debra every time they talked about the fifty thousand dollars. "There's no tellin' how much money I've turned over from what I've been doin'. And look at you—workin' day and night in the clinic. Do you know how much it would cost Kirtanananda to hire a nurse to come out here to replace you?"

"But Kirtanananda needs the money more than we do," Debra said. "He needs every penny. There's nothing we could do with it that's more important."

"I'm not sayin' we shouldn't do something for Kirtanananda," St. Denis said. "All I'm saying is, we should do something for ourselves, too."

The idea hit St. Denis when he walked into the living room one morning and looked around him at the plants Debra had used to decorate the place. It was an inspiration. He got so excited, he jumped in his 1973 Blazer and drove right over to the commune's makeshift clinic, where he found Debra stitching a gash in a five-year-old boy's hand. As soon as she finished, St. Denis walked her outside.

"I got it! We'll start a nursery!" he said. "We're both good with plants. We'll buy some land from Kirtanananda and do it right here. I even got the name: Blue Boy Nursery. It'll go. I know it'll go."

Debra loved the idea. There is no bad karma in watering plants and planting flowers. The nursery would enable her to phase out her nursing job and spend more time with her children.

She and Chuck talked it over and agreed that, like devotees everywhere who live and work outside the temple, they would turn 50 percent of the nursery's profits over to their guru. Kirtanananda agreed. Chuck and Debra paid him $17,500 for twenty-three acres of land. Actually, they paid $2,500, and Debra's mother gave the commune a $15,000 "donation"—a scheme designed to save the commune a few dollars in taxes.

There was one small hitch: a devotee named Thomas Drescher was building a house on their land and didn't want to move. St. Denis agreed to negotiate separately with Drescher for his house. Debra wanted Drescher's small, half-finished place because it was perfect for her mother, who was living alone in Exeter, New Hampshire. She and Chuck would build a new house next to the nursery.

After buying the land, St. Denis threw himself into the project like a madman. He drove around West Virginia's panhandle, interviewing every florist in the Moundsville-Wheeling area. He found there was a steady market for plants in Pittsburgh, eighty miles northeast of the commune, where interior decorators needed hearty tropicals for offices and homes.

Chuck also developed a side business that would ensure the success of Blue Boy Nursery. His interest in horticulture dated back to a trip he took to Garberville, California, a small logging and fishing town in Humboldt County that became the world's unofficial sinsemilla capital in the 1970s. (Sinsemilla is one of the most potent marijuana hybrids.)

While in Garberville, St. Denis had purchased two pounds of primo weed from two friendly, bearded growers. After sharing a joint to seal the deal, they drove into town to have dinner at a small health-food restaurant run by a bunch of ex-hippies. One of the growers had a master's degree in botany. With real passion, he explained how he planned to do for cannabis what grape growers had done for *Vitis vinifera*. From vinifera vines, the grower patiently explained, winemakers produce varietals like Pinot noir, Cabernet Sauvignon, and Chardonnay. He was now selecting strains of cannabis to produce different smokes—sweet, fruity, herbal, and spicy. Better yet, he claimed to have bred weed that produced distinctly different highs, highs he described poetically as sleepy, sexy, and electric.

St. Denis was fascinated. When he left the redwood empire, he took along a dozen small Ziplock plastic bags, each containing two custom-bred sinsemilla seeds that cost between five and fifteen dollars apiece.

St. Denis planted the seeds in a secret place high in the West Virginia mountains. A few plants died, but most were prospering. St. Denis figured that between selling tropicals to interior decorators and high-power smoke to his marijuana connections, Blue Boy Nursery would be a cinch.

Like most dealers, St. Denis was addicted to the big score. If he ordered enough material and bought enough plants, if he kept hammering away at the 250-foot-long greenhouse, he thought the nursery would come together in a flash, just like a dope deal.

When the nursery was half finished, St. Denis borrowed a truck and shot down to Florida to buy tropical plants. He took along Dr. Nick Tsacrios, a short, intense Florida native who had settled in New Vrindaban to run the commune's clinic and live with the fringies. They had just crossed the Georgia state line on their way home when the plywood frames in the back of the overloaded truck collapsed, crushing thousands of dollars' worth of plants.

"Chuck, man, you're way overzealous," Dr. Nick said. "You want everything to happen at once. Slow down. Start small and build."

"You worry about fixin' up people—I'll worry about gettin' plants to grow," St. Denis snapped. He slammed the truck's rear doors shut and stomped back to the cab.

Dan Reid hurried up the stairs to Kirtanananda's office; it was in a converted barn next to the Temple of Understanding. Although St. Denis's friends had assured Reid that St. Denis had never raped his wife, Reid was certain he had. Brenda had described it all in detail.

"Hare Krishna," Reid said when he walked into Kirtanananda's office. Then he stopped in his tracks to offer the required obeisances. He kneeled, laid his palms flat, and touched his forehead to the floor. He got up, faced the guru, and got right to the point.

"Chakradara raped my wife," he told Kirtanananda. "I want to kill him."

The guru was fond of saying, "Not a blade of grass blows in the wind at New Vrindaban without me knowing about it." He knew about St. Denis's affair with Brenda Reid. He did not know about the rape and questioned Reid carefully.

"I thought Chakradara was too wrapped up with Ambudrara and the nursery to do anything like that," Kirtanananda said.

"That's what I thought," Reid replied. "When I heard what had happned, I didn't believe it, so I went and asked Brenda. She said yes, it had happened. Not only that, it happened only a few weeks after she had the kid. The guy's an animal; he hurt her bad."

The guru was silent for a moment.

"So who's gonna care?" he said finally. "Maybe you should go talk to Drescher about this."

Reid drew in a deep breath. He was hoping Kirtanananda would say something like that.

Kirtanananda may not have cared about the rape; he did care that St. Denis and Debra Gere had not turned her inheritance over to him. He needed every penny he could get his hands on to build Krishna's American playground; if devotees started keeping their money instead of giving it to their spiritual master, New Vrindaban's raison d'être would be destroyed and chaos would ensue.

When Prabhupada, the Krishnas' founder, had to kick a devotee out of the movement for doing something especially bad, like embezzling money, he would refer to the Indian parable of the monkey on a stick. "Let him be the monkey on a stick and let us have no more of that," he would say.

When a monkey breaks into a banana plantation in India, the farm's owners kill the monkey, impale him on a stick, and leave him to rot outside the plantation. Other monkeys see him hanging there and stay away from the bananas.

Chuck St. Denis would be the monkey on a stick.

Dan Reid thanked the swami, left, jumped on his Yamaha, and rode straight to Tirtha, Thomas Drescher, the commune's enforcer.

"You're kidding!" Drescher said when Reid told him the story. 'Kirtanananda sent you to me? He really said,

'Go tell Tirtha'? Take me through it again; I wanna hear *exactly* what he said.''

Reid repeated his story.

"All right," Drescher said. "I'll do it. I take it as an order from the swami to help you."

At first glance, Drescher looks like the manager of a Denny's restaurant, with short, neatly trimmed blond hair and a bland face that would be expressionless if his lips weren't pursed in a perpetual pout. But a closer look reveals a cold, steely gaze behind the brown-tinted glasses. Tattoos run up his forearms.

Drescher grew up in foster homes and juvenile detention centers in Buffalo, New York. At eighteen, he enlisted in the Army and was shipped to Vietnam with the "blood-and-guts" 101st Airborne. Drescher returned to the States in 1972 and joined the Krishnas. He told gory stories about his time in 'Nam with relish and bragged about all the "gooks" he had killed.

When he came to New Vrindaban in the mid-1970's, his first jobs were driving a bus around the commune and guarding the palace. He drove the bus as if it were an Army jeep. A pregnant devotee remembers that every time she got on the bus, Drescher would floor the gas pedal, then slam on the brakes. Then he would look in the mirror and give her a big grin. One time she fell. Drescher laughed and laughed.

By 1977, he'd been promoted to commune enforcer, a position that combined the roles of cop and goon. He spent hours every day firing a .45 on a range hidden deep in the hills. When Kirtanananda wanted people thrown out of the commune, Drescher drove them to Highway 250 and dumped them beside the road.

The day after talking to Drescher, Reid was lying in bed in his studio, drifting in and out of a late-afternoon nap. When he heard a truck straining to climb the steep hill, he groaned and lifted himself up on one elbow to look out the window. It was Drescher's white pickup. Reid jumped out of bed and ran to meet Drescher outside the shack.

"We're gonna do it," Drescher said. "I got it all figured out."

The two went inside the shack and sat down. Drescher took Reid through it one step at a time. Reid's job was to lure St. Denis to the Artist's Studio.

"Tell him you got some coke" Drescher said. "He'll be sure to come when he hears that."

"I'll do it," Reid said.

"And get yourself a gun," Drescher said.

Fear that the *karmis*—meat-eating Westerners—would someday attack the commune had turned New Vrindaban into an armed camp. The commune had had a number of armorers over the years, beginning with Eugene Braeger, who had built an arsenal of AR-15's, Mini-14's, .45's and nine-millimeters. Braeger was succeeded by Keith Weber and Todd Schenker, two survivalists who liked to walk around New Vrindaban dressed in camouflage, as if they had just stepped out of an ad in *Soldier of Fortune* magazine.

"It's all gonna happen right in the Artist's Studio," Drescher told Reid. "We can't be bringing cannons in here. We'll blow holes in the walls. We need small caliber weapons. There's a twenty-two in the treasury where you work. *Borrow* it. Nobody will miss it. You ain't gonna have it long."

"I'll do it," Reid said.

"First thing tomorrow, you go find him," Drescher continued. "Set up a time when he's gonna come up here. As soon as that's done, come over to my place and let me know. We'll take it from there."

Reid nodded.

Drescher left and drove half a mile down an old logging road to a small stream. He got out of the truck and walked up and down the stream looking for a place where the water flowed evenly and not too quickly.

He found it and started throwing the biggest rocks he could lift into the stream. When there was a big pile, he took off his shoes, waded into the shallow water, and built a crude dam by plugging the cracks in the rocks with mud. When the water flow was reduced to a trickle, Drescher returned to the truck and got his shovel. Directly below the dam, he dug a shallow grave in what had been the middle of the stream.

*   *   *

"You guys better be ready to work, 'cause I'm a monster with this thing!" St. Denis told the fringies gathered for the planting party. He was standing beside the greenhouse, waving a hole puncher in the air. Everyone but Dan Reid laughed. Standing alone at the edge of the group, he forced a smile.

"Here's the way we do it: I go ahead punchin' the holes; you guys come along behind, plantin' the daisies. If you even come close to keepin' up with me, we'll be done by sunset."

"If I know you, you'll sneak back here and get into the beer and pizza while we're out there, slavin' away," teased Kurt Cleaver, St. Denis's best friend.

St. Denis raised the hole puncher like it was a baseball bat and threatened to chase Cleaver.

"Watch me burn out there," he said. "We'll have this baby knocked off in no time."

It was a perfect spring evening. The leaves on the maples, elms, birches, and oaks on the hillsides were a lush green. Swallows, diving over a nearby pond, did aerial acrobatics as they took insects.

St. Denis was as good as his word, punching row after row of holes while the fringies, on hands and knees, crawled along behind, putting daisies in the ground and covering the roots with soil. It was after dark when they finished and went over to Kurt and Janet Cleaver's house to pop open beers and dig into vegetarian pizzas. Every fifteen minutes or so, St. Denis ran out to the greenhouse to move a jerry-rigged watering system.

"Wait'll you see that field in bloom!" he yelled after one trip. "It's gonna be bee-ooo-tiffff-llll!"

The party broke up around ten o'clock. St. Denis and Debra packed the kids in their Blazer and were on their way home when Chuck stopped at the intersection of Stull's Run Road, a mile from the nursery. Dan Reid was there, waiting on his Yamaha.

St. Denis leaned out of the driver's window. "I'm beat, Daruka," he said. "I don't wanna drive Deb and the kids home and then go all the way up to your place. Let's do it another night."

"Hey, don't do that to me, I'm really up for this," Reid said.

"Well, all right, I'll tell you what. Let's just go from here," St. Denis said. "The kids will be asleep by the time we get there."

Reid looked at Debra and began shifting the weight of the bike from one foot to the other. When he spoke, his voice was an octave higher than usual.

"Naw, let's forget it; it's no big deal. Go home and get the kids to bed. I'll come by tomorrow and we'll set something up."

Chuck threw the Blazer into gear and drove on to the old farmhouse. There he helped Debra tuck in the two kids. Then he popped a Molson's, went upstairs, took a bath, and put on a pair of jogging pants. He and Debra had just gotten into bed and were about to turn off the lights when the phone beside the bed rang. It was eleven thirty.

"Hari bol," St. Denis said, answering with the traditional Krishna greeting.

He listened for a few seconds. Then he chuckled and said, "You're so mental." A few seconds later he added, "All right. I'll meet you there," and hung up.

"That was Reid," he told Debra as he climbed out of bed. "He was calling from the pay phone outside Ma Eddy's. He owes me fifty bucks. He had it on him when he saw us, but forgot to give it to me. He wants to get it to me now before he forgets again."

St. Denis pulled on his pants. He didn't like lying to Debra, but like Reid had said, he had been working hard. He deserved a party.

"I'll be right back. It shouldn't take more than ten minutes to get up there and back."

St. Denis grabbed his Molson's and walked out to the Chevy Blazer. He got in and drove past Ma Eddy's, the general store where he told Debra he was going to meet Reid. He turned onto the road that leads to the Palace of Gold, then onto a narrow dirt road that got narrower and more deeply rutted as it snaked up the mountain. He drove slowly, taking a slug now and then from the beer he had stuck in a plastic holder mounted on the dash.

St. Denis parked in front of the Artist's Studio, got out, and waited for his eyes to adjust to the dark. After a few moments, he walked slowly down a path that led around the studio to the only door. He was approaching the door when Thomas Drescher stepped out of the shadows and aimed a .22 pistol at him.

St. Denis froze. He heard something rustle in the woods behind him and took his eyes off Drescher for a split second. Dan Reid was standing beside a maple tree, aiming another .22 at him.

"Get inside, we wanna talk to you," Drescher said.

St. Denis turned to run back up the path.

Pop! Pop! Pop! Pop!

Drescher rapid-fired his .22.

Reid let his gun drop to his side.

"Shoot him!" Drescher screamed at Reid, "Shoot him!"

St. Denis was hit twelve times. He crumpled and went down. But then, almost immediately, as Reid and Drescher watched in amazement, he struggled back onto his feet and half staggered, half ran back down the path toward the Blazer. He stumbled like a drunk who has been decked in a bar fight.

Drescher dropped his gun and ran after him. He lowered his shoulder and dove into St. Denis, hitting him behind the knees. The big man went down. Drescher rolled him over and climbed onto his heaving chest.

"Get a knife!" he yelled at Reid. "Get a knife!"

Reid felt like he was going to vomit. For an instant he thought about running away, but he was afraid if he did, Drescher would come after him and kill him, too. He ran into the cabin and came out with a kitchen knife.

"Chant!" Drescher was screaming. "Start chanting!"

Drescher thought he was doing St. Denis one last favor. As Sri Krishna says in the *Bhagavad-Gita,* "Those who remember me at the time of death will come to me. Do not doubt this." By forcing St. Denis to chant, Drescher thought he was guaranteeing him a more spiritual life in his next incarnation.

But St. Denis would not die. Coughing blood and gasping for breath, he tried to throw Drescher off his chest. Drescher grabbed the knife and stabbed him. Again and again. Hard and deep. Finally, the blade hit a rib and snapped. St. Denis kept struggling.

Reid ran back to his cabin and grabbed a screwdriver. Drescher stabbed St. Denis with that. St. Denis fought on, screaming in agony. Reid found a hammer and Drescher hit him with that, punching a one-inch hole in his skull. St. Denis went limp and stopped fighting. Breathing deeply, Drescher climbed off him. He and Reid were looking down at the bloody body when St. Denis started emitting long, high-pitched screams like a German shepherd that has been hit by a truck.

Drescher and Reid dragged St. Denis down the logging road to the dammed-up stream. They dumped the body on the swampy ground and stumbled around trying to find the grave Drescher had dug.

It had disappeared.

Reid was mentally numb. Part of his mind denied it was all happening; the other part screamed, "Get it over with. Get it over with!" He ran up and down, back and forth across the stream bed. Suddenly, he fell in water up to his waist. He had found the hole. Water had seeped up from the ground, filling it. While Reid bailed it out with a shovel, Drescher unfolded a sheet of plastic.

"Get over here and help me get him in this," Drescher yelled.

Reid put down his shovel, walked over to the body, and picked up one end of the plastic. They were about to wrap St. Denis's head when he opened his eyes.

"Don't do that, you'll smother me," he said.

Reid screamed, a long, piercing scream of pure terror. He stopped, glanced at the body, and screamed again. Then he bolted into the woods.

Drescher watched him go. He had expected as much out of the little wimp. Killing didn't bother Drescher; he had found that out in Vietnam. He finished sheathing St. Denis in plastic and was dragging him to the hole when Reid reappeared.

"It's a good thing for you that you came back," Drescher said in an even, menacing voice. "Get over here and help me get him in."

Reid walked around to the other side of the body and

helped Drescher drop St. Denis into the hole. St. Denis was still breathing when the first shovelfuls of dirt hit him.

Reid and Drescher filled the grave; Reid working fast, Drescher at a steady pace. When the hole was covered, they knocked down Drescher's dam.

"Ever do this when you were a kid?" Drescher asked.

Reid flinched.

"I used to build dams all the time," Drescher said.

Within fifteen minutes, the stream had covered St. Denis's grave, and the gurgling current had carried away all the loose soil. The killers walked back to the artist's studio. Drescher got into St. Denis's Blazer and drove to Bridgeport, a small town across the Ohio River from Wheeling. Reid followed in Drescher's pickup truck. Drescher parked the Blazer near the home of Big John, a friend of St. Denis's and a marijuana dealer. He wiped the car clean of fingerprints, returned to the pickup, and rode back to the Artist's Studio with Reid.

When they returned across the Ohio River, they threw the .22s they had used on St. Denis out the window and into the water below the bridge.

The eastern sky was turning violet when Dan Reid walked into the tiny cabin where Brenda and his kids were sleeping. It was his first visit in weeks. Brenda woke up frightened and snapped on a light. Dan was soaking wet and covered with mud. His skin was as white as tofu and there were deep black circles under his eyes.

"What happened? What's going on?" Brenda asked.

Reid said nothing. Without bothering to undress, he lay down on the bed, took his wife in his arms and held her. It was a long time before he let go.

Dig a Hole

The instant Debra Gere woke up alone, she knew that Chuck's lame story about going out to collect fifty dollars from Dan Reid had been an excuse to party. She got out of bed angry. Oh well, she thought as she went down to the kitchen to prepare breakfast, he'll soon come stumbling in, make himself some tea, and go right to work. Chuck's recuperative powers had always amazed her.

Debra dressed the kids and fed them, then drove over to the nursery and started repotting plants. An hour went by and Chuck didn't show. Debra became worried. She took off her gloves, brushed the dirt off her clothes, scooped up the kids, and walked over to Kurt and Janet Cleaver's house. Kurt opened the door and Debra gave him a wry grin.

"Chuck snuck off to party with Dan Reid last night," she told Cleaver. "I'm a little worried because he hasn't come back. Could you go up there and check on him?"

Kurt returned an hour later; he was frowning.

"Reid says Chuck never showed," he told Debra. "He says he called Chuck last night and told him to come up, but Chuck must have changed his mind because he never made it. Reid ended up stayin' up half the night gettin' coked all by himself. He was really acting weird."

Debra felt suddenly weak.

"He must have driven off the road," she told Cleaver. "We've got to find him."

While Janet Cleaver looked after the kids, Debra and Kurt drove off to search the narrow, winding road that snakes up to the Artist's Studio. They checked every place where Chuck might have driven off the road and gone tumbling down a ridge. A couple of times they found tire tracks, and Kurt got out and investigated. Debra held her breath. But all he found were places where people had driven off the edge to dump garbage.

By the time Debra got home, it was late in the evening. She ran up to the bedroom and pulled out the top drawer of the nightstand on Chuck's side of the bed. She grabbed his address book and thumbed through it. There were many names she did not recognize. She skipped them and began calling mutual friends. None had heard from Chuck. Panicky, she called the Moundsville barracks of the West Virginia State Police.

Debra never got past the dispatcher. And she didn't get far with him. He refused to accept a missing-person report until Chuck had been gone forty-eight hours. "Those are the regulations, Ma'am," he insisted. If she did not hear from Chuck by tomorrow, she should call back. He hung up quickly to take another call.

Debra kept calling Chuck's friends until well after midnight. She spent the night wandering through the house, sobbing uncontrollably. Before dawn, she was back on the phone.

Nick Tsacrios, New Vrindaban's medic, laced up his New Balance running shoes, walked out of his small trailer, and began his daily warm-up. It was already seven o'clock and Thomas Drescher was uncharacteristically late for their morning run. Nick didn't quite know whether he was pleased or annoyed. He liked having company on his five-mile jog, but he didn't really like Drescher. As he stretched, touching his head to his knees, he berated himself for letting the guy bull his way into his life.

It had started in a neighborly way. Drescher showed up one day and said, "Hey, Nick, there's no shower at my place. Can I use yours?" Nick said sure, and from then on, Drescher would walk in and take a shower any time he wanted. Then he began showing up at night, uninvited, with a six-pack or two.

"Hey, Nick," Drescher would say as he walked into the trailer. "I need some company."

"I can appreciate that, but I want to read," Nick would reply.

"Forget that, we're gonna party," Drescher would say, pulling up a chair and opening a beer.

Drescher had eased up on his late-night visits after they started running together. The way Nick figured it, the guy just needed a friend. As long as he ran with Drescher, Drescher was satisfied and left him alone the rest of the day. Nick didn't mind running with him. It was a lot easier to do the five miles with company.

Tsacrios is short, maybe five foot six, with tight, wiry muscles and long black hair that he ties in a ponytail. His face is deeply lined, but he keeps himself in good shape and looks younger than his forty-five years. In 1972, he graduated twenty-first in a class of seventy-two from the University of Florida Medical School. He did a year's residency in internal medicine at Tulane, and a year's residency in psychiatry at the University of Syracuse. He hated both specialties and returned to Jacksonville, where he did a residency in family practice. Along the way, he became an addict. From 1972 to 1978, Nick shot cocaine, and sometimes heroin. He was arrested in Gainesville in 1975 and convicted of selling cocaine. He was placed on ten years' probation, but allowed to keep practicing medicine. He kept mainlining cocaine. In 1977 he was arrested again, this time for forging a prescription for Percodan. He received a two-year sentence to Raiford, the Florida state penitentiary, and lost his medical license.

A condition of this relatively short sentence was a nine-month stint in a state-operated drug rehabilitation program. He graduated the star of his class. Nick's first job was washing dishes in a health-food restaurant. He was happy—until his parole officer told him it was time to find work worthy of his ability. Nick answered a classified ad for a lab technician and quickly ended up in trouble again.

This time it was for practicing medicine without a license. He knew he was going back to prison, so he ran. Friends brought him to New Vrindaban to hide out.

Tsacrios hired a lawyer and eventually straightened things out in Florida. By then, he had fallen in love with rural life. He spent long days scouring West Virginia's woods for exotic plants and became a first-rate herbalist.

With Debra Gere, he set up New Vrindaban's first clinic. Nick developed a close working relationship with emergency-room doctors at Reynolds Memorial Hospital in Glen Dale, twelve miles from the commune. When he saw patients who might have a serious problem, he referred them to the ER. That took the pressure off him.

He was still doing his warm-up stretches, waiting for Drescher, when his phone rang. This early, he figured it had to be a mother with a sick kid. His premonition seemed to be confirmed by the high-pitched, hysterical voice on the other end of the line. It was a few seconds before he figured out the caller was Debra Gere.

"Chuck's been gone two nights." Debra announced between sobs. "Something's happened to him!"

"Maybe he just took off for a while; maybe he needed some time alone," Nick said.

"That's not like him," Debra wailed. "We've been together two years and he's never spent a night away without telling me. He's dead. I know it. I know it!"

Nick tried to comfort her, but Debra wouldn't listen. She slammed down the phone, leaving Nick holding a dead receiver. He put it back in the cradle and immediately thought of Tom Drescher.

Drescher had been obsessed by Chuck St. Denis for weeks. While running with Nick, he would moan and complain and curse St. Denis. The feud had begun when St. Denis bought the land for his nursery. In the middle of his plot was Drescher's half-finished house. St. Denis had tried to convince him to sell; Drescher refused. It seemed like much ado about nothing to Nick, but Drescher couldn't stop talking about it. Each morning, he insisted on telling Nick the latest outrage.

"That son of a bitch offered me eight grand for it yesterday," Drescher complained one morning. "It's worth twenty-five easy. Fuck him, I'll wait him out. I ain't got nowhere to go."

Nick thought eight thousand dollars was generous. Drescher, his common-law wife, and their two kids had been living in the basement for several years. It didn't look like Drescher would ever finish the place. Take the money and run, Nick told Drescher.

"No way," Drescher replied. "I can get more. His old lady inherited a pile."

A few days later, Drescher arrived chuckling. He had big news.

"We got a deal," Drescher said. "But I've got a surprise for that asshole. He's gonna pay me twelve grand and help me finish the house. He knows how to do wiring and complicated shit like that. In exchange, we get to live there a couple more months. Or so Chakradara thinks. Why should I do all that work and then move out? Fuck him. I'm stayin'."

Drescher and St. Denis finished the house. The deadline for Drescher's move came and went. Drescher stayed and stayed, despite St. Denis's stomping around and threatening him. Then one day, Drescher showed up at Nick's white with anger.

"You know what that fuckin' dirt bag did yesterday?" Drescher yelled. "He cut off my goddamn water. He says he needs it for the nursery. Bullshit, he needs it—he did it to get me out of there. Well, fuck him, I'm goin'. I found a trailer down on Wheeling Creek. But I'm not gonna forget this."

Drescher moved his family later that day. But as a going-away present, he ripped out the sink and the hot-water heater.

"I fixed his ass but good," he told Nick.

After that, Drescher stopped talking about St. Denis. Nick figured that was it; the feud was over. He was sick of hearing about Chuck St. Denis. But actually, Drescher was burning. He felt St. Denis had humiliated him, shown him up and made him look weak. How could he, the enforcer, let St. Denis get away with it? He was sure devotees were laughing at him behind his back.

"You know, there are some people here who would like to see Chakradara done away with," he told Nick one morning.

Nick flinched. "Tirtha, please, whatever is going on, don't get involved," he said as seriously and as warmly as he could. "I'm telling you as a friend, stay out of it."

Nick was sitting by the phone in his living room, thinking about Debra's frantic call and his conversations with

Drescher, when the door flew open. In strode Drescher. He was wearing his jogging suit and his usual pout.

Nick stared at him. Then, slowly, he got up from his chair. "You did it," he said quietly. "Goddamn it, Tirtha, you did it!"

Drescher's eyes widened. He took a few steps back toward the door.

"Listen, man, forget the run," he said. "Let's go for a walk."

Nick followed Drescher out into the warm morning and they turned down a dirt road. Drescher was silent; Nick felt a rising panic. He kept his eyes downcast, as if he had to watch his feet to keep them from taking him the hell away from there. Birds and the two men's footsteps were the only sounds.

Drescher finally spoke.

"Nick, I've killed a few people in my life and I've never seen anything like what happened," he said. "I shot the guy twelve times and he wouldn't die. He actually got up and tried to run away. You're a doctor, tell me how he could do that."

Nick remained silent. He kept his eyes on his feet: left, right, left, right.

Drescher went on, "The most amazing thing is, the whole time we were getting ready to plant him, the guy was making these incredible sounds. I didn't realize what was happenin' until later. It was his karma coming out. He passed through all his animal lives. You should have heard it. I swear, there were bears, tigers, camels, every animal you can think of."

Nick and Drescher walked up and down the road for almost an hour. Drescher kept talking about the murder. He wouldn't stop. When Nick couldn't take any more, he told Drescher he had to go over to the clinic. He was turning to walk away when Drescher grabbed his shoulder.

"I don't need to tell you, do I, Doc, not to tell anyone about this?"

Nick only nodded. Then he got in his beat-up Pinto and drove away. His hands were trembling so badly the steering wheel shook. He knew Drescher would kill him if need be, and describe his murder as nonchalantly as he had described St. Denis's.

Debra spent the day calling every name in Chuck's address book. Nobody had heard from him. That night, she drove into Moundsville and filed a missing-person report with the state police. She asked the desk sergeant if the state police had an airplane.

"Sure," he said, but he couldn't see any reason to call it out.

Debra had convinced herself that instead of going to Reid's, Chuck must have gone for a ride. He liked to drive around the steep hills, pushing the truck over the sudden crests and swinging it through the tight switchbacks. On the way home, she thought, he must have fallen asleep and driven off a mountain. The Blazer had to be in the bottom of some ravine with Chuck inside.

If she could get a plane, she could fly over the hills and find him. So after filing the report, Debra went to the Cleavers and talked it over with Kurt and Janet. Kurt then got out the *Yellow Pages* and made a few calls. They pooled their money and chartered a plane.

Early the next morning, Kurt and Debra spent an hour in the air, flying over the commune and the surrounding hills. It was beautiful; soaring over thick green forests in the hills, surrounded by brown and green farmland. No sign, however, of the cinnamon Blazer with its distinctive black fender. But Debra wasn't about to give up.

After paying off the pilot, she asked Kurt to drive her to a friend of Chuck's, a guy she knew only as "Big John" or "John from Athens." She'd been calling him for two days without getting an answer.

They knocked on Big John's door in Bridgeport. Before opening it, his wife peeked out and asked who they were. As Debra was telling her about Chuck's disappearance, Big John emerged from the basement. He listened quietly for a few minutes.

"Something funny's going on," Big John's wife said to him.

"It's weird, is what it is," Big John said. "Chuck's

Blazer is parked just down the block. We've been wonderin' what it's doin' here."

The keys were in the ignition. Chuck's checkbook was in the glove compartment. A half bottle of flat Molson's was sitting in the beverage container. Debra called the West Virginia State Police. They told her that since the car was found in Ohio, it was not their case. Debra called the Bridgeport police. An officer was finally dispatched. They waited for him in the street, but the cop missed them. He stopped at the end of the block and backed up to where they were standing. He was an old guy, and if he had any enthusiasm for his job, he kept it hidden. He spent less than twenty minutes filling out a standard report and had the Blazer impounded. Then he left.

"I don't think the cops are going to do anything," Debra said to Kurt on the way home. "They couldn't care less."

Cleaver nodded. They drove on in silence for a while.

"Why don't you talk to that county cop who's always coming around, asking questions. You know, the guy with the fat mustache. He's always trying to find out who people are, where they came from, stuff like that. Maybe he could find out where Chakradara went?"

Sergeant Tom Westfall parked his black Ford cruiser behind the dilapidated stone courthouse and walked into the dreary offices of the Marshall County sheriff.

"Teletype for you," the desk officer shouted. It had become a standard greeting. "The Hairy Kritters again. I put it on your desk."

Tom Westfall has a stomach that threatens to burst through his uniform and an easy-going disposition that hides a first-rate analytical mind and a ferocious desire to uncover the truth. He looks like a classic back-country deputy sheriff, the kind who is so bored he has forgotten he's bored, or even that he's a cop.

The son of a large contractor, Westfall grew up in Wheeling hating cops. But he wasn't the classic delinquent rebelling against authority. Westfall hated cops because cops were corrupt. He had seen them drive their shiny cruisers up lonely roads with women in the front seat; he'd seen them going in the back door of restaurants that were little more than fronts for gambling, and he had seen them drinking in bars in the middle of the day in uniform.

In 1967 he enlisted in the Army. A recruiter told him he would be a clerk. He ended up an MP in Okinawa, a tough place to be a military cop. Japanese students were protesting America's military presence with bamboo poles and Molotov cocktails; GIs fresh from Vietnam were celebrating their survival with raging drunks.

After his discharge, Westfall enrolled in West Liberty State College and worked in a grocery store while trying to decide what to do next. His neighbors convinced him that the police force would never improve until honest people became cops. He took the test, finished first, and became a deputy sheriff. He liked to think of it as nothing more than a temporary gig. It probably would have been, if it weren't for the Krishnas.

When Westfall joined the force in 1971, the Krishnas might as well have been invisible. The other members of the small police department did not want anything to do with them and pretended they weren't there. Westfall watched them coming and going to New Vrindaban and became curious: Who were they? Where did they come from? Why did they choose this exotic religion? He let devotees sell him a couple of the movement's books, and he read them. The Krishnas were harmless enough, he concluded—until he ran a few routine license checks. Because Caucasians with Hindu names have trouble buying insurance, most devotees registered their cars in their Western, or karmi, names. When Westfall traced devotees' license plates, obtained their names, and ran them through the FBI's computers, he was amazed how many came back with long rap sheets. What could be going on out there? he wondered. He decided to keep an eye on them.

Every Saturday, he rode a battered bike along the pot-holed roads that skirt the commune. When he passed a devotee, he stopped to chat. He was careful not to judge them, and to avoid religious arguments. Too many officers wanted to lecture devotees. Westfall listened, drew devotees out, made them feel that what they had to say mattered. On Sundays he sat in front of his television, watching the Pirates or the Steelers and organizing his few kernels of information on three-by-five index cards. He'd done the same thing in the Army, only then he was keeping track of deserters.

The work paid off almost immediately. When parents called trying to locate their children, or when a missing-person report came over the teletype, it was Westfall who went out to New Vrindaban. He became the "Krishna cop," both in his department and on the commune. During orientation tours for new devotees, Kuladri, the temple president, used to say, "That road leads to the swami's house. There's a general store where you can buy gas a half mile down this road, and that guy over there in uniform, he's the police. He keeps track of us better than we do."

Over the years, the inquiries from other police departments became more and more frequent, and more and more serious. License checks turned into criminal reports as *sankirtan*, the traditional public chanting to propagate the faith and raise money, turned into "scamkirtan." Westfall knew that in 1979 devotees had followed the Pope around the country selling bumper stickers and claiming they were collecting for Catholic charities. At Christmas, they dressed as Santa Claus and stood on street corners, ringing bells and collecting money. His file was full of similar reports.

So Westfall wasn't surprised to get to his desk and find one more teletype inquiring about sankirtan. This one came from a small town in Connecticut. Westfall read it, picked up the phone, and called the chief of police.

"These Hare Krishnas, are they legitimate?" the chief asked when he got on the line.

"That depends," Westfall said. "If you're talking about their religion, I'd have to say, yeah, they're legitimate. It's a form of Hinduism that goes back centuries in India. If you're talking about raising money, the answer is no way."

"Do they have anything to do with a Vietnam Veterans' organization?" the chief asked.

"Nothing at all," Westfall replied.

"I'm glad to hear that," the chief said. "They're up here claiming to be collecting for Vietnam veterans. Let's just say some of the boys got a little upset. They took it kind of personal and kicked the shit out of a couple of 'em."

"Well, I guess that's a risk they run," Westfall said. He hung up and was making notes for his file when the phone rang. It was Debra Gere.

"My husband's gone!" she blurted to Westfall. She was almost incoherent.

"What do you mean, gone?" Westfall asked.

"He was on his way to see a guy called Dan Reid and he disappeared," Debra said. "There's rumors all over the place that Reid and a devotee named Drescher killed him."

Westfall told Debra to come in and see him right away. He didn't need Debra to tell him about St. Denis or Drescher. Westfall knew them. He walked over to the stack of cabinets that held his Krishna files and pulled out two. One was Drescher's, the other St. Denis's. The years spent collecting information were paying off. He knew St. Denis was a marijuana dealer. He also knew that Drescher was the commune's enforcer. Westfall had opened a file on Drescher the first time he'd seen the so-called bus driver. With his Krishna dog-collar encircling his neck, the guy had looked at him the way a pit bull does just before it attacks. Westfall took the files back to his desk and thumbed through them. So, he said to himself, it's come to murder.

He opened a drawer and pulled out his dog-eared copy of Prabhupada's nine-hundred-page *Bhagavad-Gita*. As he waited for Debra, he flipped idly through it. He was genuinely puzzled: How come a religion that was supposed to save somebody like Chuck St. Denis had ultimately destroyed him? And how had the Krishnas got into swindling and dealing drugs? More to the point, how had people who started out searching for spiritual truth wound up behaving like hoodlums and common criminals? It seemed like the pattern was always the same. Timothy Leary thought you could use drugs to find peace and light and had ended up spreading death and addiction. The Students for a Democratic Society had started out protesting against violence and had ended up using it. It had happened every time. Somehow, the movements of the sixties all ended up becoming the opposite of what they had started out to be.

"Hi, sorry to disturb you. I'm Sergeant Tom Westfall from the sheriff's office. I'm out here investigating the disappearance of Chakradara, Chuck St. Denis. Mind if I come in for a moment?"

The devotee, a tall, thin woman with long blond hair, stood speechless behind the screen door. She didn't seem to know what to say.

"Well, I guess it would be all right," she finally answered. "Except that I don't know anything."

For weeks, Westfall had been driving out to the commune in his spare time to knock on doors. The investigating he had already done had convinced him he wasn't going to bust the case wide open. He simply wanted to keep the pressure on.

At first, most of the devotees had been afraid of him. Kuladri, Arthur Villa, the temple president, had ordered them not to talk. But Westfall's devotee contacts had called him at home to tell him what they'd heard. Some new sources had also called. They all had one thing in common: they hated Drescher.

"Who called the fucking sheriff?" Drescher asked Nick Tsacrios. "I just saw the son of a bitch going into a house down by Wheeling Creek. Did Ambudrara call him? It had to be Ambudrara. What the hell's the matter with her? Can't she forget about it?"

Drescher then started ranting about Kurt Cleaver. Kurt Cleaver was one of the few devotees who weren't afraid of Drescher. "Murderer. You're a murderer!" Cleaver screamed every time he saw Drescher. "What are you doing here, walking around? You should be behind bars!"

"Your neighbor better watch his goddamn mouth," Drescher told Dr. Nick. "Tell him. Tell him if he doesn't keep his mouth shut, he's going to have an accident."

*   *   *

Debra was a haunted woman. Lying in bed at night, unable to sleep, she heard Chuck's voice. Every time the old farmhouse creaked, she would jump up, thinking he was back. Then she would lie till dawn hugging her pillow, convinced one moment that Chuck would be coming home, terrified the next that Drescher had snuck into the groaning house to kill her.

She was now certain Drescher and Reid had murdered Chuck. But she couldn't understand why. It couldn't be that bullshit story about rape. It had to be something else. The more she thought about it, the more she came back to the kids.

One morning only two months before, Radheya, St. Denis's four-year-old son by another woman, and Reid's four-year-old, Rohini, had taken off. That wasn't unusual, and it was hours before anyone realized they were gone. Kuladri, the temple president, began calling devotees, asking if they had seen the boys. Nobody had. In growing desperation, Kuladri organized search parties to make sure every corner of the commune was covered.

Debra Gere was one of the first people he called. As soon as he hung up, Debra drove over to the Cleavers to see if they had heard anything. She walked into the kitchen to find Dan Reid playing cards with Kurt and two other devotees.

"Daruka!" she said, "Haven't you heard? Rohini is missing. Half the community is out looking for him."

"Yeah, I heard," Reid said nonchalantly. "Don't worry, he'll turn up."

Debra lost control. She ran across the kitchen and began to scream at Reid, "How can you sit there while everyone is out looking for your son? It's getting dark and cold—don't you *care?*"

Reid didn't say a word. He threw his cards on the table and walked out.

They found the bodies late that night. The boys had suffocated inside an old refrigerator. It was standing out in the open, near the nursery, a makeshift storage shed for flowers that were used to decorate deities in the Palace of Gold. Scrunched between the bodies was a dead pet rabbit.

Dan Reid walked up to the refrigerator and looked inside. When he saw the boys, he fell to the ground, screaming and pounding his fists.

Lying awake at night, Debra wondered why Reid had killed her husband. It couldn't have been just the house. Could he have twisted things so that somehow he blamed Chuck for the death of his son? Or, maybe it was Drescher who held a grudge against her because of what had happened with Jayadeva, Drescher's two-year-old stepson.

Debra had stopped by Brenda Reid's place early one Monday morning to talk to her about her schedule as assistant-midwife. When Debra walked in, Brenda was sitting on the floor, playing with the two Drescher children.

"Tom and Suzanne are out of town for a couple of days," Brenda said. "I'm keeping the kids while they're gone."

Debra took one look at Jayadeva and her eyes widened in alarm. There was a knot on his head the size of a golf ball.

"How in the world did that happen?" she asked Brenda.

"That's nothing," Brenda said. "You should see his back."

Debra went over and kneeled down behind Jayadeva. She ran her hands through his fine hair and found six or seven marble-sized bumps. She lifted the little boy's shirt and saw that his back was black and blue.

"Jayadeva, who did this to you?" Debra asked.

"My momma," the little boy replied.

Debra stood up.

"Why didn't you tell me about this?" she asked Brenda.

"My husband told me not to get involved," Brenda replied.

"Well, I'm going to get involved," Debra said.

She told Nick about Jayadeva that morning and took it to Kirtanananda that afternoon. The guru said he wanted an investigation. When Drescher and his common-law wife returned the next day, they heard that Debra had reported them. Both denied harming Jayadeva. The guru's investigation never took place.

Debra kept turning the whole thing over in her head. She had reported Jayadeva's injuries on Monday. Chuck had been killed that Friday. Could Reid and Drescher have killed Chuck because of the kids—Reid because of some crazy notion that St. Denis could be blamed for the death of his son, Drescher because he wanted to get back at her for her report on Jayadeva?

About a month after St. Denis disappeared, Debra decided she had to get out of the farmhouse. Her only alternative was to move into Drescher's old house, the one she had set aside for her mother. It was right in the middle of Tolavan, the fringies' enclave, and only a couple of hundred yards from her friends the Cleavers. She felt she would be safer there.

The day after she moved, Kirtanananda walked into the New Vrindaban accounting office.

"So, Ambudrara has moved," he said to Howard Fawley, the New Vrindaban treasurer. "What do you think we should do with the place, now that it's empty?"

"It's not worth fixing up," Fawley replied. "We've got too much other stuff going on. I pulled the file. The place is insured for forty thousand dollars. It's worth more burned down than standing."

"See what you can do," the guru said.

"If we do, we got to do it soon," Fawley replied. "The insurance policy has a vacancy clause. If the place is empty for more than two-hundred-seventy days, the policy is automatically canceled. We won't get a dime."

"See what you can do," Kirtanananda repeated.

Fawley summoned his assistant, Dan Reid.

"I think Kirtanananda wants to burn down St. Denis's old place," Fawley said. "Go confirm it. If he says yes, Drescher's ready to do it. I've already talked to him about it."

Reid searched for Kirtanananda and found him near the Palace of Gold.

"Fawley says he spoke to you about burning down the old farmhouse." Reid said. "He wants to know if you want it done, because Drescher is willing to do it."

The guru nodded his head, yes, he wanted the farmhouse burned.

"So, you want it done?" Reid asked again to make sure.

"Yes," Kirtanananda said.

Reid went back to Fawley, who opened his desk drawer and gave him $450.

"Drescher wants a gun as payment for setting the fire," Fawley told Reid. "Get him something decent."

Reid looked up Todd Schenker, one of the commune's two armorers. He himself knew nothing about guns. Schenker would make sure he bought exactly what Drescher wanted. Reid and Schenker drove into Moundsville together and purchased a Python .357 magnum at Sullivan's Gunshop. Reid gave the gun to Drescher when he got back to the commune.

In the middle of the night on July 14, 1983, Drescher walked into the deserted farmhouse. Loose floorboards squeaked under his boots. He was in the living room when he heard a noise upstairs and pulled the .357 magnum out of his belt.

"If somebody's here, you better come out!" Drescher yelled. "I got a gun."

There was no answer. The house was still.

Drescher tiptoed upstairs, keeping close to the wall to muffle his footsteps, and began searching each room. He walked into the bedroom where St. Denis had kissed Debra goodbye for the last time and pulled open a closet door. A hat fell off a shelf.

It was St. Denis's favorite hat. He'd worn it every day when he was working on the Blue Boy Nursery.

"Holy shit!" Drescher shuddered and backed out of the room.

He went out to his truck and got a can of gas. Then he went back in the house and doused both the upstairs and downstairs. He pulled out the antenna on a small radio-controlled ignition device he had built and put it in a pool of gasoline at the foot of the stairs. Then he returned to his truck and drove away. A few miles down the road, he pulled into a small clearing and stopped.

Drescher took out the transmitter and hit the switch. Then he turned on the police scanner he had installed in his truck. He kept waiting for the dispatcher to sound the fire alarm. There was nothing but static.

Drescher started the truck, turned around, and drove back to the farmhouse. It was still standing—the ignition device hadn't worked. He parked his truck and walked up to the front porch. He picked up an old board and smashed in a window. Then he took a pack of matches out of his pocket. He lighted one match and used it to set fire to the pack. Then he tossed it through the window.

The blast of the first explosion blew out the windows and sent Drescher reeling. He steadied himself by grabbing hold of a post. He was running back to the truck when the upper floor exploded, sending slivers of glass into the weeds in front of the house.

The Inland Mutual Insurance Company investigated and found a gas can near the house. Inland concluded that the fire was suspicious, but honored the claim. In December 1983 it sent New Vrindaban a check for $40,000.

Arthur Villa, Howard Fawley, Dan Reid, and Thomas Drescher were later convicted for their roles in the arson. Kirtanananda was acquitted.

A few days after the fire, Drescher and Reid both left the commune. Reid went back to Gardena, California, where he had grown up. He eventually got a job working for an accounting firm in Beverly Hills. Drescher and his common-law wife, Suzanne Bleudeu, traveled through Oregon and Montana, living on scams Suzanne had perfected as a member of New Vrindaban's women's sankirtan team.

Back in New Vrindaban, Debra and Nick, who had always been good friends, were growing very close. Nick arranged for 84 Lumber to pick up the wood it had sold St. Denis and to refund the money to Debra. Every weekend, he dug plants and flowers out of the Blue Boy greenhouse and trucked them to swap meets, where he sold them. He gave the money to Debra.

But Nick still did not tell Debra that Drescher had confessed. Nick told himself that everybody in the commune knew who had done it, and before long somebody was sure to finger Drescher and Reid. When they did, he would tell the cops what he knew.

Debra was losing weight. Her shiny red hair had become dull and had lost its luster; her skin was so pale she looked embalmed. She decided the only way to get Chuck out of her mind was to throw herself back into Krishna Consciousness. Every day, she chanted sixteen rounds of the Hare Krishna mantra. Every morning, she got up before dawn to shower and drive to the temple for the 4:30 morning service. She was on her way back one foggy day in September when she passed Drescher on Highway 250 in his white pickup. She drove up the twisting dirt road in a frenzy, stormed into the house, and grabbed the phone.

"He's back! Drescher's back!" she screamed.

"I'll be right out," replied Sergeant Westfall.

It was little more than a ploy to calm her. Westfall was one frustrated cop. He felt he had developed enough information to arrest Drescher and Reid for murder. He knew that Reid was weak, that if he woke up one morning in jail facing a life sentence, chances were good that he would turn state's evidence in return for the promise of lenient treatment. But Westfall was stymied. He couldn't get anybody interested in the case. Until he came up with a body, an eyewitness, or a murder weapon, it was just a missing-person case. Westfall spent hours trying to convince Tom White, the Marshall County prosecutor, to file charges. But White wasn't interested. He wasn't about to take a case to court that he could not win.

"No body, no conviction," he told Westfall each time the cop brought up the case.

"You know what it comes down to?" Westfall asked his wife, Martha, an elementary-school teacher, one night after they had put their children, Sarah and Tommy, to bed. "Nobody gives a damn. They just think the Krishnas are a bunch of gooks."

"But this is murder," Martha replied. "If cops aren't interested in murder, what *are* they interested in?"

"Cops figure their job is to protect the regular Joe," Westfall said. "The Krishnas aren't regular because nobody in their right mind would do something crazy like joining the Krishnas. So when a Krishna ends up missing, the cops shrug and say, 'What do you expect from those Hairy Kritters?' "

Westfall didn't have much hope he would break the case anytime soon. But he wasn't about to give up. As he drove out to Tolavan to see Debra, he decided to level with her. She beat him to it.

"They're never going to do anything to those guys, are they?" she asked. "They're gonna go free, aren't they?"

"I promise you, I'm going to arrest them," Westfall said. "It may take twenty-five years, but I'm going to do it."

While Westfall was visiting Debra, Drescher was on the other side of the sprawling commune, knocking on Nick's trailer.

"How you been, Doc? Ready to start runnin' again?" he asked when Nick answered the door.

Two days later, they resumed their routine. It was late fall. The trees were bare, their leaves covering the backroads with a wet blanket. As they set off, the air was cold and they could see their breath. Nick was quiet, except for an occasional grunt. Long before Drescher had left, he had come to hate these runs together; now it was worse than ever. He could barely look Drescher in the eye. Saying hello without showing fear was becoming impossible.

About midway along their route Drescher glanced at Nick and broke the steady rhythm of their running.

"Doc," he said, "if you wanted to dissolve a body, what would you use?"

Nick was stunned. He slowed to a halt.

"I don't know," he said, trying to keep his voice even. "I've never thought about it."

"Aw, come on, Doc. You know," Drescher said.

"Well, traditionally, I guess it's lime," Nick replied.

"Lime, huh? Would acid work?"

"I suppose. Why? What are you going to do?"

"No body, no evidence."

"You mean you would actually go back and dig up the body? You would actually do that?"

Drescher shrugged. Without thinking, Nick added, "Where's it buried, anyway? Near here?"

Drescher gave Nick a long, icy stare. "Come on, Doc. You don't think I'd tell, do you? Why'd you ask, anyway?"

"No reason," Nick replied. "You just shook me up. Come on, let's finish the run."

They jogged on in silence. It was the last time they ran together.

Early one morning several days later, Drescher snuck into the commune's garage and removed a half-dozen five-gallon plastic jugs of muriatic acid, which devotees used to clean the cement and bricks around the Palace of Gold. He loaded the jugs into the back of his pickup truck and drove to the stream where St. Denis was buried.

Drescher spent most of the morning rebuilding the dam. When it was finished, he stood over St. Denis's grave and bored holes down to the body with a pinch bar. Then he poured the acid into the holes.

A yellow film slowly formed on the puddle above the waterlogged grave.

Two weeks after his run with Drescher, Nick Tsacrios was washing his dirty clothes at a laundromat in Moundsville. He stuck his head into the industrial-sized drier and felt the clothes. He figured he had timed it just right. It was 10:45 on a Saturday night, just fifteen minutes to closing. They'd be finished in moments. He did not notice the headlights flash in the plate-glass window or see the white pickup park next to his Pinto. He was still staring at the drier when Drescher walked in.

"Hey, Nick, what's goin' on?" Drescher asked, nonchalant as could be. "I was just drivin' around, killin' time, when I saw your car parked outside. I said to myself, Hey, I'll pick up the Doc and we'll go get us a couple of beers."

Nick felt a shiver of fear, but for the moment he said nothing. He walked over to the drier and opened the round door. He reached in and grabbed an armload of hot, fresh-smelling clothes before turning to face Drescher.

"Tirtha, what do you take me for, an idiot? There's no

way I'm going to get in that truck with you. You'd kill me. You think I know too much."

"Doc, I'm surprised at you," Drescher said, trying to imitate a hurt puppy. "You and I are friends. If I can't trust you, who can I trust?"

Nick worked hard to concentrate on folding his laundry. His mind was blank; he had no idea what he should do.

"Come on, Doc. Let's take a ride and talk this over. I never imagined you felt like this."

Before Nick could answer, the glass door to the laundromat opened and a short, bald-headed man walked in.

"Time to go, fellas. I'm gonna lock it up," the man said.

"Be done in a minute," Nick said. "We'll all leave together."

Drescher shot the laundromat owner a quick look.

"OK, Doc, if that's how you feel," he said. "We'll talk another time."

Drescher left. Nick didn't dare look as Drescher returned to his truck and drove away. He stacked his laundry in a plastic basket, loaded it into his Pinto, and drove home. He couldn't sleep that night. Early the next morning, he borrowed a neighbor's truck, hooked up his trailer, and hauled it up to Debra's house.

She saw him coming and went out onto the porch. He parked the truck and ran up the steps.

He threw his arms around Debra. "Ambudrara, we have to talk!"

They went inside the small cabin and Nick told her everything. He began with the walk he took with Drescher the day after St. Denis's murder, and ended with his escape from the laundromat. Debra begged him to go to Sergeant Westfall and report everything.

Nick refused.

"The cops know who did it, and they haven't done a thing," he insisted over and over. "If Drescher finds out I'm talking to Westfall, he'll kill me for sure. The best thing we can do is lie low and hope that Drescher goes away again."

Weeks passed. Nick moved out of the trailer and into

Debra's house. When they went to bed at night. Nick tucked a .45 under his pillow.

Gradually, Debra and Nick built a routine. They put in long hours at the clinic together, and with time Chuck no longer dominated Debra's every thought. Debra was still going to Mangal aratik every morning with Janet Cleaver. They got a late start one day, and when they walked into the Temple of Understanding, the service was already in full swing. Devotees were pounding *mridanga,* drums, clicking *kartal,* cymbals, and dancing and jumping in ecstatic devotion. And dancing directly in front of the deities was Drescher's common-law wife, Suzanne Bleudeu.

"Look at that," Janet said, nudging Debra. "I can't believe she's here."

"Let's get her," Debra said.

The women marched across the temple, grabbed Bleudeu, and dragged her outside. They hit her in the face and in the head. When Bleudeu fell down, they kicked her. They left her lying on the ground, sobbing.

"You blew it, Ambudrara!" Nick screamed when Debra told him about it. "You totally blew it! How could you do something like that?"

"I don't know," she said. "I guess I had to do something. If I was a man, I'd attack Drescher. But I'm a woman, so I went after his wife."

"Tirtha's sure to come after us now," Nick said. "What are we gonna do?"

It was after midnight when the phone rang. Nick and Debra were in bed, asleep. They both woke up and listened to the ringing. Finally, Nick picked it up.

"Dig a hole!" Drescher screamed. "Dig a hole!"

Dr. Nick could not just sit around and wait for Drescher to try to kill him. He had to do something. He couldn't kill Drescher; he was a vegetarian who did not believe in killing animals, let alone humans. He thought of running away, but he had run from things in Florida and had sworn he would never run again. There was only one thing to do: take Debra's advice and go to the cops.

Dr. Nick told his story to Sergeant Westfall, and he

told it to the state police. Westfall believed him; the state police did not. They decided that because of his drug record, Dr. Nick was an unreliable witness. And Tom White, the Marshall County prosecuting attorney, was not about to put a witness on the stand whom the state police considered unreliable.

The question of Kirtanananda's involvement eluded the authorities. And the guru continuously denied he had anything to do with the St. Denis murder.

Westfall kept his file open, hoping that somehow, something would happen that would bring the case back to life. But for all intents and purposes, the investigation into the disappearance of Chuck St. Denis was as dead as St. Denis.

Blind Faith

The Messiah and the Mott Street Gang

Howard Wheeler, a tall, pasty-skinned bohemian, spotted him first. The old man with the shaved head was walking down Houston Street in New York City. His face was deeply lined and his eyelids drooped, but the old man radiated an energy that made him seem young. He stepped nimbly around drunks and pools of urine on the sidewalk and seemed so unperturbed by the filth, he could have been a native of the Bowery.

As the old man approached, Wheeler felt a mounting excitement. He knew that the old man had to be a *sannyasi*, a Hindu monk who has cast off the world. With his saffron robe, he was unmistakable. Wheeler liked to think of sannyasis as materialism's living dead, the visible souls of believers who have renounced all possessions, severed all relations with their wives and children, declared themselves celibate, and left home to wander in search of God. In India, the vow is understood to be so profound and final that a soon-to-be sannyasi must appear in court, where his will is read. The magistrate then declares him dead under civil law.

It was June 1966. Wheeler had been searching for the right sannyasi for years—sometimes it seemed like all his life. He had read ravenously. In the process, he had completed his Ph.D. in English literature at New York University. He had devoured Thoreau, Emerson, and Whitman. He had been through Camus, Sartre, and Aldous Huxley, and had studied Saint Augustine, Buddhist sutras, and Zen Buddhism. All had touched him, some had challenged him, but none had satisfied him. If anything had come close to striking a resonant chord, it was the *Bhagavad-Gita,* or "The Song of the Lord." The

47

Hindu equivalent of the Bible, the Koran, and the To-
rah, the *Gita* is a how-to manual on finding God. The
main character, a great warrior named Arjuna, is the
Hindus' Everyman. He is confused and depressed because he must fight a battle against relatives and friends.
His charioteer explains to him why the battle must be
fought, and much, much more. Suddenly, Arjuna, a plain-
speaking man of action, realizes that his charioteer is
Krishna, the lord of the universe. He can unlock the
gates to eternal joy, eternal life, eternal knowledge. "Let
me be your disciple," Arjuna begs Krishna. "I have
fallen at your feet, give me instruction."

Like Arjuna, Wheeler was willing to begin his spiritual
journey by falling to his knees and subjugating himself.
Searching for the right sannyasi, he and his companion,
Keith Ham, had gone to India the previous summer. The
trip was a disaster. They had approached dozens of saffron-
robed sannyasis. Some did not speak English. Others
remained remote; they did not want to be pestered by
anxious young Americans burdened with philosophical
questions. Educated sannyasis who spoke English tended
to be administrators of small temples tucked along the
cluttered side streets of Bombay or Delhi. To Wheeler
and Ham, they seemed more like CEOs than bona fide
gurus.

Wouldn't it be a cosmic joke if, after traveling halfway
around the world, I discovered my guru in the Bowery?
Wheeler thought as he watched the old sannyasi walk up
Houston Street. He approached the old man, but was
tongue-tied by anxiety.

"Are you from India?" he asked.

"Yes," the old man said. "Indeed, I am. I have come
to give classes on the *Bhagavad-Gita*. Do you know the
Gita?"

"Almost by heart," Wheeler responded.

"Oh, very good, very good," the old man said. "Maybe
you can help me. I have just rented a place around the
corner for my classes. Perhaps you would be so kind as to
accompany me and tell me if you think it is suitable?"

Wheeler remained a step behind the old man as they
walked around the corner to a storefront at 26 Second

Avenue. The place was dilapidated. The windows were streaked with grime, and garbage almost blocked the narrow entry hall. Over the door hung a faded sign that said Matchless Gifts in wavy psychedelic letters. A small handwritten note in the window announced that A.C. Bhaktivedanta Swami would give lectures on the *Gita* every Monday, Wednesday, and Friday from 7:00 P.M. to 9:00 P.M.

"Guess what I found?" Wheeler burst out as soon as he got back to the dank apartment on Mott Street he shared with Keith Ham. "A swami. A swami on Houston Street!"

Ham held his silence. He knew better than to interrupt when Wheeler was excited. The two had lived together ever since they arrived in New York—Wheeler to go to graduate school at NYU, Ham to work on a doctorate in American religious history at Columbia University. They were the leaders of a loose collection of East Village bohemians who liked to call themselves the "Mott Street Gang" after the row of ratty tenements they shared in the East Village.

The gang members were young, smart, and verbal. Intellectual thugs. In the evenings, they gathered in the coffeehouses and bars on MacDougal and Christopher Streets to watch Keith Ham's intellectual assassinations.

Ham didn't look like the traditional hit man. He usually walked with a cane and his stomach bulged, giving him a gnomish look—the result of childhood polio. He would sit back, listening to half-baked poets or would-be artists holding forth on art or religion. Then, when they had argued themselves into a dark alley, he would move in for the kill. In his clipped, squeaky voice, he mugged them with sources they had not read and errors in logic they had not perceived. His skills in argument were so keen, his friends threatened to drag him into Washington Square to debate all comers while they collected quarters from the audience.

It was with this air of intellectual superiority that the Mott Street Gang went to check out Wheeler's swami. They had the evening scripted. They'd sit quietly while the old geezer went through his rap. Then Keith would ask a few pointed questions that the swami would not be able to answer. Or Keith would floor him with a few basic points he'd failed to consider. Then they'd go get a beer and laugh at Keith's latest victim.

Six members of the Mott Street Gang and about half a dozen of the simply curious were sitting on mats in the empty store when the swami appeared in the doorway. He stopped to remove his shoes, walked to the front of the room in his bare feet, and sat down on a rug facing the small audience. Wheeler looked at his friends. They were studying the swami with real curiosity. Their flippant attitudes seemed to have evaporated, even though the old man had not yet said a word. Wheeler smiled.

The swami picked up a small set of finger cymbals and began striking them together, creating an infectious *ching-ching-ching* rhythm. In a deep, pure voice, he began chanting the maha-mantra, exactly as he had done countless times in India. Long after the swami stopped, his listeners kept hearing the mantra. It raced through their minds, repeating itself like a ditty from a hot pop song. The swami seemed to know this. He sat silently while his eyes danced from one person to another.

"Krishna is God," the swami said, finally breaking the silence. "Not merely an incarnation of God, Krishna is God, the supreme lord of the universe. He is a person, an eternally youthful, playful child with blue skin. His name means 'reservoir of pleasure.' "

There are many ways to approach God, the swami continued in his monotone. There is a way to God through work, *karma* yoga; through knowledge, *jnana* yoga; and through the body, *hatha* yoga. The swami said that he had come to America to introduce a new form of yoga, a better yoga, a form that was superior to all the others. It was called *bhakti* yoga. It was a way to God through love and devotion. Bhakti, the swami explained, is superior because love is more powerful than the intellect or the body. Because bhakti stresses serving God, it incorporates karma yoga; because it stresses clean living, it incorporates hatha yoga. Bhakti, the swami added, is what Krishna teaches Arjuna in the *Gita*.

The swami's English was clunky. He often added "ing"

to words that did not require it. ("Krishna is meaning, must seeing the truth.") But he held the small audience spellbound when he told them the story of Lord Chaitanya Mahaprabhu (1486–1533), the founder of bhakti yoga. Chaitanya was an arrogant young schoolteacher in Bengal before he became a devotee of Krishna. Bengal at that time was under Turkish rule and Islam was the state religion. Hinduism and its practitioners were considered inferior. But so fervent was Chaitanya's devotion that he ended up converting the Turkish governor.

As Keith Ham listened, he realized the swami was a Hindu fundamentalist, one who believed that the battle described in the *Gita* was a historical event. That didn't bother Ham. Although he knew that most interpreters of the *Gita* believed the battle was a metaphor for the internal struggle between man's higher and lower natures, he was comfortable with the fundamentalist view— he'd grown up with fundamentalism and had never really rejected it.

Much of Ham's life, his work at Columbia and his search for spiritual truth, had been shaped by a revolt against his father, a fundamentalist Baptist minister in Peekskill, New York. But it wasn't a revolt against his father's orthodoxy; Ham liked that. For all his sophistication, he wanted absolutes. He was pleased that the swami and his father were both convinced they possessed the truth. The difference between the two preachers was that his father taught fear and punishment; his God was the vengeful, white-bearded Jehovah. The swami preached love; his God was a playful, sensual, blue-skinned boy.

Ham and Wheeler exchanged glances. There was no need to speak. They knew they had at long last found their spiritual master.

The lecture ended and the swami asked everyone to join him in chanting the mantra. He explained that Krishna and his names are one and the same. *Hare* is the spirit of the Lord, the infinite energy that pervades all living things; *Rama* is a name for God the supreme enjoyer. When you chant the names of God, God is actually on your lips. You have established a direct link.

Ham, Wheeler, and the rest of the small audience tried

chanting the mantra. They were halting and self-conscious at first. But then they were caught up in the rhythm and began chanting more and more loudly. Soon winos and passersby were pushing up to the grimy window to see what was going on. They shook their heads when they saw the hippies sitting cross-legged, swaying and chanting.

The chanting stopped quite suddenly. Without uncrossing his legs, Prabhupada sprang off the straw mat, bowed, and left the room. The Mott Street Gang dropped a few coins in a wicker basket and walked out to Second Avenue. There was none of the usual verbal sparring. They went back to Ham and Wheeler's apartment and tried to figure out why they felt so good. The swami's English was difficult to understand. He was certainly no glib evangelist; he spoke in a monotone and at times seemed almost pedantic. And yet, he had power.

Hans Kary was lying on the couch of his fourth-floor walk-up in Hoboken, New Jersey, studying the front page of the October 15, 1966 issue of *The East Village Other*. The twenty-six-year-old freelance photographer thought the hippies who threw the rag together had finally lost it. They had blown out the whole front page to run a two-color picture of an old man with a shaved head in a long robe. He was standing under a tree in Tompkins Square Park, talking to a crowd of freaks.

"Save the Earth Now!!" the headline screamed.

"What is this guy, an ecologist from Mars?" Kary cackled to himself. "Is he gonna zap New York if we don't clean up the East River?" Kary opened the underground paper and started to read.

"In only three months, Swami A.C. Bhaktivedanta Prabhupada has succeeded in convincing the world's toughest audience—bohemians, acidheads, potheads, and hippies—that he knows the way to God. Turn Off, Sing Out, and Fall In," the article began. "This new brand of holy man, with all due deference to Dr. [Timothy] Leary, has come forth with a brand of "Consciousness Expansion" that's sweeter than acid, cheaper than pot, and non-bustible by fuzz. How is all this possible? 'Through Krishna,' the Swami says."

Far out, Kary thought as he tossed aside the paper. Here's a guy who isn't out to make a buck selling mantras, like that whiny-voiced Maharishi. This guy is taking it to the streets. He is definitely worth checking out.

An intense, good-looking man with high cheekbones and deep-set brown eyes, Kary wore his long brown hair in a ponytail. But he bristled when people assumed he was a hippie. Hippies were lazy. They had no discipline! They got stoned and talked nonsense. That wasn't for him. Born in 1941 to Catholic parents in Brunswick, Nazi Germany, Kary had been brought up strictly. His father had always taught him that without discipline, nothing is possible. A chef who had once cooked for Hitler in Berchtesgaden, the führer's Bavarian hideaway, Kary's father was declared a displaced person after the war, and he emigrated to the States in 1946. The family eventually settled in Florida, and Kary's father became the pastry chef at the Palm Beach Country Club, where his delicate creations were enjoyed by President Kennedy and other celebrities.

Hans did well in high school, but chose the Navy over college. He thought of himself as a man, not a kid. He wanted to see the world, not sit in an economics class. But the Navy turned out to be intolerable. Hans did not mind taking orders; he minded taking orders from idiots. He felt like a zombie. It was like a hit tune of the day, Santo and Johnny's "Sleepwalk." Whenever Kary heard it, he thought, Yeah, that's me. I'm sleepwalking.

After he was discharged, Kary wanted to obliterate his memories of the Navy. He decided to become an artist and rented an apartment in a bohemian section of Hoboken, New Jersey. He had learned photography in the Navy and figured he could support himself as a freelancer while learning to paint. Eventually, he would combine painting and photography, like the photo realists. In his apartment building he met Helena, a fellow tenant and they were soon dating. Within a year, Kary and Helena, a self-possessed young painter, were married.

Helena spent hours teaching Hans to paint. At first it was ideal. But Hans soon discovered that he wasn't a very good painter and didn't much like painting. And he hated Helena's artist friends. He found them egotistical, a bunch of jerks.

When the acid craze hit, Hans thought he'd find answers in the hallucinogen. He kept a steady supply in his refrigerator, right next to the grass. But after about a year, Hans gave up on acid. It wasn't leading anywhere. The first time he came home tripping, stuck the key in the lock, and found himself becoming the lock, the world turned over. But after a dozen or so trips, the fractured psychedelic perceptions were no longer new. Hans's attitude was, OK, I became a lock. Now what?

He sank into a depression. Gracious, even-tempered Helena would come home from her job in an art-supply store, make dinner, and listen while Hans rattled on for hours. Helena believed that talking helped, but Hans saw no evidence of it. He was trapped in himself. He accepted fewer and fewer free-lance assignments and spent more and more time on the couch. When he went into New York to check out the old guru, it was the first time in weeks he had left his building.

Walking down Second Avenue, Kary passed the Fillmore, Bill Graham's East Coast temple of rock and roll. Kary knew it well. He had been there to hear Jimi Hendrix, the Rascals, the Yardbirds, and the Animals. It was early evening and the Fillmore was dark, but Kary heard music. He thought a band must be inside, rehearsing for its big gig.

Then he realized the music was coming from two giant speakers mounted in the windows above the little storefront temple at 26 Second Avenue. They were blasting a recording of the swami and his devotees chanting the maha-mantra. In the street under the speakers, several dozen people were dancing, banging drums, clanging finger cymbals, and chanting Hare Krishna. The mantra was ecstatic, contagious. It was rock and roll.

Kary worked his way through a crowd of Puerto Rican kids, derelicts, and assorted losers. The dancers did not have that spacey expression he saw in the eyes of girls at the Fillmore who raced to the front of the stage and raised their arms to do the LSD shuffle, as if they were

incarnations of Isadora Duncan. For all their hot dancing
and chanting, these people looked serene and happy.

He caught a whiff of the pungent smells that were
drifting out of the temple and inched his way behind the
dancers to peek through the window. He was surprised to
see a circular picture of a young man and a woman
hanging above a dais covered with fresh flowers. The
man in the picture had a blue face and was playing a
flute. Kary studied the strange portrait. Then he looked
around and noticed a handwritten sign taped inside the
window near the front door! He moved closer to the
dancers to read it.

> All initiated devotees must attend morning and eve-
> ning classes.
> Must not be addicted to any kind of intoxicants,
> including coffee, tea, and cigarettes.
> They are forbidden to have illicit sex connections.
> Must be strictly vegetarian.
> Should not extensively mix with non-devotees.
> Should not eat foodstuffs cooked by non-devotees.
> Should not waste time in idle talks nor engage
> himself in frivolous sports.
> Should always chant and sing the Lord's Holy names.
> Hare Krishna Hare Krishna Krishna Krishna Hare Hare
> Hare Rama Hare Rama Rama Rama Hare Hare
>
> Thank you.
> A.C.
> Bhaktivedanta Swami, Acharya

Kary was excited by the message's sternness. If a religion did not demand discipline, he thought, it was no
good. That was the trouble with his father's Catholicism.
You confessed your sins, sinned again, and confessed
again. And sentimental hippie-dippy gurus like the Maharishi were too easy. If everybody chanted some weird
syllables for fifteen minutes a day, there would be world
peace. Right! Tell that to Richard Speck.

Kary thought finding enlightenment must be the hardest work in the world. Holy men didn't climb the Himala-

yas to spend their days meditating on a ledge just because they wanted solitude. Obviously, this swami understood discipline. Here, finally, was someone who was not selling instant salvation—just add hot water, stir, and discover God.

When the sankirtan ended, Kary found himself surrounded by smiling devotees. They were friendly, but not pushy. They invited him into the temple to share *prasadam.* When Kary responded with a blank look, they explained that prasadam is mercy. It is food that is holy because it is first offered to Krishna.

Kary joined the feast and enjoyed the mung bean soup, freshly cooked vegetables, white rice, pear chutney, and *chapati,* a kind of whole wheat tortilla. He sat next to a small, crippled man with a shaved head and smiling eyes, who introduced himself as the cook, Kirtanananda. Chuckling, he added that he was known as "Kitchenananda"—an honor bestowed by the swami in recognition of how well he had learned to cook prasadam. Kirtanananda told Kary that before the swami initiated him, his name had been Keith Ham and he had been a graduate student at Columbia. But, he added in a matter-of-fact tone of voice that belied his pride, he had decided to *make* religious history rather than write about it.

Kirtanananda looked around the small room, where people were sitting on straw mats and eating prasadam from tin plates. He pointed out a young man with rich black hair wearing a string of beads over a blue workshirt. That, he said, was Mukunda, a jazz musician whose Western name was Michael Grant. The dark haired man with the goatee sitting next to Mukunda was Hayagriva, Howard Wheeler, Kirtanananda's best friend. Hayagriva was helping the swami translate the *Bhagavad-Gita.* Kirtanananda paused for a moment to let the magnitude of the honor sink in. Then he continued giving Kary thumbnail sketches of all the devotees. The picture Kirtanananda painted was idyllic. He did not tell Kary that only a few months earlier, he had been locked away in Bellevue.

* * *

Kirtanananda—Keith Ham—woke up hungry. The temple was steadily gaining devotees, but was continually short of money. The spare change people tossed in the wicker basket at the end of a sankirtan or one of the swami's lectures was never enough to cover the spiraling expenses. There was never quite enough food to go around.

He climbed out of bed and, in the traditional sign of devotion, anointed thirteen places on his body with *tilaka,* a mixture of clay and water that comes from the sacred rivers of India. It was an important day, and he wanted to do everything right. He donned his *dhoti,* an Indian robe, and ran his fingers through his *shikha,* the tuft of hair at the top of his shaved head known by devotees as Krishna's flag.

It was shortly before nine o'clock when he left the temple. He turned heads as he walked through the Village on the way to his interview at the welfare department. He figured going on welfare would be an easy way to help the movement get money. New York would not notice one more person on its bloated welfare rolls.

Kirtanananda arrived at the welfare office a few minutes after nine-thirty. There was already a small crowd, and he had to wait. He sat quietly in one of the hard green chairs, chanting his daily rounds. He didn't seem to notice the kids and their mothers staring. It was almost an hour before he was directed to a small cubbyhole.

"Hare Krishna," he said to the interviewer as he entered. There was no response. Ham hadn't even sat down when the interviewer began rattling off a list of questions. Ham told him that his name was Kirtanananda. The interviewer scribbled a few notes at the bottom of the page. After that, he didn't let Ham finish answering a question before firing off another. A few minutes later, he pushed a form filled with minuscule print across the desk and told Ham that to qualify, he would have to take a psychiatric test.

Ham quickly signed what he thought was a form consenting to an examination. Actually, it gave doctors the power to commit him. The psychiatric intern conducting the initial interview decided Ham's dress and answers were bizarre enough to warrant further probing. He signed Ham into Bellevue for observation.

There Ham languished unable to convince the doctors to release him. He was kept awake most nights by the wails of his fellow patients. Soon his eyes were sunken and surrounded by dark circles. The hospital refused his requests for a razor to shave his head, which sprouted a thick stubble, giving him a wild, almost demented look. He refused to talk to the other patients and spent all his time reading. The doctors soon concluded he was antisocial.

Wheeler and several other devotees visited almost every day. They tried to get him to relax. They told him to play the game, and eventually the doctors would release him. Ham took their advice and tried to make friends with the other patients. He told them about the swami and his blue god, Krishna. But that only convinced the psychiatrists that he was even sicker than they had imagined. They diagnosed him as a malignant schizophrenic, a potential danger to himself and perhaps others. It looked like he was headed for a steel cell in a back ward.

The swami took the incarceration of his favorite disciple as certifiable proof that the world was completely insane. To the guru, spending your life working for money so you can buy a house and a car and raise a family, just so your children can do the same thing, was crazy. Kirtananda, the swami thought, was a boy making some nice spiritual progress. What did America do? It poked him and prodded him and locked him up. America, Prabhupada became convinced, was a crazy place.

It was Howard Wheeler who figured out how to play the game and spring his friend. He called the poet Allen Ginsberg, who often came to the Second Avenue temple to chant and talk with Prabhupada. Ginsberg was more of an amalgam of Buddhism, impersonal Hinduism, and Walt Whitman than a follower of Krishna. But he admired Prabhupada and believed there was great spiritual value in chanting the mahamantra. Wheeler told the poet that Ham was trapped in the dungeons of Bellevue and asked for Ginsberg's help. Ginsberg contacted a Jungian psychiatrist named Dr. Edward Hornick, who examined

Ham and wrote a report stating that he was a sane follower of an authentic Eastern religion.

Bellevue wasn't about to give up its patient without a fight. It refused to release Ham. The authorities declined to let Ham go unless a family member signed the release papers and accepted custody. Even though he was thirty years old.

Getting that signature was almost as tricky as convincing the psychiatrists that Ham hadn't lost his mind. Relations between Ham and his fundamentalist Baptist father were strained, to put it mildly. Ham spent days listening to the wild ravings of his fellow inmates as he pondered what to say to his parents. When he couldn't take it any longer, he worked up his courage, picked up the phone, and called his father collect.

They exchanged pleasantries. Then, in one sudden burst, Keith explained where he was and why. The Reverend Ham's reaction was even worse than Ham had feared.

"Satan!" the Reverend Ham shouted into the phone. "Satan! It's the work of the Devil."

Ham explained, cajoled, and argued, all to no avail. The Reverend Ham refused to be swayed. He said he would far rather have his son in some faceless institution than in the clutches of some wild-eyed guru. The preacher absolutely refused to spring Keith unless he promised to come back home. Keith tried every trick he could think of to change his father's mind. They all failed. Desperate, he gave in and promised to return.

The Reverend Ham drove down to New York the next morning to sign his son out of Bellevue. When Keith was led into the waiting room, the Reverend Ham stood up and they shook hands. The minister was cold and emotionless, but lightened up when Keith climbed into the front seat of the family car. Keith was bubbling over about how excited he was to be going home again.

They started working their way through the midday traffic toward FDR Drive and Peekskill, a town of thirteen thousand, north of New York on the Hudson River. Keith explained that he hadn't slept a whole night through since he was admitted and slumped in the front seat. He appeared to sleep, his fuzz-covered head barely clearing the dashboard. The Reverend Ham concentrated on his driving. They stopped at a red light near the FDR's entrance ramp.

Keith seized the moment. He threw open the door, jumped out of the car, and hobbled away as fast as his cane and one good leg could carry him.

"Satan!" he heard his father yelling as he turned the corner. "Satan!"

Ham had escaped the psychiatrists' clutches only two months before Hans Kary walked into the temple. So many devotees were joining the movement, and so much was happening, the incident seemed like ancient history. The new devotees were raising money, and the temple had more than enough prasadam to feed hungry souls who happened to wander in.

Each time Kary cleaned off his tin plate, Kirtanananda stood up, walked into the kitchen, and returned with more prasadam. Kary loved it, but soon he had had enough. He pushed away his plate and declined one last helping, claiming he was expected at home. Kirtanananda gave him a copy of Prabhupada's *Easy Journey to Other Planets* and invited him to return for one of the swami's lectures.

Kary walked to the car he had borrowed from a lawyer friend, intending to drive back to Hoboken. He slid behind the wheel and glanced at the pamphlet's first page. He didn't stop until he'd finished. Kary got out of the car and returned to the temple. He told a devotee he had to see Kirtanananda now, right away.

"This is what I've been looking for!" he said when Kirtanananda appeared. "Every word hit home."

Kirtanananda gave him an enigmatic smile.

"I was raised a Catholic," Kary continued. "I hated it. But until I read this, I never knew why. Now I do. With Catholicism, you sin and confess, sin and confess. It says here that Krishna Consciousness is like unplugging a fan. Your soul keeps spinning because it has built up a lot of karma. But eventually, the spinning will stop. Everything in this book is clear and scientific."

"It is," Kirtanananda replied. "But wait until you read

the *Gita*. That's where you'll really learn what karma is all about. The *Gita* explains the *atman,* the Hindu conception of the soul, that divine part of every living being. Wait till you find out that life is—"

"I don't want to wait for anything," Kary interrupted. "I want to join. I want to be a devotee. I'll do whatever I have to."

Kirtanananda taught Kary the mantra. Kary walked out of the temple chanting. He walked all the way uptown, chanting Hare Krishna at the top of his voice. People looked at him like he was crazy.

"Go ahead and stare," Kary sang out. "I'm liberated. I have nothing to do with this world."

He walked crosstown, chanting all the way, before doubling back to his car. When he finally arrived at his house in Hoboken, it was well past midnight. He woke up Helena and told her all about his discovery. The next morning, she accompanied him to the temple. And every day after that. A month later, Prabhupada initiated both of them.

The ceremony began with Prabhupada building a ceremonial fire in the middle of the temple! Goblets holding water, ghee (clarified butter), barley, sesame seeds, powdered dyes, and bananas—symbolizing the karma that has been accumulated in countless lifetimes—were arranged in a circle around the fire. Prabhupada then lighted two sticks of incense and performed a purification ceremony, spooning water from a goblet, sipping it, and sprinkling some on the ground. Hans and Helena imitated him.

They then chanted a mantra of purification. Hans and Helena handed their master the *japa-mala* beads, the Hare Krishna rosary of the 108 beads (one for each of the gopis) that are used to count repetitions of the mantra. Prabhupada chanted hare krishna on each of the beads and gave them back, along with their new spiritual names. Hans became Hansadutta; Helena became Himavati. Prabhupada then lighted the fire. One by one, he threw the ghee, barley, sesame seeds, and bananas into the flames. The fire sizzled and crackled as it consumed the symbolic karma. When the ceremony ended, Hansadutta and Himavati were born again.

Now they were Krishna's true servants.

The service was hard.

The temple was almost an island paradise. But every time Kary stepped into the streets, his dhoti became a magnet for abuse. Passersby seemed to take pleasure in taunting him and the other devotees. Only Kirtanananda was able to tolerate it. He seemed to have been born in a dhoti, and to draw strength from the endless confrontations. He radiated so much confidence and had such a lightning-quick tongue, he made sankirtans fun.

One cold afternoon, a middle-aged man dressed in a summer jacket, a wash-and-wear white shirt, and brown slacks kept circling the midtown sankirtan party like a shark waiting to swim in for the kill. As he walked, he held a beat-up, black, leather-bound Bible over his head.

"Devil worshipers!" he finally began shouting in a deep voice that rolled along the street like a clap of thunder.

"Blasphemers! Tear off those bedsheets. Wipe that filth from your faces. Repent. Get down on your knees and pray. Get down and beg forgiveness from the Lord Jeeesuuus, your savior!"

Hans and the other devotees ignored him. They chanted louder, the man thundered louder. Office workers walking past the New York Public Library stopped to watch and grin. Finally, Kirtanananda held up his hand. The devotees stopped chanting and anxiously watched Kirtanananda approach the man.

"What, my dear sir, do you know of devils?" Kirtanananda asked. "May I assume you have read *Rosemary's Baby*, which is a prerequisite to any erudite discussion of the subject?"

The crowd laughed.

"Laugh not, for Jesus Christ cast out the devils!" the man shouted.

"Yes, he did, he cast them into the streets of New York," Kirtanananda shot back. "You can tell them by the clothes they wear. Light summer jackets on cold winter days; the fires of hell burning deep within keep them warm. You can tell them by the way they talk; demons shout at the top of their voices."

The Jesus guy shuffled on his way, muttering to himself. The devotees smiled and resumed chanting. The crowd applauded. But it didn't throw more than a few quarters into the collection; it never did. Hansadutta had been thinking about that. If only he could raise the take, Prabhupada would take notice of him.

During a temple ceremony a few weeks later, Hansadutta was nodding off when a devotee startled him by blowing a conch shell. The idea came to him at that moment. He knew that people only give when asked. Why not blow the conch in the street during sankirtans and ask for money? He tried it the next morning.

"Surprising how loud this thing is, isn't it, ladies and gentlemen?" Hansadutta asked after stepping to the front of the small group of devotees. He blasted away on the conch shell again. "That little girl over there has her hands over her ears and I don't blame her," he said when he'd stopped. "Now, ladies and gentlemen, we're going to pass the hat and I'm going to blow on this shell until it's filled. The sooner it's filled, the sooner I'll stop. Who knows, maybe the little girl will get her hearing back by tomorrow. So help us out, folks. Krishna remembers everyone's generosity."

"Look at this," Hansadutta told Kirtanananda as soon as the sankirtan party returned to the temple. He then spread a stack of dollar bills over a table. "There's a little over one hundred fifty dollars here. Any other day, we'd be lucky to come back with fifteen dollars."

From that day on, a devotee blew a conch shell at every sankirtan. Soon, money was pouring in. So were new converts and spiritual thrill-seekers. They crammed Prabhupada's lectures, pushing and shoving to squeeze into the temple at 26 Second Avenue.

One night, Prabhupada surveyed the packed room and waited for the bustling to stop.

"The time has come," the guru finally said. The temple became very quiet. "We are getting along quite nicely. Every day new devotees are coming to us. But we must do so much more. Look around you. See how the world hungers for Krishna. We must take this Krishna-conscious movement to the world. You are Krishna's messengers. He has chosen you for this important service."

The room buzzed with excitement. Devotees felt they were witnessing a turning point. They were going to make religious history. They were the chosen. They would go forth and do for Krishna what the apostles had done for Christianity.

"Kirtanananda, I wish that you go to Montreal and open a temple," Prabhupada said after a few moments. "They will soon have this affair, this world's fair, called Expo Sixty-seven. People from around the world will be coming. I wish that you, Hansadutta, follow as soon as possible and join Kirtanananda. I am thinking that if all goes well in Montreal, Hansadutta can return to Germany, the land he came from!"

"Mukunda," Prabhupada continued, looking at the former jazz musician Michael Grant, "you and your new wife, Janaki, will be leaving soon for India. I wish that you would stop in San Francisco and see if the conditions are auspicious there to open a temple. There are many hippies in San Francisco looking for something new. We will make sure they find Krishna."

Hansadutta soon joined Kirtanananda in Montreal. The two devotees rented an abandoned bowling alley and began chanting and preaching in the streets. It didn't take the Montreal newspapers long to discover the strange pair. They published nice, fluffy stories, complete with pictures of the bowling alley/temple and the two Krishnas talking to serious-looking college students.

The publicity worked its magic. Kirtanananda and Hansadutta, who had vowed to convert one new devotee each week, were soon surpassing their goal. Kirtanananda and Hansadutta puffed with pride. Like children looking forward to Christmas, they couldn't wait for Sundays, when they could tell Prabhupada all about their latest triumphs.

Prabhupada was very much a nineteenth-century gentleman, who preferred writing letters to using the phone. Nevertheless, every Sunday afternoon, he called the Montreal temple to talk to each devotee. Kirtanananda always made sure it was he who answered the phone on Sundays. He talked to Prabhupada first, then passed the phone to the other devotees.

Hansadutta was always nervous before the calls. He wanted to tell Prabhupada what a great preacher he had become, and boast about all the devotees he had personally brought into the movement. But Hansadutta couldn't tell his guru anything. Kirtanananda monitored each conversation, telling devotees when to get off the line.

Hansadutta and Kirtanananda were no different from any other ambitious young executives clawing their way up the corporate ladder. Both wanted to impress Prabhupada. They knew the goal of Krishna Consciousness was to kill the ego. According to the swami's teaching, the atman, the Hindu equivalent of the soul, was like a light burning deep within. It had been buried by several lifetimes of accumulated dirt—residue from the senses that demanded constant gratification, and the ego that demanded money, power, and prestige. The senses had to be harnessed, the ego defeated. That was done by renouncing the world, by meditating and chanting, and by living for God. But neither Hansadutta nor Kirtanananda could vanquish his ego. Both hungered for approval.

"Hansadutta, it is very good so many nice new devotees are coming to Krishna," Prabhupada said during one Sunday phone call.

"Yes, Swami, it is very good," Hansadutta replied. The slow, Indian voice excited him. His heartbeat quickened. Suddenly, he was talking as fast as he could, rushing to get all his accomplishments out. "I've done a lot of wonderful work up here, and I plan on doing a lot more—you'll see. I've set myself a goal: I'm going to do such great service for you, you are going to write a letter just to me. Not to the whole temple, just to me."

Kirtanananda, who was standing nearby, grabbed the phone. Then he covered the receiver with the palm of his hand.

"You know how many letters he's sent to me?" he asked in his nastiest voice. "Four! You've got some catching up to do, young man."

Drop Out,
Fall In, Sing Out

Mukunda, Michael Grant, couldn't believe it was all happening. He thought back to his days as a musician, to all the performers who practiced until their fingers were raw but couldn't dent the music business. Prabhupada comes along, and overnight he becomes a rock star. It had to be Krishna's mercy.

Mukunda and his wife, Janaki, had opened a storefront temple on Frederick Street, in the Haight, two blocks from San Francisco's Golden Gate Park. Prabhupada had arrived in January. Suddenly, the temple was the "in" place to be, and not just for hippies. Wealthy, establishment types from Pacific Heights were also dropping in, thanks to two stories in the *San Francisco Chronicle:* "Swami Invites Hippies to Hippieland Temple" and "Swami in Hippieland!" It seemed that everybody wanted to meet a real swami.

Mukunda decided to capitalize on Prabhupada's popularity to fuse Krishna Consciousness with rock and roll. He spent weeks organizing a "Mantra Rock Dance" at the Avalon Ballroom on Sutter and Van Ness. He'd already signed up a couple of hot local bands, including The Grateful Dead, Jefferson Airplane, Moby Grape, and Big Brother and the Holding Company with their incredible lead singer, Janis Joplin. As a final touch, he'd convinced Allen Ginsberg to introduce the one and only septuagenarian rocker from India—Prabhupada.

By the time Mukunda arrived at the Avalon on the afternoon of the concert, a two-block-long line of freaks was already waiting for the doors to open. They were wearing a mad collection of tie-dyed shirts and leather vests, Mexican ponchos and woven robes. Many wore headbands. Some had feathers in their hair, others flowers. The air was thick with the smell of incense and marijuana.

Mukunda was looking over the crowd when he heard a tremendous roar. He looked up to see a phalanx of Hell's Angels turn the corner onto Van Ness. They stopped their choppers in front of the ballroom, climbed off their bikes, adjusted their chains and war helmets, and cut to the front of the line. The hippies cheered.

Inside, San Francisco's wizards of light, Ben Van Meter and Roger Hillyard, had transformed the ballroom into an LSD fantasy. From the balcony, three movie projectors beamed travelogues and a continuous stream of television shows and commercials onto three walls; slide projectors superimposed images while strobe lights flashed, bouncing blinding shafts of pulsating colors around the swirling ballroom.

The doors opened, and Mukunda and the devotees collected $2.50 a head. Even the Hell's Angels paid. But a tall young man wearing a coat and tie walked right past the ticket takers.

"Hey, what do you think you're doing?" Mukunda yelled at the guy.

"Let him go, man," said a hippie who was watching. "That's Owsley!"

"Who's Owsley?" Mukunda asked.

"Augustus Owsley Stanley the second," said the hippie. "He's the guy who figured out how to synthesize LSD."

"Oh, yeah?" Mukunda said. "I'd like for him to talk to Prabhupada. Somebody once asked Prabhupada if LSD could help you find God. He said, 'Is God so cheap that a chemical can lead you to him?' "

Mukunda yelled after Owsley, but he floated into the crowd, oblivious.

When Prabhupada arrived, dressed in a saffron robe and wearing a garland of gardenias, the place went wild. Devotees blew conch shells, and Big Brother's drummer slid into a prolonged roll. The light show stopped and the ballroom went dark. Suddenly, pictures of Krishna flashed on the walls—Krishna stealing butter, Krishna playing his flute, Krishna and Arjuna in their chariot. Without any direct instructions, the crowd parted. Prabhupada walked from the rear of the ballroom to the stage, where the bearded poet Allen Ginsberg waited.

"With rock 'n roll, the sound is all," Ginsberg said in introducing Prabhupada. "With Krishna Consciousness, the sound leads to God. Listen to the master."

Prabhupada sat on a cushion. In his usual monotone, the same voice he used whether talking to one person or addressing five thousand, he explained the benefits of chanting the mantra. Ginsberg cranked up his harmonium and started the chant. The devotees immediately joined in. After a half-dozen repetitions, so did the rest of the audience. The bands returned to the stage and played along. Picking up the chant, the hippies climbed onto the stage and surrounded Prabhupada, who was beaming. The celebration went on for hours. Ginsberg thought it was the "height of Haight-Ashbury spiritual enthusiasm." To Mukunda, it was like being on a spaceship rocketing toward the stars.

That winter, Prabhupada got less sleep than a methamphetamine freak. He awoke each morning at three o'clock to chant his sixteen rounds. He lectured, led sankirtans in Golden Gate Park, and met with devotees, would-be devotees, and the simply curious. Before he went to bed, he spent long hours alone in his cubicle above the temple, working on his translation of the *Gita*.

After five months in San Francisco, Prabhupada returned to New York to be with his East Coast disciples. He saw everybody who wanted to see him and attended every function he was invited to, including a "Cosmic Love-In" held one afternoon at the East Village Theater and featuring Ginsberg, Timothy Leary, and a half dozen rock bands.

It was late evening when Prabhupada returned to the storefront temple on Second Avenue. He had been up since three o'clock that morning and was exhausted. He sat on his bed, holding his head. Suddenly, a white-hot bolt of pain tore through his head, twisting his face into an obscene grimace. Then his left arm began twitching. A moment later his whole left side was twitching uncontrollably.

"Prabhupada, what is it!" asked Kirtanananda, who had come down from Montreal to be with his spiritual master.

"Give me my beads and chant for me," Prabhupada said.

"I'm calling a doctor," Kirtanananda said.

"No," Prabhupada ordered. "No doctors. Get my beads."

When Kirtanananda returned with the beads, Prabhupada asked him to massage his heart. Kirtanananda laid his hand over Prabhupada's heart. It was fibrillating.

"Prabhupada, we've got to get you to a doctor!" Kirtanananda said.

"Just massage here," Prabhupada said, rubbing his hand over his heart to show Kirtanananda how to do it. "Massage is good."

Prabhupada closed his eyes. When he opened them, some color had returned to his face.

"Why are you just massaging? You must also chant Hare Krishna," Prabhupada said and closed his eyes again. He fell asleep, and Kirtanananda crept out of the room.

"What should we do? What if he has a heart attack and dies?" Kirtanananda asked Brahmananda, the New York temple president. Tears were streaming down his face.

"He won't die. Krishna would never take him from us!" Brahmananda said.

They agreed to keep an all-night vigil. While one slept in the room next to Prabhupada's, the other stayed with the spiritual master. Prabhupada woke up in the middle of the night. When he saw Kirtanananda, he asked for another massage.

Prabhupada remained in his room the next day, Memorial Day. By midafternoon, he was strong enough to sit up and listen to the kirtan that was going on downstairs. He had got out of bed to walk to the bathroom, when the spasmodic twitching began again. His eyes rolled up and his face contorted in agony. He jerked back and began to fall. He would have landed on his head if Kirtanananda had not caught him.

"Hare Krishna," Prabhupada gasped as he struggled for air.

"Brahmananda!" Kirtanananda yelled! "Call a doctor! Get an ambulance!"

The ambulance rushed Prabhupada to Beth Israel Hospital. In addition to a bad heart, doctors found he was suffering from diabetes. Because Kirtanananda refused to leave his spiritual master's side, the doctors finally agreed to let him move into Prabhupada's room and sleep in the bed next to the guru's.

"I am thinking the best thing for me is massage," Prabhupada whispered to Kirtanananda one morning. "If I was home in India, that is what the *ayurveda* physicians would prescribe. Massage will bring life back to the left side of my body."

Kirtanananda and the New York devotees gave Prabhupada hundreds of massages. The eager devotees arrived in shifts laden with prasadam, fruit, and flowers. Two devotees took turns, rotating around the clock in four-hour shifts. Prabhupada was massaged every moment he was awake. It worked. The old man was soon able to move his left arm and leg. A few days later, he even took a few steps around his room. His doctors were astounded.

"Good morning, dear," the middle-aged nurse said to Prabhupada one day as she came into the room, wheeling a steel tray. "Aren't you the spry one, sitting up all by yourself?"

Prabhupada was chanting quietly to himself. He opened his heavy eyelids and gave the nurse a look of benign indifference.

"Now, this will be over before you know it," the nurse said as she filled a syringe. "You just roll over and close your eyes and say those magic words of yours while I do all the work."

The nurse gave Prabhupada a shot and left. As soon as the door closed behind her, Prabhupada motioned for Kirtanananda to approach the bed.

"I am having no more needles," the old man whispered. "Seven days here, nothing but needles, needles, more needles. No more needles."

"But, Prabhupada, you're getting better," Kirtanananda responded. "You mustn't stop. Please."

"It is not the needles," Prabhupada said. "It is massage and the prasadam. Take me away from these needles. We will go where I can have plenty of massage and prasadam, some place where I can walk and get strong. We will leave here today."

"Not today, but soon, Prabhupada," Kirtanananda said. "I promise."

The devotees rented an oceanside cottage in Long Branch, New Jersey. They knew the hospital staff would not release Prabhupada, who was still suffering from chest pains, so they kept the plan secret.

The escape began when three devotees in a rented car pulled up to the front entrance of Beth Israel. The driver waited while the other two went up to room 607 to help Kirtanananda rush Prabhupada out of the hospital.

They collected Prabhupada's things and put him in a wheelchair. They were rolling it down the hall on the way to the elevator when a nurse spotted them and sounded the alarm. Three interns and three nurses quickly intercepted the fleeing Krishnas.

"Turn around and get him back to his room," one of the doctors snapped.

"This man is very dear to us, more dear than you can imagine," said Brahmananda, who was pushing the wheelchair. "He will get the best of care. We'll make sure he takes his medicines and comes back for checkups."

"If you take him out of here, you are condemning him to death," the intern said.

The devotees looked at each other. Their determination faltered.

"But he doesn't want to stay!" Kirtanananda said firmly. After Bellevue, doctors did not intimidate him.

"I wish to leave," Prabhupada said from the wheelchair.

Brahmananda pushed the wheelchair forward. The doctors and the nurses formed a human wall in front of the elevators.

"Let us through," Brahmananda commanded with an

authority that he did not feel. "This is a hospital, not a prison."

"If you leave, this man is going to die," one of the interns replied icily. "It will be your fault. Remember that when you bury him."

The doctors and nurses stepped aside and the devotees pushed Prabhupada to the elevator. Emotionally shaken, they got in the elevator and did not look at the doctors and nurses. But Prabhupada did. Smiling serenely, he waved good-bye.

Prabhupada prospered in Long Branch. He spent his days resting and eating the rice, *dal,* and chapatis prepared by Kirtanananda. As soon as he could, he began walking along the beach. Each day, he went a bit farther. The stronger he became, the more eager he was to return to San Francisco. Krishna had given him much work to do there; hippies were joining the movement by the dozen.

Three weeks after fleeing Beth Israel, Prabhupada returned for a checkup. He walked into the hospital unaided, trailing a small group of devotees. The doctors were amazed at his recovery. They had no objection to Prabhupada jetting across the country to San Francisco.

"Nobody's here. Wanna do it?"

Twenty-year-old hippie "Beth Ann" awakened, propped her head up on an elbow, and looked around the room—a crash pad in an old Victorian mansion in the Panhandle. It was strewn with backpacks and sleeping bags, blankets, and clothes. *Fabulous Furry Freak Brothers* comic books lay where they had been tossed, and psychedelic posters ripped from street lights adorned the walls. The place smelled of stale incense, rotten socks, filthy underwear, spilled wine, and old marijuana.

"So, you wanna do it?" her boyfriend "Dasher" repeated. "I figure we might as well. When's the last time you can remember being alone here?"

Beth Ann blinked a couple of times and looked out the window. It was morning. The fog still hugged the moist trees. The room was damp and chilly.

Dasher lit a wake-up joint, took a deep drag, and handed it down to Beth Ann. She took it and toked.

"Get in quick," she told Dasher. "It's fucking freezing in here."

She watched Dasher unbuckle the wide belt with the big brass buckle he had bought on Haight Street. When he dropped his stained bellbottoms, she unzipped the sleeping bag and scooted over.

"I've been out already," Dasher said proudly, pointing to the paper bag next to his clothes. "I got us some pirozhki. We'll have 'em for breakfast."

They finished the joint. Dasher slid his hands under his ass to warm them up, then he lifted the white Mexican muslin dress Beth Ann lived in. He stroked her little breasts and rolled her nipples between his dirt-ringed fingers.

Beth Ann moaned slightly and they kissed. Dasher's tongue darted into her mouth. He started rubbing against her. Beth Ann moaned again.

"Might as well do it now," she said, breaking the kiss.

Dasher raised his hips and pushed Beth Ann's right hand down to his cock. She guided it, and Dasher pushed. He slid in and started pumping. A friend came into the room, paused briefly to watch them, picked up one of the backpacks, and left. Beth Ann and Dasher ignored the interruption and kept on screwing.

He came. She didn't.

Without bothering to straighten her dress, Beth Ann sat up and devoured a cheese pirozhki. The grass had made her ravenous. When she lay down again, the gloom rolled over her like fog from the Pacific.

"It's all shit," she said to herself. "Fucking shit."

Unlike a lot of hippies, Beth Ann, a skinny, green-eyed blond who liked wearing headbands and bells on her toes, did not come from a broken family. Her father was a civil engineer in Worcester, Massachusetts; her mother had stayed home to raise her and her two brothers. Beth Ann loved her parents; she just didn't want to be like them. She didn't think her parents had any vision, any sense of possibilities. They assumed their daughter would be their clone.

"You're a smart girl," her mother would tell her. "You'll go to college and get a degree. You'll become a teacher; you're good with kids. That way, you'll always have something to fall back on. Teachers are always needed. You'll get married, have a nice house and a family."

Beth Ann went to Northeastern University in Boston. Dasher, her high-school boyfriend, dropped out and went to work for his father's electrical company. At night, he got stoned.

Beth Ann finished her freshman year. Her grades were good, if not spectacular, but she was bored. She kept telling Dasher that she was different from her parents, she wanted more. She was about to start a summer job at a neighborhood Tastee-Freeze when Dasher suggested they cut out to San Francisco. You keep saying you want to be different, Dasher told her. Well, here's your chance. They left early the next morning in Dasher's Chevy pickup. Beth Ann called home from a phone at a Howard Johnson's on the Mass Pike. Her mother cried.

The thrill of their adventure quickly dissipated as they struggled to live up to the hippie philosophy that more is better. At first, Beth Ann loved the freedom. They smoked grass, dropped acid, and made love with wild abandon. But more sex wasn't better. And more drugs only made her listless.

Soon after arriving in San Francisco, Beth Ann and Dasher hooked up with some kids who had a job growing Christmas trees in the mountains above Santa Cruz. All they had to do was plant a few trees every day. But they all stayed so stoned that they never got around to planting the trees. Pretty soon, the owner of the tree farm kicked them out. One of the kids knew somebody, who knew somebody, who had a place in the Haight. The tree farm group took over a room in the moldy Victorian house in the Panhandle.

A few hours after their morning romp, Beth Ann, Dasher, and a half-dozen other hippies from the crash pad were walking up Haight Street, goofing on the tourists who cruised by in the Gray Line buses. Beth Ann waved to a straight who had his face pushed up to the window. The guy recoiled. Beth Ann stepped into the street, pulled her dress open, and showed the guy her tits. The straight's mouth dropped open. Dasher and their hippie friends doubled up with laughter.

The group continued into Golden Gate Park and settled in their favorite eucalyptus grove. They arranged a mattress of blankets and sleeping bags. A hippie from Miami pulled out a harmonica and played Paul Butterfield riffs while everybody dropped acid. Beth Ann knew she was starting to trip when the trees began to wah-wah to the harmonica. She wrapped her arms around herself and swayed with the trees. After a while, the harmonica player fell silent; but a new music had become clearly audible, wilder, more rhythmic. It echoed through the park. Beth Ann was transported. Before she knew it, the sun was rising.

"Did you guys hear that music last night?" a hippie asked as they rolled up their bedding. "Man, was it ever far out."

"Those were Krishnas," somebody said. "They chant in the park every day. Let's go over to their temple. I hear chanting with the Krishnas is a great way to come down."

They walked to the storefront temple at 513 Frederick Street and entered under a sign that said, Stay high all the time. Discover eternal bliss. The morning service was over and the temple was empty except for two devotees who were talking a couple of kids down from bad acid trips. Beth Ann was impressed. These people were helping people. A devotee came up and asked if she was hungry. She nodded. The devotee left and returned a few minutes later carrying plates piled high with prasadam. He stepped back and smiled and Beth Ann thought he looked beatific.

It was the best food Beth Ann had eaten since she had left home. The vegetables tasted clean and fresh and made her feel good. The last time Beth Ann had tripped, she had gone into a McDonalds and ordered a hamburger. When it arrived, she smelled burning flesh and opened the bun to see large, thick pools of blood oozing out of the charred meat. She had run out of the restaurant and had vowed to become a vegetarian.

The prasadam seemed like some kind of sign, an answer to an unspoken prayer. From then on, Beth Ann returned to the Frederick Street temple almost every day. Her hippie friends were no longer even paying lip service to peace and love. They got high and got laid and then did it all again. The Krishnas had found a way to make love real. Beth Ann decided to become a devotee.

Krishna was easy to sell to Beth Ann. Like most hippies, she had rejected Christianity when she rejected her parents' values. Every time she saw a hippie wearing a "Kill a Commie for Christ" T-shirt, she smiled. And like most hippies, she did not want to hear about death, even Christ's death. Death was a bummer.

Krishna was a far more appealing figure than Christ. Krishna was cool. He played the flute and hung out with beautiful girls. He wore flowers and feathers and went barefoot. Krishna was eternally young, eternally free.

"You're a fuckin' idiot!" Dasher screamed when Beth Ann told him she was going to join the Krishnas. "They'll fry your mind and turn you into a robot."

Beth Ann started to cry. "I've been telling everybody for as long as I can remember that I want to lead a good life and help people," she told Dasher. "I've found the place where people are really doing that. I've got to join. I know I'll have to give up my independence, but I've got to do it."

"Without independence, you ain't got nothin'," Dasher said contemptuously.

"What does independence matter if all it comes to is this?" Beth Ann asked, looking around the crash pad. "This is gross. Decadent. People need guidance, Dasher."

"People need to leave people alone," Dasher said angrily and stormed out of the room.

That night Dasher left San Francisco for a job as a caretaker of a motel on Highway 101, near the estuary of the Russian River. Beth Ann moved into the temple.

A short time later, Beth Ann and a small group of devotees drove out to the cabin devotees had rented for Prabhupada in Stinson Beach, a beautiful town on the edge of the redwood-crowned mountains north of San Francisco. Beth Ann felt completely, wonderfully fulfilled. Sex and drugs no longer played any part in her life. Male devotees called her *mataji,* meaning "mother," even though she was only twenty. It helped break down the sexual stereotypes. Men and women traded jobs, sharing the cooking and cleaning. They took turns decorating the deities. It was fun, a lot more fun than being a hippie.

Later that summer, Beth Ann and the San Francisco devotees all piled into cars and drove out to the airport. Everyone was somber; Prabhupada was leaving, returning to India. He had been talking about going home ever since his stroke. He thought Vrindaban, the most sacred site on earth, was the best place to finish recovering. He was eager to consult with ayurveda physicians, whose practice is based on the Vedas, India's sacred books. And if he did not recover, he wanted to die in Vrindaban.

There was a second reason for the trip. Prabhupada was taking along Kirtanananda, his favorite disciple. He wanted to show Kirtanananda Krishna's shrines, to immerse him in Indian culture and give him an advanced crash course in his chosen religion. If something did happen to Prabhupada, the bond between East and West would continue to gather strength. Kirtanananda would carry on.

The devotees drowned their sadness by putting on an ecstatic sankirtan in the Air India terminal. The noise attracted travelers from the far ends of the airport. Hansadutta, who had flown in from Montreal to say goodbye to his spiritual master, danced with more fervor than any other devotee. He jumped and chanted like he was totally possessed. But his eyes never left Prabhupada.

Hansadutta was desperate. The spiritual master still hadn't sent him a letter. Prabhupada was jetting off to India, perhaps to die, and he still hadn't given him the special acknowledgment he craved. Like a little boy starving for affection, he started to cry. The tears rolled down his cheeks and dropped onto his tightly muscled chest. Other devotees, caught up in the emotion of the sankirtan and Prabhupada's departure, started crying, too.

Suddenly, Hansadutta had an idea. He walked over and kneeled in front of Prabhupada.

"Swami, there are a lot of people here," he said, keeping his head bowed. "Can I take a collection?"

Prabhupada nodded. Hansadutta jumped up, went into his street rap and passed the hat. It was soon full. He fell to his knees again and presented it to Prabhupada just as the flight was called. Prabhupada looked at Hansadutta.

"So, our trip has an auspicious beginning," he said. "We have had a nice kirtan and have taken up a nice collection. It is Krishna's mercy."

Hansadutta started to cry again. Prabhupada had noticed him and spoken to him alone. He had attracted Prabhupada's attention by raising money. It was a lesson he would never forget.

Ten days after Prabhupada flew off to India, George and Patti Harrison arrived in San Francisco. They had read a cover story on San Francisco's hippies in the international edition of *Time* magazine and had decided to check out the Summer of Love for themselves.

The trip was more than the whim of an impossibly rich rock star. Harrison ardently believed that anything was possible. And why shouldn't he? He had grown up poor in Liverpool. Now the entire Western world was singing along with *Sergeant Pepper's Lonely Hearts Club Band.* If the Beatles could revolutionize music, why couldn't the hippies be harbingers of a better world?

George and Patti had made a point of keeping their trip secret. They didn't want a rose-colored, watered-down tour. They wanted to see the real Haight, just like anyone else. George pictured a medieval village of happy craftsmen turning out everything, from leather boots to scented candles.

A cab dropped them off in the Panhandle. George and Patti made their way to Haight Street and started walking toward Golden Gate Park.

"Hey, man, got any spare change?" asked a filthy young hippie, too stoned to recognize them.

"Spare any change? We need to eat, man," said a young girl, grabbing George's arm.

He shook her off.

A boy wearing a black turtleneck stopped directly in

front of George and thrust a tambourine into the Beatle's face. "Acid?" he asked, shaking the tambourine.

Harrison was silent.

"Mescaline?" the boy asked, shaking the tambourine again. "Meth?"

Harrison was speechless; the drug dealer moved on down Haight Street.

The Harrisons walked on, past tawdry Day-Glo poster shops and second-hand clothing stores. George was in shock. His New-Age Eden was a behaviorial sink, a slum. As he strolled with his wife, the impression he got was of a West Coast extension of the Bowery.

"Could it be?" one passerby asked aloud. "Nah. No way."

One kid walked past George three times, trying to work up his courage.

"George?" he asked on the fourth pass. "Are you George?"

Harrison reluctantly nodded.

"It's George!" the kid yelled, skipping up the street. "It's a fuckin' Beatle. George is here. Hey, George is here!"

The Harrisons kept walking. They passed a robed group chanting a catchy rhythm Harrison recognized as a mantra, but the growing crowd pushed the Beatle pied piper along before he could check them out. When they reached the park, somebody handed him a beat-up acoustic guitar and George ran through a medley of the Beatles' early hits. Then he and Patti hailed a cab and fled.

On the flight back to London, Harrison was heavy with guilt. He thought the Beatles were partly responsible for what was happening in the Haight. They had presented LSD as a mind-expanding adventure in "Lucy in the Sky with Diamonds." They had pushed marijuana as a viable way to escape mind-deadening reality in "A Day in the Life." By now, it was obvious to Harrison that drugs did not lead to a better world beyond; they led down a dark, dirty alley. But he tried to keep alive the thought that there might be a bright spot somewhere in the trip—those robed chanters he had spotted in the park. Who were they? he wondered.

Harrison, along with John Lennon, was keenly interested in Eastern religions and culture. He had jumped at John's idea to use sitars in some of their songs. They had talked Paul and Ringo into going to India the previous summer to stay on the Maharishi's ashram. He started humming, trying to recall the chanters' tune. It wouldn't quite come.

"As soon as we get back to London," he told Patti, "I'm going to find out about those people in the park."

Ambitious Pupil

Prabhupada leaned over to smell the vegetable curry the Air India stewardess had placed on the tray in front of him. The plane was an hour-and-a-half out of San Francisco and thirty-six-thousand feet over Colorado, on its way to New York, London, Moscow, and—its final destination—New Delhi.

"Yes," Prabhupada said, picking up the plastic fork. "I already feel I'm home."

"Where exactly is home?" Kirtanananda asked. "I've been working with you over a year, and I don't even know where your home is. You never talk about yourself. Loosen up, talk a little."

"My home is with Krishna in Vrindaban," Prabhupada said. "But much of my mundane life was spent in Calcutta. It is of no consequence."

"Please," Kirtanananda begged. "We have many hours to spend together. You know how I found Krishna. I would like to know how you did."

"It is enough that you are my devotee," Prabhupada replied.

"It's important to me, Prabhupada," Kirtanananda pressed.

Prabhupada looked around the plane. Most of the passengers were enjoying their meal. A few were already sleeping.

"All right," he said. "But I'll talk only a little. Then we must chant and sleep."

Prabhupada's religious awakening in Bombay was not nearly as dramatic as Saint Paul's on the road to Damascus. His zeal built gradually, like the momentum of a boulder rolling down a gentle hill.

This spiritual boulder, he said, was dislodged by a guru named Bhaktisiddhanta, a gaunt master with a rich black beard and thick, rimless glasses. They met in 1922 when Prabhupada was a twenty-six-year-old householder and businessman named Abhay Charan De.

A friend had dragged him to see the guru. When the two young men entered, Bhaktisiddhanta was on the roof enjoying a respite from the oppressive heat. He welcomed them politely. Sitting crosslegged on the roof watching the sunset, the two began discussing religion and politics. The guru, Prabhupada recalled, was horrified to hear that he'd abandoned Krishna to work for Indian independence.

"You're an educated man," the guru had responded. "You put politics above Krishna? What absolute nonsense. Krishna is above all else. You are educated; you should preach Krishna Consciousness throughout the whole world."

Prabhupada said he looked down at the traffic in the street below to hide his embarrassment. He had tried to impress Bhaktisiddhanta by exaggerating his devotion to the independence movement. In reality, he acknowledged, he had done little more than promise fealty to Gandhi. For, despite the independence leader's call to boycott all foreign schools, Prabhupada had spent four years at the Scottish Churches' College in Calcutta, one of India's best colleges. He said he hadn't found the work hard. But his conscience had turned each lesson into a torturous internal battle.

"I was very young, very ambitious," he told Kirtanananda. "I wanted to be a very great man, a very rich man. So I didn't make a choice. I tried to satisfy my conscience and my ambition. I completed my schooling, but boycotted the graduation ceremony and refused to accept my diploma."

Prabhupada went on. He spoke quickly, describing, in his slightly clipped English, his boyhood devotion to Krishna. Every day, he told Kirtanananda, he had worshiped in a small temple across the street from his home.

But like many other young men in his neighborhood, he had forsaken religion to concentrate on family and career. Many times, he said, he was nagged by doubts about the wisdom of that choice. But he had always dismissed his misgivings and convinced himself that he'd made the right decision.

"When Bhaktisiddhanta asked me why I didn't preach, it was very difficult," Prabhupada told Kirtanananda. "At first, I didn't want to tell him about leaving Krishna. So I said I had a wife and five children."

Prabhupada stopped again and Kirtanananda could see that he was reluctant to continue.

"So what happened then?" he prodded.

Prabhupada didn't answer immediately. Then he said, "I told him that before we could spread Indian culture anywhere, we must reclaim our country from the British. But Bhaktisiddhanta replied, 'What nonsense! God comes before politics. God comes before anything. If that is not true, what is?' "

Prabhupada told Kirtanananda the story as if he were still trying to make peace with himself, to forgive himself for an unforgivable indiscretion. Bhaktisiddhanta's simplicity and certainty had shattered his well-constructed armor.

"How could I refute him? His words struck me as correct. From that day forward, devotion to Krishna replaced my dedication to Gandhi. I began to read the sacred literature. I discovered Lord Chaitanya Mahaprabhu."

"Wait," Kirtanananda interrupted. "I know you're going to start on Lord Chaitanya—you always do. But let me remind you that you're talking to your best student. I know Chaitanya invented the sankirtan and revitalized Hinduism. I know he even converted the Islamic governor in Bengal. But I want to know about you."

"I am of no importance," Prabhupada replied, closing his eyes. "I am a simple devotee of Krishna. I am forever remembering that I am a servant of the servant of the servant."

"Come on, Prabhupada," Kirtanananda persevered.

"Don't preach to the initiated. If I'm going to be like you, I have to know about you."

"You can be like me by always remembering Krishna," Prabhupada said simply and with finality. "Now let's chant together for a little while. Perhaps we will talk more later."

Kirtanananda frowned. He watched the old swami's face relax, his lips moving as he silently chanted.

After Prabhupada finished chanting, he took a nap. Kirtanananda was waiting when he woke up.

"Tell me about your family," Kirtanananda asked, after the stewardess brought them some juice. "You never mention them. All I know is, you were married and had—what is it, five children?"

Prabhupada didn't say a thing. He sat motionless in the narrow seat, his head bowed, his arms resting on the armrests. Kirtanananda was about to speak when Prabhupada looked up and glanced at his devotee.

"I will tell you," Prabhupada said. "But only because through my story you will see that to find Krishna, to find true happiness, you must renounce the world. There is no happiness if you embrace the world. It is as Krishna says in *Srimad-Bhagavatam:* 'When I feel especially merciful toward someone, I gradually take away all his material possessions.'"

Prabhupada let out a deep sigh. "For thirty years, from the day I met Bhaktisiddhanta, I was a householder who went about preaching Lord Chaitanya's message of Krishna Consciousness. Every year, I did more and more for Krishna and less of the things one must do to live in the world. I was so busy chanting, studying, traveling, and writing that my businesses failed, one after another. It was Krishna's mercy."

A stewardess came up the aisle, pushing a cart and offering passengers coffee, tea, soft drinks, and cookies. Prabhupada accepted several cookies but declined the forbidden stimulants. He took a bite of one cookie and chuckled.

Kirtanananda looked up in surprise.

"This is very funny," Prabhupada said. "The cookie

reminds me of Raharani, my wife. She did not share my devotion."

For the next forty minutes, Prabhupada described his wife's bitter disillusionment with him. Kirtanananda listened carefully, his excitement growing.

Raharani, Prabhupada began, couldn't understand why he had changed. She had married an ambitious young businessman and ended up with a Krishna preacher.

"Did she object?" Kirtanananda asked.

Prabhupada searched for the right words.

"She wanted to be more English than the English," he said finally. "She was Westernized. She would get very angry if she missed her afternoon tea. I ordered her to stop, but she ignored me. Every time I went out to preach, she asked why was I abandoning her. When I told her Krishna comes before everything, she always said, 'But Abhay, I'm your wife. You have a family. You have responsibilities.' It was not easy for her. We had little money. One day, when I was out doing my service, she took one of my sacred texts and sold it. I came home and immediately noticed the book was gone. When I asked her what she'd done with it, she started crying. I was very stern. I still remember it very clearly. She said she needed some cookies for her tea and had sold it. I was very, very angry, but I didn't say a word."

Following that, Prabhupada said, he had packed a few belongings and walked out.

"What happened to her?" Kirtanananda asked.

"She moved into her father's house with the children who were still living at home. I have not seen her since."

"When did that happen?" Kirtanananda asked.

"It was 1954," Prabhupada said, his voice filling with fondness at the memory. "I went directly to Vrindaban, where I lived for most of the next eleven years. Those were the happiest days of my life. Everything I did, I did for Krishna. I chanted sixty-four rounds a day. Not sixteen rounds, like you American devotees. *Sixty-four* rounds. I never missed a day, even when I was sick. I began my translation of the *Srimad-Bhagavatam!* I published my little magazine and sold it on the streets."

Prabhupada went on to describe the majesty of Vrinda-ban's myriad temples in lavish detail. He said he'd lived in their shadow in a series of sparsely furnished rooms. He had been completely content and in 1959 had taken a vow of sannyasa. The next year, he had published *Easy Journey to Other Planets,* the first of his many books about Krishna Consciousness. He had finished translating the first canto of the twelve-canto, sixty-volume *Srimad-Bhagavatam* five years later and presented a copy to Lal Bahadur Shastri, the prime minister of India.

"He recommended that the volume be placed in every library in India," Prabhupada recalled, obviously pleased.

"This is great stuff!" Kirtanananda said. "I'm glad you told me. This is important. I know exactly what we should do. We should tell your story. A book, yes. Maybe a movie. We must use it to make devotees understand that Krishna comes first, families second. We'll use your marriage as the perfect paradigm."

"There is room for both *grihasthas* and sannyasis in the movement," Prabhupada said, referring to householders and celibates who have renounced the world.

"Sure, there is," Kirtanananda said. "We don't have to argue about that. Go on, tell me more. Tell me how you decided to come to America."

"It was my spiritual master's wish," Prabhupada said. "He wanted me to take Krishna Consciousness to the West. India is a very spiritual land. Yet for all those many years, it was Western missionaries who brought Christianity to us. I was getting old. I knew I had to try to obey my master before I died!"

Prabhupada said he had sought help from Mrs. Sumati Morarji, the owner of the Scindia Steamship Company and one of the angels who had financed the publication of his *Bhagavatam.* He said he went to her office without an appointment in May 1965 and asked her secretary to announce his arrival.

"She saw me right away," he said. "She is a very good woman. I told her I wanted to go to America to preach Krishna Consciousness. I said, 'I must go before it is too late. You have many ships. Will you send me on one going to America?' "

"That's the most ridiculous thing I've every heard!" Mrs. Morarji had replied. "You are much too old to go anywhere, and America is much too cold. Americans care nothing for Krishna. Stay here and preach to your own people. We need you."

"Krishna is not just for India, Krishna is for the world," Prabhupada told Mrs. Morarji. "Please, just a little room on one of your ships. Say yes today so I will not have to come back tomorrow."

Prabhupada said they had a long argument. Mrs. Morarji finally relented and gave him a ticket on a tramp steamer called the *Jaladuta*.

"It was a miserable trip," Prabhupada told Kirtanananda without complaining. "I had brought along my own prasadam, but I was much too sick to cook. One night, I had a terrible pain in the left side. The pain went away, but I was unable to move. The next morning the pain returned, even more terrible than the day before. I lay in my bunk, chanting and waiting for the pain to come one more time and carry me away. It was Krishna's mercy I recovered. He intervened because he had a mission for me.

"When the boat docked in New York City in September of 1965, I came down the gangplank with only the clothes I was wearing, a trunk full of books, an old typewriter, a bag of cereal, a pot to cook it in, and a few dollars' worth of rupees."

"Prabhupada, this is wonderful!" Kirtanananda said, his words spilling out. "I can't believe you haven't told me about this before."

"It is of no consequence," Prabhupada said dryly.

"No, no," Kirtanananda said. "This is the key. Try to understand."

Prabhupada turned away.

"Please," Kirtanananda begged, "let me teach you something about America. Americans love heroes, okay? Try to see it as a movie: You sacrifice everything for your faith—your wife, your children, your business. You come alone, without money, to the land of hippies and heathens. You have two heart attacks on the way here and nearly die. But against all odds you succeed. You convert the infidels. You fulfill your master's wishes. John Huston would do this film. I can see it now."

Prabhupada looked at Kirtanananda and smiled.

"That is all very nice," he said. "Now let's be silent and chant a little while."

"Wait," Kirtanananda said. "I've got some ideas for the movement. If we—"

"Chant," Prabhupada interrupted, closing his eyes.

When the plane landed in Delhi, Kirtanananda was in a funk. He had not been able to wheedle anything more out of Prabhupada. Worse, he couldn't convince the guru to listen to his ideas. Prabhupada just kept repeating, "It is all in Krishna's hands. We will succeed if we will only chant Hare Krishna."

Damn stubborn old mule.

He had forgotten how much he hated India until he stepped off the plane and was assaulted by Delhi's heat and stench. It was two o'clock in the morning, but the crowd in the terminal made it feel like the rush hour in Grand Central Station. They had to stand in a seemingly endless line waiting for an officious Indian in a white uniform to check and recheck their passports and visas, stamp them, and send them to the next line, where another clerk did the same thing. Flies buzzed while slow-moving fans churned the heavy air. By the time they cleared customs, Kirtanananda's black wool suit was soaked with sweat.

Walking out of the airport was even more depressing. They were surrounded by a mob of joyous people welcoming their loved ones. But no one was there to greet them. Prabhupada and Kirtanananda were alone.

Kirtanananda must have been disappointed. He had probably imagined a scene from a Cecil B. DeMille epic, with thousands of robed devotees dropping to their knees, offering obeisances to their spiritual master on his return from conquering America. They would rush to his side with a palanquin and hoist him over their heads. Then they would bear him through the cheering, orchid-throwing crowd.

As it was, their only greeting came from barefoot kids,

bedraggled porters, and pushy taxi drivers, who fought to
carry their bags and get them in a cab. Prabhupada cut a
deal with a driver and they piled into a beat-up taxi for
the drive through the deserted streets to Chippiwada, a
district in Old Delhi.

Thirty minutes later the driver stopped in the shadow
of a crumbling building and turned around with his palm
out. Prabhupada dug forty rupees out of his billfold and
gave them to the driver, who immediately pocketed the
money.

"My change," Prabhupada demanded in Hindi.

"What change?" the driver said.

"We agreed: thirty rupees," Prabhupada said. "Give
me my change."

The driver refused, and they began arguing with each
other. Annoyed, Kirtanananda got out of the car.

"You sound more like a pissed-off New Yorker than
Krishna's anointed messenger," he said irritably, pulling
on Prabhupada's dhoti. "Let him go. We don't need
money, we need sleep!"

But the argument raged on. Finally the driver got out,
opened the trunk, threw their luggage on the road, and
sped off.

"He cheated me," Prabhupada said.

"Hari Bol to the most spiritual country on earth,"
Kirtanananda said sarcastically, following Prabhupada to
the door of the darkened temple.

It was locked. Kirtanananda pounded on the door. A
sleepy Hindu finally appeared. He recognized Prabhupada
and his face lit up with a smile. He bowed, asked them to
enter, led them to Prabhupada's old room, and unlocked
the door.

The cubbyhole was filthy. Dust covered every hori-
zontal surface. Black bugs the size of Kirtanananda's
index finger darted into crevices in the walls as soon as
Prabhupada turned on the naked light bulb. Piled in the
corners were copies of Prabhupada's *Srimad-Bhagavatam*.

"This is where I lived when I did my *Bhagavatam*,"
Prabhupada said cheerfully. "Every day I woke, chanted,
typed, cooked, typed, and slept."

The swami had described the Jerusalem of Krishna

Consciousness as a paradise. The vision was soon shattered. Vrindaban was worse than Delhi. When they arrived, the temperature was 110 and there was no place to hide from the heat. The little town reeked of raw sewage! Many of the temples were abandoned and crumbling. Krishna Consciousness was dying in the land of its birth.

The trip got worse. A week after they arrived, Kirtanananda was leveled by a wicked attack of dysentery. He couldn't eat. It was days before he gained enough strength to sit up. Lying in a miserable, bug-infested little room in a small temple one hot afternoon, he heard a noise outside and looked up to see Prabhupada washing his hands at the outdoor well. A swarm of flies descended on the guru, completely covering him. Prabhupada was oblivious to the bugs and went right on washing his hands. Kirtanananda doubled over, wrenched by an attack of the dry heaves.

Eventually Kirtanananda recovered, and in August the monsoons arrived, breaking the heat. The stupefying routine broke, and devotees began preparing to celebrate Krishna's birthday.

On August 28, Krishna's birthday, Prabhupada anointed Kirtanananda as the first American sannyasi. It was a great honor for so young a man—one Prabhupada would not have bestowed had he not needed a successor to take over the movement and carry on his spiritual master's wishes. Prabhupada was sixty-three when he first put on the saffron robes. Now he was making a thirty-one-year-old into a master.

It must have been a heady moment for Kirtanananda. But the following days brought unrelenting torture. Kirtanananda and Prabhupada rose every morning at three o'clock to chant for several hours; Kirtanananda then had to spend the rest of the day listening to the old man drone on about the *Bhagavatam* and the *Chaitanya Charitamrita,* the long, interpretive biography of Lord Chaitanya. The routine must have galled Kirtanananda. He was a religious scholar; if he needed to, he could read texts on his own.

The visit to India became a crisis for Kirtanananda. It was clear he and his spiritual master disagreed on how devotees should dress, how they should be recruited, how the movement should grow. And Prabhupada did not seem to understand the Western mind. He was too old to change. Kirtanananda could picture himself stepping up to a lectern at Harvard and looking out at a room full of hip theologians like Harvey Cox. He would be so much more effective than Prabhupada. He knew the Western mind; he knew the Bible. He could dazzle them with cross-cultural comparisons, knock their intellectual socks off.

The old man had fulfilled his mission; he had enlightened Kirtanananda. But now it was time for him to surrender to Kirtanananda, just as Kirtanananda had surrendered to him. It was time to complete the cycle. Only then would Krishna Consciousness go forward.

"Prabhupada, I want to go home," Kirtanananda said one day. "Send me back to America. I can do great service there. Here, I do nothing."

"There is still much you must learn," Prabhupada said. "We have only made a beginning. America can wait; things are going very nicely there. Just see. All the letters say we are making new devotees every day."

"Prabhupada, I want to go home," Kirtanananda persisted.

"You may go," Prabhupada finally told him. "But not to America. You must go to London and start a temple. My spiritual master sent sannyasis there in the 1930s and they never made a devotee. Not one. You will go and make many devotees, as you did in Montreal. I have here a letter from a very important English lady who writes to say she is interested in Krishna Consciousness. You go find her and she will help you start a temple. When everything is going nicely, I will come and initiate."

Kirtanananda bowed. He took Prabhupada's money and bought a one-way ticket. To New York.

The Krishna honeymoon was over. Kirtanananda's refusal to go to London was the first crack in a movement that would eventually shatter into a thousand pieces.

Winds of War

A Guru Defects,
the Beatles Enlist

In early September, 1969, Brahmananda, the president of the New York temple, was walking along Houston Street, thinking about the temple's upcoming move to a larger building at 61 Second Avenue. He turned the corner and spotted a familiar figure farther up the block: a small man with a shaved head, who, despite his cane, was walking with a limp.

It looks like Kirtanananda, Brahmananda said to himself. Nah. No way. It couldn't be. Kirtanananda's in India with Prabhupada. Besides, this guy's a Catholic priest.

Brahmananda was haunted by the resemblance. He quickened his pace to get a closer look.

"Kirtanananda, what are you doing here!" he cried in astonishment when he caught up with the dark figure.

"Hare Krishna, Brahmananda," Kirtanananda said. "Prabhupada sent me back. I have to go up to Boston to deliver a speech at Harvard."

"So soon?" Brahmananda exclaimed. "Look how you're dressed. When I first spotted you, I thought you were a priest."

"That's Prabhupada's idea," Kirtanananda said eagerly. "He wants us to go mainstream. We talked about it a lot in India. We've decided it's the only way to build a broad-based movement. What do you think?"

"Prabhupada wants us all to dress like that?" Brahmananda asked. "I can't believe it."

"He's been through so many changes," Kirtanananda said, his animation increasing. "It's really exciting. It just goes to show Krishna's greatness. That a man his age can still have so supple a mind is an example of what true enlightenment is."

"What kind of changes?" Brahmananda asked, stopping in front of the temple.

"You'll hear all about them tonight," Kirtanananda said. "I'm jet-lagged out, but I can't wait to preach. Our movement is just beginning to catch fire, Brahmananda. Five years from now, this country will be electing Krishna congressmen."

The word spread quickly through New York's Krishna community that Kirtanananda had returned with big news. That night, every devotee and would-be devotee in the city jammed into the Second Avenue temple to hear his lecture. What he said was even more shocking than his white collar and black clerical garb.

Kirtanananda barely mentioned Krishna. He talked about Brahman, the all-pervasive spirit of God emanating from everyone and everything. The devotees exchanged looks. Kirtanananda had turned into a *Mayavadi,* an impersonalist who believes that God is shapeless and without personality because he is everywhere. Mayavadis believe that Krishna is only one of God's many manifestations. For that reason, they were regarded as heretics by the old enemy of Hindu impersonalism, Srila Prabhupada.

Brahmananda was appalled. He stormed out of the service without saying a word and went directly to his room. There, he sat down at his desk and fired off a letter to Prabhupada. He tried to recall the whole sermon and, whenever he could, quoted it directly. He also included a detailed description of the black frock.

"Did you authorize this?" Brahmananda concluded. "Please write and tell us as quickily as you can."

For weeks there was no answer. The New York temple split into pro- and anti-Kirtanananda factions. The devotees who supported Kirtanananda pointed out that he was the movement's first American sannyasi, Prabhupada's most trusted disciple. He was a great devotee, a visionary, and the best preacher in the movement.

Anti-Kirtanananda devotees were convinced he was a false prophet and soon began calling him Black Keith.

Rumors abounded that he was once again living with Howard Wheeler, and that the couple had resumed a long-standing homosexual relationship. And not only did Black Keith overlook Krishna in his sermons, he hardly ever mentioned Prabhupada.

Every day, Brahmananda was waiting when the mail clattered through the slot in the front door. Day by day, his disappointment mounted. If only Prabhupada wasn't in Vrindaban, where there were no phones.

The tissue-thin international letter finally arrived in the middle of October 1968. Brahmananda slipped it under his dhoti and ran up to his room. His heart was beating so fast, he had to stop and catch his breath before tearing it open.

"Unbelievable!" he screamed—so loudly that devotees chanting downstairs heard him. He sat down, got up, and began walking around the room. Then he stopped and read the key paragraph a second time.

"News of Kirtanananda's activities has given me much pain. . . Kirtanananda has not rightly understood KC[Krishna Consciousness] philosophy . . . the best thing will be to prohibit him from speaking at any of our functions. It is clear that he has become crazy and he should once more be sent to Bellevue."

"Hare Krishna," Kirtanananda said as he walked into the temple that night. "It's nice to see everybody together for once."

The devotees were silent. Kirtanananda walked over to the prasadam table and picked up a tin plate.

"Put that down," Brahmananda snapped.

Kirtanananda whirled around. "What did you say?"

"This came from Prabhupada today," Brahmananda said, advancing toward Kirtanananda and waving the letter in his face. "You are exposed."

Kirtanananda took the letter and read it.

"Everything I did, I did for you," Kirtanananda said, looking around the room. "I'm the only one who can take this movement forward. Prabhupada knows that. That's why he took me, only me, to India!"

"Don't even mention his name!" Brahmananda yelled.

"You have betrayed him. It's clear. You are guilty of false preaching. There is no more serious crime."

"Come off it," Kirtanananda said. "I'm doing what you'd do if you had the chance."

"Hey, man, fuck you!" shouted a devotee, a street kid from Brooklyn who had been one of Kirtanananda's most ardent supporters. "Prabhupada knows what's best, not you!"

"Yeah!" other devotees joined in. "Right on!"

"Get out," Brahmananda ordered in a fury. "Get out and don't come back. Ever. You are banned."

The devotees parted to form an aisle. Kirtanananda took a few steps toward the door. Then he stopped and looked around the room. "Each of you, this is the worst mistake you have ever made."

The devotee from Brooklyn pushed his way through the crowd. "The mistake we made was not gettin' rid of you the day you showed up wearin' that black shit," he said to Kirtanananda. "You're an asshole, man. Anybody who puts himself above Prabhupada is an asshole."

The devotee hawked noisily and let a honker fly at Kirtanananda. The gob hit him on the shoulder.

The devotees cheered. Another devotee spit. Then a third. As Kirtanananda bolted for the door, he was showered by a steady barrage of mucus.

"Those animals!" Kirtanananda screamed to Howard Wheeler when he burst into their apartment. "They spit at me. Look at this shirt. Just look at it."

"What happened?" Wheeler asked.

"Brahmananda got a letter from Prabhupada," Kirtanananda replied. "I'm banned from the temple."

"Forget about it," Wheeler told Kirtanananda. "We don't need that bunch of shits. They're garbage we scraped off the streets. Where would Prabhupada be if we hadn't found him? We'll start our own movement. When we're finished, Prabhupada and ISKCON will be ancient history."

"It's over, Howard," said Kirtanananda. "You can't just start a movement for the hell of it. Without Prabhupada, we haven't got a hook. We don't have a foundation."

"Aren't you forgetting something?" Wheeler asked. "We've got something better than Prabhupada."

"What?" Kirtanananda demanded.

Wheeler walked over to his desk. He picked up a massive manuscript and held it over his head.

"We've got his book," Wheeler crowed. "What more do we need?"

Wheeler had been editing Prabhupada's translation of the *Gita* ever since he joined the movement. "You know best how to put it nicely," Prabhupada had told him when he asked for help.

Although the *Gita* is relatively short, Prabhupada's *Bhagavad-Gita As It Is* ran to more than nine hundred pages. The bulk came from the explanatory notes. Macmillan had agreed to publish it, but only in a shorter version. Wheeler was slaving away, trying to cut the tome to an acceptable length.

The next morning, Wheeler started offering the book. He told editors that he and his coauthor, Keith Ham, were Hindu scholars who had spent years working on the *Gita*. They had come up with a translation that was sure to appeal to the counterculture. It stressed action, he said over and over, not philosophy.

Wheeler was unable to make a sale. Perhaps the editors had heard that Macmillan had a contract with the founder of the Krishna movement and weren't about to publish a competing edition. Or perhaps they could not believe that such young men could translate the *Gita* and produce hundreds of pages of analysis in just a couple of years.

Howard Wheeler and Keith Ham were walking up a street in McMechan, West Virginia, an up-and-coming ghost town five miles up the Ohio River from Moundsville. Most of the houses on the narrow street were identical tacky boxes, sporting the same little front porches. Jammed tight like matchsticks, they were separated by pencil-wide walkways, too narrow for the sun to penetrate for more than an hour or two a day.

After the cacophony of New York, the town seemed unnaturally quiet. The only sound was an occasional, muffled melody from the jukebox at Jerry's, the bar at the end of the block that billed itself as the "Home of the Barflies."

Ham and Wheeler had arrived early that morning to talk to Richard Rose. Rose had placed a small ad in the *San Francisco Oracle,* the nation's first psychedelic newspaper, offering the free use of a farm. He envisioned turning it into something of a countercultural convention center and commune, a combination of a nineteenth-century Chautauqua and a school of philosophy like the one Bronson Alcott had established in Concord, Massachusetts.

Ham saw the ad and thought that a farm in the pine-crowned West Virginia hills would be a perfect place to start his movement. He exchanged letters with Rose; in his last letter, Rose had written that if Ham came to West Virginia, they would talk it over.

"This is it," Wheeler said as they approached a small, red brick house. "You knock."

"No, you knock," Ham said. "I wrote the letters; you knock."

Wheeler knocked. The door was opened by a small man with a thick white mustache. He was wearing a black turtleneck with a black beret.

"Which one of you is Keith Ham?" he asked before they could introduce themselves. "I want you to know I had you come all the way out here because you write an intelligent letter. I got a flock of letters after that ad ran, and most of them are terrible, just terrible. Most of those hippies can't put two words together. By the way, I'm Richard Rose."

Rose invited them in. He led them through the living room, which had piles of yellowing magazines stacked knee-high, to a small kitchen at the rear of the house, where he told them to sit down.

"Before we get started, there's a couple of things you should know about me," Rose said as he pulled out a chair. "I'm a muckraker, a rebel in search of the truth. The first thing I ever muckraked was the Catholic church. I went into a seminary to study to be a Franciscan. I read church history and found out how organized religion was used to beat hell out of the peasants. I've met hundreds of priests; I've never met one I considered sincere."

Rose got up to make some coffee.

"It's nice to meet someone who's searching in a place like this," Ham said. "Not that it isn't really nice here. You just don't expect to find people like you in West Virginia."

Rose nodded and walked back to the table.

"I went into the seminary to find the truth and wasn't about to stop looking just because I left," Rose continued. "I've been all through the world's religions looking for the truth. I've looked under a lot of rocks, and I've written about what I found. I've published a couple of books and started a journal to pass along what I've found. You know what I found? We're inundated with bullshit, that's what I found."

Ham and Wheeler kept silent.

"That's not to say I haven't discovered a couple of things worth knowing," Rose continued. "Here they are: no one person, and no one religion, owns the truth. There is no price on the truth; whoever tries to sell the truth is a charlatan. There is no religion greater than friendship. Now, that's enough about me. You fellows tell me who you are."

"Well, first of all, we're living proof that everything you just said is true," Ham said in his most charming tone. "I won't lie to you. I won't ever lie to you. We're former Krishnas. We took a wrong turn. We're here because we want to start over."

"Krishnas? You two were Krishnas?" Rose asked.

Wheeler nodded.

"I've read about the Krishnas," Rose continued. "Why'd you leave?"

"Prabhupada, the founder, is locked into his own truth," Ham said. "He doesn't have any vision. He's way too fundamental. The movement is doomed because he won't let it adapt to Western culture."

"You're waking up," Rose said. "I like that."

Rose told them that in addition to being a philosopher he was also a building contractor who owned two farms up in the hills above Limestone, a one-blink village with a couple of churches, a school, and a mom-and-pop market and gas station on Route 250, ten miles above Moundsville. On one 160-acre farm, Rose raised goats. On the other, a 130-acre place, he ran cattle. Neither farm made any money, but the cattle had given Rose's father something to do. For years, the old man had looked after the scrawny herd, living in a ramshackle nineteenth-century farmhouse perched on the side of a hill.

"He's gettin' so feeble, I had to sell off the herd and move him into town," Rose told Ham and Wheeler. "I kept imagining him up there going after a stray and takin' a fall and bangin' his head on a rock, or sufferin' a heart attack and dying up there all alone."

The land was too poor to farm, he explained, and nobody wanted to live out in the middle of nowhere, without electricity. Hunters and kids shot up the place and tore through the vegetable garden in their trucks. The farm had been on its way to becoming another Appalachian eyesore when Rose read a magazine article about Haight-Ashbury. That gave him the idea to turn the place into a commune where hippies could pursue the truth without the sex and drugs that were sounding the counterculture's death knell.

The three men piled into Rose's pickup and drove out to see the farm. They parked the truck at the foot of the unplowed driveway and walked three quarters of a mile to the house through knee-deep snow. Ham and Wheeler made it only because Rose blazed a trail.

The small gray farmhouse looked like a Matthew Brady picture from the Civil War. It hadn't been painted in years. Most of the windows were boarded up with scraps of rotting plywood. The others were broken, giving the house a lopsided look.

"It's perfect, absolutely perfect," Ham said. "Would you consider selling it?"

"Selling it?" Rose said, surprised. "You two don't look like you could afford a cup of coffee. Where would you get the money?"

"We've got friends," Ham said.

"What do you want to buy it for?" Rose asked.

"We'd like to start a commune," Ham said.

"You mean on your own?" Rose asked, surprised.

"That's right," Ham said.

"You fellas are city boys. You'd freeze to death out here before it even got really cold.".

"We'll get by," Ham said. "Friends will help us."

"Nah, I don't want to sell," Rose said. "I'm not interested in making anything on this place. I want to start a commune where anybody who wants to can come and search for the truth."

"That is precisely what we want," Ham replied. "Anyone would be welcome."

They returned to town and talked into the night, as well as most of the next day. After Wheeler and Ham left, they exchanged letters with Rose and talked almost daily on the phone. Ham finally convinced Rose that their commune would welcome all seekers, not just Krishnas. But Rose still resisted. He was worried that if he sold the farm, he wouldn't have any say in how the commune was run. But if he leased it, he could keep a hand in. He ended up selling Keith Ham a ninety-nine-year lease for four thousand dollars.

After Kirtanananda defected, Prabhupada sent Mukunda and Janaki and two other couples to London to open a temple. Mukunda, the former jazz musician, had been propelled into the upper leadership cadre by his success in Haight-Ashbury. He had seen the power of fusing rock and roll with Krishna Consciousness. Now he wanted to do it again. But bigger. If he could interest the Beatles, the Krishna mantra would be on the lips of every kid in the Western world.

Mukunda, Janaki, and the two married couples who went with them to London tried every trick they could think of to hook the Fabulous Four! They sent an apple pie to Apple Records with "Hare Krishna" written in saffron icing across the top. There was no reply. They sent a wind-up walking apple with the mantra printed on the side. Still no reply. They sent a tape of a kirtan. They received a preprinted rejection letter.

"We've got to come up with another way," Mukunda said one afternoon.

"It's impossible. Everybody wants a piece of the Beatles," Janaki said. "I feel like Dorothy going down the yellow brick road."

"We're different," Mukunda replied. "We're not asking for something. We want to give them something. I really think we've got a shot because they're hip to Eastern religions. They went all the way to India to stay with the Maharishi."

"Sending them stuff isn't the way to go," said Syamasundara, a tall, handsome devotee. "No way, it'll never work. The only chance we've got is to get close to them. We've got to impress somebody who's connected to them. If they see us, they'll know we're sincere."

"But that's my point," Janaki said. "Everybody wants to meet the Beatles! It would be easier to serve prasadam to the Queen in Buckingham Palace."

"I'll camp out at Apple Records," Syamasundara said. "I volunteer—for however long it takes."

When Syamasundara arrived at Apple's headquarters early the next morning, it looked like an employment office specializing in the placement of recently released mental patients. Pallid musicians with scraggly hair hung around listlessly, hoping to play a song or convince somebody to listen to a demo tape. Crazed fans from all over the world waited outside on the sidewalk or, if they were lucky enough to get in, sat on the edge of their chairs, ready to mob any Beatle who appeared. Hucksters with incredible schemes paced the floor, waiting for one of the four to come by, touch them with a magic wand, and make their dreams, whatever they were, come true.

George Harrison hated running the gauntlet in the outer office. He had just come out of a conference and was steeling himself to duck through the room when he spotted a tall guy in robes sitting in a chair.

"You're a Hare Krishna, aren't you?" Harrison asked, walking up to him. Everybody in the room ran over to surround them.

"You know us? That's great," Syamasundara said.

"Know you? I've been trying to meet you people for over a year. Where have you been?"

"Trying to meet you," Syamasundara said.

"I saw you in the park in San Francisco," Harrison said. "When I got back home, I picked up the recording of the mantra Prabhupada made with the New York devotees. I've played it over and over. I've even started chanting a little!"

"That's wonderful!" Syamasundara said, trying to make himself heard above the shoving mob. "Wait'll Prabhupada hears about this. He'll be so pleased."

George invited Syamasundara into a back office, where they talked for almost an hour. George said his interest in Eastern religions was so deep, he sometimes thought he must have been a yogi in a previous incarnation.

"Listen," he said finally, getting up, "I've got to be somewhere. But why don't you come to my house for lunch tomorrow." He took a pad of paper out of his pocket and scribbled the address. "Come around twelve-thirty, or so. A couple of friends will be there."

His friends turned out to be John, Paul, and Ringo. They told Syamasundara all about their trip to India. George had loved it; the other Beatles had been disappointed by the trip and the Maharishi. John Lennon seemed especially unhappy.

"How do you know when you've found a real guru?" Lennon asked. "That's what I want to know."

"You'll know when you meet Prabhupada," Mukunda replied.

Syamasundara and Mukunda began spending so much time with George, they became an almost inseparable threesome. The Beatle started to describe himself as a "plainclothes devotee" and offered to rent a place for them to open a temple. The devotees thanked him, but didn't push it. They didn't want George to think they were interested in his money. Besides, they had bigger plans. What they really wanted was a record.

"What would you say to the Beatles recording the mantra?" Syamasundara finally asked one night over dinner at George's house.

"I'd say no," George replied.

Syamasundara's heart sank. He'd blown it. George was probably thinking Syamasundara was trying to use him, just like everyone else.

"You guys record it," George said. "I'll produce it, and we'll put it out on Apple."

"You'd do that, you'd really do that?" Syamasundara asked, leaping to his feet.

George laughed.

"Sure," he said. "Let's do it."

They started at George's house. The half-dozen London devotees chanted. George taped them and dubbed in a guitar. A few days later, they went to Trident Studios in Saint Anne's Alley, where George's friend, keyboard artist Billy Preston, helped make a tape.

They cut the record on Abbey Road, at E.M.I. Recording Studios. Mukunda and Syamasundara arrived in George's big Mercedes. When they got out, a crowd of teenagers shrieked and started singing Hare Krishna. Syamasundara was stunned. The kids were chanting. Well, almost chanting. They were singing the words, but to a tune he had never heard before.

"Where'd they get that?" he asked George.

"What?" the Beatle asked.

"The tune."

"Oh, that's the soundtrack to *Hair*, George replied. "You'd hear it if you ever listened to the radio."

"I guess I'd better start listening," Syamasundara said.

"Not really," George said, kidding him. "You'd find out how big you are and you'd lose your purity."

It took four takes to cut "Hare Krishna Mantra." George played the organ, Mukunda played mridanga drums, and Paul and Linda McCartney worked the control console.

"You thought 'Hard Day's Night' was big?" George yelled at Paul as the session wound down. "Wait till this hits. We'll release it on a Monday, and when we wake up Tuesday it'll be number one in thirty countries!"

The joke was almost prophecy. "Hare Krishna Mantra" sold seventy thousand copies the day it was released and broke into the British top ten in under two weeks.

Apple pushed it by throwing a big promotional party, stuffing reporters and photographers into a psychedelic-colored bus and driving them to a blue-and-white pavilion, where George and the devotees chanted. The next day, the devotees sang their hit on "Top of the Pops," an English version of "American Bandstand" and the hottest show in the United Kingdom.

"I'm glad to see your record's doing well," John Lennon said to Syamasundara one day when they ran into each other in the Apple offices. "What are you going to do with the royalties?"

"Build a temple," Syamasundara said. "We've found a nice five-story building near the British Museum. The owners weren't real anxious to sell it to us. But they changed their minds pretty fast when George wrote a letter saying Apple would guarantee the payments."

"When you movin' in?" Lennon asked.

"That's the problem," Syamasundara said. "They say we don't have the proper permits to gut the place. Getting through the red tape is going to take months. And we've only got a few weeks until Prabhupada gets here."

"Going to do the work yourselves, are you?" Lennon asked.

"We are," Syamasundara replied.

"You fellas good with your hands, are you?"

"Yeah. We've got some real fine carpenters."

"Tell you what, then," Lennon said after pausing a moment. "I just bought a place near Ascot that needs plenty of work. You help me do a few things out there and you can stay with me and Yoko till the temple's ready."

"John, you just made yourself a great deal," Syamasundara said. "We'll work harder than anybody you could pay."

Tittenhurst, Lennon's new estate, had belonged to the Cadburys, the chocolate family, for generations. It was seventy-six acres of forest and English gardens with a huge manor, a half-dozen guest buildings and servants' quarters.

In the next week, fifteen devotees moved into the servants' quarters. Some worked in the manor, ripping out the hardwood floor and laying black and white marble tiles. Others worked in the garden, helping restore the shrubs and hedges to the geometric exactitude demanded by English custom.

One evening, the devotees were sitting on the lawn making a tape to send to Prabhupada, when Lennon strolled by. Mukunda stopped him and asked him if he would like to say something to their spiritual master. Lennon walked up and leaned over the microphone.

"Hello, Prabhupada, Your Grace," he said in his most whimsical voice. "I have a question for you: What's your secret? What do you do that inspires people to work so hard for you?"

"That's easy," Mukunda replied. "It's love."

"But where does the love come from?" Lennon asked.

"Krishna," Mukunda replied.

Lennon smiled and walked away.

Prabhupada flew into Heathrow Airport on September 11, 1969. After a short press conference, he was driven to Tittenhurst in Lennon's white Rolls-Royce. Surrounded by a huge stereo system, a television, and a fully stocked bar, the Krishna mendicant sat back, closed his eyes, and chanted Hare Krishna. When he arrived at the estate, he was taken to a small room in the servants' quarters.

The guru's first visitors were George, John, and Yoko. Prabhupada took off the garland of flowers he was wearing and gave it to Syamasundara, indicating that he should hang it around George's neck. George smiled, thanked the swami, and welcomed him to England.

"You are anxious to bring some peace to the world," Prabhupada said. He stated it as a fact. "Every saintly person should be anxious to bring peace to the world."

Prabhupada gave them a quick summary of the universe as presented in the *Gita* and asked what philosophy they were following.

"Following?" Yoko said. "We don't follow anything. We just live."

"We're still sifting—sort of like looking through the sand to see who's got the best philosophy," John cut in, springing to Yoko's defense.

"I do meditation, mantra meditation," George added.

"Very nice," Prabhupada said, and went on with his lecture.

When John and Yoko left Prabhupada's little room a short time later, they were impressed.

"Look how simply he's living," John said to Yoko as they walked back to the manor. "Could you live like that?"

Harrison's reaction was much stronger. Prabhupada had captivated him. He returned to visit the guru often.

John and Yoko were polite, but kept their distance. John couldn't get over the disillusionment of his trip to meet the Maharishi and didn't want to risk another letdown. He had been so excited about going to India and had talked the three other Beatles into joining him. But when they arrived, they found the Maharishi had a woman. John was crushed.

"There are so many gurus, so many people going around saying they're it," John told Prabhupada several times. "How are we supposed to know who's for real?"

Prabhupada looked into John's eyes. He smiled, but did not answer.

He was working on the purports to his *Gita* late one night when John and Yoko knocked on his door, which was slightly ajar. Without waiting for a response, they peeked into the room and asked if Prabhupada had a moment to speak with them. The guru invited them in. They entered, sat down on the floor, and held hands.

"We have something to ask," John said.

"We are very much in love," Yoko said, picking up the thread. "We want to know if there's any way you could fix it with Krishna for us to be together always, even in the afterlife."

"Impossible." Prabhupada blanched. "When you go back to godhead, you can be united with Krishna. But husband and wife—this is simply a mundane relationship. It ends with the body at the time of death."

After that, Yoko wanted nothing to do with Prabhupada and his devotees. She avoided them and began badgering Lennon to send the Krishnas on their way.

A few evenings later, John walked into the kitchen, where several devotees were preparing the morning prasadam, and said hello. Without another word, he strolled over to an upright piano that had been stripped down to the wood and left unvarnished. Then he began banging out the Krishna mantra.

Lennon started it in rock and roll. Then he rolled into a blues rendition. The devotees stopped what they were doing and ran over to the piano to sing along. Eyes twinkling behind his granny glasses, John did a bluegrass version of the mantra; then a classical version. He was doing the mantra as a slow, sexy ballad when the spell was shattered by a scream.

"John!" Yoko yelled. She was standing in the doorway, wearing a nightgown. "I have a terrible headache! Stop all that and come upstairs with me!"

Lennon left the piano without closing the key slip and climbed the stairs with Yoko.

A few days later, John and Yoko invited Prabhupada to the manor to hear a demo of "Cold Turkey," a song John had just finished recording. Prabhupada showed up with a two-bit portable tape recorder and a tape of himself singing one of the Krishna mantras.

Prabhupada sat down on a couch opposite a large fireplace. On a wall facing the spiritual master was the famous, lifesize, full-frontal nude photo of John and Yoko. Running down another wall were black-and-white silhouettes of couples making love in almost unbelievable positions.

Although he often preached that sex was "stool," Prabhupada did not react. He waited patiently while Lennon fiddled with his state-of-the-art tape player. John pressed every button and turned every knob, but he couldn't get the "Cold Turkey" tape to play. Frustrated and embarrassed, he finally gave up and sat down next to Yoko.

Prabhupada grinned, pressed a button on his little tape recorder, and played his version of one of the Krishna mantras. When it was over, he thanked John and Yoko and went back to his little room. It was their last meeting. The paths of John, Yoko, and the Hare Krishnas would not cross again.

Before dawn the next morning, Prabhupada summoned Mukunda.

"It's not good for us to be here," the swami said when Mukunda entered his room. "It is time to go. We must open our temple."

The Pretender's Throne

"It's time you ate a little crow, Mr. Ham," Howard Wheeler said on a beautiful spring morning in June 1968.

"That would appear to be so, Mr. Wheeler," Ham replied.

"How do you want it prepared?" Wheeler teased.

"Curried, of course," Ham said.

Kirtanananda and Hayagriva, Keith Ham and Howard Wheeler, were back in the Village, crashing in the apartment of an old friend and former Mott Street Gang member. Ham had spent the winter there, trying to recruit new members for the West Virginia commune. He was selling it as a spiritual "heavenly hash," an oddball synthesis of the best in Krishna Consciousness, impersonal Hinduism, and Christianity. There weren't many buyers.

Wheeler had spent his winter working as an English instructor at a community college in Wilkes-Barre, Pennsylvania. He used class time to teach students to chant and to talk them into joining the West Virginia commune. He had even less success than Kirtanananda. All he got was a couple of passive maybe's and a quick boot when the dean found out what he was doing.

"Hansadutta keeps writing, begging me to make up with Prabhupada. He says if I throw myself at his feet, all will be forgiven."

"Enjoy your crowwwww," Wheeler taunted.

"What do you think we did wrong?" Ham asked. "How can that old Hindu take the Haight when we can't get anybody to go to West Virginia?"

"Prabhupada's venerable; we're not," Wheeler immediately replied, showing he had thought about the question for some time. He held up one finger on his right hand to check off his point.

Then he raised another. "He's exotic; we're not."

Wheeler smiled and raised a third finger. "He's fatherly; we're not."

A fourth finger went up. "He's the king; you're the prince who would be king."

The index finger on his left hand shot up. "He's—"

"Enough." Kirtanananda barked. "Okay, Okay. I'll write the damn letter."

Prabhupada sat on his *vyasasana* in the San Francisco temple, watching ecstatic devotees dance and chant in a command-performance kirtan. Like a floral neck brace, layers of orchid garlands were piled high around his neck, tickling his ears.

He had recovered from his heart attack and had returned to the United States from India four and one-half months before. From the moment his Air India flight landed, Prabhupada bounced across the country, initiating new devotees and dedicating temples that had sprung up in Los Angeles, Seattle, Santa Fe, and Boston. He seemed to thrive on the movement's growth. The children of Baptists and Catholics, Jews and agnostics were flocking to Lord Chaitanya's movement. Some were street people, some were seeking spiritual salvation. Others were trying to shock their parents or establish an identity they had been unable to forge on their own. Each new devotee seemed to give Prabhupada a burst of new energy.

I have fulfilled my spiritual master's wish a thousand fold, he thought, smiling as he watched the kirtan from his throne.

"It is such a great honor to have our spiritual master with us once again," said Govinda das, the ranking San Francisco devotee. "We have many questions."

"With Krishna's guidance, I will answer them," Prabhupada said. "Ask as you wish."

"Do you think I could give devotees a temporary initiation in your absence?" Govinda asked. "We are growing so fast. We have so many devotees who want to take initiation immediately."

"No," Prabhupada quickly replied. "Only the spiritual master initiates. You may make them members, and they will serve through you until I arrive to initiate."

"Last year we staged Rathayatra, the festival of the cars, here in San Francisco," another devotee said. "As you know, it was the first time the chariot procession to honor Lord Jagannatha was held in the West. We want to do it again and we have a permit. But there is no money. Can you help us with the money?"

Prabhupada smiled again. These Americans! They had so much energy. And now it was being channeled to Krishna. What a great blessing.

"Yes, you will have the money," he said.

Beth Ann, the ex-hippie who had split with her boyfriend Dasher to join the Krishnas the previous summer, stood up. This was the first time she had dared speak to Prabhupada and she was nervous. She spoke hesitantly.

"Kirtanananda is building a commune in West Virginia," she said. "It is very beautiful there. Is it permissible for devotees to go?"

"No!" Govinda shouted before Prabhupada had time to answer. "How dare you ask that? Black Keith is a heretic, a traitor."

Beth Ann turned ashen white. A murmur broke out among the other devotees. Prabhupada raised his hand and a hush fell over the room.

"It is all Krishna's mercy," Prabhupada said. "Only this week I have received a letter from the fallen godbrother. He humbly admits he had been taken prisoner by *maya*. He sees now that he had advanced too rapidly and tried to do too much."

"But he lied to you; he betrayed his spiritual master!" Govinda interrupted.

"Krishna used maya to lead Kirtanananda to a beautiful farm," Prabhupada continued, ignoring Govinda. "There, he will build an ideal village where devotees can practice plain living and high thinking. It will be a perfect replica of Vrindaban, where Westerners can come to meet Krishna and Radha and experience the infinite love and joy of the Lord of the Universe. It is a great service. I am very pleased."

"Prabhupada, are you telling us that you've forgiven Kirtanananda after what he's done?" Govinda asked. In the hushed room, pain was clearly audible in his deep voice.

Prabhupada looked around the temple, his gaze alighting on every devotee. One after another, they sat up a touch straighter. Each thought Prabhupada was talking to him or her directly. He seemed to be looking into their hearts, chastising them. To Beth Ann, still shaking after her admonishment, it seemed hours passed before he resumed.

"Sometimes I silently cried and prayed to Krishna, 'How have I lost this child, Kirtanananda?'" Prabhupada said. "I was so glad to receive his letter. I was so happy, my heart went out to him. He is doing great service. My gladness knows no bounds. It is exactly like finding a lost child."

The guru fell silent.

"You see what our spiritual master is teaching us?" Govinda said, standing up and stepping in front of the silent devotees. "You see from his example that Krishna is love and forgiveness? Let us stop condemning Kirtanananda. We must follow our spiritual master's example and welcome him back into our midst like a lost brother."

The session ended with Govinda's impromptu lecture. After Prabhupada left the room, Naranayana, Nathan Zakheim, a craftsman who specialized in restoring Victorian houses before he joined the Krishnas, sought out Beth Ann.

"I'm glad you asked about Kirtanananda," he said as he followed her into the kitchen.

"Thanks," she said, relieved. "I was scared. I didn't know if it was okay."

"I've been thinking," Naranayana continued. "I really want to go to New Vrindaban. You see, I'm a carpenter and I could do really great service there. I hear they need devotees who can work with their hands. I could make spiritual progress very quickly."

"That's great," Beth Ann said, her excitement obvious. "I hear it's really beautiful. I want to go with you. Let's go together."

The next week, Naranayana, Beth Ann, and two other devotees piled into a beat-up VW microbus and set off for West Virginia.

Richard Rose took a deep breath and knocked on the front door of the old farmhouse. Wheeler answered and ushered Rose into the kitchen. When he walked in, Rose was hit by an emotional sledge hammer. He had come prepared to find the farmhouse transformed into a temple—after all, he kept seeing the Krishnas' VW van coming and going on Highway 250 loaded down with lumber and cement and other building materials—but this was awful. The house looked even worse than when his father had lived there. The front porch still sagged; the windows were still broken. And it was much, much dirtier. Even the curtains surrounding the altar the Krishnas had installed were filthy. And the kitchen was disgusting. Piles of dirty dishes cascaded out of the sink and onto the counter.

It'll take at least a week to get this place livable, Rose thought, mentally kicking himself for letting the Krishnas move onto the farm. Still, he'd soon take care of that. The first thing to go would be that altar.

Kirtanananda motioned Rose into a seat with a flick of his wrist. Rose couldn't figure out why the guy looked so strange. Then it struck him: Ham had shaved his head. When he smiled, Rose saw that several teeth were missing.

Rose shook his head: And they made fun of hillbillies.

"Hare Krishna," Kirtanananda said.

"Hare Krishna yourself," Rose answered tersely.

Kirtanananda's smile only broadened. The ultra-smug, Cheshire Cat smile made Rose seethe with irritation.

"I'm gonna get right to the point. No sense screwin' around," Rose said sharply. "I want you and your people out. You lied to me. You broke our agreement. That makes your lease null and void. This place was supposed to be for everybody, but you've made it just for Krishnas. You've gone and turned it into a run-down Krishna temple. The neighbors are pissed off and I won't have it. I'll give you a week to pack up and get."

"The lease is valid," Kirtanananda said with the assurance of an English aristocrat.

"We agreed: no single religion, no single philosophy," Rose shot back.

"But Krishna Consciousness is all religions, all philosophies," Kirtanananda said. "It's the original religion. Let me give you a paper I've written. It explains everything I'm saying."

"I don't need to read any of your papers," Rose said. "I've been reading up on what Prabhupada has written. And I'm gonna tell you something: There's no truth that's deeper than a man keeping his word."

"On the mundane plane, that's certainly true," Kirtanananda replied. "But on the spiritual plane, there's a higher truth. All things are justified when they are done in God's service. How can you compare a tiny lie to the spiritual city we're going to build that will change thousands of lives?"

Kirtanananda paused for effect.

"You see?" he resumed, tapping the table to emphasize his point. "There is no comparison."

"I'll tell you where the higher truth is," Rose shouted, jumping to his feet. "It's in the courts. I'm going to sue your ass all the way back to New York."

Kirtanananda sighed.

"I've been expecting that," he said wearily. "Dear, dear Mr. Rose. Please don't waste your obviously limited resources. We have consulted a lawyer. The lease is ironclad; the farm is ours. And it'll be ours long after you're dead."

"We'll see about that," Rose sputtered. "I've got a damn good lawyer."

"Mr. Rose, believe me, ours is better," Kirtanananda said quietly.

Rose spun around to leave and saw that Howard Wheeler was standing in the kitchen doorway, grinning. Rose pushed him aside as he stormed out.

Rose drove home, did some work around the goat farm, and turned in early in an upstairs bedroom of his farmhouse. A half-dozen counterculture types were asleep in other rooms in the rambling building, the headquarters of Rose's countercommune. He couldn't let the hippies who had answered his ad in the *Oracle* fall into the clutches of the Krishnas. Whenever people called to tell him they had arrived in Moundsville and to ask directions to the commune, Rose sent them up to his farm and lectured them about the Krishnas. Some left after a few days; others were content to stay and pursue Rose's version of the truth.

Rose was just dozing off, when he heard what sounded like a car backfiring. He didn't move. Son of a bitch should tune the damn thing, he thought. *Bang!* There it was again. But this time, a piece of plaster fell onto the covers.

"What the hell? That's shooting!" he shouted as he came awake. He rolled out of bed and crawled out of the room and into the hall on his stomach. He reached the back stairway, jumped up, and ran downstairs. The shots were coming steady now: *bang, bang, bang!*

"Everybody get down and stay low!" Rose yelled.

He reached the gun cabinet and grabbed a .22 rifle. The he ran into the hall and slid his hand along the wall until he found the switch. Rose and his hippies had spent the better part of two weeks building a fence around the farmhouse, posting No Trespassing signs, and stringing up rows of floodlights. Rose hit the switch and raced to the front window. The yard was so bright, it looked like a ballpark.

Three cars were stopped on the road in front of the farm. A rifle was sticking out of the back window of the first car. Rose slid his window up, aimed at the car, and fired.

He heard a scream. The driver of the first car stomped on the gas, spinning his tires and kicking up a cloud of dust. The two others followed and disappeared into the night.

Rose rushed outside and looked down the road. Then he ran to the small trailer where his fifteen-year-old son had been sleeping.

"You all right?" he asked as he burst in and turned on a light. The boy didn't answer; he was lying in bed curled up in the fetal position and whimpering. There was a bullet hole in the trailer wall not more than two inches above his head. Rose sat down on the bed, took his son in his arms, and let out a long sigh. He was still hugging the boy when he saw the red flashing lights of the cop cars speeding up the twisting road.

"Mr. Rose, we're gonna have to make some arrests here," a state trooper informed Rose after introducing himself.

"My farm gets attacked, a bullet comes within an inch of my boy's head, and you want to arrest *me?*" Rose asked, more amazed than angry.

"Somebody here fired a shot that hit a seventeen-year-old Moundsville boy," the trooper said.

"Oh God!" Rose said. "Is he all right?"

"He's in the hospital in Glen Dale," the trooper said. "He was real lucky. He bled all over, and it looked real bad, but it's just a flesh wound. The bullet went in and out of his shoulder. But whoever shot him could have killed him."

"I won't tell you it wasn't me, but what the hell am I supposed to do?" Rose said. "They started the whole damn thing. Tell me what you'd do. I was in bed trying to get some sleep and they start shooting. I didn't know what the hell was happening. Don't tell me that you'd let your place get shot up without shooting back!"

The trooper looked at him.

"Mr. Rose, you are under arrest. We're gonna have to take a ride into the barracks. I'm going to read you your rights."

"What the hell for?" Rose said.

He wasn't worried about being arrested; he'd lived in West Virginia long enough to know that no jury in the state would send him to jail for defending his property. (Indeed, all charges against Rose were later dropped.) But he couldn't shake how low he felt, sitting in the back of the patrol car. Somehow, things had gotten out of hand.

"I wanted to create a place for people who cared about something more than getting a couple of nickels together to spend at the store," Rose told the trooper on the way into the state police barracks. "And look what happens. The Krishnas steal my farm and I end up shooting a seventeen-year-old punk. How do you figure that?"

Rose had been right about one thing. He had thought the Krishnas would not survive the wind-whipped winter of 1968–1969. And they didn't. They closed up the farmhouse and scattered. Kirtanananda rented an apartment in nearby Pittsburgh and traveled the country on recruiting drives. He was particularly interested in devotees who could work with their hands. Hayagriva, Howard Wheeler, took a job at Ohio State University and once again spent more time teaching Krishna than Hemingway.

The snows melted in March. Wildflowers sprouted on the hillsides; cardinals, the West Virginia state bird, returned to build their nests and start the cycle of life anew. And to the dismay of Richard Rose and the folks who lived on McCreary's Ridge, the Krishnas came back, too.

This time they returned en masse and worked around the clock. They cleaned out the farmhouse, rebuilt the porch, and fixed the windows. The sawing and hammering was incessant. They built small apartments in the old barn. They ordered new clothes from India for the deities and replaced the curtains around the altar. Kirtanananda drove the devotees hard. He inspected their work endlessly, demanding that everything be made perfect. It had to be. Prabhupada was coming for his first visit.

"This beautiful place truly shows the spirit of Krishna," Prabhupada said the day after he arrived. He was in high spirits. He had come to the farm from Ohio State, where Hayagriva and Allen Ginsberg had put on an ecstatic kirtan. On Monday, May 12, 1969, more than 1,000 students had packed into an auditorium that normally held 750.

"These hills are a perfect place to build our temples," he said to Kirtanananda, pointing, one after another, to seven crests surrounding the spiny ridge. "We will replicate the holy Vrindaban. Seven temples on seven hills. What a great service it will be. What a monument to Krishna."

Prabhupada was sitting under a flowering persimmon tree surrounded by his books and a cadre of devotees. The setting was perfect. It was late afternoon. The sun sinking behind the ridge looked like a flaming halo and bathed the hills in soft light.

"Perhaps I will make my headquarters here in this blessed land," the guru said. "Why return to Vrindaban when Vrindaban has come to America?"

Kirtanananda stopped dead in his tracks. He had been circling the group, listening, and snapping photographs. Now he pounced.

"Do you all hear what the spiritual master has said?" Kirtanananda asked, stepping over devotees in his rush to reach Prabhupada's side at the front of the group. "Do you hear the blessed task he has given us? We are to recreate Vrindaban here. It will take great labor, but it will be a great service. And we will get a great reward. Our spiritual master will always be with us, at our side. Always. No place on the planet will be more sacred than the ground you are now sitting on!"

Kirtanananda was ecstatic. It was just a matter of time until devotees around the country heard about this. When they saw the pictures, no other temple would be able to hold a disciple. They'd see that New Vrindaban was the most important project and they would rush there. To him.

They did. When word spread through the movement that the peripatetic Prabhupada was planning to settle permanently in New Vrindaban, devotees flocked to the West Virginia commune. Between June and August of 1969, membership almost tripled, to 250 members.

"My heart breaks for the devotees who are still doing service in New York," young Beth Ann said while waiting for the daily meeting with Kirtanananda. "It's terrible there during the summer. Hot and humid."

"Kirtanananda says it's Krishna's mercy that we were selected to come here," replied Amala-dasa, a former street kid from Philadelphia.

"Nothing in Krishna Consciousness comes close to the purity of New Vrindaban," Beth Ann said.

Amala-Dasa, Beth Ann, and several other devotees were gathered on a lawn near the persimmon tree where Prabhupada had passed his days writing and lecturing. It was early evening. Prasadam had been served, and now it was time for *darshan*, an audience with the spiritual master. As usual Kirtanananda was late. But nobody thought much of it. Kirtanananda was so spiritually advanced, so close to Krishna, that the devotees believed it was a privilege just to wait for him.

"When I first came, I couldn't believe how bad the conditions were," said one devotee in the group. "Cold showers out of a pipe that drained onto a dirt floor. No indoor plumbing, living above the cows in a dirty barn. Terrible prasadam."

"It's all part of our service," Beth Ann reminded him sharply. "Krishna sees everything. He knows the sacrifices we make for him. It's a blessing to perform austerities for him. Just think of the rewards that are waiting for us!"

"I had a hundred-and-three-degree fever and just went on hauling bricks," one devotee boasted, trying but failing to hide his pride.

"Imagine doing that if you weren't chanting. Chanting gives you strength," Beth Ann said.

"It gave me the strength to kick heroin cold turkey," another devotee, a former junkie, said to point out his devotion. "I swear, we could clean up the whole country if we could get dopers to accept Krishna and surrender to Kirtanananda."

The devotees were quick to prostrate themselves when Kirtanananda came out of the farmhouse. The guru was dressed in his usual filthy dhoti. Even the heavy incense couldn't mask his body odor. The devotees admired that. They thought that Kirtanananda was so spiritually advanced, he had transcended his body. Prabhupada would have been enraged—had he witnessed the scene. Only Prabhupada, the spiritual master and God's representative, was supposed to receive that kind of reverence. Kirtanananda had ignored those strictures. He not only encouraged devotees to prostrate themselves in his presence; he demanded it.

Kirtanananda waved his hand, and his devotees rose to their feet. While they watched, Hayagriva handed him a tin tray filled with cookies. Kirtanananda looked at the devotees and then tossed the cookies into the air. The devotees screamed and scrambled. A few of the more agile caught a cookie in the air; the others dove to the ground to snatch them up. It was a nightly ritual. By throwing cookies into the air, devotees thought, Kirtanananda was showering them with love. They considered him so holy that anything he touched was imbued with great spiritual power. They took great pains to walk literally in his footsteps.

"That collection of five karmis called the Rolling Stones are giving a concert in Veterans Stadium in Philadelphia next weekend," Kirtanananda told the devotees after they had regathered and eaten the cookies. "That presents us with a great opportunity to gather *lakshmi* for Krishna. We'll leave early Tuesday and stay in the Philadelphia temple. Remember, everything there belongs to Krishna. Remember this also, there is no bad Karma attached to any act done in Krishna's name."

A wild-eyed man wearing a T-shirt and dirty Levi's stood up.

"A bird in that tree over there just shit," he said. "Is birdshit Krishna?"

Kirtanananda stared at him. Two devotees quickly stood up and spoke to him gently for several moments. The wild-eyed man sat down again.

"Don't worry too much about the birds, Joe," Kirtanananda said.

"He's crazy," the ex-junkie complained. "Let's get rid of him."

"Joe was released from Bellevue not long ago and Krishna guided him to the New York temple," Kirtanananda said to the group. "He was given prasadam and soon felt at home there. Unfortunately, he wandered around the temple at night and interrupted the kirtans;

so they kicked him out. That is why he has joined us here."

"He's always interrupting our kirtans, too," the ex-junkie complained. "We've got wackos from every temple in America. How come they all come here?"

Kirtanananda's eyes flashed with anger.

"Who are we to reject anyone sent by Krishna?" he said. "Everyone is needed to help build our spiritual city. Besides, many of our most advanced people are mistakenly placed in mental institutions. Do not question that."

Beth Ann nodded. She spent the next ten years nodding at Kirtanananda. She married a devotee Kirtanananda told her to marry and divorced him when he told her to do that. In 1979, only weeks after he had ordered her divorce, Kirtanananda told Beth Ann to marry again. She did as she was told and moved into a small house in Tolavan, the fringie community. Their neighbor was Tom Drescher, who was living in the basement of his unfinished house.

Her second husband decided that Drescher was the coolest guy on earth. He tried to walk like Drescher, talk like Drescher, and most of all, be tough like Drescher. He started beating Beth Ann. Drescher would come over and, while Beth Ann was preparing their lunch, they would laugh about wife beating.

Beth Ann told Kirtanananda about the beatings; he told her she had no choice but to submit to her husband. Finally, she couldn't take it anymore. She took her two children—a boy by each of her husbands—and defected.

It was the day before the Stones concert, and the president of the Philadelphia temple, Ravindra Svarupa, William Deadwyler, was rushing around greeting the devotees who were arriving by the busload from temples across the country.

Ravindra was overjoyed by the communal spirit that imbued the movement. Whenever a major rock concert or antiwar demonstration was announced, the devotees showed up. They chanted and sold candles, incense, and copies of *Back to Godhead* magazine, giving all the money they collected to the local temple. In return, the host temple provided visiting devotees with a place to sleep, worship, and share prasadam.

Ravindra, a tall, soft-spoken man who was working on a Ph.D. in religion at Temple University when he joined the movement, stopped to watch two devotees greet each other in the parking lot. One was black, the other white, and they greeted each other as brothers. This is the way Krishna meant the world to be, Ravindra thought. So much joy, so much brotherhood.

"Hare Krishna. I must speak with you."

The voice broke into Ravindra's reverie. He turned to see one of his senior aides.

"You're upset," Ravindra said. "What is it?"

"Things are missing," the devotee answered.

"What kind of things?" Ravindra asked.

"Dhotis, blankets, candles, incense, silverware. Several devotees have even reported that their shoes were stolen."

"What do you mean, *stolen?*"

The devotee looked embarrassed.

"That's the only thing I can call it. We've looked everywhere, just in case things were moved because so many devotees were coming. We can't find anything."

"Nobody broke in and took these things?" Ravindra asked.

The devotee shook his head no.

Ravindra became solemn.

"You know what you are saying, then?"

The devotee nodded.

"Why are you so upset?" Kirtanananda asked calmly.

"Because I found all our missing stuff in one of your vans," Ravindra barked.

Ravindra had always acknowledged that Kirtanananda was an advanced devotee, a sannyasi, a highly spiritual being who had escaped the earthly traps. But that didn't mean Ravindra liked him. Kirtanananda seemed to relish making Ravindra feel inferior, a mere grihastha, a householder tied to his wife and children.

"And why were you snooping around in our vans?" Kirtanananda asked, arching his eyebrows to drive home his point.

Ravindra paused. He had hated going into the vans. It went against everything he stood for. To spy on one's own godbrothers—men initiated by the same guru—was low. But he was determined not to let Kirtanananda bully his way out of this.

"Because I had looked absolutely every other place, and your vans were the only possibility left," Ravindra said. "And also because I've heard from other temples that your devotees steal. You're going to have to do something about this, Kirtanananda."

"But why?" Kirtanananda asked casually. "They only did it out of love."

"What do you mean, love?" Ravindra asked.

"Love for Krishna. They were simply taking what they have to to use in his service."

"What about us? Aren't we engaged in Krishna's service?" Ravindra cried.

"Not as we are," Kirtanananda purred. "Your little temple is very nice, very nice indeed. But how can you compare it to what we are doing at New Vrindaban? You know how important our spiritual city is to Prabhupada. We cannot allow anything to come in its way. Besides, you're in a city. You can always go out and get plenty of lakshmi from the karmis. We're stuck out there in the hills. We have to take advantage of every opportunity."

"You know what you're doing? You're introducing sectarianism into this movement!" Ravindra said, working hard to swallow his anger.

Kirtanananda just smiled.

"Purity must come before unity," he said finally.

"You're justifying theft, even theft from other devotees." Ravindra cried.

"All I'm doing is practicing the rather simple philosophy that the end justifies the means," Kirtanananda said smugly. "Krishna smiles on every endeavor, as long as it is done in his service. You know that."

Kirtanananda turned and walked away to prove he was above such petty disputes. He took a few steps, stopped, and turned back to Ravindra.

"I might as well say good-bye," he said. "Don't look for us after the concert. What we collect stays with us. Hare Krishna, *Prabu.*"

Clouds of Change

It was early on a beautiful Saturday morning in June 1973. Most of the three hundred or so devotees in New Vrindaban were gathered in the enlarged temple room of the farmhouse. Kirtanananda was sitting in front of the group, paging through the first canto of the *Srimad-Bhagavatam*, the massive scripture that describes and explains Krishna's life in Vrindaban.

"Notice, please, the parallels between Krishna's story and the story of Moses from the Bible," Kirtanananda was saying. "We have the parting of the waters of the Jamuna River. We have—"

Suddenly, the sound of glass shattering echoed through the farmhouse. Devotees jumped up and turned around. The two rear windows were empty frames with a few jagged glass shards sticking to the rotten putty. In the smashed windows stood two men aiming twelve-gauge shotguns into the room.

Booooooommm.

The blast deafened the devotees. They froze in a split second of pure terror, then began screaming and diving for cover.

"I'm hit!" one devotee yelled.

"Me too!" another screamed.

The front door banged open and two men burst into the room, their shotguns cradled under their arms. The first had a big pot belly, which sagged over his brass belt buckle like a water balloon and made him look even shorter than his five feet six inches. His square head was topped by waves of greasy hair. An older man, wearing a black leather jacket over a T-shirt and dirty blue jeans, followed, dragging a club foot and struggling to keep up.

"Shut the fuck up!" the greaseball screamed.

"Anybody who moves is gonna be pickin' birdshot out of his ass," Clubfoot added. His thick voice sent shudders through the devotees.

"You, chief pinhead, get back here," Pot-belly ordered.

"Me?" Kirtanananda asked, pointing to his chest.

"Who the fuck else am I lookin' at?" Pot-belly yelled, waving his gun.

Kirtanananda walked slowly past the devotees. Pot-belly stuck the shotgun in his back and nudged him out the door. The door closed. Clubfoot stayed inside, keeping the other devotees hostage.

Tom Westfall was driving through Moundsville feeling especially good. He was on his way to work the annual Lion's Club Street Fair. Last year it had rained; this year, it promised to be a glorious day. There wasn't a cloud in the robin's-egg blue sky.

The fair was always a lot of work. In previous years, Westfall had been stuck directing traffic all day. But he didn't mind. Like other small towns across the country, Moundsville came alive during the summer ritual. Churches and civic organizations spent months planning their booths. The whole town seemed happier. All day, the air was filled with the rich smells of ribs and chicken barbecuing over an open pit fire. And no matter how tired he was, Westfall always went home just before dark and picked up his girlfriend, Martha, and brought her back for the street dance.

"Officer Westfall, come in, please," his radio crackled as he drove. Absorbed in his thoughts, he reached over automatically, grabbed the mike, pressed the button, and gave the dispatcher his location.

"Get right on out to the Krishnas," the dispatcher ordered. "They're under attack. The place is surrounded by armed men and shots have been fired. The state police have the call and will back you up."

Westfall pulled his cruiser off the road, jumped out and ran back to the truck. He opened the trunk and, as quickly as possible, slipped into his tactical coveralls. Then he unzipped a gun case and pulled out an AR-15

semi-automatic rifle and four loaded magazines. The devotees had often complained to him about locals riding by
and throwing rocks and even taking pot-shots at some of
the Krishna buildings. This could be it, Westfall thought
as he climbed behind the wheel. This could be the all-out
attack some of the devotees have been afraid was coming.

Westfall hit his siren and lights and floored the acceler-
ator of his Ford cruiser, with its big V-8 Interceptor
engine. He went flying past the Fostoria Glass Works at
eighty miles an hour and began the climb to New
Vrindaban. It took him less than fifteen minutes to cover
ten miles of twisting mountain switchbacks. Roaring up
the final dirt road to the farmhouse, he hit the brakes
and skidded sideways to a stop. He grabbed the AR-15
and took cover behind the front of the car.

Devotees were walking around in a daze, but Westfall
saw no armed men. Then Kirtanananda came down the
steps.

"What took you so long?" he demanded.

Westfall was dumbfounded.

"They're gone," Kirtanananda said calmly.

"How long ago? How many were there?" Westfall
yelled, his words running together. He heard sirens screaming up Highway 250 and reached into the car for the mike
to warn the troopers off before someone had an accident.

"An hour or so," Kirtanananda said.

"An hour?" Westfall said angrily. "I got a call just
fifteen minutes ago that said you were under attack."

"The devotee who made the call was very upset,"
Kirtanananda said. "We don't have a phone here. He
had to run all the way down to the general store on the
highway. Come with me. Several devotees are wounded."

Westfall pulled his first-aid kit out of the cruiser's
trunk and followed Kirtanananda into the farmhouse.
Shards of glass were strewn throughout the main room.
The altar was overturned and the deities lay smashed on
the floor. But only three devotees were wounded, and
those only slightly. One had been hit in the wrist, and two
others had pellets in their arms.

"What happened?"

"A motorcycle gang attacked us. At least six, possibly

more," Kirtanananda replied. "I was leading a class when they broke the windows and fired at us. They took me out at gunpoint. They made me get a shovel and marched me up the hill."

Westfall asked him to point it out. Kirtanananda did.

"I walked as slowly as I could," Kirtanananda continued. "One of them hit me with the barrel of the gun and said, 'Faster or I'll blow you away now!' But I wouldn't go any faster. He said, 'Here, motherfucker, dig your own grave.'

"I was just about to start digging when I heard a tremendous crash in the farmhouse. A few seconds later there was another crash. It sounded like a huge fight. 'Let's go,' one of the bikers said. They left me and rushed back down here.

"The thugs in the farmhouse were smashing our deities, that's what caused all the noise. When the devotees saw them do that, their rage knew no bounds. The bikers sensed that, because all of a sudden, they ran out and left. Some of us now regret that we did not give up our lives to protect the deities."

By now, the commune was swarming with cops who were interviewing witnesses. Westfall was still talking to Kirtanananda when a state trooper interrupted and asked to speak to him in private.

"You're the expert on these people," the trooper said after they had walked to a grassy knoll out of earshot of the porch. "Tell me why I can't get a straight answer."

"What d'ya mean?" Westfall asked.

"Well, some of 'em are saying there were a dozen guys with guns out here," the trooper said. "Others are saying six; and that short, fat girl over there with the black hair just told me it was only two. She says they had shotguns. The others say automatic weapons."

"Maybe they're just shook up," Westfall said. "Put yourself in their position. You're in a Bible-study class and somebody sticks a shotgun through the window—"

"But that's what's got me confused," the state cop interrupted. "The ones I've talked to seem pretty calm. The guy who told me there were a dozen bikers is just as certain about what he saw as the girl who told me there were only two . . ."

Westfall never made it to the street fair. He spent the whole day at the commune talking to devotees, collecting as many accounts as possible. He asked each devotee for a description of the raiders; no two accounts were the same. He asked every devotee if he knew the number of the attackers' license plates; none did. Shaking his head, he left just before sunset and drove to the Marshall County sheriff's office to write his reports. When he finished, it was much too late to take Martha dancing.

He went home and fell into bed, exhausted. He had just closed his eyes when the phone rang.

"You the Krishna cop?" a voice asked.

"Yeah, who's this?"

"I wanna talk about what happened today."

"Okay," Westfall said, reaching for the paper and pen he kept stashed near the phone. "Who am I talking to?"

There was silence.

"I don't think you'll remember me," the voice finally said. "We met a couple of months ago. You were riding your bike. I talked to you about the sanitation problems we were having on the commune."

Westfall mentally scrolled back through his years on the Krishna beat.

"Right, sure, I remember," he said. "You must be Drutaka Dasa."

The phone went silent. Westfall wanted to kick himself. Lying in bed with the silent receiver pressed to his ear, he figured he'd spooked the source.

"Hey, you still there?" Westfall asked, just to break the silence.

"Listen," Drutaka finally replied. "Whatever I tell you didn't come from me."

"Agreed," Westfall said.

"Some heavy karma could go down if anyone ever found out I called the cops."

"Anything you say," Westfall said.

There was another long silence. Westfall figured Drutaka must have scared himself and would hang up any second.

"You're doing the right thing," Westfall said quickly.

"Krishna rewards honesty. This is what Prabhupada would want you to do."

"That's the only reason I'm getting involved," Drutaka agreed.

"So, what happened today?"

"I recognized one of the guys who attacked us," the devotee said. "He was out here yesterday, yelling and screaming that we'd kidnapped his daughter. He said if we didn't give her up, he was gonna come back with a gun. None of us thought he was serious. His last name is Delmore, or Elmore, or something, from Louisville. That's all I know. Hare Krishna."

"Is his daughter up there?" Westfall asked.

"Hey, that's all I know," Drutaka snapped.

The line went dead.

The next morning Westfall swore out a warrant and called the Louisville police. A few days later, they picked up Charles Elmore, the owner of a motorcycle bar, and Buddy Clements, a biker friend of his with a club foot. They were charged with assault with a deadly weapon. They could not afford to post bail and were jailed for a month—until Westfall arrived to take them back to West Virginia.

Louisville was steaming when Westfall rolled up to the city jail in his black squad car. He spent an hour filling out reams of paperwork in triplicate before an officer led Elmore and Clements, bound in handcuffs and leg irons, to Westfall's waiting car. The three began the trip back to Moundsville in silence. Dusk seemed only to increase their gloom. By the time they passed the sign marking the West Virginia state line, it was almost dark.

"Welcome to Wild, Wonderful West Virginia," Westfall read aloud to break the tension.

Clements started to cry. "Oh shit, man, we're going to jail!" he howled as they rolled north on Interstate 77. I don't wanna go to jail!"

"Why'd you go shoot up the Krishna place?" Westfall asked sternly.

"All I wanted was my daughter back," Elmore said, coming to life. "None of this woulda come down if they hadn't taken her and lied about it."

"So you got a bunch of bikers together and went up there to get her back," Westfall said.

"What are you talkin' about?" Elmore asked.

Westfall noted the confusion in his voice. It didn't sound feigned.

"What bikers?" Elmore added. "It was just me and Buddy in his beat-up Caddy."

The two prisoners leaned forward and spilled their story. It had all started months earlier when a New Vrindaban sankirtan bus broke down in Louisville, stranding a group of *brahmacharis*—celibate male students. Since it was going to take at least a week to get parts for the old diesel, the brahmacharis moved into a boarding house next to Elmore's bar.

"One of those shaved-head creeps starts sniffing around my daughter," Elmore told Westfall. "I'm not saying she wasn't responsible in part. But hell, she ain't but fifteen."

Elmore paused to think a moment, then continued.

"These guys were out workin' the streets, sellin' magazines and all, makin' like they're priests. And all the while, one of them has a thing goin' with my girl. Like I said, she's only a kid. She thought he was cute.

"So they get the bus fixed, and when it rolls out, my daughter's gone. I figure she's got to be on it. So I get Buddy, and we go after her."

When Elmore and Clements reached New Vrindaban, the Krishnas denied Elmore's daughter was there. They were a religious movement, they said. The girl was a minor. Why would they open themselves to a kidnapping charge?

"I bet I've listened to a thousand drunks try to weasel just one more," Elmore told Westfall. "I know when somebody's lying, and those weirdos were lying. I told 'em if they didn't bring her to the motel we were stayin' in, we'd be back."

"My guess is that they snuck her out of there and hid her in the woods, or something," Buddy Clements added.

"Which one of you took Kirtanananda up the hill and told him to dig his own grave?" Westfall asked.

"Shit, what are you talkin' about?" Elmore said. "We never did nothin' like that. I took him outside and made him go with me while I searched the place. We were gone maybe ten or fifteen minutes at the most. I couldn't find her, so we split. Tell you the truth, I got a little spooked. All those statues and spaced-out people. Is that stuff what you call voodoo?"

"Terrible news," the devotee who was acting as Prabhupada's secretary said as he ran into the guru's quarters in a temple in Mayapur, India, the birthplace of Lord Chaitanya. He was carrying a letter. "New Vrindaban has been attacked."

"What's that?" Prabhupada asked, rising from his small desk to take the letter to read for himself.

The letter from Kirtanananda made it sound like New Vrindaban was under siege by hordes of bikers. Kirtanananda wrote that he'd caught two of the bikers, but a karmi grand jury had let them go. It just proved how maya was turning people against Krishna's movement.

Prabhupada read the letter without raising his heavy eyelids. He'd been expecting this. It was, in fact, a good sign. Maya, illusion, the enemy of those who climb the spiritual path back to godhead, only attacked when threatened by spiritual progress.

Prabhupada thumbed through the *Bhagavad-Gita* on his desk. He stopped at a page describing the turning point in the battle between the Pandavas and the Kauravas —a struggle for succession usually seen as a metaphor for the internal struggle that goes on within us all. But Prabhupada, a fundamentalist, believed the battle was a historical fact. Obviously, the lord of the universe condoned violence.

"You will take a letter to Kirtanananda," Prabhupada told his secretary. He waited for the devotee to get his notebook and pen, and then began dictating the letter:

When New Vrindaban has been attacked twice, thrice, why are you not keeping guns? Where violence is, there must be violence. We are not followers of Gandhi's philosophy. Ours began on the fields of war. If somebody attacks you, you must protect yourselves to your best capacity.

When Kirtanananda read the letter, he must have smiled. The attack served to unite the New Vrindaban devotees: now they busied themselves building up an arsenal and recruiting a new type of devotee.

Tom Westfall's eyes widened when he ran the names of the new disciples through the police computer. New Vrindaban had always attracted an odd lot of counterculture types, often with rap sheets for possession of marijuana or vagrancy. But the new devotees were a harder, more violent breed, with longer police records. Many had served time for crimes like armed robbery and assault with a deadly weapon.

Westfall watched the changes sweeping the commune from the vantage point of his telex machine. Almost every day, he received some inquiry or report from one police department or another. Meanwhile, informants at the commune were reporting that Kirtanananda had collected an arsenal and was forming a defense force.

Westfall's apprehension grew day by day.

"Anything can happen out there," he told Martha, his fiancée, one night, "Anything."

Thomas Drescher cupped his left hand over his right and steadily lowered the Colt .45 automatic until the black silhouette of a human figure filled the sights. He took a deep breath and ripped off nine shots that punched fist-sized holes in the target's head and neck.

"Wow, man, you shoot like a bitch!" said Walt Parry, the newly appointed commander of the New Vrindaban temple. Before joining the Krishnas, Parry rode with the Warlocks, an East Coast motorcycle gang that practiced black magic. He left the motorcycle gang to join the Marines, then went AWOL to join the Krishnas.

"In a couple of weeks, you'll be pretty good yourself," Drescher said as he reloaded the .45. "You'll get as much practice as you want here. You gotta remember that shooting is an art. You can't hurry it. You gotta learn to feel it."

"I swear I've seen more guns since I've been here than I did in all the time I was in the Marines," Parry said.

"AR-fifteens, Mini-fourteens, forty-fives, nine millimeters —where's this stuff coming from?"

"Two guys take care of our weapons," Drescher said. "One's Keith Weber, the other is Todd Schenker. You've probably seen them around wearing jungle fatigues and bush hats. They really know their shit when it comes to guns. Weber drinks a lot but he's a good guy."

Parry shook his head. He took hold of a .45, aimed at the target, and rapid-fired five shots that formed a haphazard low-to-high pattern.

"Got to watch that kick," Drescher said. "You'll get used to it."

Parry heard a vehicle coming up the road to the firing range, which was hidden deep in a ravine in the hills behind the commune, and he whirled around. The heavy gun swung past Drescher's crotch.

"Take it easy," Drescher warned. "That's just Kirtanananda; I can tell by the sound of the engine. He likes to come by the range and check out his army."

A Toyota Landcruiser drove up, and the guru got out smiling.

"Hare Krishna," he said. "It's nice to see New Vrindaban's first line of defense out on maneuvers."

Drescher grinned like a little boy whose father has just appeared.

"Watch this," he said. He aimed the .45 at the target and riddled it with nine shots. The gunfire rattled Kirtanananda; he jumped back, but never took his eyes off the target.

"That's magnificent." Kirtanananda said. "I really pity anyone who's dumb enough to come up here and mess with us."

"Who'd try, anyway?" Parry asked. "We're not botherin' anybody."

"There's a simple answer for that," Kirtanananda said condescendingly. "From eternity past to eternity future, there has been, and always will be, a great struggle between devotees and demons for the hearts of men. That struggle is what this material world is all about."

Kirtanananda got back in his Landcruiser and drove away.

"Ain't he something?" Drescher asked. "He's about ten times smarter than anybody I ever met."

Parry nodded and began picking up some of the spent cartridges that littered the area.

"There must be a fortune in brass just layin' here," he said, throwing a handful into the back of Drescher's white pickup. They landed in the steel bed with a staccato clatter.

"Forget it," Drescher said, holstering his .45. "Let's get out of here. That's too much like work."

"But if we pick up the spent shells and reload them like the Marines, we'd save a ton of money."

"Money ain't a problem." Drescher shrugged. "Kirtanananda gives Weber and Schenker all they need. He's been buyin' ammo a thousand rounds at a time. Why bother reloadin' when we're gettin' more fresh shells than we'll ever be able to use. Come on, let's get goin.' I need a beer."

Chicago devotee "Gary Dienstel" watched the last few commuters hurry home. It was seven o'clock on a cold night in March 1974. Only an hour ago traffic had been bumper to bumper. A bitter wind, one last reminder of the mean winter, had emptied Randolph and Michigan in Chicago's Loop in a hurry.

The cold didn't bother Dienstel. He'd grown up in Green Bay, the icebox of the north, and had become accustomed to freezing long ago. He'd joined the Krishnas eighteen months earlier, after dropping out during his freshman year at the University of Wisconsin in Madison. Now he hustled the streets, ignoring the weather and selling Prabhupada's books and *Back to Godhead* magazines.

Dienstel watched a blue Ford drive up the street and stop in a spot reserved for taxis. A man got out and walked toward a newsstand tucked between the stairs that led down to the Illinois Central Railroad and the Chicago Public Library. Dienstel approached him.

"Hare Krishna," he said, handing the man a copy of *Back to Godhead*. "Please take one."

"I was just gonna pick up a copy of the *Sun Times*," the guy said as he accepted the magazine. He leafed through the lavishly illustrated pages for a moment and then looked up at Dienstel.

"This looks pretty good," he said. "I'm interested in Hindu religions."

Dienstel's face lit up. It was rare that anyone showed interest.

"We're the first Eastern religion to make inroads in the West," Dienstel said rapidly. "Our spiritual master calls the West 'the blind man' because America is so spiritually impoverished. He calls the East 'the lame man' because India is so poor. If the two were united, they would heal each other."

"Or, you'd get a blind man with a limp," the man said, pulling his heavy coat around him.

Dienstel's spirits fell. The guy was mocking him.

"Only kidding," the man said with a smile. "I know something about your movement. My neighbor had a kid join back in sixty-nine. You're doing a lot of good work."

"We've published a lot of great literature," Dienstel said, perking up again. "Our spiritual master has produced the greatest translation of the *Gita* ever done. It's called *The Bhagavad-Gita As It Is* and it emphasizes the practice of bhakti yoga, not the watered-down philosophy they give you in college."

"My neighbor said something about that," the man said. "You don't happen to have a copy with you, do you?"

"I did earlier, but I sold them all," Dienstel said. "I can have one for you tomorrow. Do you work in the Loop?"

"I do," the guy said. "Come on over to the car. I'll give you my address and you can drop it off tomorrow."

They walked to the curb.

"That's Donnie, my partner," the man said, pointing to a redheaded driver. "We got a little car-rental business over on Wabash. You're younger than I am. Reach in there and hand me that briefcase on the backseat, and I'll give you a piece of our stationery. It's got the address on it."

Dienstel reached in for the briefcase. The man pushed him into the car, jumped in behind him, and slammed the door. The driver floored it and went fishtailing onto Michigan Avenue. Dienstel screamed and tried pulling open the door. The man jerked Dienstel's arm behind his back and slapped the palm of his hand over Dienstel's mouth.

"Relax, Gary, we're here to help," the man said.

Dienstel stopped struggling; the man took his hand off Dienstel's mouth but kept it hovering only inches away.

"Who are you?" Dienstel asked.

"Your parents sent us. Think of us as family friends," the man replied.

"They hate Krishna!" Dienstel screamed. "I'll sue them! I'm twenty years old, I've got a right to lead my own life."

"Of course you do, Gary, that's why we're here," the man replied. "We're gonna help you live your own life. Not some life you've been programmed to live."

"You're deprogrammers!" Dienstel shouted.

"You got it, Gary," the man said. "I'm Sam and you've already met Donnie. We're gonna have some nice long talks. Tell you what: If you'll lie down on the floor here so you won't know where we're goin,' I won't tie you up and blindfold you. What'a ya say?"

Dienstel curled up on the floor, the drivetrain bump cramping his side. He closed his eyes and began chanting.

"Gary, what you're doin' there is the first thing we gotta talk about," Sam said. "You need to stop that chantin' right now."

"Chanting the Lord's names is the purest form of worship," Dienstel said. "When you chant, God is actually on your lips. Chanting burns off bad karma. It—"

"It's brainwashing, is what it is," Sam interrupted. "You got to stop repeating that mumbo jumbo and give yourself a chance to think."

"I know how to think. I think a lot better now than I did before I surrendered to Krishna."

"Gary, this is America. What made this country great is, you don't have to surrender to anybody."

Dienstel stared up at Sam. He stopped moving his lips, but continued to repeat the chant furiously in his mind.

The two deprogrammers drove him around before taking him to a safehouse in Homewood, a suburb twenty miles south of Chicago. They bundled him into the clapboard house, sat him down on the couch, and asked him if he'd like to talk to his parents.

He shook his head, but they went ahead and called. Sam said a few words and held the phone up to Dienstel's ear. He listened to his father explain why he had hired the deprogrammers. Sam tried once again to convince Dienstel to say something to his father. Again he refused.

The deprogrammers led him to the rear of the house and locked him in a room. A sheet of half-inch plywood was nailed over the inside of the only window. Dienstel lay down on the cot and tried to figure out what to do. He was small and thin—no physical match for the deprogrammers. There was no way he could overpower these guys and escape. He was going to have to outthink them.

The door opened an hour later.

"Come on out and have a little dinner," Sam said.

Dienstel walked into the living room. Donnie was sitting on a couch, taking a bite out of a hamburger.

"Got you a Big Mac, fries, and a chocolate shake," Sam said. "If you don't want the shake, I'll trade you my Coke."

"This really reeks!" Dienstel said. "You know I'm strictly vegetarian."

"Why, Gary? Why won't you eat meat?"

"We don't believe in killing animals," Dienstel said. "An animal dies in an act of violence. When you eat meat, you ingest that violence. It's taking on bad karma."

Sam walked over and pushed his face up close to Dienstel's.

"Bullshit, Gary." he screamed. "Bullshit! I'm gonna tell you the real reason you're a vegetarian. It's to weaken your body. That's how these people work, Gary. When they weaken your body, they weaken your mind."

"What people? Who's 'they'?" Dienstel asked.

"The Krishnas, Reverend Sun Myung Moon's Unification Church, the Children of God, the Scientologists, Synanon, Guru Maharaji Ji's Divine Light Mission. They're all the same, Gary. All cults operate the same way."

"You're saying ISKCON's a cult?"

"That's it. Exactly."

"We're a religion!"

"And Prabhupada's God?"

"He's a representative of God. There's a big difference," Dienstel said.

"He's a hustler in robes and you're a sucker, Gary. A real sucker."

Dienstel winced. Sam and Donnie smiled.

"Why do you live in the temple, Gary? Why a goddamn temple?"

"In a communal setting, people help each other along the spiritual path," Dienstel said.

Once again Sam stuck his face in Dienstel's.

"Bullshit, Gary. A commune is a concentration camp. They keep you together to control you, to control everything you do and everything you think."

Dienstel refused his Big Mac, and Donnie pushed him back to his room. An hour later, they hauled him back into the living room and tore into him again. After a couple of hours, they sent him back to his room. Dienstel was so exhausted, he went right to sleep.

It seemed like just a few minutes, but it was almost an hour later when he opened his eyes to find Donnie shaking him.

The questioning began again. So did the lectures. It went on like that for three days. One of the deprogrammers would work on him for a couple of hours, then the other would take over. They played anticult tapes produced by other deprogrammers and devotees who had deserted the movement. Every evening, they took time out to call his parents. Dienstel steadfastly refused to say a word to them. After the call, Sam and Donnie would let him sleep for an hour or two, then wake him up and continue the assault on his faith.

Dienstel loved talking about Krishna and arguing about religion. He looked on his abduction as a test of his faith and was determined not to give in.

The more the deprogrammers attacked, the more obstinate he became. He blocked each of their logical thrusts with quotations from Prabhupada and the sacred books.

So far, Dienstel felt, he was easily handling the intellectual competition.

But he knew he was losing the physical combat. He was weakening. He was still refusing to eat the fast food they served and, day by day, was losing weight from his already bone-thin frame. The sleep deprivation also was working. His eyes were pulling into their sockets. His cheeks, topped by dark bags under the eyes, were becoming sunken like an old man's.

Lying on his unmade cot at the end of the third day, Dienstel got smart. The only way to win, he figured, was to appear to lose. The next morning, he picked up his Egg McMuffin and took a tentative bite. It almost made him gag. But he choked down his revulsion and finished the sandwich.

"I've been thinking about something," Dienstel said after the deprogrammers had cleared the table. "You might be right about life in the temple. It really is pretty regimented."

"How so?" Sam asked. "Tell me exactly how?"

"Well, just take a look at our day. When do we have any time for ourselves?"

"Right, Gary. Right. And why is that? Tell me why that is?"

"I'm beginning to wonder about that," Dienstel replied.

That afternoon, they were sitting around the living room, making small talk.

"Ever been out to Wrigley Field?" Donnie asked. "Ever seen a game in the Friendly Confines?"

"Never have," Dienstel replied. "I'd like to, though. I was a big Milwaukee Brewers fan before I joined the movement."

Dienstel paused, deep in thought.

"I gotta admit, there's things I miss," he confessed.

"Like what, Gary?" Sam asked. "Tell us like what."

"Like Creedence Clearwater Revival. I used to listen to them all the time. I don't think I've heard a Creedence song since I joined the movement. The Krishnas think rock and roll is maya."

The next afternoon, Donnie slid a cassette into the small tape deck. Dienstel steeled himself for one more boring anticult tape. He was surprised to recognize the first few beats. And when the deep country twang of John Fogerty singing "Proud Mary" echoed through the room, he forced a smile. Soon he was tapping out the beat on his knees and singing along. He'd forgotten most of the words and had to improvise.

Over the next few days, the atmosphere in the safehouse changed from a Marine boot camp to an interrogation room where a couple of friendly detectives were questioning a cooperative witness. At the beginning of the second week, Dienstel agreed to say a few words to his parents. Soon the nightly conversations were lasting half an hour. He even appeared to enjoy the diet of Big Macs, fries, and milkshakes.

"I'd forgotten how good these were," he said, wiping ketchup off his chin one night during the third week. "The taste of America."

Sam and Donnie grinned.

The next morning at four o'clock, Dienstel got up. Carrying his shoes in his left hand, he tiptoed into the living room in his socks. Donnie, who was supposed to be guarding him, was asleep on the couch. His keys were on the coffee table. Dienstel took them and clasped them lightly in the palm of his hand so they wouldn't jingle. Then he walked to the front door, unlocked the shiny new deadbolt, and opened the door so slowly, he felt like time had stopped.

It was freezing outside. He was wearing only the wash-and-wear shirt and off-brand blue jeans the deprogrammers had given him. Shivering with cold and excitement, he put on his shoes and ran up one dark street and down another. They were all the same, lined with two-bedroom houses that had fake brick facades.

Dienstel started to panic.

He came to a corner and stopped. He looked to his left first and then to his right. He could just make out a red traffic light far down the street. He ran toward it and discovered a major road. He turned left for no real reason and began running. When he got tired, he slowed to a walk. Then he started running again—until he found himself in downtown Homewood, standing in front of the entrance to the Illinois Central Railroad. His heart pounded with joy. The train would take him back to Chicago and the ISKCON temple.

Standing in the doorway of a greasy-spoon diner across the street from the station, Dienstel saw his ticket home—a few early-bird commuters waiting on the platform. He knew that if he went over to them, he could beg the money for his fare. But something restrained him. As soon as Sam and Donnie found he'd split, this was the first place they would come looking for him. And who knew how often the trains ran at this hour? He could be stuck up there on the platform for twenty or twenty-five minutes. If the deprogrammers arrived before the train, he'd be trapped.

Still, he thought, it's worth the chance. If he could catch the train, he was home free. He was about to step into the street when he heard an engine roar. He looked to his left and saw a pair of headlights bouncing toward him. He ducked back and hid in the recessed entryway of the dark restaurant.

The blue Ford made a U-turn in the middle of the intersection and came to a rocking halt in front of the train station. Sam jumped out and raced up the stairs. Donnie got out of the car and looked up and down the street. He waited for a car to go by and crossed to Dienstel's side of the street. It was after five o'clock now and starting to get light. A few more feet, Dienstel knew, and Donnie would spot him.

"Donnie!"

The voice echoed up and down the empty streets. Donnie stopped and turned around.

"He's not up there! Let's go check the bus stops on the Dixie Highway!"

Donnie turned and ran back to the car. The two deprogrammers piled into the Ford and raced off, tires squealing. For a few moments, Dienstel was afraid to move. He wanted to cross the street and climb the stairs to the platform so desperately, he could almost feel his feet moving. But what if Sam and Donnie came back? It wasn't worth the risk.

Instead, he walked along the shadows until he found a

side street that headed south and began picking his way through the suburban maze, always making sure to move parallel to the railroad tracks. He finally worked his way into Chicago Heights, the town south of Homewood. He found the train station and walked onto the platform. He told a commuter he'd been so sleepy when he left home that he'd forgotten his wallet. If he went back to get it, he'd miss his train and would be late for work. The man gave him a couple of bucks and his business card. Dienstel promised to mail him the money.

An hour later, he walked into the Chicago temple and a hero's welcome.

"We're at war with maya!" shouted the Chicago temple president. He pointed to Dienstel, who was sitting in the front row of the devotees gathered in the main room of the elegant stone building that housed the temple.

"The kidnapping of our godbrother who returned to us today through Krishna's mercy is not an isolated case. Devotees are being taken by body snatchers all over the country."

The president paced in front of the devotees.

"In a war, it is us against them," he continued. "You are with us or you are against us. The measure of sincerity is initiation. Therefore, from now on, only devotees who have surrendered to Prabhupada will be allowed to worship and take prasadam in this temple."

The room was silent. People exchanged glances. After a few moments, a man with thick, curly black hair wearing a yellow Arrow shirt and light brown slacks got to his feet.

"For anyone who doesn't know me, I'm Frank Sterns," he said calmly. "I teach English at Roosevelt University downtown. My wife is Hindu. We have been coming to the Chicago temple with our kids since it opened four years ago. Even though we've never been initiated, we've always felt that this is our temple and that Krishna Consciousness is our religion. But now you're telling me that we are no longer welcome here because we've chosen to stay in the world and raise a family?'

"I thought I made myself clear," the president said

sternly. "Either you take initiation or you leave us. What is so difficult? You have shown great interest in Krishna Consciousness. Why not take initiation?"

"I'll be initiated when I'm ready to be initiated," Sterns shot back, his voice rising in anger. "I've never felt anyone should be initiated until they are ready to commit themselves totally, twenty-four hours a day, seven days a week."

"That is the only kind of devotee we are interested in," Bhagavan said icily. "Now, are you with us or against us?"

The English teacher turned to walk out of the room. Then he stopped and looked at the president.

"Maybe I've been teaching kids from Chicago too long, but I'm going to tell you something just the way those kids would tell you: This is really fucked up and you are one dumb fuck. This 'Us against them' mentality you're shoving down peoples' throats is going to hurt the movement more than a battalion of deprogrammers."

The president stared at the English teacher. Sterns shook his head and stormed out, never to be seen again in the Chicago temple. He didn't bother closing the heavy door.

"Just see," the president said, raising his voice and imitating Prabhupada's way of speaking. "My point is made. This man is no loss. We are better off without someone who would speak to a representative of Srila Prabhupada in such a way."

The president stared at the devotees until several of them nodded.

"Now, to continue. These deprogrammers are being sent by parents. It is therefore required that devotees sever contact with their families. They are not to be trusted. Devotees must also cease to associate with friends made prior to joining the movement. You are in danger. So-called friends may be working with parents to set you up for a kidnapping."

One of the female devotees raised her hand. The president looked around, inviting a male devotee to ask a question. None did. Finally, he nodded at her.

"Excuse me, but it seems to me you are proving Dr.

Sterns's point," the woman said. "I mean, I joined because my best friend joined and brought me to a temple. Sananati, who's sitting here beside me, joined after her big brother joined. We all know that you don't make devotees on the street, because we've all tried. You make devotees by introducing people you know to Krishna. How can we make new devotees if we can no longer bring Krishna's message to people we care about?"

"Woman," the president hissed. "Woman, I'm going to tell you something I shouldn't have to. Srila Prabhupada has said he would have been happy if he had come to this country and made one pure devotee who was willing to sit under a tree and chant Hare Krishna with him. One pure devotee, woman. This movement has never been about numbers and never will be. It's about purity!"

Stocking
God's Treasury

Prabhupada was in his small room in the temple in Mayapur, chanting his morning rounds. He finished and rang a small silver bell. His new secretary—a different devotee assumed the honored position every few months—appeared carrying a silver tray loaded with a plate of freshly sliced fruit and a stack of letters.

Prabhupada glanced at the unopened mail and was overcome with sadness. He used to look forward to reading his mail. The letters once had been filled with declarations of love for Krishna and the spiritual master. But that had all changed. Now the letters were full of troubles. They were little more than lists of complaints: temple presidents complaining about devotees, devotees about temple presidents; wives complaining about husbands, husbands about wives. The divorce rate was running around 80 percent, his temple presidents wrote him.

Perhaps he had made a mistake in trying to build the movement around grihasthas, householders. At first, the Americans—with their inflated sense of romantic love—thought the procedure strange. Prabhupada would walk around a room, picking out devotees almost at random and matching them.

You and you will do nicely," he liked to say, pulling devotees forward by their hands. The ceremonies had been just as simple: a few words, then the newlyweds exchanged flowers.

When Westerners tried talking to him about physical attraction and other nonsense he'd heard in their pop songs, he always gave the same explanations: "What sounder foundation could a marriage have than devotion to Krishna? Surely, Krishna is a stronger bond than your transitory feelings?"

But the letters proved that the devotees had simply not advanced far enough. Prabhupada sliced the flap of the first envelope with an engraved silver letter opener given to him by one of his eager secretaries. He ran his eye down the page: another complaining husband.

Prabhupada sighed and slit open another envelope. Here was a letter from a devotee in Chicago reporting that the temple president had delivered a speech saying that the number of devotees the movement attracted was no longer important. Prabhupada shook his head. This is all nonsense. The president was in maya.

So many were in maya.

"This is too much for one sick old man to handle," he said to his secretary, who was still standing by his side. "If only Krishna had sent me help in the form of one enlightened devotee. But none of these boys has experienced *samadhi,* none is advanced enough to be my successor."

Then, he smiled at the irony. Maybe it was just as well. If there was only one successor, the others would surely gang up to destroy the man.

Prabhupada once again rang his bell. Another devotee entered.

"I will take massage now," he said, placing himself on the massage table. "As I once called Kirtanananda Kitchenananda, I should call myself 'Problempada.' "

The masseur didn't respond.

Once a year, in March and early April, ISKCON regional secretaries and temple presidents came to Mayapur, a rural town in Bengal, from all over the world to celebrate Lord Chaitanya's birthday and to hold ISKCON's annual meeting. It was quite informal. Temple presidents delivered speeches about how many devotees they had attracted and all the wonderful projects they had going. The days were passed chanting, gossiping, and enjoying prasadam.

But this year was different. The tension was high. Rumors had spread that Prabhupada would announce major changes. He had indicated many times that he was unhappy about the inconsistencies among independent temples. Daily worship of the deities varied too widely. He hadn't dropped any definitive hints about how he planned to handle the problem, so the rumors swirled.

When Prabhupada called a special meeting, everybody knew that the moment had come. The temple presidents and regional secretaries arrived early, eager to get a place at the front. The sannyasis were particularly excited. They all knew how much the divorce rate had disappointed their guru. Maybe he'd finally come round to their point of view: The traditional Indian way of running a religious order, the celibate way, was right, even for the West.

Prabhupada walked into the temple slowly, showing his age, and sat on the lavish red *vyasasana*. His disciples offered obeisances.

"I am announcing today the formation of a Governing Body Commission, a GBC," he began. "Twelve devotees will be responsible for twelve parts of the world. The GBC members will travel always from one temple to another within their zones, inspiring the devotees and making sure that services are uniform. To do that, they must be sannyasis. They must always be thinking of Krishna, not of wives and children left behind."

Prabhupada waited a minute, then raised his hand and asked for silence.

"The GBC must also spend much time in India," he said firmly. "The leading devotees must study. For this, we will build three temples, one in Bombay, one in Vrindaban, one here in Mayapur. They will be the seminaries of Krishna Consciousness. There, the leaders will advance to the highest levels and continue building our movement, even after I am gone."

Prabhupada paused and nodded to his secretary. He began distributing a preprinted list of members on the new Governing Body Commission.

Kirtanananda's name was not on the list. Hayagriva's was.

Evidently Prabhupada had not forgotten Kirtanananda's defection.

"The GBC will meet tomorrow to discuss its various duties," Prabhupada said. "There is only one thing I must say now: If you fight each other, what will happen is plain; revolutions lead to no solutions and then to dissolution. I am asking one thing above all else: please cooperate. Your love for me will be shown by how much you cooperate to keep our movement together after I am gone."

Prabhupada knew better. He knew his disciples would compete to succeed him. But he may have figured he had found a way to use that competition. Undoubtedly, every member of the GBC would push to make his own area the strongest. By trying to outdo each other, they would almost certainly make the movement grow, despite their feuds.

"Now there is this," Prabhupada said, looking out over the room again. "It has come to my attention that some leaders are saying it is no longer important for us to make devotees. This is not so. We must always be making devotees, even though maya is attacking and making it ever harder for us, especially in America."

Prabhupada paused. The temple was silent.

"The way to defeat maya is to counterattack with force," he continued. "We have established this Bhaktivedanta Book Trust this BBT, to publish *The Bhagavad-Gita As It Is,* the *Srimad-Bhagavatam,* and other sacred books. We must distribute these books everywhere in the world. These books are Krishna's most potent weapon against maya."

Nobody had sold those books better than Hansadutta. And nobody could have been more ecstatic to find himself on Prabhupada's list.

Hansadutta, an exotic, handsome figure in a fresh white dhoti, stopped a middle-aged, blond-haired German woman on a street in downtown Frankfurt. She tried to step around him. He moved to block her.

"I have no time for this," she said in German, once again trying unsuccessfully to step around him.

"Give me an answer to one question and you can

proceed," Hansadutta replied. All that is required is a yes or a no."

Before the woman could reply, Hansadutta stepped close and looked deep in her eyes.

"Are you happy?" he asked.

"That's it? That's the question?" the woman asked with a laugh.

Hansadutta moved so close they were almost touching.

"Yes," he said. "Don't hesitate; just answer."

The woman looked at Hansadutta. Then she broke eye contact and looked down at the sidewalk.

"No, since you insist on asking, the answer is no," she said. "My mother is dying of cancer. She is in terrible pain."

"I'm truly sorry," Hansadutta said. "Rest assured you're not alone in your suffering. I ask that question all day long. I very rarely get a yes."

Hansadutta reached into a cloth bag hanging on his left shoulder and pulled out the German edition of Prabhupada's *Gita*.

"There's no happiness in this world," he said, pressing the book into the woman's hands. "Nothing lasts. Your mother will die; we'll all die."

The woman looked at the *Gita*.

"It's about finding eternal happiness," Hansadutta said. "It's about transcending grief. Take it. It's a gift for you and your mother."

"But why would you give me such a thick book?" the woman asked. "It must cost a fortune."

"I give it to spread the joy of Krishna Consciousness," Hansadutta said. "If you feel you can't accept it without donating something, that will be fine. The money we collect goes to feed starving children in Bangladesh."

The woman opened her purse and handed Hansadutta a bill.

"Now you're the one who is being generous," Hansadutta said. "Hare Krishna. I will chant for you and your mother."

Hansadutta stuffed the bill in his *japa* bag and walked around the corner to a parking lot where two devotees were waiting in a brand new VW van.

"Great morning," Hansadutta said. "The old master

should get out more often instead of relying on his devotees. The master has definitely not lost his touch. I just took fifty marks off a woman whose mother has cancer."

Hansadutta got in the van and they drove out of Frankfurt to Kettershof Castle, the famous German *Schloss* Hansadutta had purchased a year earlier. He had opened ISKCON's first German temple in Hamburg. When it was up and running, he had moved on to Munich and opened another. He came to Frankfurt because the castle was up for sale. It was an eye-popper, exactly the kind of lavish place Prabhupada had wanted.

Even in America, Prabhupada seemed preoccupied with glamor. In Detroit, Alfred Brush Ford—great grandson of Henry—and Elisabeth Reuther Dickmeyer, daughter of Walter, the former president of the United Auto Workers, each contributed $150,000 so that ISKCON could purchase the lavish Fischer Mansion, which had been built by Lawrence "Body by" Fischer, the founder of Cadillac Motors. In New York, the ISKCON temple was now located in a beautiful, multimillion-dollar midtown landmark, a twelve-story building at 340 West Fifty-fifth Street. ISKCON owned the whole building.

Hansadutta had wanted the Kettershof Castle in Frankfurt because it kept him in the forefront of the Krishna status competition. Bhagavan had turned an estate in Florence that had once belonged to Machiavelli into a temple. He had then gone on to France, where he bought a château near Paris that was once Jean-Jacques Rousseau's retreat. Germany's guru wasn't about to let himself be outclassed. Nor were any of the other GBC members.

As the van carrying Hansadutta rolled up to the entrance of his castle, it passed a dark green BMW parked in the shade under a row of elms. The man sitting behind the steering wheel glanced at the van's license plate and wrote down the number in a notebook. He checked his watch and also noted the time.

Hansadutta went directly to his quarters for his day's nap. He was soon awakened by shouts coming from the ground floor of the castle. It was dark outside; he had slept longer than he intended. Within seconds, somebody was pounding on his door.

"Hansadutta, quick!" a devotee outside yelled. "It's a raid. The police are raiding us."

"Open up and come out with your hands up!" a voice ordered.

Hansadutta did as he was told. A German cop grabbed him as he was coming through the door and slammed him face-first into a wall.

"You are under arrest," the cop said as he snapped on a pair of handcuffs. "You have cheated your last German citizen."

The cops searched the castle and found Hansadutta's arsenal. They confiscated a Walther, several Colt .45s, and a number of semiautomatic rifles. They also took along boxes of ammunition and fourteen devotees, including Hansadutta. All were charged with fraud, larceny, and a half-dozen postal and weapons violations.

"It's a little more difficult than I thought," Hansadutta's lawyer said in a conference room after bailing everybody out. "The police have collected a lot of evidence. They've been tailing you for seven months. The charge sheet is three pages long. The cops say you've collected over four million marks for charity, and that not one mark—not one—has actually been donated."

Hansadutta looked at the attorney and shrugged.

"When you're working for God," he said, "you have to cut some corners."

Prabhupada woke at three, as he always did, no matter what part of the world he happened to be in. For a moment, he thought he was still on the airplane from India—he always seemed to be on an airplane. It was March 1976. Just the other day a devotee told him that in the last three years Prabhupada had circled the globe ten times.

Prabhupada looked around the dark room. Yes, now he remembered: he was in the apartment reserved for him in the Los Angeles temple. He had arrived late in the evening and gone directly to bed. Today, he would tour the BBT, the world's largest publisher of books on

Hinduism. Millions of copies of Prabhupada's books were circulating around the world. That was good. His books would spread the knowledge of Krishna long after he was gone.

Other things were not so good. Every time he returned to America, the problems were worse. Prabhupada climbed out of bed in a somber mood, trudged into the bathroom, and turned on the shower. Even after doing it every morning for more years than he could remember, he was never prepared for the cold water. But it was invigorating. The shock cleared his mind of all his mundane problems and allowed him to focus on Krishna.

He smiled ruefully as he toweled himself dry. Before he had left Calcutta, a newspaper reporter had asked him what he most wanted in this life. He had said the obvious: to see Krishna Consciousness spread to every city and village on this planet. Now he admitted to himself that he'd told a small lie. What he wanted more than anything else was to be left alone. He wanted to chant and translate the sacred texts and prepare to meet Krishna.

He had tried to make things easier for himself by creating the GBC. One sick man could not possibly oversee a movement that had nearly two hundred temples in almost fifty countries. But the GBC was a disaster. Its members had been at each other's throats from the first moment. Trying to win his favor, they came running to him with tales of perfidy, stealing, and scheming. Prabhupada understood the problem: They didn't want to serve him. They wanted to *be* him.

Prabhupada picked up his japa bag and took out his beads. As soon as he began chanting, his mundane cares disappeared. After he had finished his rounds of the maha-mantra, he attended the morning devotional services. Whey they concluded, he returned to his room. He had just sat down when Ramesvara, Robert Grant, president of the Bhaktivedanta Book Trust and Governing Body Commission member for Los Angeles, knocked and entered, followed by a train of devotees carrying prasadam. The devotees offered obeisances and left.

"Prabhupada, there are no words to express what a joy it is to have you with us," Ramesvara said.

Prabhupada smiled. Ramesvara was the son of a New York City real-estate developer. He was very ambitious and very immature, but he was also a first-rate businessman. Prabhupada decided he could be frank.

"I leave tomorrow to deal with this nastiness in the New York temple," Prabhupada said. "Tell me what is happening in America."

"Even though you did not appoint Kirtanananda to the GBC, he continues to claim he is your true successor and that everyone else is subservient to him," Ramesvara began. "He says he was not appointed because he is higher than the GBC."

Prabhupada nodded. He would have been disappointed if Ramesvara had not mentioned Kirtanananda first. They hated each other. Kirtanananda had even stopped his devotees from selling books because the money went to the BBT and Ramesvara was the BBT president. Kirtanananda was keeping every penny for New Vrindaban. That infuriated Ramesvara, but Prabhupada didn't mind. New Vrindaban was important.

"I am always hoping that Kirtanananda will learn humility," Prabhupada said. "What else?"

"The way I see it, we have a major problem with sannyasis, even though I myself have taken the vows of renunciation," Ramesvara said. "Since you appointed only sannyasis to the GBC, people think that the road to power begins with a vow of celibacy. Everybody wants to take sannyasa. I am afraid that many are homosexuals. This has led to problems for women. Women are now regarded as inferior in almost every temple. In New York, a sannyasi has even spit on a woman."

"A sannyasi did this? Who?"

"His name is Gargamuni," Ramesvara said.

"This is terrible," Prabhupada said.

"Worse yet is Tamal," Ramesvara said.

Prabhupada was surprised, but did not show it. Tamal, Thomas Herzog, had done excellent service since being appointed to the GBC. After spending several years in India, Tamal had returned to America with a few brahmacharis. He bought an old Greyhound bus, converted it into a rolling temple, and began touring college campuses. He had made many devotees, so many that Prabhupada had authorized a dozen buses for Tamal. Even as they spoke, the buses were rolling across America.

"What is this with Tamal?" Prabhupada asked.

"He's like Kirtanananda," Ramesvara said. "He's stealing devotees from other temples."

Prabhupada leaned forward. "This is not true. He is bringing us devotees from college campuses. I myself have seen many pictures."

Ramesvara shook his head.

"The sixties are over, Prabhupada. American kids aren't interested in seeking enlightenment anymore. They want to go to business school."

"But these pictures of new devotees Tamal sends me?"

"They're mostly people he's stolen," Ramesvara said. "It's part of this sannyasi thing. He goes into a temple where the president is a householder. He comes up to a brahmachari and says, 'You're a celibate student, that's good, you're making spiritual progress. But look at your situation. You're under a householder. Householders are in maya, they're controlled by their wives. To advance spiritually, you must surrender to a sannyasi. If you're really serious about Krishna Consciousness, come with me. There's room on the bus.' "

"This must stop," Prabhupada said angrily. "We are devouring each other."

"How can I help?" Ramesvara asked eagerly.

Prabhupada looked at Ramesvara. It was obvious he was more interested in scoring a coup against an enemy than in spreading Krishna Consciousness.

"Bring me a devotee who can take dictation," Prabhupada sighed. "I will write some letters about all this."

Prabhupada was glum when he settled into his first-class seat for the flight to New York the next morning. He had created the GBC to solve just the kind of problems plaguing the New York temple. But it hadn't worked. Here he was, busier than ever, dealing with one snafu after another, all by himself.

"Prabhupada. You've arrived. This unexpected visit is a blessing from Krishna," said Balimardan, the new president of the New York temple, when he met Prabhupada at the John F. Kennedy Airport terminal the next evening. "Come this way; we have a limousine waiting. Prabhupada, you're gonna love New York. Wait till you see how far the movement's come from that ratty old storefront down on Second Avenue."

Prabhupada was silent; he had a matter of some urgency on his mind.

"Your wife," he asked as soon as they were seated in the stretch limo. "She is not who she claimed to be?"

Balimardan shifted uncomfortably in the padded leather seat.

"At the time I wrote you, yes, I believed she was Natasha Toyota, the heiress to the automobile fortune," Balimardan said. "That, in fact, is why I married her—you told me to. As it turns out, no, she isn't an heiress. But, Prabhupada, I'm still glad I married her. Everything has worked out fine. We have a nice Krishna-conscious marriage."

"But who was she then?" Prabhupada asked.

"I don't really know. But anyway she's been reborn as a devotee. Wait'll you meet her. She's as sweet and innocent as any woman in the movement."

Prabhupada did not reply. The limo pulled up in front of the West-Fifty-fifth Street temple.

"Now, this is the real New York, Prabhupada," Balimardan said. "Look at all the skyscrapers. And here we are, right in the middle of them. Talk about making inroads into America."

"Let us enter," Prabhupada said.

When the spiritual master walked into the temple, two hundred devotees fell to their knees and offered obeisances. Prabhupada acknowledged them by briefly bowing his head. Then he looked around for his vyasasana, his elaborate preaching chair. It was gone.

"Why is this?" Prabhupada asked, pointing to the place on the altar where the huge chair should have been.

"We took it out to have it cleaned," Balimardan explained. "When we went to pick it up, the cleaners was closed. There was a sign on the door saying there had been a death in the family. We will get it and have it here tomorrow. I promise."

Prabhupada faced the New York devotees.

"There are demons in this movement disguised as devotees," he said and walked out.

The devotees gasped. Balimardan and his wife, Natasha, scurried after him.

"Prabhupada, we're sorry about this," Natasha said. "We'll get your vyasasana tomorrow. We had no idea this would upset you so."

"Show me my quarters," Prabhupada ordered, ignoring her.

They took an elevator up to the top floor. As they walked down the hallway, Prabhupada stopped in front of each door to ask what was inside. Balimardan patiently explained how the temple used each room, and pointed out each devotee's quarters.

"And this?" Prabhupada asked, stopping by a door halfway down the hall.

"Oh, that's nothing," Natasha said.

"Nothing?" Prabhupada asked.

"It's kind of our personal temple," Balimardan said. "It's where we worship Krishna together."

"I will see it," Prabhupada demanded.

"Prabhupada, it's really too late for you," Natasha said. "You need your rest. Perhaps in the morning."

"I will see it now," Prabhupada commanded.

Balimardan dug a key out of his japa bag and opened the door. The room looked like a suite in a Catskills honeymoon lodge. Under a ceiling mirror in the center of the lavish room was a huge bed.

"This place is known as the Bower of Bliss, is it not?" Prabhupada asked.

"Well, you see, Prabhupada, in New York you sometimes kinda have to do things a little differently," Balimardan said.

Prabhupada walked over to a small, leather-covered refrigerator, opened the door, and began unloading the contents, one expensive gourmet item after another. He held up a tin of clams.

"This is what you offer the deities?" he demanded of Natasha. "This is an abomination!"

"What of it?" Natasha shot back. "I was new to the movement then."

"I am told your devotees eat poorly. I am told they scrounge for vegetables in trash bins behind supermarkets. And you live like this?"

"I guess we've gotten a little loose," Balimardan said softly.

Prabhupada looked at Natasha.

"You're not an heiress," he said. "Who are you?"

"I'm a devotee," she replied.

"You are not a devotee!" Prabhupada said, raising his voice for the first time. "A true devotee of Krishna would never live like this."

Balimardan sank into a black leather couch.

"Prabhupada, I'm sorry," he said.

"Your devotees spend every day on the street, peforming sankirtan," Prabhupada said.

"Yes."

"They raise much money."

"Yes."

"You do not turn this money over to ISKCON."

"Not all," Balimardan admitted.

"I want one hundred and fifty thousand dollars," Prabhupada said.

"That's a lot of money," Balimardan said.

"You have it."

"Yes."

"You will bring it to me in the morning. A cashier's check will do nicely."

"If I do, will everything be cool?" Balimardan asked, getting off the couch. "We've gone a little overboard, there's no hiding that. When you can do anything you want, you sorta start seein' what you can do. We'll clean up our act, I promise, Prabhupada."

"The cashier's check in the morning will do nicely," Prabhupada repeated. "Now show me to my quarters."

Balimardan was up by dawn the next morning. An hour after the banks opened, he knocked on Prabhupada's door. He was admitted and delivered the check.

"I will teach the *Srimad-Bhagavatam* class this afternoon myself," Prabhupada said as he took the envelope. "Make sure all the devotees are there."

"Yes, Prabhupada," Balimardan said. "I was going to get them together, anyway. I have an important announcement to make."

That afternoon, Balimardan ushered Prabhupada into the temple and onto the freshly cleaned vyasasana. The temple was packed with devotees, who bowed and scraped. Prabhupada nodded and smiled.

"I have spent the night in agony over the spiritual master's statement that there are demons in the movement disguised as devotees," Balimardan said. "Nothing could present a more terrible threat to our movement. But with Krishna's mercy, I have found the demons. The two devotees who took Prabhupada's vyasasana to the cleaners but did not bring it back are no longer devotees. I kicked them out of the temple this morning."

Balimardan smiled and nodded at Prabhupada.

"You must bring them back," Prabhupada said.

Balimardan looked puzzled.

"But, Prabhu—" he began.

"It was not them I was referring to," Prabhupada interrupted. "It was you—you and your wife. You are the demons. I am casting you out of the temple. You will go. Now."

Balimardan stared at Prabhupada.

"We had a deal," he said under his breath. "You're double-crossing me."

"You can't do this!" Natasha screamed. "You have no right. My husband is the master here, not you!"

She leapt to her feet in the front row and turned to the devotees.

"Tell him, tell him he can't do this!"

Prabhupada sat on the vyasasana, his face expressionless as Natasha ranted on. Finally, he stood up and pointed at her.

"Enough. You will go!"

The look in his eyes withered Natasha. She fell silent, then she began to sob. Balimardan took her by the arm and led her out of the temple. The devotees cheered.

Prabhupada sat back down on the vyasasana and closed his eyes. He began to chant solemnly. One by one, the devotees joined him. The tension relaxed as the soothing rhythm built. Finally, when the chanting ended, Prabhupada spoke.

"I am having two minds about you," he said. "You have been very good devotees. You have worked very hard to carry on Lord Chaitanya's movement. I am grateful to you for that. But you have let yourselves be led astray by two infidels who departed from our philosophy. How could you allow this? Krishna Consciousness is very simple. If your leaders chant and obey the regulative principles, they are practicing Krishna Consciousness. If they do not, they are demons disguised as devotees.

"It is all very good for you to be humble devotees and take orders. But you must always remember that your leaders must be humble, too. If they are not, if they demand service and are not humble, then those who serve them are fools. Tomorrow, I leave for London to see our devotees there. I leave you to clean up this mess.

"Hare Krishna."

The
Primrose Path

Marriage and Murder
Made in Godhead

"You know what I need? I need what you've got."

Steve Bryant paced back and forth in the small room of the dingy apartment in London's East End. The place was made even more drab by the gloomy April rain falling outside. He was jumpy and irritable, like a truck driver who's been popping Benzedrine for several days. Bryant always acted this way when he was worked up about something.

"What have I got that you don't?" asked "Jerome Greene," his best friend. Built like a basketball player whose weight program had failed, Greene was draped across an overstuffed chair, his fingertips propped against his cheek.

"Come on, you know," Bryant said.

"If I did, I wouldn't have spent the last half hour waiting for you to tell me," Greene said wearily.

"A wife!" Bryant yelled. "I want to get married."

Greene jumped up in the chair.

"You're not serious," he said. "You can't be, not after the way you put me down when I got married. I can still hear you ridin' me: 'Householders are in maya. Sex is maya. You can't love a woman and make spiritual progress. Krishna demands undivided attention.' What happened? What happened to you, Sulocana, the perfect brahmachari? What made you change your mind all of a sudden?"

"It isn't all that sudden," Bryant said, sitting down for the first time. "I could really get behind being a celibate when I joined. It made a lot of sense. But here it is, years later, and here I am, still a brahmachari. It'd be different if they made me a temple president or something. But they won't."

They stared quietly for a while in opposite directions.

"Listen, you married an English girl," Bryant said after a few minutes.

"That I did," Greene replied.

"Well? Think she knows anybody?"

"For you?"

"For me."

"I don't know," Greene said, "I'll ask."

In the late 1960s, just before Steve Bryant joined the Krishnas, he was a typical screwed-up American teenager. He had dropped out of junior college, laid some carpet, then quit to haul cement. For a while, he had toyed with the idea of becoming a masseur. He built a fancy table, but then dropped the idea.

His only real interests were drugs, motorcycles, muscle cars, and bodybuilding. And more drugs. Six foot one and 210 pounds, with thick blond hair, he had a taste for black leather jackets and acid. He also liked driving fast, tearing through the suburbs into Detroit to cruise Woodward Avenue. He eventually racked up enough speeding tickets to lose his license.

If Bryant hadn't been spiritually inclined, if he hadn't been intrigued by metaphyics, he probably would have settled down eventually, become a mechanic or a cabinetmaker, and raised a family. But he wasn't and he didn't. Instead, he chased nirvana. Little did he know that the search would take him down the road to a private hell.

"I've found the answer," Bryant announced one night while sitting with his parents in the den of their suburban Royal Oak home. "Krishna is God. This guy Prabhupada is his messenger!"

His father, Jack, a retired Air Force major, put down his newspaper and tried not to sigh. Jack prided himself on his ability to hang in there with Steve. He wasn't a ramrod-straight military man whose spit-and-polish view of reality had alienated his only son. He'd spent the last eleven years teaching math in junior and senior high school. He knew about the antiestablishment line then in vogue with young people. He knew that the smartest thing to do was to listen to his kid. Still, it was sometimes hard not to preach or threaten.

"Does this have to do with that Scientology course you were going to take?" Jack asked, trying to sound genuinely interested.

Steve bristled.

"Naw, that turned out to be a drag," he said. "Krishna's the real thing. I had this great meal at the temple today. Even their cooking tastes better then anyone else's."

"Who cooks better than me?" Steve's mother, Helga, interrupted with mock hurt. Entering the den, she'd caught the tail end of the conversation. Helga was always looking for ways to get her son to lighten up. He was so serious, so intense.

"Steve was just telling me about this new Krishna religion he's found," Jack said.

"*The* religion," Steve snapped. "And it's not new. It's a lot older than Christianity."

Helga couldn't hide her disappointment. Not another religious lecture. She hadn't minded the first few. It was interesting when Steve went to the Unitarian church with one friend, to a Catholic church with another, and a Methodist chapel with a third. He'd come home and tell her all about the rituals and beliefs. But her interest had evaporated several "answers" ago.

What upset Helga was that Steve didn't distinguish between magic and religion. All through high school he'd been wrapped up in astrology. Now he was taking his religion of the month just as seriously as he'd taken astrology. Hunching over his charts, he'd drone on and on about how the stars revealed everything. He'd even bought a crystal ball, Helga recalled, sighing inwardly.

"Prabhupada says that eating meat is a great sin," Steve continued severely. "You two should think about the consequences of eating Krishna's creatures. You are creating extra karma with every cheeseburger."

Helga allowed Steve to launch into a lecture about karma. It's better to let him get it out, she reminded herself. She tried to listen, but finally couldn't take it anymore. She yawned and got up to go to bed.

"You know what's wrong with you, Steve?" she said as

she left the living room. "You're boring. If you didn't take things so seriously, you'd be a lot more fun. And a lot happier."

"There's nothing more serious than Krishna Consciousness," Steve replied. "The future of the whole planet depends on people coming to Krishna."

With speed born of certainty, Bryant became devotee Sulocana, spending 1974, his first year in ISKCON, in the Detroit temple. From Detroit he went to Los Angeles; from Los Angeles to Gainesville, Florida; from Gainesville to London. His frequent moves slowed his advance up the ISKCON hierarchy. But he was even more seriously handicapped by his personality. The same thing that bothered his mother irritated fellow devotees.

Shortly after arriving at the London temple, he was doing the work of decorating the statues of Radha and Krishna. Bryant took great pride in his ability to adorn the deities.

Every morning, the deities are lovingly dusted and bathed in a mixture of milk, rose water, and a small amount of cow's urine. When done, the devotees drink the concoction. Then the statues are lavishly dressed and presented with an offering of prasadam.

No devotee performed the ceremony with more attention to detail than Sulocana did. And nobody knew more about Krishna Consciousness. Or so he thought.

One day, while Bryant was busy decorating Krishna, a woman working alongside him reached out to put a bouquet behind Radha. Bryant glanced up and saw the strap of her bra slip down her shoulder. With his eyes, he followed it back across her shoulder, into her sari. He imagined the smoothness of her breast and her brown nipple pressing against the white bra cup.

Bryant turned white with rage. He jumped up and immediately sought out the woman's husband.

"Your wife!" Bryant shouted.

"What?" the man said warily.

"She distracted me," Bryant complained, almost screaming. "She destroyed the mood of reverence I need for decorating the deities."

The husband leaped to his feet.

"But how?" he asked. "What did she do?"

"She let her bra slip off her shoulder and I saw it!" Bryant said.

The devotee shook his head. Then he looked at Bryant, his smile full of disgust.

"You know what, Sulocana?" he said finally. "You and your supercelibacy act are a real pain in the ass. A real pain in the ass."

Bryant's friend Jerome Greene had heard the story— several times. That was another reason why he was so surprised that Bryant now wanted to get married.

"There's somebody we think you should meet," Marianne Greene, Jerome's English wife, told Bryant a few days later.

"A girl?" Bryant demanded.

"Yes," Marianne said.

"Who? Tell me."

"An old friend," Marianne said. "Her name is Jane, Jane Rangely. She's twenty or twenty-one. She and John, her ex-boyfriend, have a two-year-old boy, Rinnian. They split up a few months ago."

"Tell him the best part," Jerome said.

"The best part? What's the best part?" Bryant interrupted nervously.

"She wants to be a devotee," Marianne said. "It's all she talks about."

"I wanna meet her," Bryant blurted out. "When can I meet her? Are you gonna have us both over, or what?"

"I don't like him," Jane said as soon as Bryant had left after their first meeting. A pretty woman with green eyes, pale white skin, and full lips, Jane had long brown hair and a cute figure. "He's so full of himself. Is he always that puffed-up?"

"He was just nervous about meeting you," Jerome said. "He'll be calmer next time."

"It was like I wasn't even there. I mean, he just went on and on about Krishna, like he was Prabhupada or something."

"Sulocana is very, very devout," Jerome explained. "If you marry him, you'll make spiritual progress. Women need someone to guide them."

Jane paused.

"Well, maybe liking him isn't important. I liked John and it didn't work out with us. If we're both devotees and really dedicated to Krishna, that should be enough, shouldn't it?"

Jerome didn't answer.

Two weeks after Steve and Jane first met, they were married in a civil ceremony. The newlyweds moved into the Greenes' apartment together with Jane's two-year-old. Right from the start, there was trouble. Jane wanted a spiritual master, someone to guide her.

Bryant wanted more.

"Where do you think you're going?" he demanded a week after the wedding as Jane headed for the door.

"Just out for a walk," Jane said. "Rinnian needs some fresh air. We've been cooped up here all day."

"You didn't ask," Bryant said.

"Ask who?"

"Me," Bryant said.

"Ask you if I can take a walk?" Jane said, her eyebrows rising.

"Absolutely," Bryant said. "You must. In Krishna Consciousness, the man makes every important decision. And I think it's important when and where you take a walk. I don't necessarily want my wife out on the streets alone."

"But we're just going around the block!" Jane cried.

"Around the block or around the world, a Krishna-conscious wife gets her husband's permission first."

"Marianne, what is all this?" Jane pleaded.

"Another thing," Bryant said before Marianne could reply. "Your hair—it's too long. And you're way too proud of it. You must surrender your pride. Prabhupada says a Krishna-conscious wife must be modest. Nothing about her should call attention to sex."

"Marianne, what's he saying?" Jane cried, the tears begining to roll down her cheeks. "You never told me these things."

Marianne looked at the floor and kept silent.

"We'll talk about your hair later," Bryant said. "You can go for a walk now. You can probably go for a walk anytime you want—if you ask first."

Bryant's demands were in line with Prabhupada's philosophy. He preached that women were controlled by their passions and must be subservient to men. But Bryant ignored the rest of his master's message: in return for subjugating themselves, Prabhupada taught that women must be protected and given love, kindness, and respect.

Bryant treated Jane as a worthless inferior. He was more military than his Air Force-trained father, more of a dictator than a husband. Deep down, he did not really want a wife; he wanted a devotee. If he could not be a guru in ISKCON, he would be a guru to a woman. That way, he thought, he could show everyone his devotion and authority.

"Baby, your new old man's totally fucked." The words came from John Morgan, Jane's old boyfriend and a part-time guitar player, one day when Jane snuck out to meet him.

"It's Krishna's way," Jane said, glancing around in fear that someone would notice them talking.

"Listen to me," John said, oblivious to her concern. "You're a very spiritual bird. I can dig that. But this guy's taking advantage of you. All the Krishnas take advantage of their women. They're into this heavy male trip. This one's worse 'cause he's totally paranoid about me coming back on the scene. You've seen what he's like when I come around. You're a dog on a very short leash."

"Don't talk like that," Jane said. "You mustn't. He's a very advanced spirit."

"Sure," John said, kissing her good-bye. "Advanced macho."

Later that evening, Jane had her hair cut short.

As Bryant approached the temple, he heard the soft *ching-ching-ching* of the cymbals. Then came the steady beat of the drums and the first chants of "Hare Krishna, Hare Krishna, Krishna Krishna, Hare Hare . . ."

It was six o'clock in the morning. Deep feelings of

pleasure and spiritual well-being swept over him as the rhythm built. His first impulse was to hurry into the temple and join the kirtan.

He held back because he was exhausted. It wasn't because he'd gotten up at four to take a cold shower and attend Mangal-aratik, the morning devotional service. Or because he'd spent an hour carefully decorating the Radha-Krishna deities with flowers. And certainly not because his wife of less than a year had exhausted him.

Bryant was drained because yesterday he had danced and chanted for five hours. He had reached a state of high ecstasy. He had felt so much joy, his whole body ached. Krishna had definitely been present.

And yet he was troubled. If the kirtan was spiritually purifying, if Krishna had really been present, why did he feel hung over, like he'd polluted his body with drugs and alcohol? *Hare,* the spiritual energy of the Lord, was the purest, most potent force in all the universe. If he had truly connected with that divine force, why did he feel tapped out? A devotee filled with Hare is supposed to be absolutely calm and, at the same time, filled with boundless energy.

"Something's wrong," he muttered, but then dismissed the thought almost as soon as it occurred. He came to the same conclusion he always reached when attacked by doubts: his faith wasn't sufficiently pure. He tried to convince himself to enter the temple and join the kirtan to purify himself and do penance for his dark thoughts. Instead, he decided to take a walk.

He returned around noon for his meal of prasadam. The kirtan was still going on. The noise was deafening. The temple smelled like a rank gym, heavy with sweat and body odor. Devotees were pounding drums and smashing cymbals, screaming the mantra at the top of their voices, jumping up and down like their legs were pogo sticks, and waving their arms above their heads.

Jayatirtha, James Immel, the GBC member in charge of the United Kingdom, was writhing on the floor in front of his vyasasana. Bryant stood by the door, watching him roll three times to his left, then three times back to his right. Jayatirtha lay still for a moment. Then his

whole body began to shake. He struggled onto all fours
like a baby and crawled onto his vyasasana. Tears streamed
down his face.

Suddenly, Jayatirtha began howling like a coyote. It
was spooky, a long, terrifying shriek that boosted the
kirtan's frenzy one more notch. Then he shrieked again.
The drummers pounded the blue drums harder and faster.
The dancers jumped higher and chanted louder. The
same thing had happened yesterday, when Bryant was
one of the dancers. This time, he backed out of the
temple and began walking home to the Greenes' apartment.

As he strolled, he began thinking about Jayatirtha.
Bryant and other London devotees liked to congratulate
each other about how fortunate they were to be serving
Jayatirtha. His bizarre kirtans, his high-profile ecstasy,
surely meant that Krishna had revealed himself and that
Jayatirtha was overwhelmed by the vision. When he bab-
bled frantically on his vyasasana, he clearly was speaking
to the Lord. Often, Bryant had pushed in close to see if
he could hear the sacred words.

True, a few devotees remained skeptical. Prabhupada
never put on such a public display of ecstasy. He regarded ostentatious demonstrations of emotion as false
and cheap. Was Jayatirtha claiming to be on a higher
plane than Prabhupada? Bryant wondered.

He walked faster, struggling to put the question out of
his mind. He didn't want to question Jayatirtha's legiti-
macy; he wanted to believe.

"Jerome says you're to go right back to our bedroom,"
Marianne said when Bryant entered. "He's been waiting
for you. Something's up.

"What is it?" Bryant asked. Jane was on the couch,
reading her son, Rinnian, a story. As usual, Bryant ignored them.

"He hasn't told us yet. He wants to speak to you first,"
Marianne said. "He's all excited about it."

Bryant rapped on the Greenes' bedroom door and
walked in. Jerome was sitting on the bed, writing a letter.

"What's up, Prabhu?" Bryant asked jauntily, using the

Krishna equivalent of "Bro"—or, literally, "one who has taken shelter at the feet of the Lord."

"Brace yourself," Jerome began. "A mystery has been solved."

"Oh yeah?" Bryant said, sitting down.

"Why does Jayatirtha hold such wild kirtans?" Jerome asked. He stopped and waited for Bryant to respond. When Bryant didn't snap at the bait, Jerome couldn't contain his excitement.

"Why does he roll on the floor? Why does he talk to Krishna?"

Jerome stopped once more to look at Bryant. He kept staring until Bryant succumbed.

"Well, why?" Bryant finally asked.

"Because he's tripping."

"He's *what*?" Bryant screamed.

"He's on acid. He takes a hit almost every day."

"How d'you know?" Bryant asked.

"Read for yourself," Jerome said, handing Bryant a letter. "It came this morning."

Bryant turned his back to Jerome and began reading. The letter was from a devotee in Berkeley who had known Jayatirtha before he joined the movement in 1967. Back then, Jayatirtha had been an acid freak, one of Timothy Leary's most devoted disciples. He had stopped taking acid to follow Prabhupada. But now he was back to tripping. The devotee had written Jerome to find out if other temple members were also taking acid.

"I knew he was bogus," Jerome said. "I just knew! I've been saying that all along."

Bryant stared silently at the letter.

"Didn't I tell you Jayatirtha was bogus?" Jerome pushed.

"This can't be true," Bryant said coldly. "Krishna would never let such a blasphemy occur. He's defiling our kirtans. He's making a mockery of everything Prabhupada taught us."

"That's exactly right," Jerome broke in. "And he's getting away with it because Prabhupada isn't here to stop him."

"What should we do?" Bryant asked.

"I don't know," Jerome replied. "But we can't stay here."

It was exactly 5:00 A.M. when Jayatirtha emerged from his chambers at Bhaktivedanta Manor, the estate George Harrison had bought for ISKCON on the outskirts of London. He walked the estate and chanted his rounds every morning at this hour. Devotees knew all about this routine. That morning one was waiting for him, hiding behind an ancient oak tree.

She wanted to take Jayatirtha's picture. Like many other members of the temple, she considered him the most spiritually advanced man in the movement—after Prabhupada, of course. She had built a little altar at her home and planned to mount the picture there, right under Prabhupada's.

Fearing she would disturb his chanting, the devotee followed Jayatirtha at a respectful distance. He walked through the shady grounds and onto a path that led into a meadow full of wildflowers. Jayatirtha stopped; the devotee knelt in the grass, focused the camera, and began snapping away.

Suddenly, she noticed a strange movement. She watched Jayatirtha reach down and help a woman to her feet. They embraced and started kissing. Jayatirtha untied her sari; she lifted her arms, danced a couple of circles, and spun out of it. Then she helped Jayatirtha out of his dhoti. The photographer watched as the couple embraced. The woman fell to her knees and took Jayatirtha's penis into her mouth. The temple president groaned. Then he threw back his head and howled, just like he did at his ecstatic kirtans. The photographer lost sight of him in the tall grass when he sank to his knees and joined the woman on a blanket.

The photographer crawled closer until she could see them making love. Their white bodies were grinding together in the green grass. The photographer inched still closer, aimed her camera, and began shooting.

"I have something for you," a male devotee, holding out an envelope, said to Jayatirtha after evening prasadam, three days later.

Jayatirtha looked at the envelope.

"What is it?" he said.

"Pictures," the devotee replied.

"How nice," Jayatirtha said, reaching out to take the envelope. "Let's have a look."

The devotee pulled the envelope out of his reach.

"You will want to see these in private," he said. "I suggest we go someplace else, someplace very, very private."

Jayatirtha's eyes narrowed.

"What is this?" he asked.

"You won't know till you see, will you?" the devotee said.

Jayatirtha rose to his feet. The devotee followed him into his office, closed the door, and locked it.

"Now," Jayatirtha demanded. "Give it to me!" The devotee handed him the envelope. Jayatirtha tore it open and pulled out a thick pack of five-by-seven-inch photographs. When he looked at the first picture, his head snapped back. His eyes hardened and he stared at the devotee. Then he flipped through the rest.

"Where'd you get these?" Jayatirtha asked. His voice was little more than a whisper.

"My wife wanted your picture," the devotee replied. "So when you left the temple on your morning rounds the other day, she followed."

"It was a small indiscretion, a mere contretemps," Jayatirtha replied almost airily.

He was bluffing. And the devotee knew it.

"You really think the GBC will see it that way?" he asked.

"You mean you'd take these to the GBC?" Jayatirtha asked, his voice once again fading.

"Hey, I'm only a devotee and you're on the GBC and everything," the devotee replied. "But I've got my duty. I have to help preserve the movement's purity. Hey, where would we be without purity?"

"Wait," Jayatirtha interrupted. For a moment he paced in silence. "All right," he finally continued. "Let's say you've done your duty. You've brought this to me. I've confessed. I must admit I'm badly compromised. But it was a mistake, nothing more than a slip. I promise never, never to engage in such disgraceful behavior again."

Jayatirtha paused.

"There, that's over and done with. Now, since there's no need for this to go any further, you'd be doing a great service by presenting me with the negatives."

"Well now," the devotee said. "I don't know, my wife went to a lot of trouble to get them."

"Of course, of course," Jayatirtha said. "She has done a great service. She has helped me see the error of my ways. She should be rewarded. Did you have something particular in mind?"

"We were thinking like, how about a trip to India?" the devotee replied.

"That's a very good idea," Jayatirtha said. "I'll arrange it. India is so spiritual. It'll be very healthy for you. You'll forget all these worldly pressures. You'll be able to set your minds at ease."

The first letter had a Bombay postmark.

The Governing Body Commission ignored it.

The second came from LA.

The GBC filed it and forgot about it.

But day by day, letter by letter, the file grew. It was soon too thick to ignore. Jayatirtha's behavior was just too bizarre to remain secret. Or to cover up.

Reluctantly, the GBC launched an investigation. It concluded that Jayatirtha's "emotionalism" was caused by his continuing relationship with his wife. The answer seemed simple. Suspend him for a year and force him to take a vow of sannyasa, celibacy.

But the diagnosis was wrong. The problem wasn't Jayatirtha's wife. It was sex and drugs. That became clear as soon as the guru's probation expired. Once again he started dropping acid and seducing devotees. And once again, devotees started writing to complain. A few even quit the movement.

Finally, at the annual meeting in Mayapur in April 1982, the GBC hotly debated Jayatirtha's fate. Several members said they didn't have the authority to discipline one of their own. That, they warned, could only introduce sectarianism and doom the movement. But most members felt they no longer had any choice. They argued Jayatirtha couldn't be saved. His sacrilege was poisoning the entire movement.

They won. Jayatirtha was excommunicated.

"They can't do this to you," protested John Tierney, Navaniticara, Jayatirtha's most devoted disciple. "They're just jealous of your spiritual powers."

Jayatirtha laughed.

"Those fools," he said. "They chant and chant and chant, and nothing ever comes of it. They're too blind to see that acid is a sacrament, as necessary and powerful as chanting."

Jayatirtha had pursued samadhi, the unification of man and God, for ten years. He had chanted and read Prabhupada's books. He had done everything he was supposed to do. But it wasn't enough—he was spiritually frustrated. One day, he had taken a hit of acid and made his discovery: LSD turbocharged chanting. Or was it chanting that turbocharged acid? He wasn't sure and didn't care. Acid chanting took him so high. It made him Krishna. And if he was Krishna, should he not sport with the gopis, as the Blue Lord had done? Of course, he must. Jayatirtha began mixing sex and chanting, chanting and acid. It was heaven. He was Krishna; his partner, Radha. Religion was great. Why couldn't the GBC understand? he wondered over and over again.

"We don't need them," he finally told Tierney.

Jayatirtha was reborn as Tirthapada. His sex-to-drugs-to-God philosophy was an immediate hit. The Peace Krishnas, as he called his group, quickly attracted devotees from all over the world. Jayatirtha-Tirthapada was soon jetting first class from the United States to India and back to Canada. For a while, he indulged in the sacrament in Santa Rosa, California, where he and his band opened a small firm called Spirit of Liberty Marketing. Then he was off to India. He returned to celebrate the opening of the Peace on Earth Crafts Store in Victoria, British Columbia. Then he was off to Nepal.

He was in Nepal when a prospective devotee, a former member of ISKCON named Nataipada, made contact. A friend in Santa Cruz, California, had told him about the Peace Krishnas' ecstatic kirtans and their close relationship with God. Nataipada was bubbling with excitement when he finally tracked down Jayatirtha-Tirthapada and his group. But it didn't last more than a few days.

"Drugs are maya," Nataipada complained to Jayatirtha when he found out about the acid. "Using drugs and smuggling them are evil. I want nothing to do with you or your movement."

"Suit yourself," Jayatirtha replied.

"I need plane fare home," Nataipada demanded. "I've been misled. You people are not practicing true Krishna consciousness."

"How you feel has nothing to do with us," Jayatirtha said. "You got yourself here, you can get yourself home."

"Let me ask you something: How long do you think your organization would last if the cops found out what you were into?"

Jayatirtha stared at him. Nataipada was determined not to be intimidated. He tried not to blink.

"See me tomorrow," Jayatirtha said, ending the contest. "I'll have an answer for you then."

Nataipada knocked on Jayatirtha's door bright and early the next morning.

"Ah, it's you. Come in," Jayatirtha said, stepping away from the door. "I've been expecting you."

Nataipada walked into the room and sat down on an intricately woven rug. Four different shades of red fibers fused and parted in a hypnotic swirl on the floor.

"Listen, I'm sorry things didn't work out," the guru said soothingly. "Please understand that what we do, we do in all sincerity. With us, LSD is a sacrament. We don't abuse it. I'd like you to see that first hand. I'm not trying to keep you here, the plane fare's no problem."

Jayatirtha stopped and handed Nataipada an envelope containing five hundred dollars. Nataipada tucked it away in a pocket under his dhoti.

"Thanks," he said.

"But you really ought to stay and see one of our kirtans," Jayatirtha continued. "We're going to row across a lake and have a kirtan on the far shore. Why don't you

come along. At the very least, it'll be something to tell
your friends about when you get back to the States."

Nataipada agreed.

The next morning, Nataipada, Jayatirtha and his band
of disciples piled into a small boat and began rowing
across the lake. The plan, the guru explained, was to set
up camp on the far shore, drop acid, and stage a spectacular kirtan. Nataipada sat in the bow, marveling at the
ice-clear water and the sun rising over the crown of
snow-capped mountains. The gentle rhythm of the bob-
bing boat relaxed him. He quietly started chanting! He
had no idea how far out the boat was, when he was
shaken by a sudden, violent rocking. He looked around
to shout a warning and saw Jayatirtha standing in the
stern, pointing at him.

"Kill him!" Jayatirtha screamed. "He's Judas Iscariot."

Nataipada went pale. He was still sitting motionless
when three devotees grabbed him from the rear. Two
snatched his arms and pinned them behind his back. The
third grabbed him around the neck in a headlock.

"I won't tell anybody. I promise!" he screamed.

Nataipada fought. He freed one arm and punched and
scratched. The boat rocked violently. Finally, a devotee
grabbed his free arm and immobilized him. All three
then began pushing him backward. Nataipada took a
deep breath as he fell into the water. But the icy-cold
glacier water knocked much of the air out of him. He
surfaced and grabbed onto the side of the boat.

"Please!" he screamed. By the time he heard his echo,
he was shivering violently. The devotees stopped, turned,
and looked up at Jayatirtha. He was still standing in the
stern, swaying with the rocking boat.

He didn't seem to notice. "Kill him," he finally said.

The devotees pushed Nataipada's head down. But he
pulled on the side of the boat, struggling to keep his
mouth above the water. One devotee grabbed his fingers
and wrenched them upward. Bones cracked; Nataipada
screamed again.

This time, he never heard the echo.

The Nepalese authorities discovered the body several
days later, washed up on the shoals of a river that drained

the lake. During their halfhearted investigation they found an envelope containing five hundred dollars in Nataipada's pocket. They also noticed that several fingers were broken. But they ruled that the drowning was accidental.

The case was closed.

Jayatirtha's story ended four years later in London. It happened in December 1987, when Navaniticara, Jayatirtha's s most devoted disciple, decided that his guru was Rasputin. Seven months earlier, in May 1987, Jayatirtha had abandoned his wife and taken up with a younger woman. How could he do that? Navaniticara wondered. Jayatirtha was Krishna; his wife, Radha. How could Krishna leave Radha? Impossible. Navaniticara pondered the paradox so much, his brain seemed ready to burst. At night, he dreamed about it and woke up screaming. During the day, he thought about it until his head pounded.

The answer came unexpectedly.

His guru wasn't Krishna.

He was Rasputin.

Rasputin, the mad monk, an evil spirit, Krishna's enemy. Rasputin had used his black magic to fool Navaniticara and the other Peace Krishnas. Rasputin had seized control. As if by magic, the painful pounding in his head stopped for the first time in months. He knew at once what he had to do.

Navaniticara descended the narrow stairs to the kitchen and grabbed a butcher knife. He waited for the guru in a brass shop, a small antique firm called Knobs and Knockers that was owned by a Peace Krishna. For the first time in months, Navaniticara felt at peace. When he heard the key turn, he stood up and squeezed himself behind the door. He didn't give Rasputin a chance. Before the mad monk could say a word, Navaniticara plunged the knife into his chest. It slid in cleanly. Blood spurted, gushing over Navaniticara's face. The guru clutched the knife and fell to the floor, dead.

Navaniticara wiped his eyes with the back of his hand, leaving long streaks of blood across his cheeks and forehead. He sat down beside the body, took the guru's hand, and for a long time, watched the blood gurgle out around the blade. He began to cry.

Then the rage hit him again. Rasputin was dead, but he wouldn't die. His eyes were still open. Navaniticara cursed. He grabbed the kitchen knife, yanked it out, and plunged it back into the guru's chest.

"A stake through the heart!" he muttered as he sat down again.

It wasn't enough. Navaniticara could still feel the evil spirit lurking in the room. He was going to have to do more. Once again, he yanked the knife out. Then he rolled the guru over, grabbed his hair, and pulled his head off the ground.

The back of the guru's neck was exposed. Navaniticara whacked it with the knife as hard as he could. He hit a nerve and the head twitched in his hand. Navaniticara dropped it and watched it bounce back. He was right: the evil spirit still controlled the body. Navaniticara steeled himself and grabbed the hair again. He hacked and he sawed. It took a long time before the job was done and the spirit banished.

The London police discovered the scene the next morning, Friday, December 13, 1987. Navaniticara was sitting next to the decapitated body, cradling the severed head against his chest. His face was still streaked with blood and tears.

"I've done my work," he was muttering. "I've done my work. I've done my work."

Conning for Krishna

The alarm went off at 5:00 A.M. on a summer morning in 1976. Sharon Wilson lunged for the clock radio and hit the off button just as Robert Plant reached his crescendo: "And she's climbing the stairway to heaven . . ."

Sharon immediately looked over to make sure that Dharmatma, Dennis Gorrick, the leader of the New Vrindaban women's sankirtan team, was still asleep. Thank goodness. If the alarm had woken him, she'd be in trouble.

Sharon eased out of bed, careful to avoid disturbing Dharmatma. She put on a robe and walked downstairs to the kitchen of the small house near the Pittsburgh airport. She filled a tea kettle, set the oven to four hundred degrees, and prepared a tray of fruit—oranges, apples, bananas, canteloupe, honeydew, and persian melon—on a thick bed of lettuce. She garnished it with sprigs of fresh parsley and put it back in the fridge. She popped a pan of six muffins into the oven, hurried back upstairs, and woke the other four women. She took a quick shower and put on a short black skirt and a white blouse, taking care to leave the blouse's top two buttons open. Dharmatma always insisted she display her large, firm breasts.

She returned to the kitchen and set the table for Dharmatma. She tried not to think about her work at the airport. But there was no way she could keep it out of her mind for long.

"It's for Krishna," she kept telling herself. "It's for Krishna."

Sharon endured the Pittsburgh International Airport because she understood that the path back to godhead was rough. If reaching God was easy, every karmi would have found salvation long ago. You had to suffer to

attain the ultimate goal. She'd drummed that into herself
ever since she was a little girl growing up in San Luis
Obispo, an old mission town nestled in a fertile California
valley between the rocky shores of the Pacific and the
brown Lucia Mountains.

The town's slow, orderly pace of life and her friends'
comfortable middle-class existence only emphasized the
horror at home. Home was chaos. Her mother drank
heavily and had married and remarried five times. Sharon
had four brothers and sisters, and each had a different
father.

Sharon compensated with discipline. Her room was
always tidy; she was never tardy with her homework. All
the way through elementary school, she was the top
student in her class. She was so nice, and had so many
friends, nobody was ever jealous. But her mother was
too busy and too screwed-up to pay much attention. She
pulled Sharon out of high school, away from her friends,
and dumped her in a program for gifted students. Sharon
found herself taking freshman English classes at a local
community college. She got A's there, too.

But that didn't bring the stability she craved. One by
one, her siblings scattered—her sisters into early marriages, her brothers into jobs and the military. Her mother
continued to drink heavily and didn't seem to care whether
they stayed or left.

Sitting in class one day, Sharon was struck by a revelation: She was wasting her time in school. School didn't
matter. Her mother didn't matter. Her brothers and sisters didn't matter. All that mattered was God.

There was no one to talk it over with.

She left home a few weeks later at sixteen to find God
in a commune in the hills behind Carmel, 125 miles up
the coast. Her mother said it probably was a mistake, but
didn't try to stop her. If Sharon was old enough to take
college courses, she was old enough to run her own life.

The commune turned out to be about getting stoned
and staying stoned. Sharon decided to split and explore
the country. She stuffed a few things in a backpack,
walked out to Highway 1, and stuck out her thumb. Two
weeks later, a trucker dropped her in Denver, where she

moved in with a devout fundamentalist Christian family and joined their church.

The pastor welcomed her with hosannas. A few weeks later, he summoned her for their first prayer session. When she entered his spartan office dressed in her Sunday finest—a white blouse, dark skirt, and knee socks—he offered her a seat on his couch. He then began leading her in prayer.

The pastor closed his eyes and beseeched the Lord. Then he reached over and put his hand on Sharon's thigh. He just wants me to feel the Spirit, she thought. She closed her eyes. The pastor's hand inched higher. Sharon grabbed his wrist and jerked his hand away. Then she ran out of his office.

She stopped going to church, but gave no explanation to the family she was living with. They cajoled and preached, but she refused to go. They were close to kicking her out, when she met a Krishna sankirtan party that was working a shopping mall across the street from the Wendy's where Sharon flipped burgers. During breaks, she'd walk over and talk to the devotees. She liked their sincerity and energy and made a small contribution. They gave her Prabhupada's books, which she snuck into her room and read at night, when everybody else was asleep.

Sharon soon decided to join the movement. She left the fundamentalists without telling them where she was going and moved into the Denver temple. Once again, she was welcomed. Because she was so young, the temple president told her she had to have a man to protect her. He presented her to a devotee who was fifteen years older than she was and explained that they were now engaged—an arrangement that did not include sex. The temple president said he would marry them as soon as they got to know each other.

Sharon's fiancé immediately talked her into moving to Los Angeles with him. He bought the tickets and they boarded a Greyhound bus early the next week. He didn't touch her the entire journey, but he kept nipping on a bottle of apricot brandy hidden in his japa bag.

A few days after they arrived, he split. Several of the older women took Sharon under their wings, but she was miserable in "Loose Angeles," as the Los Angeles temple was called throughout the movement. Sharon wanted discipline and structure. But Ramesvara, the president, didn't seem to care what devotees did as long as they performed sankirtan and the money kept rolling in. Devotees kept telling her that New Vrindaban was the strictest temple in America. So one day, she used the last of her money to buy a bus ticket to Pittsburgh. When she arrived, she called the commune and told a devotee where she was.

Dharmatma picked her up.

"I know how to take care of women: promise 'em everything and give 'em nothing," Dharmatma had boasted as he drove Sharon south to West Virginia.

Sharon didn't like what he said, but she liked the way he said it. He was so confident, so totally sure of himself. Her spirits picked up. But it didn't last; Sharon hated the commune as much as Los Angeles. It was the middle of winter, and devotees were taking cold showers in unheated rooms that had dirt floors. The food was terrible, and she felt trapped in the mountains.

When Kirtanananda asked if she wanted to join Dharmatma and his Pittsburgh sankirtan team, Sharon gratefully accepted. She'd heard stories about how unmercifully Dharmatma drove his women, but it was an escape. Best of all, her life would be structured and she would be serving Krishna. Didn't Kirtanananda emphasize over and over again that there was no service higher than sankirtan?

One by one, the other members of the sankirtan team filed into the kitchen and helped Sharon put the finishing touches on Dharmatma's breakfast.

"Isn't this the week Dharmatma promised we'd get Sunday afternoon off?" one of the women asked as she scurried around the kitchen.

"Yeah, that's what he said, but it's just another PEEGEN," said Debbie, the newest member of the team. Everybody laughed. They had turned Dharmatma's philosophy of "Promise 'em everything and give 'em nothing" into an acronym, PEEGEN, and a running joke.

Sharon glanced at the clock and hurried upstairs to

wake Dharmatma. Then she returned to the kitchen and waited silently with the three other women while he shaved and showered. They were lined up ready for inspection when he came down for his breakfast of granola, yoghurt, fresh fruit, freshly squeezed orange juice, hot muffins, and tea. Dharmatma sat down and looked the women over.

"You look like a schoolteacher in that stupid blouse," he snapped at Debbie. "Look at that dopey round collar you've got buttoned to the neck. Think any guy is gonna give you more than a glance? Get back upstairs and change."

"But it's the only clean thing I have," Debbie whimpered.

"I don't give a damn. Wear that black silk thing you had on yesterday. Who cares if it's dirty as long as it shows off your tits."

Debbie ran from the kitchen. She returned a few minutes later in a silk blouse that was cut low off the shoulders. Dharmatma did not even glance at her.

Dharmatma didn't look like much. He had a receding hair line, close-set eyes, big ears, a broad nose, and a wide, leering mouth. Hardly a Richard Gere. But he considered himself endowed with absolute power over women. A former bodybuilder and bartender from Vancouver, he had joined the movement in the early seventies. He spent his early years as a devotee working Los Angeles, heading up a team of women that sold books and magazines on the streets. He moved to New Vrindaban in the midseventies.

Dharmatma's reputation had preceded him to West Virginia, and Kirtanananda was anxious to see if it was true that he had a pimp's power. He took Dharmatma with him on a trip through Eastern Canada. One morning, Kirtanananda and his entourage were watching a kirtan in the Toronto temple. Kirtanananda's eyes never left two devotees dancing near the flower-bedecked altar—not because they were the most attractive women in the temple, but because they were the best fundraisers the temple had, selling more than three hundred dollars' worth of books every day.

"Take off your shirt and go in there and do whatever it

is you do to get them to come back with us," Kirtanananda told Dharmatma. Dharmatma laughed. He took off his shirt, displaying his weightlifter's body, and began dancing in front of the deities.

When the New Vrindaban party rolled out of town, the two women went with them. Shortly thereafter, Kirtanananda had appointed Dharmatma head of the New Vrindaban women's sankirtan team.

"All right, you can have breakfast now," Dharmatma said when he finished eating.

Sharon, Debbie, and the other two women pulled up chairs to the table and prepared to sit down.

"No," Dharmatma snapped. "That's mine."

"What can we eat?" Sharon asked.

Dharmatma went over to the refrigerator, opened the door, and looked in the crisper.

"An apple, a peach, and a handful of raisins each," he said. "But take it with you. We've got work to do."

"You know what Kirtanananda says when he sends out a sankirtan team?" Dharmatma was finishing his usual pep talk as he dropped the women off at the airport. " 'I don't care what you do, as long as you make your quotas.' That goes for me, too. Don't come back without your quota. Remember, Krishna and Kirtanananda are both depending on you."

The first thing Sharon did as she walked through the terminal was look around for the security guard she had nicknamed the "Golfer," as a tribute to his uniform of madras jackets and lime-green or raspberry slacks. She didn't see him at the flower stand or by the car-rental sign, his usual places. She walked into the middle of the lobby and looked up at the hotel on the second floor. Sometimes the Golfer was standing up there by the registration desk, leaning over the railing, looking down at the people coming and going. He wasn't there today.

Sharon sighed with relief. She had been working the airport seven days a week for almost three years now. It was hard work making her quota without the Golfer. With him there, it was almost impossible.

Sharon walked down to the United Airlines concourse

and stationed herself outside the security checkpoint. She looked for the right mark—preferably, a young man traveling alone and in no apparent hurry. Several young men went by carrying briefcases and suitbags, but Sharon let them go. She always started slowly. Next to Mahara, she was the best collector on the team and almost always made her three-hundred-dollars-a-day quota—provided the Golfer wasn't hounding her.

She spotted her first target and was about to approach him when she glanced up the corridor and saw Debbie running toward her. Sharon could tell she was crying. Somebody had probably said something nasty to her. Debbie couldn't take the terrible things harried travelers sometimes said to fend them off—"Why don't you forget this shit and go back home to your mother?" or "Tell you what: I'll buy a book if you'll suck my dick!" You had to steel yourself and pretend you didn't hear them.

Debbie ran up to Sharon and held out her hand. There was an angry red circular welt the size of a nickel in the middle of her palm.

"What happened?" Sharon asked.

"I can't believe it, I just can't believe it." Debbie said between sobs. Her chest was heaving. She took a couple of deep breaths and blurted out the story.

"I was working the American Airlines concourse. A flight came in from Houston and I spotted this cowboy type smoking a fat cigar. He was wearing a huge belt buckle and one of those big cowboy hats with turquoise around the brim. He was drunk—can you believe it? He gets off a plane at seven in the morning, drunk. I thought maybe he was too drunk to know what he was doing, so I went up and gave him a book."

She broke off to dab at her eyes. "He didn't even thank me; he just said, 'What's this for?' I told him it's the greatest book ever written and that I was giving it away. Then I asked him for a donation. He got all angry and started shouting that I'd given him the book. So I told him the money went to pay for a school for orphans. He pulled out his wallet and I thought he was going to give me a bill. But when I held out my hand, he crushed his cigar in it. Then he started laughing and walked away.

Debbie started crying again. Sharon put her arm around her.

"I'm gonna go to the police and have him arrested," Debbie said. "He's probably down in the baggage claim right now."

"Don't," Sharon quickly snapped. "They hate us here. They'll let him go and turn it around so that you end up getting arrested."

"But my hand," Debbie wailed. "What about my hand? It hurts."

"We could call Dharmatma," Sharon said. "But he'd only get angry at us. Let's go see what we can find."

The two women went over to the airport gift shop and bought a tin of Band-Aids and a small tube of first-aid cream. Sharon bandaged Debbie's hand and returned to the United concourse. There, she spotted a young, dark-haired man in a three-piece business suit and cut in front of him. She stood very close; the man was alarmed and took a step back. Sharon took a step toward him.

"Excuse me," she said. "I'm a missionary, trying to spread the word of God."

"You don't look like a missionary," the man said, eyeing her open blouse.

"Sometimes it's the only way to get attention," Sharon said, smiling seductively. "After all, bodies belong to God, just like everything else."

"What church do you belong to?" the man asked.

"An international church," Sharon said. She reached into her bag and pulled out Prabhupada's *Gita*. "We print these books. The money goes to feed poor children all over the world. Children in Appalachia, Bangladesh, Biafra—all over the world."

"What's the book about?" the businessman asked.

"Science, history, philosophy, geography—everything is in this book," Sharon said, handing it to him. "Here, take a look. You can have it. All we're asking is a small donation."

The man took the three-inch-thick book and looked at the picture of Arjuna and Krishna in their chariot on the dust jacket. Then he turned it over and glanced at the picture of Prabhupada.

"What do you usually get for one of these?" the man asked.

Sharon moved closer. "Well, most people give—"

"Hold it!" someone shouted.

Sharon and the man looked up the concourse. The Golfer was scurrying toward them, his walkie-talkie dangling from his belt and slapping his thigh with each step. He was wearing a powder-blue madras jacket and green checkered pants like some nightmarish vacationer. Even at this distance, Sharon saw his acne scars.

"Did you give this woman any money?" the Golfer panted.

"No, why?" the businessman asked.

"Did she identify herself as a member of the Hare Krishnas?" the Golfer asked.

"She never said anything about being a Krishna," the businessman said. He turned sharply to Sharon. "Hey, how come you're not wearing Indian clothes?"

"You're lucky you didn't give her any money," the Golfer said. "She's a short-change artist. We've had dozens of complaints."

"You've got no right to interfere like this," Sharon said, repeating Dharmatma's instruction by rote. "You're interfering with my right to practice my religion."

"Religion doesn't give you the right to cheat people," the Golfer shot back.

"Here's your book," the businessman said, handing the *Gita* back to Sharon. "I wasn't going to buy it, anyway."

The Golfer shadowed Sharon most of the day. But around four o'clock, he disappeared. Sharon sighed with relief. She made sure he wasn't lurking in some cranny and then made her way back to the fifty-cents-a-day rental lockers.

"Locker stuffing," as the Krishnas call it, probably was the trickiest part of the airport operation. To throw off the Golfer, the girls rotated the job. Today, it was Sharon's turn.

The airport security officers were trying to drive out the Krishnas by enforcing a legal technicality. The Supreme Court had ruled they could not stop devotees from selling religious books—as long as the devotees brought the books with them when they arrived each morning. But if they kept a supply of books at the airport, then they were vendors and needed a license. And there was no way the airport would ever give them a license.

The problem for the Krishnas was to resupply the sankirtan team after the women had sold the copies they arrived with. For a while, Dharmatma had used a van strategically parked in the short-term lot. But the security guards had caught on and refused to let the women back into the airport. Locker stuffing was the only way around the problem. Every day, Dharmatma walked into the airport with several suitcases stuffed with books. He loaded them into a locker and slipped the key to Sharon or to one of the other "girls."

Airport security had figured this one out, too. As soon as Dharmatma arrived, an officer followed him. In a game of cat and mouse, the Krishnas countered by sending devotees up from New Vrindaban. Lately, Tom Drescher had been dropping off the books.

Sharon was supposed to meet Drescher and pick up the key at exactly four-fifteen. She looked up and down the row of lockers but didn't see him.

"Freeze!" someone whispered in her ear.

Sharon gasped and whirled around. Drescher was standing there, grinning.

"Scared yah, didn't I?" he said.

"That's not funny," Sharon said.

"The hell it isn't," Drescher said. "You almost came out of your skirt. In fact, I wish you would have. Why should Dharmatma have all the fun?"

Sharon scowled.

"Come on, gimme the key," she said.

Drescher put down the empty suitcase he was holding and pulled a key out of his pocket.

"Walk me outside," he said.

"Are you nuts? They'll see us together," Sharon said.

"Make believe you're tryin' to sell me a book," Drescher said. "That way, I get to look at your tits."

"Hold it right there."

The Golfer and two uniformed security guards were running toward them.

"Take off!" Drescher told Sharon, stuffing the key into her hand. "Go that way and I'll make a run for the door."

Sharon ran up the corridor and ducked into a ladies' room. Drescher ran into the main terminal. The Golfer and the guards followed him.

"Stop! Stop that man!" the Golfer yelled.

Drescher shoved and pushed his way through a crowd of travelers. Any second now, some asshole who wanted to be a hero was going to grab him. He spotted a man in a brown business suit ahead of him, hurrying toward the same door he was.

"Stop that guy!" Drescher yelled. "Stop him before he gets to the door."

Two men in army uniforms jumped in front of the door and grabbed the guy.

"Good going," Drescher said as he hustled by. "The guy back there with the walkie-talkie wants him."

He ran to the curb and jumped into the Chevy pickup truck that was waiting for him. The truck was in traffic and on its way out of the airport before the Golfer and the guards were able to push past the servicemen and get out of the building.

Sharon ducked out of the ladies' room and ran through the baggage-claim area. First she caught a shuttle bus to the long-term parking area. Then she walked past the collection booths, crossed Airport Parkway, and called Dharmatma from a phone booth outside Denny's.

"Drescher just called. I'll be right there," Dharmatma said.

"I have to say this," Sharon said when Dharmatma arrived and she had climbed into the front seat. "I don't want you to take this wrong—you know how dedicated I am to doing service for Kirtanananda—but I just don't know how much more of the airport I can take. I'm afraid of what the Golfer will do when he sees me tomorrow."

"Forget it," Dharmatma said. "We're gonna give up on airports."

"We're *what?*" Sharon asked, astounded.

"It's only a matter of time till they kick us out," Dharmatma said. "They've already kicked the devotees out of O'Hare and the airport in Portland, Oregon."

"I didn't think they could do that," Sharon said. "I thought our lawyers were protecting our right to solicit under the First Amendment."

"They are, and they've done good," Dharmatma said. "They're not givin' us the boot 'cause we're a religious organization. They're kickin' us out 'cause of the scams.

"But what are we going to do? How are we going to raise money?" Sharon asked.

Dharmatma grinned.

"You'll find out when we're ready," he said. "Me and Kirtanananda have been talkin' about it. You ladies are goin' on the road. You're gonna make more money than you ever did at this fuckin' airport."

Gregory Martin Gottfried, Guru Kripa, president of ISKCON's Tokyo temple, was strolling down a crowded Tokyo street, feeling fine. It was a drizzly, overcast day in March 1975. His troupe of American devotees clustered a respectful step or two behind him. They had been working hard; Guru Kripa was notorious for making devotees put in twelve- and fourteen-hour days.

But now it was time for a little fun.

Guru Kripa looked up and down the street, making sure no cops were around. The cops had been hassling the hell out of his devotees ever since one of them slapped a little old lady who was givin' him shit. The cops were always grabbin' devotees, hustling them into a station, and threatening to charge them with extortion.

So far, nothing had come of it. The devotees had adapted by blending into Japanese society—as much as Americans ever can. They had junked their dhotis and donned suits and wigs. Other than that, nothing had changed.

Guru Kripa didn't see any cops on the crowded avenue. He held up a hand to stop the troupe, then dug two ten-thousand-yen notes, each worth about twenty-five dollars, out of his back pocket.

"Hey, you little slants, watch this!" Guru Kripa yelled. He crumpled up the bills, blew his nose in them, and let them drop to the ground.

A Japanese man scampered up, picked up the bills, handed them back to Guru Kripa, bowed, and hurried away.

The devotees thought it was hysterical, but Guru Kripa was disappointed. He had done this before and produced a much better show. One time, two Japs had started lecturing him, and another guy, who hadn't seen what he had done, picked up the bills and got a handful of snot. What a pisser.

"Looks like I'm gonna have to make it rain," Guru Kripa said.

The devotees knew what that meant. They fished yen notes out of their pockets and handed them to Guru Kripa. Then they spread across the sidewalk and held out their arms to slow people down.

"OK, Japs, it's your lucky day," Guru Kripa bellowed. "It's rainnnning monnney."

Guru Kripa threw the yen notes into the air. The bills caught in the breeze and floated down over the crowd. People gasped, put down their shopping bags, and bumped into each other, trying to snatch money out of the air. They chased down all the bills and, with the unfailing politeness of the Japanese, returned them to the stubby, pugnacious-looking American.

Japan was one big playground to Guru Kripa. He did not give a damn about converting the Japanese to Krishna Consciousness. Guru Kripa was on the island to sell Prabhupada's books and make money. And the Japanese were a soft touch. They had an ancient tradition of wandering Buddhist mendicants, and were quick to buy a *Gita* or a *Back to Godhead* magazine. And if some chump refused to come across, all the Krishna had to do was stand in front of the guy and block his way. Just to escape, he would eventually hand over a thousand yen to the devotee.

Then there was the pen trick, a Guru Kripa favorite. He had shown his men how to spot a Mont Blanc fountain pen in a businessman's suitcoat pocket, and how to use a rolled up *Back to Godhead* to flick it out. Devotees passed the pen around so that when the guy realized his pen was gone and called for the cops, the last devotee to get the pen had already vanished.

No evidence, no arrest.

Messing with people on the street was fun, but for Guru Kripa, nothing beat hitting a jewelry store. It was a simple little rip-off, but it worked every time. In fact, it was time to make a score.

"Govardhan," it's you and me this afternoon," Guru Kripa said to one of his partners in the jewelry-store scam. "I got the place all set up. I'll show you. The rest of you guys, spread out and sell some books. Prabhupada needs the money!"

As planned, Govardhan was waiting on the corner that afternoon when Guru Kripa came strolling along the street. He had changed into a three-piece pearl suit and a black wig that covered most of his forehead. Govardhan was wearing a cowboy hat over a blond wig, a Western shirt, Levi's, and cowboy boots.

Guru Kripa nodded almost imperceptibly. Govardhan nodded back. The signal meant Govardhan would follow in exactly seven minutes. Guru Kripa walked down the street and entered the jewelry store. An impeccably dressed clerk approached him and bowed.

"Yes," Guru Kripa said, "I would like to see some Rolex watches. I understand the prices are very attractive here in Japan."

"Right this way, sir," the clerk said in perfect English. He pulled out a chair covered with red felt and offered the seat to Guru Kripa. Kripa took it. Then the clerk went behind the counter, took a set of keys out of his pocket, and opened the display case.

The clerk laid a fourteen-karat gold Rolex Oyster Perpetual Date with a Jubilee bracelet on the counter. Guru Kripa examined it.

"Let me see the ladies' version, will you?" he asked. "My wife will kill me if I come home from this trip without a little something for her."

The clerk smiled understandingly and brought out the matching women's model. Guru Kripa then asked to see the platinum version. There were eight Rolexes on the counter when Govardhan walked in.

"Hi, there," he said to the clerk who approached him. "I came in to have a look at some diamond bracelets for the little lady back in the States."

Govardhan started coughing a deep, wheezing cough.

"I'll be honest with you," Govardhan said when he finally finished coughing. "I came in to get out of this damn Tokyo air." He started coughing again and laid a hand on the clerk's shoulder to steady himself.

"I live in Tucson back in the States," he told the clerk. "That's in Arizona. It's desert. You ever heard of it? No? Well, I moved there for my health seven years ago. See, I got asthma. This terrible air you got here is gonna kill me."

Govardhan barely finished the sentence when he was struck by a severe coughing fit. He reached into his jacket pocket and pulled out a yellow-stained handkerchief. Then he collapsed on top of the glass counter across the aisle from Guru Kripa.

The clerks yelled at each other in Japanese.

"Quick!" Guru Kripa yelled, "Get him some water!"

The clerk who had been talking to Govardhan raced to the back of the store. Guru Kripa and the other clerk went over to Govardhan, who was wheezing heavily.

Guru Kripa turned, scooped up the watches, and ran out of the store. The clerk yelled and ran after him. Guru Kripa stopped; when the clerk reached the glass door, Guru Kripa slammed it in his face.

He raced down the street and turned the corner, where another devotee was standing with a bicycle. Guru Kripa jumped on the bicycle and began weaving through traffic. He rode twenty-five blocks through the rush hour, until he met another member of the gang. He dismounted, gave the bicycle to the devotee, entered the jammed subway and rode back across Tokyo to his hotel.

"Any trouble?" Guru Kripa asked when Govardhan showed up a few hours later.

"None at all," Govardhan said. "One of the clerks was out on the street, jumping around and yelling; the other one was on the phone, calling the cops. I picked myself off the counter, staggered out to the street, and kept going. The clerk was jabbering about what went down and forgot about me."

Guru Kripa flew to Calcutta two days later. As soon as he arrived, he took a cab to the edge of the bazaar. Then he continued on foot. He strode purposefully through the narrow streets, pushing through the crowd and ignoring the pleas of the merchants hawking their wares from rugs on the sidewalk.

"Ah-ha, my good friend. You have come again," said a large man wearing a turban and a wide smile, who was sitting on a stool in front of an open doorway.

Guru Kripa did not know the guy's name or his nationality. All he knew was that he was reputed to be Calcutta's chief money changer. Guru Kripa called him "Chief Head" because he never failed to bring out a pipe of hash before doing business.

Chief Head got off his stool and bowed to Guru Kripa. Kripa followed him through a dark, empty store to a back stairway. They climbed it and entered the air-conditioned living quarters on the second floor. A moment later, two servants appeared. One laid a red rug on the floor while the other poured tea from an elaborate silver tea service. Both then vanished. As custom demanded, Chief Head removed the hash pipe from the cupboard, lit it, and offered Guru Kripa the stem. The American took a couple of tokes out of politeness. Then he opened his duffel bag, removed the clothes, tore out the false bottom, and began stacking Rolex watches, diamond bracelets, diamond rings, and piles of Japanese yen on the rug.

"Give me a price for all of it," Guru Kripa said.

Chief Head picked up the watches and examined them one at a time.

"Why are you always in such a hurry?" Chief Head asked in mock hurt, putting down the watches and picking up a diamond bracelet. He held the bracelet to the light, then smiled. "We have not yet finished the first pipe."

"I come here for two reasons," Guru Kripa said. "You

always give me the best deal, and you don't give me
bullshit. That's the way I like it!"

Chief Head laughed. "I wouldn't dare bullshit, as you
say, and risk losing my valued customer.

But bullshit is exactly what Chief Head did. He put an
absurdly low price on each jewel. Guru Kripa haggled;
Chief Head nodded politely and raised the offer a fraction. Guru Kripa demanded more. They settled on one
item at a time. It took hours. It was dark before they
finished.

"You are such a serious man of business," Chief Head
said as Guru Kripa stuffed bundles of rupees into the
false bottom of his duffel bag. "Don't you ever have any
fun? Perhaps I can arrange some for you. A girl? A
young boy, perhaps?"

"I'll have fun," Guru Kripa said. "I'll have fun tomorrow when I visit my spiritual master."

"Ah, I see. You have a spiritual master? And who
might he be?"

Guru Kripa glowered. "Think I'd tell you? You're so
fuckin' low, I'd get pissed off if his name ever touched
your ugly lips."

Chief Head smiled agreeably. "I look forward to these
visits so. I know nobody like you. A serious man of
business with a spiritual master. Tell me, how do you
justify what you do to bring me these lovely things."

"It's like this," Guru Kripa said. "Everything I do, I
do for Krishna. Everything belongs to Krishna. All I do
is liberate his things to use in his service."

"And the people who own them? What about them?"

"They get rewarded," Guru Kripa said. "You advance
spiritually if you help Krishna, even if you don't know
you're doing it."

Kripa rose awkwardly to his feet, his legs stiff from
sitting cross-legged on the rug for so many hours. Chief
Head led him down the stairs and into the street.

"See you next time around, probably in a couple of
months," Guru Kripa said in parting.

The next morning, Guru Kripa left for Mayapur, fifty
miles north of Calcutta. He sat in the backseat of the
rented car thinking about Prabhupada. Dealing with Chief

Head, he had been totally calm. Now he was so excited, his hands trembled.

Guru Kripa cared nothing for the ISKCON organization. His sankirtan party had traveled in America before going to Japan, and when his vans needed tires, he did not hesitate to steal the tires of the host temple's vans. One time, Kirtanananda had tried to recruit him. Guru Kripa told him he would rather flush the money down the toilet than give it to him. His loyalty was solely to Prabhupada.

Before joining the movement, Guru Kripa had been a Marine sergeant who demanded absolute obedience from his men. But that was nothing compared to the loyalty he gave Prabhupada. Anyone who questioned the spiritual master in his presence was in for a fight. No one had ever touched Guru Kripa as deeply as Prabhupada. The spiritual master was the only person he had ever met who had a purpose higher than his own self-interest. He gave Guru Kripa a reason to live, a cause that justified his life. Prabhupada was Guru Kripa's true father; Guru Kripa lived only to make him proud.

Like all devotees, Guru Kripa composed a poem every year to celebrate Prabhupada's birthday. He was especially proud of one he had written several years ago. He didn't think any devotee had ever equaled it:

> Sweet sweet
> What a treat
> Them two lotus feet

A cooling, late afternoon breeze was ruffling the trees as Prabhupada's secretary welcomed Guru Kripa to Mayapur. He was led into a twelve-foot-square Bengali hut, so primitive it had a dirt floor, and through a partition that separated the main room from the servant's quarters. Guru Kripa followed the secretary into a small garden behind the hut, with its outhouse and a hand pump for bathing. Prabhupada was sitting next to a wall of exotic red flowers, holding a Dictaphone in one hand.

Guru Kripa fell to the ground to offer obeisances. His

eyes filled with tears. The greatest man in the world lived
so humbly.

"You have come," Prabhupada said, raising his voice
to overcome the construction noises reverberating through
the village. "This is very nice."

The small town was normally so quiet you could hear
the bells tinkling on the passing cows. But Mayapur now
sounded more like downtown Chicago than an Indian
backwater. Air hammers blasted through rock, and huge
trucks rattled along the dirt streets, hauling bricks and
cement for one of Prabhupada's dream temples, which
would be crowned by a colossal four-story dome. Inside,
devotees planned to build a miniature palace where the
Radha and Krishna deities would reside, surrounded by
pillars sheathed in gold, silver, and jewels.

"Your health—I hope it's been good," Guru Kripa
said quietly.

"Sometimes I am troubled with pains," Prabhupada
replied, slowly lifting his left arm. "Nothing helps but
massage. Always massage."

"You must slow down a little and save yourself," Guru
Kripa said.

"I am sustained by doing Krishna's work," Prabhupada
said. "Just see the temple going up here. You must also
visit Bombay and Vrindaban and see the temples we're
building there. In Bombay, we will have a cultural center
that will include a theater and a restaurant. There will
also be two seven-story towers that will house a four-star
hotel. Many Western visitors will stay in the hotel and in
that way they will come to Krishna."

"Prabhupada, I have brought something for the temples," Guru Kripa said, unable to contain his excitement
any longer.

Before Prabhupada could reply, Guru Kripa tore open
the duffel bag and began stacking rupees in front of the
spiritual master. When Guru Kripa was finished, Prabhupada
was smiling broadly. He nodded, and his secretary stuffed
the money into a linen bag.

"This is very nice," Prabhupada said. "We must have
lakshmi for Krishna's service. You and your sankirtan

team have financed this Mayapur temple almost by yourselves. You have also helped feed many thousands of
hungry people. As you know, many people have fled
Bangladesh and the war with Pakistan and have come
here." Prabhupada frowned.

Guru Kripa was filled with alarm: had he somehow
offended the guru?

"There is no reason for this starvation," Prabhupada
continued. "Krishna provides for every living being. Man
brings starvation."

"Yes, Prabhupada, I know," Guru Kripa said, his voice
loud with relief. "You gave the order that no person
within ten miles of a Hare Krishna temple should ever go
hungry."

"Just so," Prabhupada replied. "We have offered
prasadam to many hundreds of thousands, here in Bengal
and at other temples around the planet. The money you
bring helps us do these things. I am very pleased with
your service. But you must bring us more lakshmi.

Guru Kripa stood up, bowed from his waist, and left.
He walked back through the hut feeling lighter than
air. He had pleased his spiritual master. He emerged
onto the dirt road, gazed moist-eyed at the marshy
green fields surrounding the temple, and drew in a deep
breath. He had almost reached his car when Prabhupada's
secretary scurried up to him and tapped him on the
shoulder.

"Yes?" Guru Kripa asked.

"I thought you should know," the secretary said. "I
read all of Prabhupada's mail before he does. He gets
lots of letters about what you're doing in Japan. Devotees are saying you've ruined the movement there by
getting in so much trouble with the police. I know
Prabhupada appreciates your service, but perhaps it would
be wise to lie low for a while."

Guru Kripa grabbed the secretary's throat, squeezed
his thumbs under the kid's Adam's apple, and yanked
him up until only his toes touched the ground.

"You little fuck," he hissed. "Who do you think you
are, criticizing me? What have you done for Prabhupada?"

"Compared to you, nothing!" the secretary gasped.

Guru Kripa let go of the kid, who crumpled to the ground like a lifesize puppet. Kripa stepped over him and walked to his car. He did not look back.

Krishna's Mules

"You should have brought it up at the meeting," said Joe Davis, a short, intense man in his early thirties. "The whole movement is losing devotees; it's not just our temple."

Roy Christopher Richard, president of the Laguna Beach temple, looked at his most trusted lieutenant and sighed. They were in the backseat of a car they had hired to take them back to Calcutta after the ISKCON annual meeting in Mayapur in April 1976. Tomorrow they would be on a Pan Am 747, flying first class back to Los Angeles.

"We've been over this and over this," Richard said. "If devotees leave, they leave. Only the strong survive. Besides, devotees aren't all that important right now. We've got to get temples built so that we'll be ready for the next wave of devotees. Have faith. Let's enjoy our last night here."

Their Bengali driver looked at Richard and Davis in his rearview mirror.

"You gentlemen will be leaving soon?" he asked.

"We're off to the States tomorrow," Richard said.

"Is that so?" the driver said. "Perhaps you gentlemen would be interested in paying for your trip? It's very easy."

Davis and Richard looked at each other and grinned. They didn't need to have the offer spelled out. Before joining the Krishnas, they had dealt marijuana and knew the subtleties of drug language.

"Afraid not; those days are over for us," Davis said.

"Very well, but I think you should meet my friends,

just in case," the driver said. "There are many opportunities."

"No," Richard said, emphatically closing the conversation.

They rode on in silence, sweating in the suffocating heat. Although it was only mid-April, the temperature was over one hundred degrees. The Bengali driver dropped them off at their hotel near the Maidan, a huge park on the Hooghly River, and earned a small bonus by returning the rented car. Exhausted after the drive, Richard and Davis went to their room. Richard took a cold shower; Davis dropped onto one of the two beds in the English-style room and listened to the running water.

"That driver hittin' on us has got me thinkin'," Davis said as Richard stepped out of the shower.

"Thinking about what?" Richard called from the bathroom.

"About the old days, what else?" Davis said. "We're knockin' ourselves out selling Prabhupada's books. We got an incense and candle business and a factory that cranks out pins and buttons by the thousand. And I'm thinkin' that's chickenshit. We're missin' the most lucrative business there is."

"And the most risky," Richard quickly added, his voice muffled by the towel he was using to dry his hair. "Get serious."

"I am," Davis yelled, jumping off the bed. "Look at it this way: You and I did drugs for years, right? We didn't quit till we came to Krishna, right? The karmis won't quit till they come to Krishna, right? Krishna is the only force strong enough to make them stop, right?"

"So?" Richard said.

"Well, suppose we use this filthy habit for Krishna," Davis continued. "Suppose we do bad to accomplish good. We get into the business and move a stash from here to the States. It would be a cinch. Customs is a joke. They never look under our dhotis. We could give the money to Prabhupada to build temples. The more temples there are, the more karmis that will come to Krishna. The more karmis that come to Krishna, the less drug users there are. One day, bingo! No more drug users."

Davis walked up to Richard.

"Don't you see it? It's beautiful! We use drugs to spread the movement. By dealing over the short run, we destroy drugs in the long run."

Richard sat down on his bed.

"I like it," he said hesitantly. "I think I like it a lot."

They talked about it some more over a vegetarian dinner. Richard vacillated; Davis pushed. They never actually agreed to the scheme. The idea was that they'd test the waters. Davis would cash in his ticket and stay in India for a while to look for a connection. If he found somebody trustworthy, maybe they would get a little something going. But only maybe.

Roy Richard was sitting behind his desk in the Laguna Beach temple, listening to Davis lecture four devotees who were standing ramrod straight against the wall.

"If any of you fuck up, you're dead," Davis barked. "I'll come after you myself. Remember, you're doing this for Krishna. It's a helluva risk, but there's a helluva gain."

Davis paced back and forth like a drill sergeant.

"You guys are mules," he continued. "Don't forget that. I want you to work as hard as a mule and I want you dumb as a mule. You don't know a damn thing."

The devotees nodded.

"Your contact's name is Aziz. He owns a small air-conditioning business in Peshawar. That's in Pakistan, near the Afghanistan border. Soon as we're done here, we're gonna go outside. We will take a Polaroid picture of each of you standing next to me. Whatever you do, don't lose it. It's your ticket. You will present the picture to Aziz when you arrive. Aziz will take it as your introduction and give you a suitcase with a false bottom. Pack your things in it and bring it back here to me. Understood?"

One of the four devotees raised his hand.

"When do we leave?" he asked.

"You're all going at different times by different routes," Davis replied. "I've got your itineraries in my room. I'll talk to you one at a time this afternoon. Any other questions?"

Another devotee raised his hand.

"We're taking a big risk. Are we gonna get paid for this, or is it just part of our service?"

"This is special service," Davis said. "Special service requires special rules. In short, yes, you will be paid. We'll determine the amount after we've moved the product. Anything else?"

There were no more questions.

"All right. Wait outside. We'll be out with the Polaroid in a moment."

"This is gonna fly, Rashadeva," Davis told Richard when the devotees were gone. "I can feel it in my bones. We're gonna make a ton of money."

"Feels real good," Richard agreed. "But to make hay, you need hay. That's why there's someone I want you to meet."

"What are you talking about?" Davis asked, alarmed.

"Everything's cool," Richard said, smiling as he rose from his desk. "I got us a partner. Wait a minute; I'll get him."

Richard went across the hall into his apartment. He returned a few minutes later with a tall, heavyset man who was about thirty years old.

"Joe, this is Alexander Kulik," Richard said. "Alex is in the substance business. He's gonna finance us. In return for bringing him in, he's going to cut the movement in for a percentage of his profits."

Davis and Kulik shook hands.

"My little brother's a devotee," Kulik said. "He got me interested in Krishna Consciousness. I'm a great admirer of Prabhupada's."

"Ah, Krishna's mercy again," Davis said.

"It's so damn complicated," Joe Davis was saying. "We're getting buried by grief."

"I know," Alexander Kulik replied.

Kulik learned over the glass coffee table in his La Costa Country Club condominium and snorted a long line of high-grade cocaine through a rolled-up hundred-dollar bill. He sniffed and handed the bill to Davis, who inhaled one of the white lines.

"It's been two years of nothin' but grief," Kulik said.

Over a three-year period in the midseventies, the mules who worked for Joe Davis, Roy Richard, and Alexander Kulik had smuggled millions of dollars' worth of hash oil into southern California. In turn, the trio had funneled millions of dollars into ISKCON, money that went to help build temples in Los Angeles and San Diego. They opened Govinda's, a restaurant on the Pacific Coast Highway in Laguna Beach, and set up the Prasadam Distributing International, PDI, to launder the money and cover the operation.

Most of the mules were now PDI "employees," receiving ten thousand dollars for each run. And Davis and Richard had decided long ago that the two of them shouldn't be the only ones out in the cold. If the mules were getting paid, the organizers should get a cut, too. After all, the mules weren't the only ones taking risks.

The benefits were heady. Like the mules, many of whom owned beachfront condos and drove BMWs, Davis and Richard lived in style. Richard now owned two homes. One was a rambling beachfront mansion, the other a mountain retreat in Topanga Canyon. He drove a Mercedes and a BMW. Davis had a place on the beach and a serious cocaine habit.

For the first year, the smuggling operation was as smooth as the top of a Krishna's head. Aziz was a consummate professional who never ran short of the product. The mules breezed through customs. The distributors sold the oil without a hitch and the money rolled in. If there was a problem, it was laundering the profits. Richard and Davis developed and marketed a health-food cookie called Bionic Bits. It ended in a million-dollar bath. The cookies were blander than bran and dry as sand. Nobody, not even devotees, bought them.

Worse yet, PDI was living proof of Bob Dylan's line, "To live outside the law, you must be honest." The drug ring was devouring itself. One after another, the mules began looking to their own interest. When they weren't on a run, they were embezzling from the company.

Cocaine and heroin dealers, who were put under PDI's umbrella by Kulik, were also milking the company. The agreement was that they could use PDI as a front to make deals and launder money. In return, PDI was to receive a cut from every deal. It didn't work. The free-lancers—in particular, a coke dealer named Steven Bovan—were robbing the company blind.

"We've gotta clean house," Kulik said, doing another line of coke. "A guy like Bovan, muscle is the only thing he understands."

"What ya got in mind?" Davis asked, taking a hundred-dollar bill, rolling it a little tighter, and placing it to his nostril.

"Well, I know a couple of guys lookin' for work," Kulik said. "They're heavy."

"How heavy?" Davis asked.

"On the heavy side of heavy," Kulik said. "Let's just say that even though they aren't blood relatives, they're self-made men in a large New Jersey family."

Davis stopped cutting another line on the glass table and looked at Kulik. "Are you serious?"

"Hell, yes," Kulik said, enjoying his coup. "These are the big boys. They're expensive, but closing down Bovan and those other fucks is worth every penny."

During the next week, Steven Bovan and the other PDI free-lancers were all visited by three men. They delivered the same message to each of them: If you don't clear out and pay PDI the money you owe, you could have a serious accident.

"I haven't heard a peep out of those guys," Kulik said several days later when he and Davis met for lunch at Govinda's. "This is beautiful. I love it. They're scared shitless. If they don't come through soon, my guys will pay them another visit and maybe leave a calling card."

Davis chuckled.

He was home alone that night, doing a little toot and watching Johnny Carson, when the phone rang.

"Joe?" Kulik said when Davis answered. "We got a problem."

Davis shivered. He thought he heard a footstep and

looked out the sliding glass doors, expecting to see armed men on his deck. It was empty. Damn coke, he thought. I'm getting paranoid.

"Tell me," he said, turning back to the phone.

"They got me," Kulik said.

"What ya talkin' about?" Davis said, "Who's got ya?"

"I've been kidnapped," Kulik said, almost shouting. "A couple of guys grabbed me as I was comin' off my boat tonight."

"Where are you?" Davis asked.

"How the fuck should I know?" Kulik said. "You got to come through for me, Joe."

The phone was wrenched out of Kulik's hand. Davis heard muffled voices, but could not make out what they were saying.

"You there, fuckface?" somebody asked.

"Yes," Davis said, almost in a whisper.

"Him or you, fuckface. It was a toss-up. Things worked out so we got him first. You're next. Unless."

"Unless?" Davis asked, holding his breath.

"Unless you come up with one hundred grand by noon tomorrow. Be in your office. We'll call and tell you how to get it to us. Now say good night to your friend."

"Joe?" Kulik asked. "Get the money, Joe. These guys mean business."

The connection was cut before Davis could answer.

The next morning, Davis took one hundred thousand in hundred-dollar bills out of a safe in his office. He was doing a line of coke to steady himself, when the phone rang at noon sharp. He looked at it, tempted not to answer. Then he picked up the receiver.

"That you, fuckface?" asked the same voice Davis had talked to the night before.

"Yes," Davis said.

"Got a pen?"

"Yes."

The voice gave him detailed instructions. He was to wrap the money inside a copy of the *Los Angeles Times*. He was to drive to Corona Del Mar State Beach. At exactly 2:15, he was to put the newspaper in a trash bin beside the entrance to the snack bar.

"Let me speak to Alex, first," Davis demanded.

"Do or die," the voice said simply. The line then went dead.

Davis did as he was told.

He got back to his oceanfront condo late that afternoon. Kulik was waiting there. He was dressed in a clean sport shirt and freshly pressed slacks. His hair was wet. He looked like a golfer on his way to the clubhouse restaurant after a relaxing round.

"Thanks, buddy," Kulik said simply, giving Davis a soul shake. "I owe you one."

"Nah, we owe them one," Davis snapped. "Who was it?"

"Had to be Bovan's boys," Kulik said. "No one else has the balls."

"We should have cut them off a long time ago," Davis said.

"I got it all set," Kulik said. "Just lend me your car for a couple hours and don't ask any questions. You'll know when it happens."

"No problem," Davis said, handing Kulik the keys. He was too burned out to care. He'd been up all night, sweating and doing lines. Now he was wiped out, ready to crash.

One week later, on October 22, 1977, Steve Bovan finished a lobster dinner at one of the best seafood restaurants in Newport Beach. He glanced at the bill, peeled some cash off a wad of twenties, left it on the table, and walked out.

He was unlocking his Mercedes when he heard a sound behind him.

The nine shots from the silenced nine-millimeter nailed Bovan to his car. He stood motionless for several seconds, then his knees gave out and he buckled from the bottom up. As the sedan rolled out of the parking lot, Bovan slid down the high-gloss paintwork, leaving streaks of blood on the driver's door. He pitched sideways, collapsing in a heap beside the front wheel, his nose against a tire.

As soon as they heard about the murder, Bovan's boys

knew it was a mob hit. And they knew it wasn't a one-shot deal. There had to be contracts out on them, too. They ran to the Newport Beach police and spilled everything they knew.

"Wake up and get the hell out of there. You're under arrest."

Six hours after Bovan was hit, Alexander Kulik opened his eyes to see an Orange County deputy sheriff holding a gun on him. He had been snorting coke for almost three days straight without sleeping, and it had finally caught up with him while driving. He had pulled into a shopping center in Mission Viejo and fallen asleep in his hundred-thousand-dollar Stutz Bearcat.

"Get your ass out here," the sheriff said, yanking the door open. Kulik was only halfway out of the car when the cop grabbed him, spun him around, and slammed him forward across the hood. The cop frisked him, slapped on the cuffs, and read him his rights.

"You got a warrant?" Kulik demanded as the cop led him to the squad car.

"You're fuckin' right I got a warrant!"

"When do I get to call my lawyer?" Kulik said. "You guys will be in deep shit if you touch that car before I call my lawyer."

The cop said something into a microphone and ignored him. Kulik looked across the parking lot and saw three police cars with flashing lights come tearing toward them. A white police crime lab was right behind them.

For the first time, Kulik knew he was in serious trouble.

The cops found a million dollars' worth of high-grade China-white heroin under the Bearcat's backseat. They obtained another warrant the next morning and searched Kulik's La Costa condominium and his pickup truck. The apartment was clean, but another five hundred thousand dollars' worth of almost pure heroin was in the truck's air cleaner.

It was an open-and-shut case.

Kulik talked. Davis, Richard, the mob hit men, and many of the mules were all arrested. At his trial, Kulik claimed he had done it all for the Krishnas. He testified that he had given more than $2 million to A. C. Bhaktivedanta Swami Prabhupada. It didn't make a difference. Kulik and the others were all convicted and sentenced to jail.

The Chosen

Prabhupada returned to Vrindaban to die in the spring of 1977.

Everything about him, even his skull, seemed to have shrunk. His skin hung slack, gray as fog. He was so weak, devotees had to lift him onto his palanquin to carry him into his quarters in the brand-new, multimillion-dollar Krishna-Balarama temple.

On good days, Prabhupada could walk a few halting steps; on bad days, he lay very still on a mattress covered by a spotless white sheet. Devotees kept a twenty-four-hour vigil by his side, constantly placing and replacing the flowers at the head of the bed. They hovered over him, straining to hear every word.

Prabhupada was happy. Every day, all over the world, tens of thousands of devotees were chanting Hare Krishna —and all because of him. He knew he had accomplished much more than his spiritual master. Not since Lord Chaitanya had anyone done such wonderful service. Krishna was sure to call him back to godhead.

And yet, Prabhupada was troubled. His guru's movement, the Gaudiya Math, had disintegrated after the death of its swami, Bhaktisiddhanta. Bhaktisiddhanta had not found any of his followers qualified to succeed him as *acharya*, the spiritual master who leads by enlightened example. Like Prabhupada, Bhaktisiddhanta had named a group of men to a governing body. But instead of cooperating, they had fought each other for supremacy until the movement devoured itself.

Resting on his white deathbed, Prabhupada worried that internecine war would consume his legacy, also. A few weeks earlier, he had finally named Kirtananda to the GBC. It was not right to hold him down any longer. Kirtanananda was doing great service in building the splendid Palace of Gold, the first of New Vrindaban's seven temples. Prabhupada knew that Kirtanananda wanted to be the new acharya. He knew that Tamal, too, wanted to be named the acharya. So did Bhagavan and Ramesvara. And Hansadutta. Hansadutta was perhaps the worst of all and certainly the most impatient. When asked several years ago what Hansadutta wanted more than anything else, Prabhupada had replied "Hansadutta wants me to die."

"After the acharya leaves, chaos enters," Prabhupada muttered, as he lay staring at the ceiling, deep in thought.

Tamal Krishna, who was standing next to the bed, leaned forward.

"What's that, Prabhupada?" he asked.

"Nothing," Prabhupada sighed. "Nothing."

"Please, Prabhupada, talk to me," Tamal begged. "Talk to us. There is so much you must tell us. We have to know what to do after you leave."

"Chant Hare Krishna," Prabhupada said softly. "Obey the regulative principles. Read my books. The answers to all your questions are in my books."

Prabhupada closed his eyes and began to chant quietly. Tamal watched for a while before tiptoeing out of Prabhupada's quarters.

"Anything new?" Ramesvara demanded as soon as Tamal entered the large room at the rear of the temple where the entire Governing Body Commission assembled every day during the drawn-out death watch.

"Nothing," Tamal sighed. "He won't talk about the future or what he wants. He just keeps telling me to read his books."

"We have to push him," Ramesvara said. "We have to go in there and make him lay it out."

"No," snapped Satsvarupa, the GBC member for the Northeastern United States. "That is unseemly. We cannot force politics on the spiritual master."

"Anything is better than this constant waiting and speculating," sighed Ramesvara. "We don't really have any choice. We've got to deal with it."

Ramesvara and the other GBC members were like kids who rise before dawn on Christmas morning, anxious to open their presents but afraid to wake their parents. For weeks they had been debating when and how to approach Prabhupada. Now they had finally decided that Ramesvara was right; they could wait no longer. Prabhupada might leave the planet at any moment.

Early the next morning, Tamal, Kirtanananda and Satsvarupa went into Prabhupada's quarters with a tape recorder.

"Prabupada, we are wondering, when you are no longer with us, how should we conduct initiations?" Satsvarupa asked cautiously.

"I shall recommend some of you as officiating acharyas," Prabhupada answered.

"Is that called *rtvik acharya?*" asked Tamal Krishna.

"Rtvik, yes," Prabhupada replied. "The rtvik initiates new disciples in my name. Just see. The new disciple becomes a disciple of my disciple."

Of the millions of words Prabhupada had written and spoken to help guide his devotees to Krishna, none was more important. He was in effect choosing his successors, handing over the movement. And yet he remained remarkably casual, as if he were naming a committee to plan next year's convention in Mayapur.

"Who will these initiating gurus be?" Tamal asked almost breathlessly.

"You can give me a list of sannyasis," Prabhupada said. "You, Tamal, can do. Kirtanananda can do. Satsvarupa can do. So too, these three can do."

"Suppose someone who wishes to be initiated is in America. Should he simply write directly to Kirtanananda or Satsvarupa?" Tamal asked.

"He can go to whomever is nearby," Prabhupada replied wearily. "Bhagavan can do. Harikesa also can do."

"Who else?" Tamal asked.

One by one, the list grew to eleven names.

Prabhupada thought he was selecting eleven bishops. Instead he got eleven popes.

*   *   *

Summer turned into autumn, and Prabhupada became weaker and weaker. He remained flat on the bed, almost motionless for days on end. His eyes remained closed for hours at a time. But devotees were always there with a microphone to record his every word.

When Prabhupada talked intelligibly, it was always about Krishna.

"Everything . . . is. . . moving, . . . acting . . . by . . . the . . . supreme . . . desire of Krishna," Prabhupada muttered in the second week of November 1977. "This . . . consciousness . . . is . . . called . . . Krishna Consciousness. . ."

Prabhupada left this planet, as his devotees say, on November 14, 1977. He was eighty-one.

5

Chaos

Krishna, the cowherd boy. This beautiful, flute-playing blue boy is God, the all-knowing, all-powerful, omnipresent, energy-giver to the cosmos. (PHOTO COURTESY OF THE BHAKTIVEDANTA BOOK TRUST, BBT)

A real guru. Hare Krishna founder Prabhupada's power came from his absolute conviction that Krishna was lord of the universe. Here he is holding *kartals*, the sacred hand cymbals used during chanting. (BBT PHOTO)

The man who would be God. Keith Ham, Kirtanananda Swami Bhaktipada, sitting in a field at the West Virginia commune of New Vrindaban in the early 1970s. (BBT PHOTO)

Let us now praise famous men. Hansadutta, where he always wanted to be: right next to Prabhupada. (BBT PHOTO)

Kirtanananda stands in front of the Palace of Gold. Built by devotees without blueprints, the palace contains two hundred tons of marble imported from Italy and Canada. The stained-glass windows are made from hundreds of pieces of hand-shaped glass. The domed roof and outside walls are coated with twenty-two-karat gold leaf. (MICHAEL BRYANT PHOTO)

A Beatle in ecstasy. George Harrison chants with devotees in London. Harrison helped the London devotees cut a hit record, "Hare Krishna Mantra," and gave ISKCON a Tudor manor outside London. "I feel at home with Krishna," Harrison told Prabhupada's biographer. "I think it's something that has been there from a previous birth." (KEYSTONE PRESS PHOTO)

The original eleven gurus in Mayapur in 1978, soon after they announced they were Prabhupada's divinely chosen successors. From left to right: Harikesha, Northern Europe, Eastern Europe, the USSR; Jayatirtha, the London guru who was beheaded by a crazed follower in London on Friday, December 13, 1987; Hansadutta, who is now managing a trailer court in a small town in northern California; Hridayananda, the southeastern U.S. guru who is based in Miami; Ramesvara, who is now selling real estate in New York; Bhagavan, who is married and living in Berkeley, California; Kirtanananda, who rules over the cult based in New Vrindaban; Tamal Krishna, the Southwest U.S., Fiji, and Asia; Satsvarupa, who remains in the movement but has resigned as a guru; Jayapataka, India and East Asia. (ISKCON WORLD REVIEW PHOTO)

Kirtanananda Bhaktipada on his *vyasasana*. (ISKCON WORLD REVIEW PHOTO)

Hansadutta, as a guru on the left, a felon on the right. Hansadutta mixed Krishna Consciousness with rock 'n' roll, guns, and rampant paranoia. (LEFT: CONGER PHOTO; RIGHT: IMPOUNDED POLICE PHOTO)

Berkeley Police Officer Joe Sanchez with the guns that were found in the trunk of a Mercedes belonging to Hansadutta. Sanchez is holding the commando-style mini-14 sub-machine gun that Vladimir Vassilievich built especially for his guru. (SACRAMENTO BEE PHOTO)

Dan Reid, Daruka. (IMPOUNDED POLICE PHOTO)

The Artist's Studio. Dan Reid lured Chuck St. Denis up to this shack by promising him cocaine. (T.R. WESTFALL PHOTO)

Chuck St. Denis, Chakradara, murdered devotee and dope dealer who was stabbed, shot, beaten with a rock, and buried alive. (PHOTO COURTESY OF CHRISLYN ST. DENIS)

Thomas Drescher was arrested for the murder of Chuck St. Denis. (T.R. WESTFALL PHOTO)

The "Krishna Cop." Detective Sergeant Tom Westfall in his office in the Marshall County, West Virginia, Sheriff's Department. (T.R. WESTFALL PHOTO)

Krishna children dance at a *kirtan*. (MICHAEL BRYANT PHOTO)

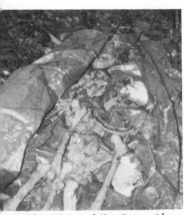

The remains of "Joe," an unidentified body found buried at New Vrindaban. A West Virginia state medical examiner found evidence of death by trauma. (T.R. WESTFALL PHOTO)

Terry Sheldon, known as Tapahpunja, fled the United States after Steve Bryant's murder. He is believed to be living in Malaysia. (IMPOUNDED POLICE PHOTO)

The would-be Krishna terrorist. Steve Bryant, Sulocana, stands in front of the Radha and Krishna deities he has just finished decorating. (PHOTO COURTESY JACK AND HELGA BRYANT) INSET: Steve Bryant in the Marshall County Jail. (IMPOUNDED POLICE PHOTO)

Plundering the Legacy

When Steve and Jane Bryant left the London temple
with Marianne and Jerome Greene, they went to New-
castle-upon-Tyne, where they worked and lived in a
Krishna-owned incense factory. The city was dreary, and
the small apartment they shared in the warehouse was
damp and drafty and infested by mice.

Most days, Steve Bryant was as gloomy as the weather.
He walked around in a funk and lashed out at Jane or
her son, Rinnian. He felt trapped. Whenever Rinnian
mispronounced a word, or Jane didn't greet him warmly,
he flew into an uncontrollable rage. Bryant had been
devout for five years, and all it had gotten him was an
insignificant dead-end job in an incense factory, a rotten
apartment, and a wife who cringed every time she saw
him.

But Bryant had ideas about how to improve things—
big ideas. Before joining the movement, he had been a
flea-market junkie, hunting bargains all over the Greater
Detroit Metropolitan Area. It was only natural that when
he had gone to India, he'd spent hours prowling the open
markets in New Delhi, Bombay, and Calcutta. He couldn't
believe the bargains available—gold, silver, precious stones
for a fraction of what they cost in the States. He had
been too broke to buy anything, except for a few trin-
kets. But he never forgot those bargains.

One of Bryant's skills was working with his hands.
Lately, he had been tinkering with a battered thirty-five-
millimeter Canon camera, and had invented a low-cost
way to put four miniature pictures on one frame. He did
it by building a lens cap that blocked out three quarters
of the film. He kept rewinding the film and reshooting,

exposing a different quarter in each shot. When he finished, he had four separate pictures on each negative.

One afternoon Bryant went into a jewelry-supply store in Newcastle and bought a cheap pendant. Returning to his apartment, he carefully fitted a miniature picture of Radha into the setting and covered it with a beveled piece of glass.

"I gotta surprise for you," Bryant said to Jerome and Marianne that evening before prasadam. "Feast your eyes on this."

He tore open a small manila envelope and let the pendant slide onto the table. Jerome picked it up and held it to the light.

"This is really nice," he said, handing it to Marianne. "I've never seen anything like it. Where'd you get it?"

"I made it," Bryant said triumphantly.

"You're kidding!" Marianne squealed, handing the pendant to Jane.

"Think devotees would buy them?" Bryant asked.

"I sure would," Marianne said.

"So would I," Jane said.

"It's yours," Bryant said to Jane. "I want you to have it. It's my way of saying that I can be more than just the chief grump."

"Oh, Sulocana," Jane replied simply. Tears welled in her eyes as Marianne fastened the pendant around her neck.

"I got plans," Bryant said.

"Yeah?" Jerome said.

"Even though we make slave wages working here, Jane and I have saved a little money," Bryant went on. "I'm gonna use it to make five or six dozen pendants. With the money I make from selling them, I'm gonna buy all the cameras and tape recorders that I can carry. Then I'm going to India and sell 'em all on the black market and make a killing."

The more Bryant talked about the plan, the more excited he became. He was soon pacing the floor, emphasizing each point by slamming his fist into his palm.

"I'll invest that money in gold and silver and precious stones," Bryant said. "There are some terrific deals in India. I'll come back and make some really nice stuff.

You guys can put together a brochure and take care of the orders that will come flyin' in from temples all over the world. We can say good-bye to this stinking incense factory."

They stayed up late working on Bryant's ideas and were more than an hour late for work. When they arrived at the factory, they were surprised to find it empty, except for the manager.

"What's going on?" Bryant asked. "Where is everybody?"

"Haven't you heard? We've closed. Prabhupada died in Vrindaban two days ago. Word reached London early this morning. Go back to your apartment and chant to help ease his soul back to godhead."

The two couples were stunned. Prabhupada had been on the brink of death ever since the *Jaladuta* arrived in Boston Harbor twelve years before, in September 1965. Yet still it was a shock. It seemed impossible that he was gone. They made their way slowly back to the apartment without speaking. It was work just to put one foot in front of the other.

They spent the day chanting and praying for Prabhupada and moping quietly.

"I had nothing before I joined the movement," Jerome said in a teary voice. "Prabhupada taught me how to act around people. He was such a gentleman. Everything I know that's good came from him."

Everybody nodded.

The silence hung over them.

"In retrospect, you know what's really weird?" Marianne asked after a while. "He kept telling us not to be dependent on him because he wouldn't always be here. He kept saying, 'Krishna Consciousness is not in my body, Krishna Consciousness is in my books. Read my books.' And yet, I haven't really read his books. I don't think any of us have."

"That's true," Jerome said, "I always thought, why bother? Why read the Bible if Jesus Christ is alive? I figured I could always sit at his feet and absorb his wisdom."

Bryant was sitting on the floor with his back to the wall. His arms were wrapped around his legs and his head was propped up on his knees. He hid his eyes and began sobbing. The others looked at each other. Their eyes filled with tears and they started crying, too.

"Prabhupada was our inspiration," Bryant said between sobs. "When things got hard, we could always think of him and find the strength to go on. Who's gonna do that for us now? Who's gonna stand guard over our spiritual lives?"

"Prabhupada appointed us rtviks, not acharyas!" Ramesvara, the Los Angeles guru, screamed.

"There's no difference!" Hansadutta screamed back.

"There is, so!" Ramesvara said petulantly. "There's a huge difference. When he named us rtviks, Prabhupada made us generals. You guys want to be emperors."

"Call me a Napoleon if you want, as long as I get Australia," put in Bhavananda, Charles Backus, the GBC member in charge of building the Mayapur temple. "I pioneered Australia. It's mine."

"I did the same in South Africa. I'm claiming South Africa with Europe," said Bhagavan.

"How are you going to handle Europe and South Africa?" Ramesvara asked. "In case you haven't looked at a globe lately, they're rather far apart."

"I have devotees in both continents," Bhagavan said superciliously. "Geography is no barrier to love."

Prabhupada's eleven successors were seated on pillows, facing each other across a long, narrow table in the half-finished GBC room in the Mayapur temple. They had been meeting in the same room every day throughout February and March of 1978. They were trying, unsuccessfully so far, to determine the movement's future. Like Mafia dons carving out exclusive territories, they were dividing the world into fiefdoms.

Bhagavan slowly got to his feet and waited until all eyes were fixed on him. A tall, strikingly handsome former medical student from the University of Buffalo, Bhagavan was already infamous as the Krishna Sun King. The faucets in his private bathroom were gold plated. He would eat only from gold plates and drink from gold goblets. He was chauffeured around Europe in a Mercedes 500.

When the silence was complete, Bhagavan pointed his finger at Tamal Krishna, whose cross-country campus crusade had irritated many temple presidents.

"I charge that man with trying to steal my devotees," Bhagavan said. "My devotees love me and regard me as Prabhupada's legitimate successor. And now I learn that Tamal has sent letters to certain devotees claiming that he and he alone is Prabhupada's successor, and that devotees must surrender to him."

"I am the only one really qualified to lead the movement," said Tamal, who claimed the American Southwest and the island of Fiji, as well as several other Pacific islands.

Kirtanananda shook his head. When this is over, he told himself, they'll see that there is only one true swami fit to lead ISKCON: Kirtanananda Swami Bhaktipada.

"Let's go back to the subject of vyasasanas," Ramesvara said. "Let's start by trying to settle this chair thing."

"Each guru must have his own vyasasana," Bhagavan said.

"Absolutely right," Hansadutta said.

"What about when another guru visits? Where will he sit?" Ramesvara asked.

"Good point," Bhagavan said. "Symbols are very important, and what talks louder than furniture? I propose that each temple have three vyasasanas right next to each other. One will be Prabhupada's forever. We'll rope it off and put his picture on it so that no one will even think of sitting there. A second will be for the local guru, and the third will be reserved for visiting gurus. That way, every devotee will instantly know that we are now equal to Prabhupada."

"If we're equal, I suppose we're supposed to get *puga*, too?" Ramesvara asked, referring to the ceremony in which devotees worship their spiritual masters.

"But of course," Kirtanananda said.

"Absolutely correct," Hansadutta added. He closed his eyes and imagined the ritual. It pleased him to think about how he would at last receive the obeisances he so richly deserved. Finally, he would be worshiped as he should be—as a "pure devotee," a link between God and man. He saw himself seated on his vyasasana. In his mind, Hansadutta watched a devotee blow a conch shell three times and ring a small bell. Then another devotee approached and offered a stick of incense.

The devotee circled Hansadutta's feet with the smoldering stick three times, then circled his chest twice and his entire body seven times. The devotee then did the same with a camphor wick, a ghee lamp, water, a handkerchief, and a flower. Hansadutta smiled. He could practically feel the devotee fanning him with a yak's-tail whisk and peacock feathers.

"Our godbrothers will never go for it," Ramesvara said, interrupting Hansadutta's daydream. "For years, we've all been more or less equal. Then Prabhupada dies, and all of a sudden we're baby Prabhupadas."

"That's your mistake," Bhagavan said, leaping to his feet. Once again, he waited for silence. "We're not demanding to be worshiped just because we want to raise ourselves above our godbrothers. We're only doing it because we love them. Worshiping a spiritual master is a vital part of every devotee's faith. We have to appear absolute, or their faith will be shaken. We have to be worshiped just like Prabhupada, or our disciples won't think we're his equal."

"Devotees will offer *puga* willingly because they love us," Kirtanananda interrupted. "You cannot check their love."

"That's right," Hansadutta added. "This movement has always been about love."

The room was silent for a moment. Ramesvara looked troubled. Bhagavan walked over to him and put his hand on his shoulder.

"Don't you see? You've got no choice," Bhagavan said. "You've got to accept puga. We all do. We've got to be absolutely consistent. If even one of us does not go along with the program, we'll all look fallible. Come on, Ramesvara, for the good of the whole movement. So, what do you say?"

Ten pairs of eyes bored into Ramesvara.

"Maybe you're right," he sighed. "Prabhupada always said we're an autocratic movement. The authority of the spiritual master has to be absolute. If you doubt him, you doubt the link to Krishna and everything falls apart."

"Absolutely right," Bhagavan said.

"I'll go along with it," Ramesvara conceded. "But I want you to know I'm not going to be comfortable, sitting up there on the vyasasana receiving puga from some devotee who knew me when I was Bobby Grant. It just doesn't feel right. I don't know, but maybe I'll get used to it."

"Of course, you will!" Bhagavan cried enthusiastically. "It's new for all of us. But we'll get used to it."

"Let's finish working out who gets what," said Hansadutta, who had staked his claim to Berkeley, the Philippines, Sri Lanka, and several temples in India. "My devotees need me."

"As mine need me," echoed Tamal.

"And mine, me," added Bhagavan.

It took another week to finish carving up the world. As soon as the meeting concluded, the newly minted gurus hastened to return to their temples. Comfortably settled in first-class seats, they congratulated themselves on the agreement.

But only a few were satisfied. The rest were scheming to seize control.

When the Palace of Gold is finished, devotees everywhere will visit New Vrindaban and see that only the true acharya could build such a splendid temple, Kirtanananda told himself as he winged his way back to the States. I don't have to take over the movement; the movement will come to me.

I'll send sankirtan parties all over Europe, Bhagavan planned. I'll buy palaces and convert them into temples and recruit the wealthiest people in every country. I'll turn ISKCON into the modern equivalent of the Holy Roman Empire.

I'm going to build a magnificent temple in Fiji, Tamal promised himself. The population is already half Hindu and growing. I'll convert them all and turn Fiji into the first Krishna Consciousness nation on earth. When that happens, no one will be able to deny that I am the next acharya.

Hansadutta's plans were simpler. His whole life, he had been controlled by authority figures. First, his father, then his commanders in the Navy, and finally Prabhupada. Even Himavati, his ex-wife (they separated because Hansadutta insisted on taking a vow of sannyas) had tried to control him in her own gentle way. But now, for the first time, he was free, free of all control. He was a guru. He could do whatever he wanted; he could tell people to do things and they would do them.

He strapped on his seatbelt and grinned. He could hardly wait to get back to Berkeley and find out what real freedom was all about.

Hansadutta:
Secretary for God

"Thank you for flying with us, sir."

Hansadutta brushed by the flight attendant on his way out of the plane and onto the San Francisco jetway without bothering to acknowledge her. He never paid much attention to women, especially not now. He was preoccupied by the memory of the big send-off Prabhupada had been given in this same airport so many years ago. He was hoping his welcome home from the Mayapur meeting as the newly appointed guru for Southeast Asia, Southern India, Sri Lanka and the Pacific Northwest would be even more fantastic.

He ran his hand along his thigh, straightening an imaginary crease in his dhoti. As he approached the end of the jetway, he checked himself to make sure he had a blank look on his face, a look that Hansadutta thought made him appear serene, yet vital; benevolent, yet strong.

"Oh yes," Hansadutta said to himself as he stepped into the terminal. "This will do."

From every direction, devotees rushed toward their new guru. Airport security guards tried to hold them back, but there were too many. And they were too eager. They pushed past the metal detectors, chanting, singing, crying with joy, and throwing flower petals.

"Hare Krishna!" Hansadutta shouted, raising his sannyasa staff above his head. He felt something poke him in the back. He turned and saw that a businessman had nudged him with his briefcase.

"Come on, buddy, let's get the hell out of here," the businessman said.

Hansadutta glared at him and turned back to his devotees.

"I said, move it. Get these freaks out of here," the businessman said.

"Please, gentlemen," said a Pan Am ground attendant who had walked up behind them. "I take it these people are here for you, sir?"

"Yes," Hansadutta answered. He paused a moment and then added, "And for Krishna."

"Well, you must do something about them, sir," the attendant said politely. "I'm getting calls from Security."

"They are only showing love," Hansadutta replied.

"They're disturbing the whole international terminal, sir," the attendant said firmly. "They're not supposed to be in here at all. Those jingle-jangle things they're wearing have set off all of our electronic surveillance devices."

"Let the damn weirdos have their love-in somewhere else," the businessman said, his face flushed red. "The flight was three hours late and now I'm late for a meeting I flew fourteen hours to make."

"Surely you can understand how important security is sir?" the airline attendant said soothingly to Hansadutta. "A man in your position? When other celebrities land here, they're very helpful in getting their fans to cooperate."

The attendant pointed up the corridor.

"If we could just get everybody past the metal detectors and into the main terminal, there wouldn't be a problem."

"Yes, of course, as you wish," Hansadutta said, motioning for his devotees—and a half-dozen reporters—to follow.

"We love you, Hansadutta!" a devotee shouted.

"Is it true you plan to set up headquarters in the Berkeley temple?" asked a karmi reporter, poking a microphone at him.

"Krishna's mercy has brought you to us," another devotee yelled, tears streaming down her face.

"What do you people believe in?" shouted a second reporter, pushing through the crowd.

Hansadutta was annoyed. He wanted to bask in the love of his devotees. But he realized he had to handle the press. He thought of Kirtanananda: Whenever a reporter or photographer appeared holding a notebook or pointing a camera, Kirtanananda was always ready with a clever quote and a satisfied expression.

"Give them what they're looking for," Kirtanananda would say. "It's publicity you can't buy."

Hansadutta raised his hand above his head, calling for quiet. The flashbulbs popped. Prabhupada used to do the same thing. Hansadutta felt a rush of power when the crowd fell silent.

"You ask what we believe in?" he said to the reporters while turning to the photographers. "We believe in chanting and dancing the holy names of God. We believe in eating and sleeping and living for Krishna."

"Is it true you're a terrific dancer?" another reporter asked.

Hansadutta smiled becomingly. "My name means swanlike, elegant. Judge for yourself."

With that, Hansadutta began to chant and twirl, bouncing and rocking his head to the maha-mantra. The devotees picked up his rhythm. In an instant they had a fiery kirtan going.

Then, just as suddenly, Hansadutta held up his hand again and the devotees stopped.

"I have a question," a short and pudgy reporter asked. "There are strong rumors that several women in the Berkeley temple have been abused. Do you have a comment?"

Hansadutta glared. "We've been the victims of hateful rumors since our spiritual master arrived in this country," he said. "This is yet another slander. Krishna women are as beloved as Radha was beloved by Krishna."

The pudgy reporter didn't miss a beat. "That's not what one of the women who blooped told me."

Hansadutta looked him hard in the eyes. "Blooped? You mean left the movement? Who are you? What newspaper do you work for?"

The two men stared at each other.

"Actually, I don't work for any paper," the pudgy man admitted. "If the papers were doing their job, I wouldn't have to be here. My sister was a devotee in the Berkeley temple. She left because—"

"Because she couldn't live up to our rigorous standards, and now she condemns us to cover her weakness," Hansadutta said, seizing the offensive. "It happens all the time."

He dismissed the pudgy guy with a wave of his hand. "Any other questions?"

"My sister—"

"Any other questions?" Hansadutta asked, his voice louder this time.

"What does it mean to be a guru?" asked a reporter from the *San Francisco Chronicle*.

Hansadutta thought for a moment, then smiled—a smile that charmed the devotees.

"To get to see a big man, you first have to see his secretary," he said. "I am kind of a secretary for God."

All morning, Hansadutta had been in his office at the Berkeley temple, a former mansion just off Telegraph Avenue. He paced back and forth across the Oriental rug, head down, deep in thought.

Then he threw himself into a chair. For a long time he hardly moved. Then he reached into his desk and grabbed a bottle of the cough syrup he had brought back from India by the case. He had stopped coughing months ago, but the medicine, which was 70-percent alcohol, helped him think. And he needed to think now. He has to figure out how to handle Jiva.

"Tell Jiva I want to see him," Hansadutta ordered Michael Ralph Pugliese, the devotee who had become his chauffeur and personal servant. "Tell him I want to see him now."

Five minutes later there was a knock at the door. Hansadutta took another hit of cough syrup, closed the desk drawer, and called, "Enter!"

James Patrick Underwood, Jiva, head of the temple's women's sankirtan team, walked through the door. He looked as humble as any burly, tattooed former inmate of San Quentin with a shaved head could look.

"Hare Krishna," Jiva said and prostrated himself at Hansadutta's feet.

Before Jiva could rise, the secretary for God jumped

on Jiva's back, pinned him to the floor, and pressed the barrel of a .38 into his right temple.

"You've got five minutes to clear out," Hansadutta hissed in Jiva's ear.

Jiva was a thug who had gone to prison for a string of armed robberies. His idea of fun was going out to the airport to steal suitcases off the baggage carousels. He liked to tell devotees that one of his ambitions in life was to be a pimp. Nothing scared him. Jiva did things for fun that other people thought were crazy.

But now Jiva was scared. This guy Hansadutta was a maniac.

"What's the matter, man? What'd I do? You been here two months and I ain't crossed you once. Not once. I swear I ain't."

The barrel of the .38 pressed harder against Jiva's head.

"Who fucks every woman on the sankirtan team?" Hansadutta barked.

"I do," Jiva admitted, his voice shaking. "But they need it. The more I fuck 'em, the more money they bring in.

"Who beats the shit out of them?"

"I do," Jiva admitted. "But I'll stop. I promise I'll stop."

"Who gives 'em uppers so they'll work eighteen hours a day?"

"Anything, man—anything you say. I'll stop. Just put the gun down so we can talk about it."

Hansadutta was having fun. He waited until Jiva started to whimper. Then he let him get to his feet and shoved him into a chair.

"You'll have to take a vow of sannyasa," Hansadutta said, holding the gun on him.

"I'll do it. No more pussy," Jiva said.

"From now on, I'm in charge of the women," Hansadutta said. "They're mine."

"They're yours, Maharaj," Jiva said.

Hansadutta placed the gun on his desk.

"Why will women no longer work eighteen hours a day?" he asked Jiva.

"Because Krishna doesn't want them to?" Jiva hazarded, slumping in his chair with relief.

Hansadutta looked annoyed. "Yes, yes, of course. But why else?"

Jiva looked confused.

"Because twenty-five women who each bring in three or four hundred dollars a day selling incense and candles and cookies is small-time shit," Hansadutta said. "I've figured out a way that's a lot less work that will bring us a lot more money."

"Hi, there!" the perky blond said to the middle-aged man on his way into the shopping mall. He had just gotten out of his car and was lost in thought, trying to decide on a birthday present for his wife.

"Oh hello, there!" the blond called again in a sing-song voice. "May I have a second of your time, sir."

The guy checked his watch. He was about to apologize and move on, when he looked at the girl. She was so fresh and clean and earnest, he had to smile at her.

"Me?" he asked, pointing at his chest.

"Sure," she said. "Could you step over here to the microphone?"

The guy looked past the girl and saw that she was standing in front of a van with a stenciled banner hanging above the rear door. "Radio KSNA," it said. He started to blush. The girl smiled again, pulled him forward, and held out the microphone.

"What's your name?" she asked, trying to put him at ease.

"Roger," he answered stiffly, intimidated by being on the air.

"I'm 'Sandy' from KSNA, Roger. Where are you from?"

"Oakdale."

"Just up the road in Oakdale. That's great, Roger, because today's your lucky day. Tell me, what kind of music do you like?"

"Ah, country and western, mostly," Roger said, loosening up a little.

"C and W! I'd have bet you'd say that, Roger. Let's see what we've got here."

Inside the van, Jiva hurried through a rack holding hundreds of albums. He pulled out three records and handed them to Sandy. She glanced at them and gave them to Roger.

"What do you think of that, Roger? Three brand-new C and W albums. They're yours to keep, Roger."

"Gee, great," he said, picking up her enthusiasm.

"Roger, you don't have to give a cent for those albums. Take them home and enjoy them. All we ask is that if you're willing, you'll do a little something to help Radio KSNA fight hunger in Africa. Now, I'm sure you know that albums like those would cost you fifteen or twenty dollars in a record store. All we're asking is, out of the goodness of your heart, could you give us a little something to feed a starving child in Africa?"

Roger reached into his wallet and peeled out his only bill—a twenty. He planned to ask for ten dollars change. But when Sandy squealed with delight and gushed into the live microphone about how generous he was, he quickly changed his mind.

"I was going to buy my wife something for her birthday," Roger told Sandy. "But these records and helping feed kids in Africa will make her a nicer present than I could ever find in the mall."

Sandy watched Roger walk away, then went into the van and laid the dead microphone on a table. Jiva was down on his hands and knees, sorting records. When he looked up, Sandy gave him a thumbs-up.

"That's over three hundred dollars already this morning," Sandy said. "You know how long I'd have to stand on a corner to make this much?"

"This is the greatest scam ever," Jiva said. "It's Krishna's mercy that Hansadutta found the warehouse down in LA. We get all the cutouts we can truck away for a dime apiece, and those idiot karmis give us five dollars."

"The starving-children bit works best," Sandy said.

Jiva held up an album.

"Look at this: *A Thousand Strings play the Music of Spain.* Who listens to this shit?"

"Stiffs," Sandy said. "Karmi stiffs."

Sandy walked over to Jiva and placed her hand on the

back of his neck, then ran it up toward his head. When she hit the band of his wig, she pulled it off and kissed his shaved head.

Jiva jumped up. "What the hell are you doing?"

"Come on, baby, relax," Sandy said.

"You stupid bitch!" Jiva shouted, pushing her across the van. "You know Hansadutta ordered me to take sannyasa. You know better than to question the order of a pure devotee."

"I'm sorry," Sandy said. "I really am. I forgot."

"Get back out there," Jiva ordered and went back to sorting albums.

Sandy jumped out of the van. Before her feet touched the ground, she had put a big smile on her face.

"Hi, there!" she shouted to a grandmotherly type walking back to her car with a small child.

The woman returned her smile.

"Could I have a moment of your time?"

He is a pure devotee. Sandy reminded herself silently as Hansadutta pulled off her sari and began biting her right nipple. A pure devotee knows all.

The day before, the first time it had happened, he had called her into his office to congratulate her for doing such magnificent service for Krishna. They had wound up screwing on the Oriental rug, right under a portrait of Prabhupada.

At first, Sandy had been scared and confused. She had felt like crying. Her unbridled female lust had caused the downfall of a pure devotee, a sannyasi who was beyond sex. She vowed not to go near Hansadutta again.

The vow didn't last a day. Hansadutta summoned her to his office, and there they were, lying on the rug while her tongue danced playfully in and out of his mouth and he pushed his knee up between her legs.

Even in this, he is advanced, Sandy thought to herself. Not like Jiva; fucking Jiva was like getting mugged. Hansadutta made beautiful love. Making love to him was like making love to Krishna himself.

I must be very special, she thought as she lay in the

afterglow. His feelings for me must be very powerful to drive him to break his sacred vow of sannyasa.

That night, Sandy stood in front of the mirror in the women's bathroom. She checked to make sure no one was watching, then pulled her sari away from her neck. It was covered with half a dozen hickeys. She stroked them lovingly.

When the door swung open, Sandy quickly covered herself. But she was too slow.

"Hare Krishna," said "Elaine," a tall, thin, brown-haired devotee. "Too bad they don't make turtleneck saris."

Sandy looked coyly at her feet. She didn't particularly like Elaine. Elaine thought she was more advanced than the other women because she collected more money than anybody else.

"I have nothing to hide," Sandy said.

"You better hide that neck, anyway," Elaine answered. "Jiva's gonna be pissed if those marks are still showing tomorrow. How are you going to be Miss Wholesome Radio with hickeys all over your neck?"

"Jiva can't say anything about this," Sandy said petulantly.

"And why not?"

"Because Hansadutta gave me these," Sandy blurted out, "and he's a pure devotee. Anything he does is Krishna's will."

For a moment Elaine looked shocked. A curious sequence of emotions—anger, hurt, fear, mockery, cynicism —passed over her face. Then she drew herself up to her full height.

"Yes," Elaine said proudly. "I too have given myself to Krishna's representative on this planet."

Eddie "Fast Fingers" Dawson, one of the most respected studio musicians in San Francisco, was looking over the score for the fifth time. Hansadutta, the composer, was leaning over his shoulder, pointing out, also for the fifth time, where he wanted the lead guitar to come in.

The shit I have to play for money, Dawson thought.

He glared once more at the song's title and shook his head: 'Guru, Guru, on the Wall'—gimme a break!

"Look," man, he said to Hansadutta, I can read music.

"You got it wrong the last time," Hansadutta said. "Musicians are such egotists. It's very important that you don't let your ego interfere. Krishna says—"

"Hold it, man," Dawson snapped. "I'll play this shit because it's a gig and I'm a pro. But I'm not about to listen to you put me down. I put up with that shit when I was on the road with Van Morrison, but you ain't him, man. Not even close."

The female back-up singers and the keyboard player broke up laughing.

"Okay, look, let's make a deal," Dawson said, winking at the singers. "You lay off my playing and my ego, and I'll back off on your lyrics. What'd you say, man? We'll get out of here a whole bunch faster."

Hansadutta nodded.

" 'Did you ever see a guru behind a gun? . . .' " Dawson read from the sheet music and gave a titter. He looked up at Hansadutta and flashed the peace sign. "Okay, keep cool. Just rehearsing. Now, everybody ready? Let's go one more time. Take it from the top."

Hansadutta walked to the microphone, aimed an imaginary machine gun, and pretended to fire as the *Rat-a-tat-tat! Rat-a-tat-tat! Rat-a-tat-tat!* that opened the song filled the studio. He boogied to the mike and tried to cut loose, even though his voice was hoarse from previous takes. What came out sounded like a cross between Bob Dylan at his thinnest and Neil Young at his squeakiest.

> Did you ever see a guru flying a plane?
> Thin as a cane? Looking insane?
> Did you ever see a guru driving a car,
> Porsche or Mercedes? Singing in a bar?

On cue, the female back-up singers came in with a Phil Spector wall-of-sound chorus:

> Guru, guru, on the wall,
> Who is the heaviest of them all?

Whose disciples are the worst?
Who could I give my last shirt?

Hansadutta threw himself into the next verse. This was his favorite. This was where he took a shot at his West Coast rival for power, Ramesvara.

I once saw a guru just like you,
New York Jew, nothing new.
I once saw a guru, a fantastic dancer,
Holy gangster, carefree prankster!

Hansadutta was in a frenzy. He flew through the other songs he'd written for the album—"Nice But Dead," the title tune, "Gas, Food, Wine, and Beer," "Hourglass," and "Helpless Awe"—like he was leading a kirtan.

'Thin as a cane, looking insane'—indeed, Dawson thought as he packed up his Fender Strat. The guy's got intensity, I'll say that for him. But intensity without talent is about as useful as a typewriter in the hands of a chimpanzee.

"Tell me really, man, why did you go through all this hassle to cut an album?" Dawson asked Hansadutta on their way out of the studio.

"Well, Western society is so obsessed with rock'n roll, I thought this might be a perfect way to spread Krishna Consciousness."

Dawson looked around the studio. Hansadutta's band of devotees was clustered by the door, waiting for him.

"Hey, listen, maybe *they'll* swallow that," Dawson said, nodding toward the devotees. "Me, you don't have to bullshit. Come on, man, the truth. Being a guru ain't enough, is it? You wanna be a rock star. Ain't that the truth?"

Hansadutta grinned.

"Sure," he responded after a moment. "Why not. Why should I say no to being a rock star? Why should I say no to anything?"

"I like it!" Dawson said, giving Hansadutta a soul shake. "Hansadutta, the rock 'n roll guru!—like I've always said: It can't get weird enough!"

*   *   *

Hansadutta was depressed. His album *Nice But Dead,* had flopped in the U.S. He had cut a couple of others and they, too, had bombed. The albums had each cost around thirty-five thousand dollars to produce. Now devotees were giving them away as part of the record scam.

Nobody had reviewed his music. Hansadutta was convinced that was the reason why his albums hadn't taken off. He had even called *Rolling Stone* himself, and they still hadn't given him so much as a mention. Well, *Rolling Stone* was in maya, everybody knew that, Hansadutta thought as he took a long hit of cough syrup.

Hansadutta had been feeling down for months. That scared him. He'd been afraid of the blues ever since his stint in the Navy and those bleak days in Hoboken before he joined the movement. And here he was, lying flat on his back on the couch in his office. The shades were drawn to block out the bright California sun; a silver bell and a bottle of Indian cough syrup were beside him on the floor. Day after day had passed like this. The only time Hansadutta got up was to go to the bathroom; the only devotee who saw him was Michael Pugliese, his personal servant, who loyally brought prasadam and took it away untouched.

Hansadutta knew what was bringing him down. Being God on earth to a bunch of devotees who were so pathetic they'd do anything he told them to was harder than he had ever thought it would be. He had to keep the temple running and look after Mount Kailasa, the 480-acre farm the temple owned in Lake County, north of the Bay Area. He had to make sure the sankirtan women were happy so they'd keep collecting. He had to write his books and publish Prabhupada's. He had to write his songs. And he had to listen to that twit Ramesvara scream at him over the phone that the record scam and the arsenal he was putting together up at Mount Kailasa were going to ruin Krishna Consciousness. Who was Ramesvara to tell him about Krishna Consciousness? Hansadutta *was* Krishna Consciousness.

That was why he was lying in the dark, staring at the ceiling.

Heavy is the head that wears the crown, Hansadutta sighed as he reached for another swig of the potent cough medicine. I got it all: women, money, cars, land, guns, devotees who do anything I tell them, too. Yet I'm miserable. I was happier when I was just another devotee chanting in the streets.

Well, he knew one surefire cure for the heavy blues. Hansadutta had been putting it off because he didn't want to admit his depression. Besides, it exhausted him just to think about it. Still, there comes a time when you've got to do something. Hansadutta rang the bell. A few seconds later, Michael Pugliese entered the darkened office.

"It's time for a road trip, Krishna style," Hansadutta said wearily. "Call the travel agent. I want to visit my temples in Asia. Book us Pan Am this time."

"How many are going?" Pugliese asked.

"I don't know," Hansadutta said, dismissing Pugliese. "Make seven reservations. If there's more, we'll make more later."

Hansadutta and his entourage were in the first-class cabin of a Pan Am 747 on their way from Manila to San Francisco. For two months, the guru and his merry men had temple-hopped across Hansadutta's empire—from India to Sri Lanka, Singapore to the Philippines. The Philippines were the best.

"If they paid royalties, we'd clear a fortune," Hansadutta said.

"That's right," replied Michael Pugliese.

Pugliese was nervous. Hansadutta was slurring his words and rolling his head. Much of the time he'd whisper so softly, Pugliese had to strain to hear him. But then suddenly he'd start shouting, and the stewardess would run over and try to calm him down.

"Gimme," Hansadutta said.

Pugliese hesitated. He couldn't say no to a pure devotee. But if a pure devotee was clearly stoned out of his mind, was he still infallible?

"I said gimme," Hansadutta demanded sternly. He

tried to sound menacing to make it clear he wouldn't tolerate having to repeat an order.

Pugliese, Hansadutta's traveling medicine kit, reached into his japa bag and pulled out a Percodan. He slipped it past the armrest to Hansadutta. Pugliese looked around to see if anyone was paying attention. No one was.

"Well, it's good for me 'cause I'm a man, and it's something called Percodan," Hansadutta sang.

He giggled and elbowed Pugliese, who giggled, too.

"Tell me about it again," Hansadutta commanded. "Tell me about the DJ one more time."

"We met a Filipino disk jockey in Cebu who likes Krishna Consciousness," Pugliese said. "He had you on his show and played cuts from the *Nice But Dead* album. As soon as he played 'Guru, Guru, on the Wall,' the request lines lit up. He played it again, and he played it the next night and every night after that. Before long, stations all over the Philippines were playing it."

"I got a hit, I got a hit record!" Hansadutta crowed. "That'll show those bastards in the States."

He tried to slap Pugliese on the knee but missed. His arm caught between the seats. Pugliese had to twist around and help him free it.

"Why ain't we sellin' albums? Why ain't I on Filipino TV, singin' my songs? Tell me again," Hansadutta commanded.

"Because there are no copyright laws in the Philippines, that's why," Pugliese said. "Before we knew it, there were four versions of 'Guru, Guru' out on forty-fives."

"Get the press release," Hansadutta said. "Go on, get it. I haven't approved it yet. I don't know if I will. But I want to hear it again."

Pugliese fished around in his briefcase and came up with a paper entitled "The Travels and Preachings of His Divine Grace, Hansadutta Swami."

"OK, here it goes," Pugliese said, clearing his throat. "I'll start with the part about the visit to Cebu: 'The Philippine devotees are religious by nature, so when they came in contact with His Divine Grace Hansadutta Maharaja, Krishna Consciousness immediately flourished within the core of their hearts.

" 'These devotees were fortunate enough to get the grace and association of a bona fide spiritual master coming in disciplic succession from Lord Krishna himself. All the Filipino devotees surrounded Hansadutta, offering their obeisances. It was a most amazing thing. They took hold of his feet and would not let go. This was simply spontaneous affection coming from their hearts.' "

"Pretty good, huh?" Pugliese asked. "I think it shows the kind of power you've got over devotees."

"Do you think my American devotees have such love for their spiritual master?" Hansadutta asked.

"Of course, they do," Pugliese said. "You tell somebody to do something and they do it, no questions asked."

"But they don't love me," Hansadutta whined, tears forming in his eyes.

"How can you say that?" Pugliese asked, genuinely concerned. "You get obeisances everywhere you go. Your devotees worship you. How many cars did they give you last year? Three? Four?"

Hansadutta's head was lolling now, back and forth and from side to side, like a crazy puppet's.

"I am not loved!" he shouted. "No. No. Not as Prabhupada was loved!"

A stewardess rushed up to his seat.

"Sir, please," she said. "You'll have to keep it down a little. People are sleeping."

"Is there spontaneous affection for me?" Hansadutta demanded. He didn't wait for a response.

"No!" he cried, shouting again. "No, there isn't. It's all give-and-take. I take you on trips so you give me love."

Devotees had come over to surround the guru.

"Chant," one said. "Start chanting. That'll calm him. It always does when he gets like this."

"No!" Hansadutta screamed. "There is no spontaneous affection. You're plotting against me. Yes, you are—every one of you. You're all jealous, jealous that Prabhupada chose me. *Me*. Hansadutta."

"Nobody's jealous," Pugliese soothed. "All we want is to serve you."

"Maya!" Hansadutta shouted, struggling to his feet.

"Sir, please stay seated," the stewardess said. "The captain has turned on the seat-belt sign."

"Woman," Hansadutta hissed, pushing her out of his way. "Woman. You're in maya. All women are in maya. Women seduced me. They made me break my vows. What am I without vows? Nothing!"

The stewardess raced back into the coach section to summon help. The airplane hit an air pocket and took a hard dip. Hansadutta slammed into the seat across the aisle. He picked up a small bottle of red wine and threw it against a window.

"The pilot is against me!" Hansadutta yelled. "We're going to crash. You'll do anything—even sacrifice yourselves—to get rid of me!"

The stewardess led two tense-looking stewards into the first-class cabin. Hansadutta saw them and leaped up onto an empty seat.

"Try to throw me off this plane!" he screamed. "Just try it!"

The stewards went for him. Hansadutta eluded them, jumping from seat to seat. In each row, he reached up and tore down the oxygen masks. The devotees didn't know whether to go for the stewards or grab their spiritual master. They ended up watching while the stewards tackled Hansadutta and wrestled him into a seat.

"I am not ready for another body!" he yelled. "I am not ready for another body!"

When the 747 landed at Oakland Airport, every devotee in the Berkeley temple was there, eager to see their spiritual master get off the plane. Jiva wanted to report how much money the stripped-down version of the record scam was bringing in. Sandy was anxious to see if things would be the same between them as they were before Hansadutta left for Asia. They were all so wrapped up in their thoughts, they hardly noticed the two Oakland police officers standing near the jetway.

The plane landed and two stewards ran down the jetway and whispered to the cops. The cops followed the stewards back to the plane. The devotees looked at each other, puzzled.

The next thing they knew, the cops returned leading

the handcuffed Hansadutta down the jetway. The devotees automatically started their kirtan. Then they realized
what they were seeing. They stopped chanting to stare.

"Hare Krishna!" somebody said to Hansadutta.

The holy gangster/carefree prankster was too wrecked
to answer.

Krishna's Arsenal

Joe Sanchez, a ten-year veteran of the Berkeley Police Department, was cruising Telegraph Avenue in his patrol car. In the late sixties, when Berkeley was really wild and crazy, Sanchez was flying missions over Vietnam. But as he drove past the mural that marked the site of the battle for People's Park, Sanchez was thinking that Berkeley hadn't changed.

Here it was in 1979, and Telegraph Avenue was still lined with tarot-card readers, jewelry makers, and vendors hawking crystals and tie-dyed T-shirts. The street was also full of human flotsam: longhairs ranting at invisible demons; barefoot, greasy-haired girls; would-be musicians dragging around guitars.

The scene didn't bother Sanchez. People could do whatever they wanted, as long as they didn't break the law. But if they did, they'd have to deal with him, and that could be unpleasant. Sanchez was one tough cop. His fellow officers referred to the area of the city he patrolled as "The Wall of Sanchez."

Sanchez turned off Telegraph and rolled past the blue-and-white Hare Krishna temple at 2334 Stuart Street. Even the religions that had sprung up in the sixties were still here, he noted. He stopped his cruiser to let a tall man with a military-style haircut cross the street. Well, maybe some things had changed. Sanchez watched the guy walk into the temple. At least they weren't wearing robes anymore. And they weren't dancing in the street and stopping traffic like they used to.

Sanchez glanced at his watch. It was almost time for his break. He was thirty pounds overweight. For months, he'd been promising his wife he'd go on a diet. But postponing its start by one more day wouldn't hurt. He thought maybe he'd cruise over to Top Dog and get himself a couple of smoked bratwursts. He was about to radio in, when he saw a tan Dodge van with Washington license plates shoot through the stop sign.

Sanchez hit his lights and went after the van. This section of Berkeley was plagued with petty crime—punks doing B and Es, kids taking joyrides, and dopers snatching purses. If you didn't stay on top of everything that moved, the vermin would swarm over decent citizens like cockroaches taking over a kitchen.

"What's the problem, Officer?" the driver, Michael Pugliese, asked as he handed Sanchez his license.

Sanchez looked him over. He was a good-looking kid with thick black hair that hung over his blue eyes.

"The problem," Sanchez said, whipping out his ticket book, "is that you ran that stop sign back there. This is a residential area. What if kids on their way home from school—"

"You got the badge and the gun," Pugliese interrupted. "That means you can stop me. That doesn't mean you can give me a lecture. Just write the damn ticket."

"Get your registration and get out," Sanchez snapped, ready to give the wise-guy punk as hard a time as he could.

The kid dug through the glove compartment and opened the door. "Here you you go, Officer," he said, pronouncing it "Off-fiss-sir." "Let's see how fast you can write me up."

Sanchez studied the license.

"You got a problem," he said. "This has expired."

Pugliese's bravado disappeared.

"You're kidding," he said. "Let me see."

Sanchez handed it to the kid.

"Oh, yeah," he said, "I forgot. I got a new one."

Sanchez took the license back, and the kid reached for his wallet and rifled through the plastic cards. When he pulled out a Washington driver's license, Sanchez caught a glimpse of a California license.

"Let me see that other license," Sanchez said as the kid handed him the Washington license.

"I don't have to show you that," the kid said.

"You'll show it to me here, or you'll show it to me down at the station," Sanchez said in his no-bullshit street voice.

The kid frowned and pulled out the license.

"Stay here," Sanchez said and went back to his cruiser. He laid the licenses out on the front seat. The expired license was issued to Michael Ralph Pugliese, born 3–13–55, five feet nine inches tall, 150 pounds, brown hair, blue eyes. The Washington license was issued to Dino Bhandu, same birthdate, same physical description. The second California license was issued to Lance Presley, same birthdate, same physical description. The two California licenses had the same address, 2334 Stuart, the Hare Krishna temple.

Sanchez radioed in the three licenses for a records check and then walked back to the kid.

"So, who the hell are you, my friend?" Sanchez asked.

"Depends on the time and the place and who wants to know," Pugliese/Bhandu/Presley answered.

"I've been working nothing but Krishnas for almost a year, and I still have no idea who some of them are," Joe Sanchez was saying into the phone. "They go up to Washington state and get their names changed. Apparently, all you have to do up there is appear in court. Even Hansadutta, the guru, has done it. He calls himself Jack London now. Can you believe that?"

"At thia point, I'll believe anything," said Sergeant Tom Westfall. "I like the name Dino Bhandu the best. It's got a lounge-lizard feel to it."

Westfall had been the Krishna cop in West Virginia for so long, he had developed a sense of humor about the movement. Sanchez had not. He was overwhelmed by what he was turning up.

"I think that guy Michael Ralph Pugliese aka Dino Bhandu aka Lance Presley may be wanted for jewelry-store robberies in Japan," Sanchez said.

"I've never heard of him," Westfall said. "He probably isn't part of Kirtananda's empire."

"I'm telling you, Tom, the Berkeley temple is like a halfway house masquerading as a church," Sanchez continued. "The whole congregation has a criminal record. Every time I run one these devotees through the computer it comes back with heavy-duty paper. I've arrested fifteen devotees in the last year and not one of them on penny-ante charges. I'm talking assault, armed robbery. A couple turned out to be German nationals wanted by Interpol."

Sanchez put an elbow on his desk and rested his head on the palm of his hand.

"The money that pours into that temple is unbelievable," he continued. "I'd say at least ten thousand dollars a week goes right to Hansadutta. I know what they're doing and I'm pulling my hair out because I can't get anybody interested. I've talked to the FBI about what's going on. I laid the whole sankirtan scam out for the IRS. I made the case for them. All they had to do was move on it. And do you know what happened? I got a form letter from them, thanking me for my interest. I'm just a local cop, Tom. I can't deal with these people by myself. I'll get a warrant to arrest somebody on a Tuesday, and on Wednesday he's in the Philippines."

"Me too," Westfall said sympathetically. "I got guns, drugs, women getting beaten up, a half-dozen fundraising scams going on at once, and I can't get the feds to shake a leg."

Sanchez and Westfall spent the next half hour exchanging information.

"Keep a list of everybody you meet, Joe," Westfall said just before they hung up. "Kirtanananda and Hansadutta are old friends. "My guess is, I'll find some of your guys out here and you'll find some of mine back there."

Hansadutta stepped out of the trailer that was set aside for him at the Mount Kailasa farm. It was early morning and the thick Pacific fog was rolling across the hills, giving the farm an eerie, otherworldly beauty. Hansadutta walked down to the World War II jeep only he was permitted to drive and put a .357 magnum on the seat beside him. Then he went charging up the road past the duck pond and the white barn with Hare Krsna Farm painted on the roof in huge red letters. The peculiar spelling of Krishna was due to believers' reluctance to spell the god's name in full.

The 480-acre farm is located at the top of the Maycamas Mountains, which separate the northern portion of California's wine country from the Pacific Ocean. It has meadows and ponds, deep woods, and grassy bluffs. Hansadutta liked to ride around and picture the karmi attack that was sure to come any day now. If they built a bunker up on that bluff, three devotees with machine guns could seal off the dirt road that wound out to Highway 175, he thought. If they laid a minefield along that row of fir trees to the north, karmi foot soldiers would be in for one hell of a nasty surprise.

Hansadutta grinned as he drove back to the farmhouse and its makeshift temple. If anything was more fun than real-life cops and robbers, it was real-life war. He walked into the temple and the devotees prostrated themselves to offer obeisances. Without looking at them, he walked up to his vyasasana and sat down.

"We are in the age of Kali-*yuga*," Hansadutta began. His words were slightly slurred, the aftereffects of last night's Percodan. "Kali is the worst stage of the four yugas, the age of war and death, depravity and ignorance. It has lasted five thousand years, four hundred and twenty-eight thousand years remain."

Hansadutta looked at his devotees. Their faces were upturned; all eyes were on him as they drank in every word. This was as it should be.

"Krishna sent Prabhupada to this planet to lead us out to Kali-yuga," Hansadutta continued. "But only a few were enlightened enough to recognize who he was and follow him."

Hansadutta paused. He glanced over the devotees, confirming that they were among the chosen few.

"We used to think the karmis would join us," he resumed. "Now we know how naïve we were. We underestimated karmi depravity. They are the spiritual descendants of men who rode with Genghis Khan. They live to kill and rape."

Hansadutta nodded at a devotee, who handed him a silver cup filled with spring water. He drained it and handed it back to the devotee.

"Genghis Khan had horses and swords. The karmis have missiles armed with nuclear weapons. It is only a matter of time before they blow themselves off this planet. That is their nature. That is their destiny.

"It is Krishna's mercy that we will survive this holocaust. That is why he led us to this secluded place high in the hills. But the karmis will come for us. We have everything they need: food, water, shelter, and clothing. Most of all, we have Krishna. They hate us most of all for that. We will have everything; the karmis, nothing.

"We must continue with the preparations we have been making for the struggle that lies ahead. Go now. I will join you later."

Vladimir Vassilievich, aka Vladimir Panasenko, or Vipra, stood up and stretched; then he began walking the quarter mile up the dirt road to his shop in the barn. A youngish-looking Ukrainian with a round head, large nose, and skinny arms, Vipra liked to think of himself as the keeper of the royal tool box. He was a superb mechanic who, by himself, kept the temple's fleet of vans running. He was also an excellent gunsmith, who could take apart, clean, and reassemble an automatic rifle in minutes with his eyes closed. It was Vipra who kept Mount Kailasa's arsenal well oiled.

Vipra kept his past a secret. Only a few devotees knew that he had been a sports-car mechanic and a part-time photographer before he joined the Krishnas in 1974. He had had a teenage wife and a 1960 short-wheelbase Ferrari Berlinetta. He had been certain the world could offer him no more. Then he discovered the Krishnas. He read their books and decided that Prabhupada was absolutely right.

"When you find the truth, you must surrender," he announced to his wife.

She went back home to her parents and filed for divorce. Vipra moved into the Berkeley temple and signed his Ferrari over to the temple president. The temple president immediately sold it for $25,000, quit the movement, and moved in with his girlfriend. He used the money gained from selling the Ferrari to enter law school.

Vipra arrived at his barn, walked into his workshop, and snapped on the lights. He thought of his ex-wife and wondered where she was and what she was doing. He missed her and often thought of her—almost as often as he thought about his Ferrari. No matter how hard he tried to concentrate on Krishna, the car kept creeping back into his mind. He closed his eyes and remembered the excitement. He could feel the adrenaline rush he used to get, racing the blood-red car through the turns on Highway 1 in Big Sur. The car had been appreciating in value faster than a Van Gogh painting. The last one like it to go on sale in America had fetched $650,000.

Vipra shook his head and walked over to the workbench. He was rebuilding the transmission of a 1975 Mercedes, one of the cars that devotees had given to Hansadutta, when the gunfire erupted. That wasn't unusual. Taking target practice by shooting at human silhouette targets was part of the daily routine for most devotees. Vipra listened and picked out the sounds of an HK-91 assault rifle, a nine-millimeter, a .357 magnum, and a .45 long Colt.

Then he went back to work. The gunfire continued for half an hour and then stopped. Vipra looked up from his work bench and listened for a minute.

"That's funny," he said aloud. "They usually shoot all morning."

An hour later, one of the sankirtan van drivers walked into the workshop.

"Bad news, Vipra," the driver said. "A five-year-old boy got shot."

Vipra dropped a socket wrench and looked up at him. "Where? How?"

"He got hit in the hand. They took him to a hospital over in Lakeport."

"How'd it happen?"

"I didn't see it," the driver said.

"Well, what did you hear?" Vassilievich asked impatiently.

"I heard what Hansadutta said."

"And what'd he say?"

"When the police come, Spencer will say he did it."

Vassilievich nodded. Spencer Lynn Joy was the acting president of Mount Kailasa.

"Spencer was cleaning a gun in one of the trailers. The gun somehow went off. The bullet went through the wall of the trailer and hit the boy in the hand."

Vassilievich picked up a rag and wiped off his hands.

"What really happened?" he asked.

"What happened is what Hansadutta said happened," the van driver said. "He's the guru, he knows best."

"Go get me some prasadam," Vipra said. "I want to keep working."

What Vipra really wanted to do was think. He sat down on the rear bumper of the Mercedes and tried to picture the accident. It wasn't hard.

He knew there could hardly be a worse cliché than the story about the gun going off while being cleaned. The first thing you did in the cleaning process was disable the firearm. Second, the chance that a kid could "accidentally" get hit in the hand defied all probability. Mathematics said it almost couldn't happen. The farm was huge. Vipra had often sat in the meadow outside his workshop for half an hour before anybody walked by.

Vipra also had often seen Hansadutta shoot in the direction of devotees. It was horseplay to him, like boxers sparring. The kid probably had his arm outstretched, holding a target for a supposedly infallible guru who was a supposedly infallible marksman. Vipra wondered if he should relate his doubts to somebody. He considered it for a couple of days.

But by then it was too late.

The boy and his mother were gone, bundled onto a plane bound for India and one of the temples Hansadutta controlled there.

Bill Benedict attended Mangal-aratik on the morning of February 2, 1980, just as he did every morning. As he left the temple, he glanced at the enlarged photograph of a Berkeley cop named Joe Sanchez that was hanging on a wall above the pay phone.

Beware: This man hates you! a sign under the photograph said. Benedict shook his head. If he had anything to say about it, the picture wouldn't be there. But he didn't. It was Hansadutta's temple, not his.

Benedict, a black-haired, brown-eyed, thirty-nine-year-old devotee, was one of the Krishna heavyweights who had been left off the GBC. He had founded the San Diego temple in the late sixties and was president of the Berkeley temple in the midseventies. With Jayatirtha, James Immel, he had started Balarama's Enterprises, a flourishing Krishna business that wholesaled incense and scented oils.

Benedict walked a block from the temple down Stuart Street, where he had parked his car. As he approached it, he noticed the driver's door was ajar. A sinking feeling came over him. He distinctly remembered having locked it.

He ran to the car and looked on the backseat. Sure enough, his aluminum Haliburton briefcase was gone. The briefcase contained three checkbooks, a twelve-hundred-dollar round-trip Pan Am ticket to India, and seven credit cards. Benedict returned to the temple and called the Berkeley police. Who but Joe Sanchez should arrive at the scene to take the report.

Two weeks later, Joe Sanchez called Benedict at home and asked him to come to Berkeley police station.

"We've got some leads," Sanchez said after they sat down in a small room detectives used to interview suspects. "People have used your checks and credit cards to purchase goods all over the place. It's the weirdest collection of stuff you've ever seen."

Sanchez opened a folder and read from a list typed on a piece of yellow legal paper: bolts of silk and velvet, horse saddles, cameras, ladies' sportswear, farming equipment, thirty-eight cases of black and white floor tiles, sewing machines, knives. Sanchez paused and looked at Benedict.

"And nine guns," he said. "Nine guns."

Benedict shook his head in dismay. "Who'd want all that stuff?"

"I can't figure it," Sanchez said. "We estimate that about a dozen businesses have been bilked out of a total of eleven thousand, four hundred fifty dollars' worth of merchandise."

"Any idea who the thieves are?" Benedict asked.

"Not yet. That's why we asked you to come in."

"Me? Why?" Benedict asked.

"We've done a lot of legwork," Sanchez said, paging through the file. ' 'We've interviewed clerks at Sears, J. C. Penney, Emporium Capwell, and a couple of gun stores. The same two men bought all this stuff."

Benedict was disturbed. "From what you're telling me, I think devotees might have ripped me off," he said to Sanchez.

"What do you mean?" Sanchez asked.

"I can't be sure. Give me a little time. I'll check it out."

"OK, but don't tell the people at the temple what you're up to."

Benedict went up to Mount Kailasa, parked beside the farmhouse, and walked into the makeshift temple.

Benedict was shocked. For a second he thought he might faint. The temple wasn't makeshift anymore. The floor had been covered with brand-new black and white tiles. Hadn't Sanchez told him thirty-eight cases of black and white tiles were bought with one of his forged checks?

Benedict glanced at the deities, then hurried to the altar to take a closer look. Radha and Krishna were both dressed in lavish new clothes made of silk and velvet. Sanchez had told him about rolls of silk and velvet purchased with one of his forged checks at the Fabric Center in Sacramento. The deities' new apparel also explained the sewing machines that had been bought in a store near the Fabric Center, with another forged check.

The next day, a Saturday, Sanchez waited all day for Benedict's call. It didn't come. On Sunday morning Sanchez finally called his home. Benedict's wife answered.

"He went to the farm, walked into the temple and

found the tiles!" she said. "And not only the tiles—one of the sewing machines!"

"Why didn't he call me?" Sanchez asked.

"He went to the Berkeley temple instead. He's blabbing it all over the place. I'm really scared. People in the temple are trying to get him to cover up what he's found out."

Sanchez wasted no time. He jumped in his car and started combing the streets of Berkeley for Benedict's car. He found it parked on Oregon Street. When he spotted Benedict, Sanchez jumped out and motioned for Benedict to walk back to him. Then, Sanchez opened the passenger door and pointed to the front seat.

"I found something out," Sanchez said as he got in the car.

"What's that?" Benedict asked.

"Your wife's got all the brains in your family."

"What're you talkin' about?"

"I've been trying to get hold of you," Sanchez said. "You won't return my calls and I can't find you anywhere. Today your wife tells me you've been running around the temple telling everybody how you got ripped off. She's afraid those guys are going to blow you away. You know something? She could be right."

Benedict kept looking at his shoes. He didn't say a thing.

"Let me ask you a question," Sanchez said. "Your wife says Hansadutta told you he was going to take care of things for you. Are the devotees who ripped you off still in the temple?"

Benedict nodded.

"Shouldn't that tell you something?" Sanchez asked.

Benedict was silent. Finally he looked at Sanchez.

"What do you want to know?" he asked.

"Tell me what you told Hansadutta," Sanchez said.

Benedict told him about the stolen goods he had discovered at the farm. He also told him that Hansadutta was preaching that Armageddon was at hand, and that the Krishnas had assembled an arsenal to prepare for it.

Two days later, Berkeley police and deputies from the Mendocino and Lake County sheriff's departments raided the Mount Kailasa farm. They were almost too late. The cover-up had begun as soon as Benedict left Hansadutta's office.

"We've been expecting you," a devotee told Sanchez. "The regular residents split yesterday. We're all new devotees."

"We have a warrant to search the farm," Sanchez said.

"Help yourself," the devotee replied. "We don't know anything. We just got here ourselves."

Whoever cleaned out the farm wasn't as thorough as the police. They found a grenade launcher, three rifles, four riot-type, short-barrel shotguns, fifteen hundred rounds of ammunition for an HK-91 assault rifle, boxes of ammunition for a nine-millimeter, a .357 magnum, and a .45 long Colt, plus stacks of human silhouette targets. The police also found a Dodge van, welding equipment, chain saws, and an electric typewriter that had been stolen from a Mendocino County farm. A devotee was using the typewriter to write a book about Hansadutta. Along with the manuscript, police found a pamphlet on how to invest in fine diamonds and a manuscript entitled "Rough Plan for Temple and Fortress Combo."

Despite the haul, Sanchez went back to Berkeley depressed. From what Benedict had told him, the raiders had found nothing more than the remnants. There should have been enough weapons on the farm to arm a couple of Marine platoons. The first thing he did when he got home that night was call William Benedict. Later that night, he met with one of the informants he had painstakingly developed in the Berkeley temple.

The informant told Sanchez that Pugliese/Bhandu/Presley was on his way to Hong Kong. Hartwig Heinrich Dalldorf and Peter Kaufmann, two German nationals who had been arrested with Hansadutta when the German police raided the ISKCON castle outside Frankfurt, had also hit the road. Dalldorf was second in command at Mount Kailasa and was in charge of the weapons arsenal. Kaufmann was the farm's schoolteacher and weapons instructor.

The informant also told Sanchez that the day before

the police raid, Vladimir Vassilievich, Vipra, and another devotee had hauled away fifty sticks of stolen dynamite. They'd stuffed as many of the guns and as much of the merchandise purchased with Benedict's checks and credit cards as they could into vans. Now the stuff was untraceable, hidden somewhere in Berkeley.

It didn't take Sanchez long to pick up Vipra and haul him down to the station.

"I did take those things off the farm," Vipra soon admitted. He was sitting in the same small room Sanchez had used to interview William Benedict, as calm as an insurance salesman explaining a policy.

"Removing stolen property is serious business," Sanchez said. "You could be looking at some serious charges here."

"I didn't take it to hide it," Vipra explained in a monotone. "I brought it down here to give to you. Just tell me where you want it and I'll bring it to you."

"You did *what?*" Sanchez cried.

Vipra smiled. "This has been very good for us. Some bad people have joined the movement lately and now they're gone. Besides, Benedict says that if everything is returned, he'll drop the charges."

Sanchez shook his head.

"You know something?" he told Vipra. "You people are unbelievable."

Three weeks after the raid, Charles E. Crane, the Berkeley Police Department inspector who was helping Sanchez with the Krishna cases, received a phone call from a police officer in El Cerrito, a small community north of Berkeley. Residents near a garage at the corner of San Pablo Avenue and Alameda Street had been calling to report gunshots late at night. An El Cerrito police officer had run a check and found that the garage was the headquarters of Sgt. Pepper's Guns, a business owned by Ronald Roy Walters. Walters had three federal firearms licenses. His address was 2334 Stuart Street, the Hare Krishna temple.

"Ronald Roy Walters? That's Darpada," Sanchez said when Crane called him. "We've looked at him for everything, from passport fraud to auto theft. But so far we can't get anything to stick."

The cops obtained a warrant and hit Sgt. Pepper's Guns a few nights later. This time they struck paydirt. They found fifty thousand copper-jacketed lead bullets for 7.65 Mauser semiautomatic rifles; sixty thousand empty brass cartridges for 7.62 automatic rifles; nine pounds of smokeless powder; dies for bullets for a .44 magnum; a .380 automatic, a nine-millimeter, a .30-.30, and a .243 Winchester.

"How's this for spiritual literature?" Sanchez asked his fellow searchers. He was going through a filing cabinet in the rear of the building. The cops looked up and gathered around.

"Here's a two-volume edition of Hitler's *Mein Kampf,* Sanchez said, handing it to an officer. "Here's a book called *Wiretapping, Tailing, Optical and Electronic Surveillance, Surreptitious Entry: How to Stop it or Do it Back.* And here's *The Protocols of the Elders of Zion.* It's an infamous anti-Semitic tract by some right-wing fanatic."

"You're under arrest," Sanchez said as he grabbed Dennis Lee Richardson aka Richard Tavares, a devotee who was on his way out of the Berkeley temple after the morning devotional service. Richardson was the devotee who had helped Vipra take the guns and stolen property out of Mount Kailasa.

"We ran a records check on you," Sanchez said after handcuffing Richardson and reading him his rights from a plastic card. "You're wanted for burglary and grand theft in Mendocino County."

Sanchez searched Richardson and found a receipt for a storage locker in Sacramento.

"What's in there?" Sanchez asked, fingering the receipt.

"Nothing much. Just a few candles and holy books," Richardson said.

Deputies from the Sacramento County sheriff's office were dispatched to search the locker. They found four rifles, four shotguns, four hundred rounds of live ammunition, and thousands of brass cartridges.

* * *

"We've got to rebuild our arsenal," Hansadutta said. He was lying on the couch in his office with his hand over his eyes. His head pounded as usual. Since the raid, he had been having more and more headaches and taking more and more Halcion, a sleeping medication he smuggled in from the Philippines.

"The cops are demons whose job is to make sure we can't defend ourselves when the apocalypse comes," Hansadutta continued. "I want a special weapon, one worthy of my position. Your duty is to make me that gun."

Vipra had long ago decided that Hansadutta was crazy. But he was divinely crazy. Nobody in ISKCON was publishing more of Prabhupada's books than Hansadutta. Nobody had more energy or was a better preacher. Vipra kept hoping that the good side of Hansadutta would eventually triumph over the evil. Now it was clear that it would never happen. The gun mania and the pill-popping were only getting worse. And now Hansadutta wanted this "special weapon."

Hansadutta wanted Vipra to build him a commando-style mini-mac 14 submachine gun with a silencer. A silenced machine gun is the ultimate intimidator. Imagine standing in line in a bank and turning around to find somebody holding one of those things.

Vipra knew why Hansadutta wanted the weapon. He and Jiva were planning to stick up Fort Ord, down the coast in Monterey, to heist the payroll. One of Jiva's longstanding ambitions was to rob an army payroll. Criminals, Vipra had quickly learned, have ambitions, just like everybody else.

Vipra vacillated. He believed in the movement, had given half his life to it. And although he knew Hansadutta was crazy, he had been a Krishna for too many years to betray a swami easily. On the other hand, he couldn't let Hansadutta do it. Robbing the Fort Ord payroll would finish Krishna Consciousness in America. Hansadutta had to be stopped, once and for all.

Again, Vipra's indecision led to paralysis. He decided he would do nothing, at least for the moment. He would go ahead and make the machine gun as ordered. Then he'd act. As soon as he gave it to Hansadutta, he would call Joe Sanchez and set the guru up. Perhaps getting busted for possessing an illegal weapon would knock some sense into the swami.

The day Vipra gave Hansadutta the brand-new mini-mac 14, the guru put it in the trunk of his Mercedes. Then he drove across Berkeley to show off his new toy to Jiva and the other members of his inner circle. Happy as a kid, he returned hours later to his white stucco home, not far from the Berkeley temple, and parked the Mercedes in his driveway.

Joe Sanchez was cruising his beat, following what had become his routine path. Down Telegraph, right on Stuart past the Hare Krishna temple, down a few more blocks, and on past Hansadutta's house. These days, Sanchez didn't feel comfortable unless he knew exactly where the guru was.

Sanchez drove past the house and noticed the car. He stopped and backed up. He looked at the black Mercedes parked in the driveway again. Sure enough, it had German license plates. Sanchez got out of the car and checked to see if a California Department of Motor Vehicles registration form was taped to the inside of the right front windshield, as required.

It wasn't.

"I could use a little help out here," Sanchez said to the dispatcher over the police radio. "There's an unregistered Mercedes parked in the driveway at my friend the guru's house."

When the cops opened the trunk, they found the silenced machine gun. They also discovered a Walther P-38, a nine-millimeter, and a Colt .45—all of which were loaded. There were also two military-style assault rifles with full clips, two .22 rifles, and eleven boxes of cartridges for a 7.62mm NATO.

Vipra was sitting in the office of the Berkeley temple president, who was talking on the phone to Ramesvara. Ramesvara was screaming into the phone so loudly, Vipra could hear his voice across the room.

"This is terrible, a complete disaster," Ramesvara was saying. "How do we explain an ISKCON guru having all those guns? Think how this makes us look."

As Ramesvara went on and on, Vipra listened. It was his fault Hansadutta had the weapon, he told himself. He had been going to set Hansadutta up; Sanchez just happened to get there before he could. Now Jiva had split for the Pacific Northwest, and Hansadutta was sitting there sweating. He couldn't let Hansadutta go to jail for this. It would destroy the movement. He had to protect Prabhupada's reputation.

"Give me the phone," Vipra said finally.

The temple president looked surprised and shook his head. Vipra insisted, gesturing for the phone. Finally, the temple president handed it to him.

"Don't worry about Hansadutta," Vipra told Ramesvara. "I'm going to solve the problem by taking the rap for the guns. It's my fault. I built the machine gun."

"You did *what!*" Ramesvara exploded.

"I built it," Vipra answered. "Like I said, I'll take the rap."

Vipra heard Ramesvara sigh in relief.

"You'll have to put some distance between yourself and the movement," the Los Angeles guru said. "We'll have to portray you as a fringe devotee. ISKCON won't be able to get you an attorney or anything."

"That's all right," Vipra said.

And then he smiled. He had made his bargain, his separate peace. Whatever happened in court, he was through, through with Hansadutta and through with Krishna Consciousness.

Hansadutta was lying on the couch in his office, watching the light flicker on the ceiling, when there was a knock on the door. A devotee stepped respectfully inside.

"Excuse me, Mahararja, I thought you should know: Jiva has been killed."

Hansadutta sat up. His head felt full of cotton.

"What did you say about Jiva?" he asked.

"He's dead," the devotee repeated.

"How? Tell me how it happened."

When Jiva, James Patrick Underwood, had left the Berkeley temple, he had gone to Washington state and hooked up with a criminal who specialized in armed robbery. They had started holding up gas stations, liquor stores, and pharmacies in Seattle all the way south to California. Outside of Visalia, a pretty little town on the eastern edge of the San Joaquin Valley, the two men got into an argument. Jiva's partner had shot him in the head and dumped his body in an irrigation ditch.

As Hansadutta listened to the story, his face was as blank as a mask. When it was over, he told the devotee to leave and lay back down on the couch.

It was just a matter of time, he told himself. He rolled over and tried to sleep.

There is one word that sums up everything: Contempt, Hansadutta thought as he took another hit from the bottle of ouzo. I have contempt for the devotees who are stupid enough to do anything I tell them to do. I have contempt for the women who let me use them to collect money, and who let me use their bodies for sex. I have contempt for ISKCON. Except for Kirtanananda, they're all worms. None of them has the balls to stand up to me.

He had a very special contempt for the Governing Body Commission. It had hemmed and hawed, debated, and argued about how to respond to the matter of the guns found in Hansadutta's car. At the annual meeting in Mayapur during February and March of 1981, the GBC had finally acted. It decided to suspend him and strip him of his guruship for one year.

His Divine Grace had been outraged. How could the GBC, mere mortals, tell him, a living representative of Krishna, that for the next twelve months, he could not be a guru? He talked it over with Tamal Krishna, who was sitting out a year's suspension for claiming that he alone was Prabhupada's true successor. Tamal and Hansadutta agreed that no one had the right to take away a position Krishna had conferred through Prabhupada.

The two suspended gurus hopped a train across the Ganges River to Navadwip, the small village where Sridhar, Prabhupada's aging godbrother, had his ashram. The old guru said exactly what Hansadutta and Tamal were hoping he would say: To remove men Prabhupada had appointed to be gurus was to question the authority of the spiritual master. Prabhupada was empowered by Krishna; how could he possibly have named the wrong people to succeed him?

Hansadutta and Tamal returned to Mayapur to proclaim that Sridhara had said they were right and the GBC was wrong. The GBC was in maya; it must correct its terrible error by immediately reinstating them both. The GBC held a meeting and capitulated. From that moment on, the eleven gurus, not the GBC, controlled ISKCON. From then on, the gurus knew that they could do anything they wanted without having to answer to any authority.

Hansadutta laughed at the memory.

"They're snails," he muttered as he gulped down more ouzo. "Slugs. Let's face it: any group that would put me back on the vyasasana has to be worthless."

Now he was getting down to what was really wrong. More than anything else, Hansadutta had complete and utter contempt for himself. He had started out determined to be Prabhupada's greatest devotee. And look how he had turned out. He'd broken his vow of sannyasa; he drank and took pills. He couldn't remember the last time he had chanted. He'd blown it.

"Hansadutta," he said to himself, "you're a fraud."

He decided he had to get out of his house and go for a ride. The blues were coming on so strong, he didn't know what he'd do if he stayed. It was a Sunday night in August 1984, and Berkeley was uncharacteristically hot. Maybe if he got out and drove around with the air-conditioning on, he'd feel better.

He got into his Bronco and drove aimlessly, up one street and down another. It only darkened his already black mood. Everything he saw—people walking down the streets eating ice-cream cones, standing in line at the movies, sitting and talking under the trees on the Berkeley campus—enraged him.

"Maya. It's all maya," Hansadutta snapped as he stopped for a light on San Pablo Avenue. "Look at these people.

They're all doing the same things and thinking the same things. And they all think they're special. They're all going nowhere. They'll be born again in new bodies and all this will repeat itself."

He was driving past McNevin Cadillac on San Pablo Avenue when he slammed on the brakes and pulled to the curb. Cadillac—the perfect symbol of American materialism. Big, fat, dumb cars for a big, fat, dumb country. Prabhupada had come and gone; his message had been ignored. Cadillac remained.

Hansadutta reached over and pulled a nine-millimeter Beretta out of the glove compartment. He rolled down the passenger window and fired thirty shots into the showroom, shattering the window and doing twelve thousand dollars' worth of damage. Then he floored the Bronco and roared away, laughing hysterically.

Ten minutes later, while every cop on duty in Berkeley was converging on McNevin Cadillac, Hansadutta pulled up in front of Ledger's Liquor Store on University Avenue. Demon Rum, he thought to himself. Prabhupada was so right to prohibit booze. Think how many people it has ruined. Think what it's done to me. He reloaded the Beretta and aimed it at the plate-glass window.

A clerk and two customers were inside the store. All at once, glass was breaking, bullets were whizzing over their heads, whiskey bottles were popping. The three people inside hit the floor.

When the shooting stopped, the clerk got up in time to see a Ford Bronco pull away from the curb. He ran to a phone and called the cops.

The Berkeley police stopped the Bronco within a few blocks of the liquor store. Hansadutta staggered out and was immediately handcuffed. In the Bronco, the cops found the nine-millimeter Beretta, a Winchester twelve-gauge shotgun, an H and R fully automatic nine-millimeter machine pistol, a .22 caliber Colt semiautomatic pistol, and box after box of ammunition.

When Hansadutta obeyed their order to empty his pockets, the cops were amazed. He pulled out roll after roll of tightly wound fifty-dollar bills held together with thick rubber bands. The cops counted it right there on the street. Hansadutta had stuffed $8,627 into his pants before he decided to go out for a ride.

"Hansadutta! So good to hear your voice! Where are you calling from?" Kirtanananda asked.

"The Haight. Remember the Haight? I'm in a drug program at the Haight Ashbury Free Medical Clinic. It's going great."

"That's wonderful news," Kirtanananda said. "Are you coming back to the movement?"

"That's what I'm calling about," Hansadutta said. "Now that I'm excommunicated, the GBC has given the Berkeley temple to Atreya Rishi. You know Atreya?"

"Of course," Kirtanananda replied. "For years. He's a graduate of Harvard Business School. He was the head of the Arthur Young accounting firm office in Tehran until Khomeini threw him out."

"Right, that's the guy," Hansadutta said. "I don't want him to have the temple. If I can't have it, you should have it."

"I see," Kirtanananda said. "But how can I get it?"

"Easy," Hansadutta said. "The devotees are still loyal to me. I swear, I could sit on the vyasasana and drink wine and smoke a cigar and they'd still be loyal to me."

"And?" Kirtanananda asked.

"And all I have to do is tell them to surrender to you and they will. All the devotees I appointed to the temple board of directors are still in place. I'll have them vote the temple over to you and that'll be that."

"And I could name you temple president and you would have your vyasasana back!"

"Kirtanananda, you always catch on so quick," Hansadutta said with genuine admiration.

"This is all very interesting," Kirtanananda said. "Here's what I propose: New Vrindaban is the perfect place to recuperate from a bout with chemicals. Why don't you come out here when you've finished your program, and we'll talk through all of this."

"I'll do it," Hansadutta said. "We'll be together again. It'll be just like the old days in New York."

Sex, Pigs, and Husbands

"You're back, Hayagriva," Kirtanananda said one cold morning in December 1978.

"So it appears," Howard Wheeler replied.

Wheeler was sprawled on the couch of the small camper reserved exclusively for him in New Vrindaban. Two young Mexican men were sitting on plastic-covered, high-backed chairs at the small counter that separated the kitchen from the living area.

"It pains me to see how low you've sunk." Kirtanananda said, smiling.

"You've met my friends?" Wheeler asked.

One of the Mexicans, a tall, skinny kid, got up, stuck out his hand, and walked toward Kirtanananda. The other reached out and pinched his ass as he passed by. The tall Mexican playfully slapped his hand away.

Kirtanananda smiled. "I assume these are close friends?"

"Oh, yes, very close," Wheeler said. "Very close indeed."

"You're always bringing friends back from Mexico," Kirtanananda said.

"Well, I seem to make a lot of friends." Wheeler grinned. "And you're chronically in need of laborers for the palace. That's the only reason I bring them back to this hole in the wall."

"I'm glad you're so dedicated," Kirtanananda laughed. "How long do you plan to stay?"

"Who knows?" Wheeler said. "Probably until I get tired of my friends and have to go back to Mexico to make some new ones."

"Well, I'm glad you're back," Kirtanananda said. "Noth-

269

ing picks me up like having my oldest and closest friend around."

Returning to his Landcruiser, Kirtanananda wondered how long Wheeler could keep going before he burned himself out. For years, Wheeler had been traveling back and forth between New Vrindaban and a house the commune owned in Ensenada, Mexico. He was supposed to be editing Prabhupada's books and working on *The Hare Krishna Explosion,* a history of the movement's early years. He did do some work. But mostly he drank, did drugs, and chased boys.

Wheeler had been through several Krishna wives. His first, Cheryl, had divorced him and gone to court to try to get custody of their boy, Devin, whose Krishna names were Dharmaraja, or Samba. She had failed. Samba had been spirited away to Mexico. Only when Cheryl gave up was the boy allowed to return to the commune. There was no way anyone but Kirtanananda was going to get Samba.

The guru always kept Samba at his side. The boy sat on Kirtanananda's lap as he drove the Landcruiser around the commune. He ate off Kirtanananda's plate. He even slept with Kirtanananda. Several years before, Kirtanananda had sent Samba to a guru kula in India, a requirement for all Krishna children. A few weeks after Samba had left, Kirtanananda's housecleaner walked into his quarters and found him weeping.

"What's the matter?" she cried, rushing to her master's side.

"I . . . miss . . . Samba," Kirtanananda sobbed. "I miss him so much."

Kirtanananda couldn't bear the separation. He became morose. He moped. Finally he booked a reservation and flew to India. A few days later, he returned—with Samba, of course.

Kirtanananda got in the Landcruiser and drove across the commune. A female devotee had arrived from London the day before and he had to welcome her. He didn't really want to meet her. He hated dealing with women. Before his weekly *darshan,* or meeting, with female disciples, Kirtanananda would always tell his male devotees, "Get out the incense, boys, it's fish night."

When a man came to him and told him he was having problems with his wife, the guru's advice usually boiled down to two words: "Hit her."

"Three things are better when you beat them: your drum, your dog, and your wife," he liked to say. That is exactly what many men at New Vrindaban did.

Still, there were times when it paid to be nice to women, and this was one of them. Kirtanananda had been told the new arrival was young and pretty. A pretty young devotee was a valuable commodity. She could do sankirtan. Or he could marry her off to some man he needed to keep happy.

"You've arrived; how splendid!" Kirtanananda said when he met the new arrival, Jane Bryant. "So tell me, what do you think of us so far?"

"It's so beautiful, I can't get over it," Jane said. "I've lived in cities all my life and have never seen hills like these. And the palace. I don't think I've ever felt so spiritual as I did yesterday when I walked in for the first time. And it's not even done yet!"

"That's as it should be, for the palace is both a labor of love and a triumph of faith," Kirtanananda said proudly. "Do you know, it was built by devotees working without blueprints. Can you imagine that? It was the first time most of them did any construction. It's magnificent, don't you think?"

"Overwhelming," Jane said meekly.

"We spare no expense to honor our master, Prabhupada," Kirtanananda said. "There's over two hundred tons of white Italian and blue Canadian marble in the palace. The onyx is from Iran; the crystal chandeliers come all the way from Austria. That gold leaf you see on the roof contains more than four pounds of twenty-four-karat gold."

"It looks like a fairy princess waved her wand and the palace magically appeared," Jane said. "I'd heard it was beautiful, but I never imagined this. I'm so glad I decided to come here."

"How did you come to New Vrindaban?" Kirtanananda asked.

"My husband, Sulocana, sent me and my little boy, Rinnian," Jane said. "He tells everyone you are Prabhupada's only bona fide successor. He's in India now, buying things for a jewelry business. He's going to start it when he joins us here."

"They tell me another little person is going to join you."

Jane smiled.

"I'm pregnant," she admitted, looking at the ground. "I found out just before we left England. The second one is supposed to be easier, but I seem to be getting just as sick as I did with Rinnian. But please don't let my condition interfere with my service."

Kirtanananda smiled.

"We'll find some service that's suitable to your condition," he said.

Jane was confused. Her shoulders slumped and she looked at the ground.

"Sulocana's told me that over and over," she said quietly. "He says a husband is his wife's guru. She can only be initiated by someone he chooses. That way, there's spiritual consistency. The husband and wife both follow the same guru."

"Maya," Kirtanananda snapped. "He's in maya. Your husband is of no consequence. Your children are of no consequence. They are bonds that bind you to the material plane. That's why we put our children in the nursery as soon as possible. We must shatter these bonds. You must submit to Krishna."

Kirtanananda paused. Thinking he was finished, Jane looked up. She was going to answer, but was hushed by the guru's fiery look. He stepped forward until they were almost touching and stared deep into her eyes.

"I am the eternal man in your life," he said. "I am your guide on the eternal journey to Krishna. How can another man, any man, even your husband, matter, when you have entered into an eternal relationship with your spiritual master?"

Kirtanananda paused again. Jane was speechless, her eyes wide with wonder.

"Take initiation," Kirtanananda ordered. "Now. It is time."

For the next two weeks, Kirtanananda was extremely solicitous. He managed to speak to Jane every other day, at least. He asked her how she liked the worship services. He gave her some pamphlets and paperbacks he had written and made a point of following up. Had she read them? What did she think of them? Had they deepened her understanding of Krishna Consciousness? Did she have any questions he could answer? Did she need anything?

Jane was flattered. She was being treated better by the most powerful guru in all of Krishna Consciousness than by her own husband.

Kirtanananda popped the question at the beginning of Jane's third week in New Vrindaban.

"You seem very devout," he told Jane. "Why don't you take initiation from me?"

"Oh, I'd love to, I absolutely would!" Jane cooed. "I'll write Sulocana right away and ask his permission."

"What?" Kirtanananda asked.

"My husband, Sulocana. I'll write him for permission," Jane said, thinking that the guru had forgotten Bryant's name.

"Why do that?" Kirtanananda said, working to suppress his irritation.

Jane blushed. "I can't get initiated without his permission. It isn't done."

"You question me?" Kirtanananda asked, his voice dropping to a whisper.

Jane was initiated by Kirtanananda three days later. She became Jamuna; Rinnian was renamed Krishna das, Krishna's servant. The next day, she started her service. She split her time between the commune's glass workshop and its nursery.

Steven Hebel, Swarup, bounded up the rickety steps that led to the loft above the New Vrindaban cow barn. Tufts of old straw stuck out of the cracks like dried-up weeds, and manure was ground into every board of the wooden structure. The air was thick with the smell of stale urine and cow dung.

How can they keep kids here? Hebel wondered as he stumbled along the dim corridor. I know these Vrindaban devotees are into austerity, but there's got to be a better place for kids than a cattle barn full of cow shit.

Hebel had flown to Pittsburgh from Los Angeles late the previous night. It was February 1979, and it had been almost a year since he had seen Scott, his four-year-old son, who was living in New Vrindaban. But now he was overcome by foreboding. He stopped in front of a dilapidated door and stared at the hand-scrawled sign.

Nursery, it said.

Inside, he heard kids crying. He opened the door. He looked into the kindergarten and froze in his tracks. The room stunk of excrement, vomit, and urine, tinged with eye-stinging ammonia. The floor was littered with soiled diapers.

There were fifteen to twenty children crowded in the small room. Some were lying in battered cribs, screaming themselves blue. Others sat in the filth on the floor, playing with a battered doll or a broken toy car or an old diaper. A pregnant woman, holding a shrieking baby under one arm, was dashing around trying to see to everything at once. She snatched a dirty diaper out of the mouth of a little boy on one side of the room. Then she rushed back to pick up a bottle lying on the floor. Then she separated two toddlers fighting in the corner.

"Hare Krishna," Jane Bryant said, barely pausing from her frantic activity when she spotted Hebel. "Can I help you?"

"I just moved here. I came to see my son, Scott," Hebel said.

Jane waved him into the room and led him to the crib where Scott was sleeping amid the chaos.

"But look at his stomach!" Hebel cried as soon as he saw the boy. "It's all bloated. He looks like he's starving!"

"It's not that," Jane said impatiently. "Don't worry, he's getting plenty to eat. He's just got some kind of a parasite. A lot of children have it. Just look around—see!"

Hebel looked at the other children and found Jane was right.

"What is it?" he asked.

"Kirtanananda says it's not serious," Jane replied unconcerned. "I just give them some medicine and it goes away after a while."

Hebel wasn't reassured. He patted his sleeping son's head, pecked him on the forehead, and left at once to look for Kirtanananda, whom he had known since the movement's first days in New York City. He found the swami supervising the last minute touches to the Palace of Gold.

"Kirtanananda, man, I've just come from the nursery," Hebel began without any greeting. "I can't believe how filthy the place is. It's disgusting. You've got to do something."

"Why, what's the problem?" Kirtanananda said. He was barely paying attention. He turned away from Hebel every few words to shout instructions at the laborers.

"My son's sick; all the kids are sick," Hebel said. "That nursery isn't fit for pigs."

"Yes, yes. We'll get to it," Kirtanananda said with the airiness he always affected when confronted by an overwrought devotee.

"You'll get to it? When? What's more important than a decent place for little kids?"

Kirtanananda turned, stood still, and for the first time, stared directly at Hebel.

"Seeking spiritual perfection. The palace. Bringing the masses to Krishna."

He then turned on his heel and walked away. He was furious that Hebel had had the gall to question him. How could Hebel doubt a pure devotee, who was so spiritually advanced that he was incapable of making mistakes?

Hebel watched Kirtanananda limp off, and shrugged. Then he took off his shoes and entered the palace to take his first look at Krishna's glory.

Steven Hebel had grown up in Hewlett, Long Island, the favorite of every Jewish mother on his block. Such a nice boy. And handsome, too. Those dark eyes, that thick black hair, those full lips and that square jaw. And so charming. When he talked to you, there was nobody else in the world. He was so smart, his mother said, they invented the honor roll for that boy. President of his student council, eight hundreds on his SATs. And as a junior, he applied for and received early acceptance at Cornell. Of course, Harvard and Yale both wanted him, too.

But Hebel hated the Jewish mothers who had smothered him with love. He hated high school, where girls, beautiful girls, were always hitting on him, calling him at home, asking him to come over. Hebel wasn't interested in their silliness. He was fascinated with death.

It had started when Hebel was ten and his father died. After his passing, Hebel spent much of his spare time sneaking into the cemetery. It was peaceful there. He'd sit on a mausoleum under the lush green trees and look at the ordered rows of graves.

"Why'd you do it? Why'd you take my dad?" he'd ask God over and over again.

It wasn't pain or unfulfilled love that drove him to ask. He had liked his dad, a former weightlifter, but didn't really miss him all that much. Steve simply wanted to know. He wanted an answer to the basic paradox of life: Why do people die?

He started reading seriously in his early teens. He pursued his quest through Camus, Sartre, Richard Alpert, Alan Watts, all the Western Easteners. He didn't find any answers.

In the spring of 1967, Hebel visited his sister, a freshman at Boston University. She turned him on to marijuana. He walked into Kenmore Square flying high and his world changed as he watched the big Citgo sign change colors against the night sky. Everything suddenly seemed fresh and alive and exciting, just the opposite of his predictable life on Long Island. He was hit by the realization that he had to do something to escape—or Long Island would consume him.

Like many kids of his generation, Hebel decided to become a hippie. He left that summer. He hitchhiked to California and spent the next year devouring huge amounts of grass, acid, speed—anything that messed up his mind and helped him escape. It wasn't enough.

He returned to New York and discovered the Krishnas on Second Avenue. He listened to devotees preach and read Prabhupada's books. For the first time, he found peace. Krishna Consciousness answered all his questions about death: You didn't die: you were recycled.

"I'm moving in with the Krishnas," Hebel told his startled mother one day.

"But you're Jewish!" his mother cried. "You can't change what you are."

"Ma, that's exactly what I'm gonna change."

"But, Stevie, you're throwing your future away!"

"No, I'm not, Ma. I'm finding a future."

"But, Stevie, why these robes and the shaved-head thing?"

' 'Krishna Consciousness is ironclad and scientific, Ma," Hebel said. "It makes sense."

"But how will you live?"

"The temple is just a hole in the wall, but it's really spiritual, Ma. It's not like the synagogue. That's just a glorified social center."

Brahmananda, the New York temple president, took Hebel under his wing and made him one of the first employees of the ISKCON Press, which grew into the mammoth Bhaktivedanta Book Trust. As the handsomest male in the New York temple, it was natural that he would attract the attention of the temple's most beautiful female, Kanka, or Susan O'Neal.

Blond-haired, blue-eyed Susie grew up in Albany, Oregon, the daughter of a prominent physician, whose hobbies were sports cars and airplanes. She was a superpopular swimming star, the girl all the other girls dreamed about being. One night, her father took a car into a turn too hard and skidded across the wet pavement and smashed into a tree. Dr. O'Neal was killed instantly.

Susan's mother was remarried to a retired Air Force officer. They began each day with Bloody Marys and ended them with scotch and sodas. Susan hated her stepfather and despised the person her mother had become.

She left home to go away to Northeastern University in Boston, vowing that she would be different.

She and a girlfriend were on a summer tour of Europe, walking down a Hamburg street, when they spotted a man in robes chanting on a corner. It was Hansadutta. Susan was fascinated. She and her college friend spent several days in the Hamburg temple, learning to chant and listening to Hansadutta preach. When they flew back to the States, Susan's girlfriend returned to school. Susan didn't. She moved into the New York temple and was initiated by Prabhupada.

Kanka, as Susan was now called, was very happy. Prabhupada was a perfect father figure; she, a perfect daughter. She dedicated her life to spreading the word that Krishna was lord of the universe. Krishna Consciousness, unlike her real father, was eternal—it could not be taken away from her. Then she met Swarup, Steven Hebel.

"Hey, Swarup, Kanka just told me she likes you," Brahmananda told Hebel one afternoon. "Maybe you should go out on a date, or something."

"Kanka?" Hebel asked. "Really? She's cute."

Their wedding, in June 1971, was not only a major Hare Krishna event, but also a sixties happening. In their September 6, 1971 issue, *New York* magazine covered it and published a long story of the idyllic couple. It was presented as the best of the sixties; the paradigm of peace and love, antimaterialism, and cross-cultural advancement. Here were intelligent, all-American kids choosing to live simply as conservative Hindus.

For years, Steven and Susan Hebel remained the model of a devout Krishna couple. They had three children and lived in Brooklyn, Boston, and Los Angeles. Like an IBM management trainee, Hebel climbed the ISKCON ladder rung by rung. He vaulted into the elite with his appointment as the movement's social secretary.

But Steven's marriage collapsed in 1977, when he started an affair with Cynthia, known in the movement as Chitta, a tall, blond, blue-eyed devotee, who wore a ring through her nose. He didn't like deceiving Susan and finally told her about it. She wasn't about to give him up, so all three moved into a small house near the Los Angeles temple. On even nights, Steven slept with Susan; on odd nights, with Cynthia. It wasn't long before Hebel was exhausted and the women were threatening to scratch each other's eyes out.

"I always wanted a *shiksa*, but this is ridiculous," he told a friend.

Susan finally packed up the kids and left Los Angeles to submerge herself in Krishna Consciousness in New Vrindaban. A few weeks later, Hebel was working in his office in the LA temple when his phone rang.

"Swarup! Long time no see," the caller on the other end of the line said. It took Hebel a moment to place the voice. It was his old friend from the Laguna Beach temple. The two men chatted a while about their personal lives before launching into a discussion of the movement.

"There's been some big changes down here," his friend said. "Really big changes."

"Like what?" Hebel asked.

"Like you gotta come down and see for yourself," his friend replied. "Believe me, it'll be more than worth the trip."

The last time Hebel had seen him, he'd been following a devotee's ascetic regime in the Laguna temple. This time, Hebel arrived to find him living in a beachfront condo and driving a shiny black BMW.

"The fruits of laboring for Krishna," his friend said with a laugh.

Hebel sank into a seamless white leather couch and listened to the Laguna Beach devotee describe his work as a mule for Joe Davis and Roy Richard.

"But I didn't get you down here just to hear me talk," his friend said, producing a razor blade and a small glass vial filled with white powder.

"Is that what I think it is?" Hebel asked as his friend began laying out lines.

"It is, and you're gonna love it."

Hebel did love cocaine. From then on, he'd spend a day in his office, playing the role of a senior ISKCON/ BBT executive; the next day, he and Cynthia were in Laguna Beach, doing coke.

*   *   *

Steven Hebel wondered how things had gotten so screwed up. It wasn't only him. The whole movement was spinning out of control, flying apart. After Prabhupada's death, Ramesvara had returned from India and proclaimed himself an acharya. But many of the older devotees in LA refused to accept the squeaky-voiced Jewish kid as their guru. Some "blooped"—returned to karmi life; others joined Swami B. R. Sridhar, Prabhupada's eighty-five-year-old godbrother, who had a small movement based in his temple in Navadwip, across the Ganges from Mayapur.

Hebel hadn't been as upset about Ramesvara as some of the other devotees. At first, Ramesvara had been pretty cool about the whole thing, laughing about his supposedly exalted state. But that didn't last. The more he was worshiped, the more he liked it. Soon he began demanding that all devotees idolize him.

Hebel rolled up a twenty-dollar bill, snorted a line, and handed the "straw" to Cynthia.

"You should have been at the temple this morning," he told her. "I was sitting around Ramesvara's office with a bunch of other senior devotees, shooting the breeze with my feet up on his desk, when that little schmuck walked in. I said, 'Hey, Ramie-swami, what's happening?' "

"He freaked out, huh?" Cynthia said. The coke had made her jittery and she was pacing the room.

"He went totally nuts. First, he storms out of the room. He comes running back in, shaking and shrieking, 'Would you act like this if Prabhupada walked in?' He starts ranting and raving about how he's on the same level as Prabhupada and should be treated that way."

Cynthia didn't say a thing. She sat down and cut a few more lines. When they were neat and straight, she handed Steven the rolled-up bill. Another line, or two, always seemed to lift his mood.

"Look, I'm sick of this decadence," he said, pushing the coke away. "Don't you miss being pure? Don't you miss the old days of being devout? The only way we're ever going to get back into Krishna Consciousness is to go to New Vrindaban and submit to Kirtanananda."

They were silent for a while.

"Besides," Hebel said. "I miss my kids. I wanna be near them."

Cynthia looked out the window, debating whether to put her foot down.

"Okay, I'll go," she tentatively agreed. "But promise that I won't have to share you with Susan."

Hebel did.

They both vowed to stop using drugs and celebrated their decision by finishing the lines Cynthia had laid out on the round pocket mirror.

On his first day at New Vrindaban, after Kirtanananda stormed off in response to his questions, Hebel drove up to his tiny cabin in Tolavan, the small fringie community at the edge of the commune. He couldn't get the condition of the nursery or Kirtanananda's odd behavior off his mind. He kept seeing his son's bloated stomach—how could a bloated stomach not be serious?

When Hebel arrived, Cynthia met him at the door. She was irate. "You know who I just talked to?" she shouted. "Dharmatma! He told me Kirtanananda wouldn't let us stay if I didn't do sankirtan."

Hebel ran his hand soothingly through her blond hair. She knocked it away.

"I won't do it," she said, her face flushed with anger. "I swear I won't—not after all the stories I've heard about how he treats women. And especially not after *meeting* that arrogant scumbag!"

"Don't worry," Hebel said calmly. "I'll get you out of it."

While Hebel was calming Cynthia, Thomas Meyers, Taru, marched his new wife, Mahara, Mary St. John, behind the old barn at New Vrindaban. Taru was an intense young man, one of the few scholars at New Vrindaban. A cum laude graduate of Cleveland State, Taru had learned Sanskrit so he could read the Hindu scriptures in their original form and was the editor of *Brijabasi Spirit,* the community magazine.

When Kirtanananda ordered them to get married, Taru and Mahara barely knew each other. They hadn't talked much since their marriage and didn't know each other much better now. Mahara had no idea why her husband had ordered her to follow him.

When they arrived behind the barn, Taru turned and hit her hard across the face.

Mahara screamed. Taru hit her again.

"Why are you doing this?" she cried.

"Kirtanananda told me to," Taru said.

" But *why?*" screamed Mahara.

"You're not submissive enough."

"But how can I be more submissive?" wailed Mahara, one of the best sankirtan collectors in ISKCON. "I've given Kirtanananda my life. I've worked day and night doing sankirtan. I've raised millions of dollars for him."

"You're not submissive enough," Taru repeated and hit Mahara again.

She fell to the ground. Taru jumped on top of her and again hit her in the face. He got up and stood over her, clenching and unclenching his fist. Mahara was curled up with her hands over her face, whimpering. Taru was crying, too.

"I'm sorry!" he sobbed. "I'm sorry!"

He looked down at Mahara one last time and then ran away.

Taru disappeared during the winter of 1980. New Vrindaban did not report his absence. Devotees were told not to mention his name. But that didn't still the rumors.

Sergeant Westfall heard the gossip and quietly began making inquiries. The story Westfall heard over and over was that Taru was in India. He checked with Immigration and the State Department; neither had a record of Taru leaving the country. Westfall slipped questions about the vanished devotee into all his conversations with members of the commune and grilled his informants. But he couldn't get a solid lead about what had happened to Taru.

"I have had a revelation," Kirtanananda announced one day. "I dreamed Taru has gone to India and jumped into the confluence of the three holy rivers. He has drowned."

Taru has never been seen or heard from again.

* * *

Sharon Wilson was back home in New Vrindaban after
five weeks on the road. She was exhausted from working
fourteen- and fifteen-hour days and crisscrossing the country at night to get to ball games and concerts. She walked
up the stairs in Dharmatma's house and knocked on his
bedroom door.

"Go away, I'm busy," Dharmatma shouted.

Sharon knew what that meant. He was in there with a
woman.

Who is it this time? she wondered as she walked back
down the stairs. One of his sankirtan bimbos, maybe? Or
one of his other wives?

Dharmatma had three wives, including Sharon. He
controlled everything they did, whether they were at
home or on the road. If a woman needed new underwear, she had to call Dharmatma to ask for permission to
buy it. One time, Sharon's clothes were so worn out,
they were literally falling off her back. She asked
Dharmatma for some money. He gave her a stolen credit
card and told her to buy a few things, but only what she
really needed. Another time, he told her to shoplift. She
was nailed liberating a blouse in Toronto, Canada, and
spent a weekend in jail. When she telephoned Dharmatma
to tell him what had happened, he called her a fool for
getting caught.

A young, heavyset woman Sharon had never seen before came down the stairs and walked out of the house
without looking at Sharon. Sharon went back upstairs
and knocked on the door.

"I suppose *you* want some?" Dharmatma asked when
she walked in. He was sitting on the edge of the bed,
naked except for his underpants.

Sharon smiled. "I missed you."

"I'll bet you did," Dharmatma snapped.

Sharon walked over and sat down next to Dharmatma.
She kissed his shoulder and began licking his neck.
Dharmatma pushed her away and jumped to his feet.

"Did you see that pig who was in here?" he asked.

"Who is she?" Sharon asked.

"A new girl," Dharmatma said. "She joined the team

a couple of weeks ago. I just fucked her. I had to, to keep her going. It was awful. I can still smell her. This whole room reeks of pussy. How can you stand it?"

"I stand it because you're here," Sharon said, walking over to him. She slipped her hand into his pants and began fondling him.

"I'm still your favorite, aren't I?" she asked. "Come on, let's go over to the bed and I'll remind you why I'm your favorite."

She took him by the hand and led him back to bed. She peeled down his underpants. It took her a long time to get him hard.

Sex with Dharmatma was always the same. Sharon always had to seduce him; he was completely passive. When it was over, she had to tell him how great it was, how nobody had ever fucked her like he did. She did it because long ago she had discovered that the better actress she was in bed, the easier life was out of bed.

Dharmatma came, rolled out of bed immediately, and put on his briefs.

"You really are a whore, aren't you?" he said. "You've really got to have it, don't you?"

Sharon's heart sank. It was going to be this way again. Dharmatma was going to abuse her. She had been hoping that this time it would be different, that maybe, just maybe, he'd be too tired.

"Did you hear what I said, slut?" Dharmatma said.

"I just missed you," Sharon said, getting out of the other side of the bed. "That was all."

"You gotta have it all the time, don't you?" Dharmatma repeated, walking around the bed toward her. "I'll bet you get it a lot on the road. I'll bet you fuck truck drivers. I bet you go into truck stops and get yourself some Peterbilt hog."

"Why are you like this?" Sharon whimpered, stepping back. "Why do you say such terrible things?"

Dharmatma hit her across the face with his open hand. Then he hit her again with the back of his hand.

"Don't you dare ask why, *bitch!*" Dharmatma screamed. "You know why! 'Cause you're such a filthy pig. Now get dressed and get your ass outta here. I want every bathroom in this house cleaned before lunch. You got that?"

Sharon nodded.

"I wouldn't have to hit you if you didn't have an attitude," Dharmatma said in a calmer voice. "I only do it 'cause I think it'll help."

"I know," Sharon hurried to agree. "I must have done something in a previous life to deserve it."

"Could be," Dharmatma said, losing interest. "Now get out of here and get the bathrooms cleaned."

Sharon scrambled into her clothes and went downstairs wondering what was worse, being on the road or being home. She hated living in a van with two or three other women and spending all day begging money from strangers. But on the road, she could at least tell herself she was doing something for Krishna.

Sharon had had three children with Dharmatma. But she'd never been allowed to spend much time with them. Like all New Vrindaban youngsters, they'd been put in the guru kula when they were five. When they were eight, the commune's children were sent to India to study. For the last eight years, Sharon had been on the road almost continuously. Even births did not keep her off sankirtan for long. She'd worked the streets until the day she went into labor with her second child. Two months after childbirth, she was back out working "the pick," as sankirtan was called.

Sharon had played so many roles working the pick that she felt like an actress traveling from town to town with a second-string repertory company. Sometimes she was a concerned mother, collecting money for the Nandegram School for underprivileged Appalachian children. Other times, she was the widow of a Vietnam veteran, collecting to help troubled Vietnam vets. She also posed as a representative of NORML, the National Organization for the Repeal of Marijuana Laws. She worked Hansadutta's record scam. At fairs where she had to wear a name tag, Sharon told people that ISKCON stood for "Interstate Kids Concern."

For a while a new wrinkle introduced by New Vrindaban

—and quickly copied by other temples—had made things more interesting.

"Excuse me," Sharon would say to a person walking across the street. "But I'm going to have to make a citizen's arrest. You were speeding through that intersection."

During the holidays, it had been a goof to approach people and arrest them for being "under the influence of Santa Claus." At ballgames, she'd arrest people for being "intoxicated with football." People were so relieved to find it was all a joke, they gladly gave her a few dollars.

But after a while, the citation line became as dull and as routine as all the other scams. And she was tired of getting arrested. It had happened so often recently—twice for theft by deception in Indianapolis; three times for soliciting without a permit in Norfolk, Virginia; and who could remember how many times in Austin, Texas, or Orlando, Florida?

Sharon got a brush and a box of Comet out of a downstairs closet and went into the bathroom. As she scrubbed the toilet, she thought about how sankirtan had changed over the years.

At first, devotees worked the crowds at sporting events, particularly football games, where spectators arrived early to tailgate. The pickings were always good because fans were drinking heavily and in a fine mood. Digging into their pockets to come up with five or ten dollars to buy some poor kid a turkey dinner or help an orphan in Appalachia only added a warm glow of altruism to their beery high spirits.

Then it occurred to Dharmatma that the money his teams collected was only a fraction of what people spent on sports paraphernalia. Why not cash in on these fans' obsession? Why not sell pennants and buttons in parking lots? The sankirtan parties would make a fortune.

New Vrindaban soon began buying hats, pennants, bumper stickers, and buttons bearing the insignia of major college and pro teams from Taiwanese manufacturers. Ignoring copyright and trademark laws, the Krishnas sold the souvenirs at games. After the sports paraphernalia operation really got rolling, the Krishnas bought a four-color printing press in Iowa for $110,000 and began turning out their own posters and bumper stickers.

Sharon thought of all the bumper stickers she had pushed: Snoopy holding a beer mug with slogans like Let's Party! Life's a Beach, and Party Till You Puke. But her favorite was Are We Having Fun Yet?

"Are we having fun yet?" she asked herself as she scrubbed around the bathroom sink.

She finished up quickly and hurried over to the nursery to pick up her three-year-old son. Seeing her children was the best thing about being home. Still, it hurt to see them. They always reminded her of her failures as a mother. She felt so guilty about spending so little time with the children. Sometimes when she looked at her little boys she would get all teary-eyed.

She took her son home, put him in a high chair in the kitchen, and started making lunch for him. She was waiting for a bowl of Campbell's tomato soup to cool when Dharmatma walked in.

"I thought I told you to clean the bathrooms," he said menacingly.

"I did," Sharon said.

"I said *all* the bathrooms. That means the one upstairs, too."

"I forgot," Sharon said. "I'll get to it right after lunch."

Dharmatma walked up to her.

"This is for being disobedient," he said and slapped her across the face.

"You hit Mommy!" the three-year-old shrieked. "Daddy! Don't hit Mommy!"

Sharon raced to the high chair.

"It's all right," she said. "Don't cry. See, Mommy isn't crying."

"Get away from him," Dharmatma ordered. "You're turning him into a wimp."

Sharon had her back turned and was stroking her son's hair. Dharmatma ran over, grabbed her by the long thick braid that tumbled down her neck, and dragged her out into the garage. He took a thick rubber hose off a workbench. He drew it back and hit Sharon across the back of the neck as hard as he could.

A white light flashed in front of her eyes. Her arms shot out, numb and rigid. She hit the garage floor, face first.

6

Shadows
of Terror

Black and Blue

Steve Bryant was working in the fiberglass shop at New Vrindaban, molding the elaborate scrolls that were to decorate the Palace of Gold's facade. There was no ventilation in the shop, and the fumes were terrible. A ferocious headache was beginning to pound.

It was April 1980. Since returning from his buying trip to India a year ago, he had been slaving away in the shop almost every day. Almost always he wound up with a screaming headache. Bryant reached over to pick up a pair of tongs and banged his arm against a hot vat.

"Fuck!" he screamed. "Just fuckin' *screw* it!"

He looked at the angry red welt already rising on his forearm and stomped out of the shop. It was a beautiful early-spring day. The first traces of color on the hardwoods that topped the rolling hills hinted that summer was on its way. As usual, Bryant was much too frustrated to notice.

He wandered over to the Palace of Gold and sat down on the red brick steps that sloped up to the front entrance. Visitors were gathered on the veranda, taking off their shoes before entering the palace on a two-hour tour that included the surrounding gardens, their elaborate fountains, and their three thousand rose bushes. Bryant watched for a while. Then he walked down the road past a small man-made lake where a twenty-five-foot gold-and-white, swan-shaped boat floated full of tourists. He continued past a large barn that was being converted into a hotel and stopped in front of the Temple of Understanding, a simple wooden building used by devotees for daily services.

There he sat down on a bench. All about him were

signs of industry and prosperity—the dairy farm, the saw mill, the brick factory, the garage where trucks and earth-moving equipment were stored, the schools—plainly, the community was thriving. But it only served to underline Bryant's feeling of failure. Nothing, absolutely nothing had worked out as he had planned. When he returned from India, he had sold every piece of jewelry he had made. Yet he ended up clearing only a few hundred dollars. The supplies had cost more than he had planned, and the cameras and tape recorders he had lugged all the way to India had brought less than he had hoped.

Shortly after his return, his wife, Jane, had given birth to Sarva Dharma, their first child. Bryant was thrilled to have his own son; yet the birth hadn't changed his feeling of helplessness.

As for Jane, she was wonderfully, ecstatically happy. That was one of the reasons why Bryant was so miserable. When Jane wrote to him in India to tell him she had been initiated, he was certain that Kirtanananda had made a fundamental mistake. No guru should ever initiate a man's wife without her husband's permission. Bryant had been angry, but the more he thought about it, the more he decided no real harm had been done. He had written back, telling Jane that he would serve Kirtanananda and she could serve the swami through him.

Now he wasn't so sure he had done the right thing. Jane clearly was in love with Kirtanananda. She had three pictures of the guru taped to the wall above her side of the bed. All day long, it was Kirtanananda this and Kirtanananda that.

Bryant was still moping on the bench an hour later when Kirtanananda drove up in his Landcruiser.

"Sulocana, how come you're sitting around when there's so much service to be done?" the guru asked, leaning through the open window.

"But that's just it," Bryant cried, getting off the bench. "You won't let me do service."

"What are you talking about?" Kirtanananda asked. "You're supposed to be in the fiberglass shop right now."

"The fiberglass shop! Who cares? Anybody can do that kind of work," Bryant said. "A devotee with my years and experience in the movement should have a more responsible position."

Kirtanananda shook his head. Bryant just did not get it.

"I've told you before, you'll advance when you surrender," Kirtanananda said.

"But I am surrendered," Bryant wailed.

Kirtanananda shook his head again. "You're not my man, Sulocana. You're just not my man."

"What do you mean, not your man?" Bryant demanded.

"You'll be my man when you do service without questioning," Kirtanananda said. "When you see that what I am doing is in accordance with Krishna's divine plan. When you work in the fiberglass shop from sunup to sundown and then get down on your knees and thank me for giving you such a wonderful opportunity to do service—that's when I'll know you're my man, Sulocana."

Kirtanananda didn't wait for Bryant to reply before driving off.

"That arrogant son of a bitch," Bryant muttered as he watched the Landcruiser disappear around a bend behind a cloud of dust. "If I'd joined the movement five years earlier, I'd be him and he'd be me. I'd be the swami of the palace."

Bryant walked across the commune to the camper shell he shared with his wife and infant son. It was a little more than a plastic hovel that lacked running water and a toilet. They used an outhouse across the dirt road. Bryant went inside, got the keys to his old Chrysler station wagon, and drove over to Tolavan.

Bryant had heard that most days after work, there was an informal party at Don McAdams's house. McAdams had designed and built the Palace of Gold's crown jewels— the fantastic peacock windows. The spectacular green, blue, turquoise, and royal purple tails of the peacocks each contained more than fifteen hundred pieces of hand-cut and handstained glass. Every day when he finished work, McAdams liked to get the fringies together and relax with a beer, and maybe even a joint or two.

McAdams's cabin was crowded with fringies when Bryant arrived. Dan Reid, Kurt Cleaver, and Steven

Hebel were all there. Bryant knew who they were, but he'd never had much to do with any of them. As a practicing devotee who strictly adhered to the principles, he considered himself far above these undisciplined part-timers.

"Hey, look who's here!" Don McAdams yelled in welcome.

Bryant didn't answer.

"Don't just stand there, Sulocana, come on in," McAdams called out.

McAdams knew Bryant through Jane, who had split her time working in the nursery and his stained-glass studio before the baby arrived. He liked Jane a lot better than Bryant. He thought Bryant treated his wife like a scab, continually picking at her and finding fault. But, hey, a party was a party.

"How about a brew?" McAdams asked.

"Sure, why not?" Bryant answered nervously.

McAdams walked into the kitchen and came out with a cold bottle of Rolling Rock. He handed it to Bryant, who studied the green bottle before popping the cap and taking a big swallow.

"Wow! It's been so long, I forgot what it tasted like," Bryant said. "Good bye, vow against intoxicants. Good bye, principles."

Across the commune, Kirtanananda was in his office talking to Walt Parry, his temple commander (the commune's sergeant of sorts), and a couple of other devotees. The door swung open. Advaita, Emile Sofsky, aka John Jenkins—the erstwhile manager of the commune's restaurant—stood there holding a chrome suitcase. No one said a word.

Advaita marched into the room and placed the suitcase directly in front of Kirtanananda on his desk. The two men looked at each other. Advaita nodded almost imperceptibly. Kirtanananda nodded back. With a flourish, Advaita reached over and popped open the suitcase.

Parry peeked inside.

It was cash heaven—rows of fifty-dollar bills, divided into neat bundles and bound with thick rubber bands,

were stacked next to each other. Parry looked at Kirtanananda. The guru's eyes had widened.

"*Jai!*" Kirtanananda exclaimed, using the Hindu word
for glory. "Jai!"

Advaita slammed the suitcase shut.

"What is it, Maharaj?" asked a devotee who hadn't
been able to get a look inside the suitcase.

"Nothing, nothing at all," Kirtanananda said. He slid
the suitcase off his desk and stashed it on the floor, next
to his feet.

"Hare Krishna," Advaita said and walked out the door.

In February 1979 Advaita's operation came crashing
down. He and three of his runners were busted as their flight
from Bombay landed in New York's Kennedy Airport, Customs officials discovered a plastic container holding hash
oil in the false bottom of a runner's suitcase. It had
leaked through and soaked the clothes.

Advaita and the runners were arrested. Bail was set at
$350,000. He put up the money and disappeared. But
before he was released, prosecutors found letters Advaita's
accomplice Syamakunda had written him from India. They
described where he had purchased the hash oil and how
the runners were to make the rendezvous. Two U.S.
Drug Enforcement Administration officers immediately
flew to India, where they enlisted the help of the Indian
police and arrested Syamakunda in New Delhi. Like
Advaita, he immediately jumped bail.

Syamakunda bought an American passport on the black
market, returned to the States, and made his way back to
New Vrindaban. Within days he was running an East
Coast drug operation with Steven Hebel.

Syamakunda had left ten kilos of hashish and three
kilos of hash oil in India. It was hidden under a chest of
drawers that was built into the wall of a room in a tourist
hotel in Haryana, a small town an hour north of Delhi.
Hebel agreed to give Syamakunda a cut of any profits he
made.

Hebel flew to India, found the stash, and flew it into
Montreal, where a dealer paid them $50,000 for the load.
Hebel and his family (Cynthia, who was now his wife,
and her seven-year-old daughter by a previous marriage)

moved to Santa Cruz, California, and Hebel became a full time drug dealer. His best clients were Krishnas.

It was the right move at the right time. New Vrindaban needed a new connection. After Advaita got busted, the commune had stopped smuggling and started dealing. New Vrindaban devotees bought drugs in bulk from dealers like Hebel and sold them in small quantities at rock concerts and other events.

Hebel was Chuck St. Denis's West Coast connection. It was Hebel who took St. Denis up to Garberville, California, and introduced him to the sinsemilla growers. They sold St. Denis the seeds that he planted in West Virginia.

Thomas Drescher, Tirtha, was another customer. Every week or so, Hebel drove over the Santa Cruz mountains to the San Jose Airport, where he air-expressed a half pound of sinsemilla to Drescher, who was dealing out of Govinda's, a Krishna-operated restaurant on High Street in Columbus, Ohio, near Ohio State University. Drescher wired Hebel his money, care of the Western Union office in Santa Cruz.

Hebel found dealing a lark. Every month or so, he flew to Pittsburgh, rented a car, and drove the ninety miles down to New Vrindaban to visit his three children. Whenever he was there, he made sure he checked in with Drescher.

"Get down here as fast as you can!" Drescher said one Friday afternoon when Hebel called. "Something big is about to come down."

Hebel drove his rented Oldsmobile down to Columbus the next morning and met Drescher at Govinda's.

"Wait'll you see what I got set up," Drescher said. "You'll never believe it."

They drove to a two-story house in a residential neighborhood on Columbus's east side. Drescher led Hebel into the house and down a hallway that skirted the kitchen. He stopped at a door, opened it with a flourish, and stood aside to let Hebel pass.

Hebel entered and found a well-stocked laboratory. It had beakers, Bunsen burners, white plastic containers, five-gallon containers filled with liquids, and a machine for pressing pills.

"What's all this?" Hebel asked.

"A 'lude factory. What else?" Drescher said. "Ain't it something? I put the whole thing together myself."

Drescher explained that he had met a guy who called himself Reno, who knew a chemist who knew how to manufacture Quaaludes. Reno introduced Drescher to the chemist, and Drescher used the money he had made selling sinsemilla to finance the lab.

"I can move all the 'ludes you can get me in California," Hebel said.

"I know. I know," Drescher said. "That's why I was so anxious to get your ass down here. I want to get the thing running. I'm going to make a million dollars and give it to Kirtanananda."

"I'm going to make a million dollars and put it in my pocket," Hebel said, laughing.

They spent the rest of the day working out the details of the operation. Hebel slept at the house Saturday night and left early Sunday morning to return to New Vrindaban and spend the day with his kids.

At seven o'clock Monday morning, officers from the DEA and the Columbus Police Department broke down the front door and raided the house. The chemist had squealed to the DEA. They had wired him and sent him back into the house. The DEA officers presented transcripts of conversations between Drescher and the chemist to a judge, who gave them a search warrant. The authorities seized the lab and arrested Drescher.

In a flurry of announcements and press releases, New Vrindaban denied any connection with Drescher. Spokesmen for the commune said he was a fallen devotee, less than a fringie, a hanger-on. Kirtanananda had tried hard to save him, the spokesmen said, but the swami had finally given up on Drescher years ago and had excommunicated him.

But while Drescher was in jail awaiting trial, his wife wrote a letter to a Buffalo devotee. It told a dramatically different story. Dealing drugs, the letter said, was one way to achieve the ultimate goal of Krishna Consciousness—uniting with God.

I've been doing my service by night and hustling around for Tirtha by day—the Federal judge, U.S. Marshals, FBI, U.S. Attorney, attorneys, Channel 10 News, ACLU, etc. etc. Then there's hearings, arraignments and trials. Medical releases. SSI money. Threatening phone calls. Krsna help me. Srila Bhaktipada said if Tirtha takes the whole thing and no other boys get caught then he'll go back to Godhead at the end of this lifetime. Perhaps I can serve his feet and go back, too.

Drescher's bust did nothing to slow down Steven Hebel. He made another hash run to India over the Christmas holidays in 1980, brought twelve kilos into Montreal, and sold the stuff to wholesalers.

He cleared thirty thousand dollars. The money was so good, Hebel decided to make one final run to India. A really big one.

In New Delhi he bought thirty kilos of hash this time, worth around one hundred thousand dollars wholesale.

Hebel was arrested in Montreal on February 15, 1981. Customs agents going through his luggage found the thirty kilos. He was convicted and given a choice of serving a sentence in Canada or the United States. Hebel picked the States and did a year in a minimum-security federal prison in Morgantown, West Virginia, eighty miles across the mountains from New Vrindaban.

Broke, his wife, Cynthia, moved back to the commune with her daughter and newborn son. She hated doing it, but she had no choice. Steven had invested every penny in the run that got him busted. At least the rent was free in New Vrindaban. Besides, it was close enough to visit the prison occasionally.

But she rarely got to see Steven. Serving time, and out of contact, he couldn't protect her from Dharmatma's clutches. Right away Dharmatma began to put the pressure on.

"Let me stay," Cynthia begged. "Please!"

"Money is honey," Dharmatma said icily. "If you can't bring in some honey, go somewhere else."

He assigned her to a sankirtan team collecting across

the Southwest. A few days later, Cynthia went off with the sankirtan team. The women spent the Christmas holidays in New Orleans, working the French Quarter. As in other cities, the devotees usually hit the streets between one and two in the afternoon and stayed until two or three in the morning, or as long as the streets were jumping.

Cynthia couldn't take the pace. Day by day her legs hurt more and more. By Christmas the pain became so severe, she could barely walk. Early one morning, she was limping back to the New Vrindaban van. She had collected almost two thousand dollars that day. Drunks kept laying ten, sometimes twenty dollars on her. Before she could thank them, they'd mumble something and stagger on up Bourbon Street.

Maybe if I skimmed some of this, I could get out of the commune and get a little apartment near the jail until Steven is released, Cynthia was thinking as she turned down a dark, narrow street that led to the lot where the van was parked.

She was only a few feet into the alley when a man stepped out of a doorway and raced up behind her. He grabbed her neck in a choke hold and slapped a hand over her mouth. She kicked, hit, and scratched. She tried to scream, but her voice was muffled by her attacker. The man wrenched her neck, pulling her off her feet, and dragged her up the sidewalk. An old Buick was parked at the curb. A second man opened the door while Cynthia's captor shoved her into the backseat and dove in on top of her.

A third man, the driver, pulled away from the curb slowly, routinely. The man who had opened the door then climbed into the back and helped Cynthia's captor bind and gag her. He found the leather bag that hung around her neck and ripped it off. Then he climbed into the front seat.

"Oh-eee! The bitch is rich!" he said, counting the sankirtan money.

They parked in an alley behind a dilapidated building and sat in the car for a few minutes to make sure no one was around. Then they took off Cynthia's blindfold, hustled her into a dingy little apartment, threw her on a bed, and locked the door.

A few moments later, Cynthia's captor came into the room and closed the door. He untied her hands, but left the gag over her mouth. He unstrapped his belt, dropped his pants and his underwear, and peeled off the black T-shirt that covered his muscular chest.

"This ain't gonna hurt none," he said. "Just relax. You're going to like it."

Cynthia closed her eyes and pictured herself walking down the beach in Santa Cruz with Steven and her children. She imagined the wharf stretching out into the ocean, carnival music emanating from the rides and washing over the boardwalk, waves crashing on the beach and gulls soaring in the air.

The captor finished raping her and the guy from the front seat came in. When he was done, the driver came in. Then the captor came back. Then the guy from the front seat. And then the driver.

Light was coming through the shade when her captor walked in carrying a syringe. Cynthia shivered.

"This ain't gonna hurt a bit, baby," he said, rolling her over. "You ain't gonna feel a thing."

Cynthia came to in a churchyard. She remembered that she was in New Orleans, but had no idea where. She looked at herself and discovered she was wearing a man's white undershirt and her underpants. Her body was covered with bruises.

A man came by walking his dog. Cynthia yelled to him and he called the police.

The police gave her some clothes and interviewed her, then drove her around the French Quarter until she spotted one of the women from the sankirtan team. Cynthia told her what had happened. They went to a phone booth and called Dharmatma.

"They raped me and beat me up," Cynthia told Dharmatma. "I'm black and blue and covered with hickeys. Can I have some money to get a motel room and lay around for a few days until I recover?"

"Hell, no!" Dharmatma shouted. "You go buy some

heavy makeup and put it on. Then you get right back out there."

Cynthia did as she was ordered. She and the other members of the sankirtan worked New Orleans through New Year's Day. Then they piled into vans and drove back to New Vrindaban.

When Cynthia walked into Dharmatma's house, he looked up and smiled.

"Hey," he said. "I heard you had a party. How come you didn't invite me?"

A Fork in the Path

It was April 1984, and Steve Bryant was driving his one-of-a-kind van much too fast. The soft road had been turned into a mud track by spring rains. He stopped in front of an old farmhouse that belonged to New Vrindaban and jumped out. He was frantic, but took the time to lock the van. Maybe the thing looked funny—Bryant had built it himself, wrapping sheet metal over an old Ford camper until it looked like an igloo on wheels. And maybe it got only six miles per gallon, but it was his creation. He loved it. It was the only place he felt really comfortable. He spent hours sitting at the table in the van, making jewelry, listening to Linda Ronstadt, the Beatles, and other favorites on his stereo.

Bryant ran down the steps of the farmhouse to the basement apartment he and his family had been calling home for the last few months. It was dark and dank. There was only one small window, and it was sealed shut. There was no heat. Ripped-up cardboard boxes were tacked to the walls for insulation. Jane was sitting in a vinyl chair nursing Nimai, the Bryants' one-year-old son. Four-year-old Sarva was in a corner, pushing a toy locomotive across the cement floor. Seven-year-old Rinnian, Krishna das, was in the guru kula.

"We're leaving!" Bryant said. "Get packed! We're not gonna spend another day here."

Jane's eyes widened and her mouth dropped open. She looked down at Nimai, who had just fallen asleep.

"What are you saying?" she asked.

"I'm telling you we're going to hit the road," Bryant replied more quietly. "We don't need this place. We've got the jewelry business and the van. We can go wherever we want. I'm thinking maybe Mexico. We could park the van on a beach and live on fruits and vegetables for next to nothing. It'd be great for the kids, and all I'd need to keep the business going is a post office."

"Why this, all of a sudden?"

Bryant walked up to his wife and leaned toward her until their noses were almost touching.

"Because Kirtanananda's a liar!" he said.

Jane jumped up, knocking the chair over backward. "Don't say that! Don't ever say that again! Kirtanananda is a pure devotee."

"He's a liar," Bryant said, his voice rising. "I just talked to Kuladri. I'm not going to get the hotel job. Kirtanananda promised it to me and now he's giving it to a drunk!"

For over a year, devotees had been working to convert the New Vrindaban barn into an elaborate resort complex, complete with hotel and time-sharing condos. Kirtanananda had promised Bryant the position of hotel manager as soon as the conversion was complete.

"Did Kuladri say why Kirtanananda changed his mind?" Jane asked.

"He didn't have to," Bryant said bitterly. "It's the same old story—I'm 'not his man.' "

Jane started to cry.

"Stop that!" Bryant ordered. "This is no time for your moaning. Start packing. You've got a couple of hours. I've gotta do a couple of things, but I'll be back later this afternoon."

Bryant only had one thing to do. He went over to Tolavan to tell his fringie friends about Kirtanananda's perfidy. When he returned to the basement apartment, he found Jane standing with her back to the sink and her arms folded across her chest. She hadn't done a thing to prepare for the trip.

"I thought I told you to start packing," Bryant said angrily. "How come you haven't done anything? Is Nimai sick or something?"

"He's fine," Jane said.

"Then why aren't you ready?" Bryant asked. He stormed across the room, pulled open a dresser drawer filled with his socks and underwear, and started throwing his clothes in a beat-up box.

Jane just watched.

Bryant grabbed a handful of her clothes and tossed them into the box.

"Leave my stuff alone," Jane said evenly.

"What?" Bryant asked without stopping.

"Sulocana," Jane said, "I have something to say: I'm staying. You can leave if you want, but I'm not going with you."

It was as if Jane had told him she was about to die from cancer. For the first time since they were married, Bryant was speechless.

"I'm not going, Sulocana," Jane said. "My home is here with Kirtanananda and his devotees."

"You're my wife!" Bryant sputtered.

"I don't have any affection for you, Sulocana. I never did."

"You can't mean that," Bryant said, on the verge of tears.

"Kirtanananda says I can stay," Jane insisted. "I talked to him this afternoon. I'm to take shelter here. You're to leave."

Bryant sank into the green vinyl chair. The angry, supermacho male who had given Jane such a hard time over the past five years vanished like a character who'd been written out of a soap opera.

"Don't do this to me," he blubbered. "My first concern has always been your spiritual well-being."

"My spiritual well-being is Kirtanananda's concern, not yours," Jane shot back.

"This is not how a Krishna-conscious wife behaves," Bryant said.

"Don't tell me how to behave—not when you're over in Tolavan every night drinking beer and smoking marijuana."

It was the first time Jane had ever talked back to her husband. She discovered she liked it.

"I want to take care of you and the boys," Bryant pleaded.

"Kirtanananda will take care of us," Jane said coldly.

"You can't choose him over me. You can't. I won't let you stay here. I won't!"

"It's already been decided," Jane replied.

Bryant decided to stay until he could change Jane's mind. For the next month, he was as relentless as a real-estate agent trying to close a deal. He begged and badgered Jane to leave New Vrindaban every moment they were together. Some nights, he came in from his van and woke her up to read a passage from one of Prabhupada's books about the sanctity of marriage.

That didn't work. So he became the model husband. For the first time in all their years of marriage, he helped with the housework, cleaning the apartment and washing dirty dishes.

Even that didn't work. Jane couldn't be bullied or coaxed away from Kirtanananda and his commune. So Bryant changed tactics once again. He began knocking the swami and deriding New Vrindaban.

"This place is a tourist trap," he told Jane. "The most spiritual thing in the whole commune is the sound of the cash register ringing."

But Bryant's rantings only strengthened Jane's determination to stay. Bryant swallowed his pride; he decided to remain in the commune with his family for a while. But pressure on him to leave mounted almost daily. He was told he was no longer needed in the fiberglass shop and was laid off. Devotees shunned him. When he sat down for a meal in Prasadam Hall, devotees at his table got up and moved. When they were forced to talk to him, they called him Bryant instead of Sulocana, a mortifying insult that meant he was no longer considered a member of the movement.

Bryant reacted by immersing himself in right-wing politics and the culture of guns. It was an interest that had first flourished when his Krishna career began to sour in the early eighties. Now it became a passion. He bought several pistols and spent hours every day practicing with them on the New Vrindaban firing range. He put himself on the John Birch Society mailing list and read every pamphlet they sent him. He sent away for several Bircher books and began preaching their view of the world the way he had once preached Krishna Consciousness.

"Politics are a farce," he told Jane one day. "The same people who control the United States control the Soviet Union."

"You know what I'd like to do?" he announced another time. "Become an assassin and bump off some of the people who are running the world."

It didn't soothe his rage. Each day, Bryant became angrier and angrier. Soon, he began to hate himself. He saw himself as a man of action hanging around and knuckling under to a woman. Enough is enough, he finally told himself. He would show Jane and the rest of these New Vrindaban creeps. They were going to find out what kind of man they were dealing with.

It was four o'clock on a June morning. The van was parked beside the old farmhouse and Bryant was lying in it, wide awake. Jane would be appearing at any moment. She never missed Mangal-aratik.

Sure enough, Jane came out of the house a few minutes later carrying Sarva, who was fast asleep. She laid him on the backseat of their beat-up old Datsun, covered him with a blanket, and then went back and got Nimai. Then she drove off.

Bryant waited for half an hour before he climbed into the driver's seat of the van. If he had timed it right, the morning services ought to be going full blast about the time he reached the Temple of Understanding.

He was right on target. The kirtan was raging when Bryant walked into the temple. He circled around to the side and entered the small room where the children stayed while their parents worshiped the Blue Lord.

"I came for my kids," Bryant told the woman who was watching the children. "We've got doctor's appointments in Moundsville."

"Kind of early for that, isn't it?" the woman asked.

"Not really," Bryant said. "The clinic opens at six."

He went to the crib where Sarva and Nimai were sleeping.

"Come on, guys, let's go," he said as he lifted them

out. He carried them out to the van, put them in his bed, and drove out of the commune.

"Dad? Did I wake you?" Bryant asked as soon as his father answered the phone.

"You did. What time is it?" Jack Bryant asked.

"Almost six. Well, a little after five-thirty."

"Where are you?"

"Moundsville, a phone booth outside the bank," Steve said, talking as fast as he could. "I'm sorry I woke you. I wouldn't have called if it wasn't important. Can I stay with you awhile?"

"Sure, why?" Jack asked.

"I've got the boys. I took them from the commune. I had to. Jane wants a divorce. She wants to keep the kids and stay there. It was the only way I could keep our marriage together."

Helga was awake and tugging on her husband's shoulder.

"What is it? What's going on?" she asked.

"Trouble," Jack answered, "Steve's taken the kids."

Then he turned back to the phone.

"What are you going to do?"

"I'm coming home to Detroit for a while," Steve said. "I need you guys to take care of the kids while we get this worked out. I'll fill you in when I get there. Right now, I gotta get out of here."

Then he hung up.

Jack had just finished telling Helga what was going on, when the phone rang again. It was Jane.

"Steve took the boys and left," Jane said.

"We know. He just called," Jack replied.

"He called me, too. He says the only way I'll get them back is if I go with him."

"What do you think you'll do?" Jack asked.

"I suppose I'll have to go with him," Jane said. "Please have him call me as soon as he gets there."

Bryant was driving up Highway 2 along the Ohio River when the van started to stink. He knew what that meant; Nimai needed a diaper change. He decided to stop in Wheeling and get diapers, milk, and something for Sarva to eat before he got on the interstate.

He pulled into the first shopping plaza he passed and

parked in front of a supermarket. Sarva was awake, but Nimai was still sleeping.

"You watch your brother," Bryant said, reaching under his seat to check that his loaded .45 was securely strapped in place. "I'll only be a second."

Then he got out of the van and locked it.

He came out of the store a few minutes later carrying a box of Pampers under one arm and a bag of groceries under the other. He put the diapers down and began digging in his pocket for the keys.

"Don't move," he heard a voice behind him say.

Bryant whirled around.

Three members of the New Vrindaban defense force were standing there, poised to jump him. The one in the middle, a devotee he knew only as Bhakti Fred, pulled his hand out of his windbreaker to show Bryant he had a pistol.

A wave of helplessness swept over Bryant: If only he'd taken his gun! He looked around for an escape route and spotted two more devotees walking toward him, one from each end of the van.

"How'd you find me?" Bryant stammered, backing up against the driver's door.

"It was a snap," the devotee with the gun said. "We knew where you were going and that van of yours is as easy to spot as a fire truck."

"We came for the boys," another member of the defense force interrupted.

"You can't have them," Bryant said.

At that moment, Jane stepped around the back end of the van.

"Please, Steve, give me the boys," she said.

"Give the lady her children," cut in the devotee with the gun. "I don't want to ask again."

"Jane, couldn't we just talk for a minute, just you and me?" Bryant begged.

Jane shook her head no.

"Please!" Bryant pleaded.

The devotee with the gun shook his head.

Bryant didn't say another word. He smashed his fist

into the van, unlocked the driver's door, and stepped aside.

A devotee scrambled into the van and came out carrying Sarva. Another devotee fetched Nimai.

"Bye, Daddy," Sarva said over the shoulder of the devotee who was carrying him away.

Bryant spent a week at his parents' house in suburban Detroit. His father kept advising him to relax and accept the situation.

"Steven, let Jane go," Jack Bryant said over and over again. "You've got a chance to start your life over. You can have more kids."

That only made Bryant angrier. The more he thought about it, the more he understood that this wasn't between him and Jane. It was between him and Kirtanananda. The swami had brainwashed Jane. He had stolen her by initiating her without permission. Then he had intentionally split them up so he could keep her, the compliant one, and get rid of him, the defiant one. Gurus weren't supposed to separate couples; they were supposed to help them stay together.

"Imagine a priest telling a woman that he was the eternal man in her life, and that her husband was of no consequence," Steve raved at his father.

"Let it go," Jack said.

Exasperated, Bryant took off for Los Angeles. He drove all day, pulling over occasionally to sleep in the van for a few hours. As soon as he awoke, he climbed back into the driver's seat and got back on the highway.

Every day, Bryant stopped at a pay phone and called Jane. Some days she came to the phone; some days she didn't. When she did, it was only to tell Bryant that she was going ahead with the divorce. When Bryant started pleading, she usually hung up.

One night in Dallas, Bryant was so upset after Jane hung up that he couldn't sleep. He took a couple of the codeine tablets he had brought from a fringie. They didn't help. He lay in bed in the van, tossing and turning, going over and over the role Kirtanananda had played in breaking up his marriage. Finally, at three in the morning, he couldn't take it anymore. He got up, pulled on a pair of pants, took his tape recorder, and called the guru from a pay phone.

"Sulocana here," Bryant said. "Guess what?"

"What?" Kirtanananda asked.

"I can't transcend this," Bryant said, meaning his anger over the breakup of his marriage.

"So surrender," Kirtanananda said simply.

"I surrendered to Prabhupada a long time ago," Bryant said.

"Well, now you'll have to surrender to me," Kirtanananda said.

"I just talked to my wife and she doesn't want to come back to me, ever," Bryant said. "And I can't allow my sons to stay there."

"All right. We'll fight for them," Kirtanananda said.

"You want to go through with a fight, huh?" Bryant asked.

"Yeah!" Kirtanananda said.

Then they traded accusations about who was responsible for the failure of Bryant's marriage.

"You tried to persuade her that you had the only relationship with her," Bryant said.

"I have the only eternal relationship with her," Kirtanananda said. "Your relation to her is noneternal."

"What does that mean?" Bryant asked.

"It means there's only one thing you can do," Kirtanananda said.

"What's that?" Bryant asked.

"You have to surrender," Kirtanananda said.

Bryant refused and Kirtanananda hung up.

Bryant was so angry, he ran back to his van, jumped behind the wheel, and drove nonstop to Los Angeles. He spent a couple of days in the LA temple, selling jewelry to devotees. Then he hit the road again, driving across the lower end of the San Joaquin Valley to Bhaktivedanta Village. A farming community owned by the Los Angeles temple, the village is near the entrance to the Sequoia National Park in Three Rivers, a beautiful little town in the foothills of the Sierras.

Bryant thought the farm would be the perfect place to

cool out. The air was clean and crisp; he had a spectacular view of snow-covered mountains; and on hot days he could wander down to one of the rivers, take off his clothes, and jump into a pool of crystal-clear, fresh mountain water.

When he arrived at the village, the first thing he did was look up his soul sister, Yuvati Matusow. They'd had a platonic, brother-sister relationship ever since their days together in the London temple. Yuvati had been three when her mother joined the movement in the mid sixties, and she had grown up in Krishna Consciousness. At twenty-two, she had been married and divorced and had three children.

"I'm sorry Jane and your boys are in New Vrindaban, but I'm glad you're out," Yuvati said. "I hated the place when I lived there. All kinds of weird things were happening."

"Like what?" Bryant asked.

"Like Jadurani, for one," Yuvati said.

"Who's she?" Bryant asked.

"You don't know about that? Oh, Sulocana, you're so naïve!" Yuvati then told him the story.

Jadurani, Judy Koslofsky, an art student in New York City in the midsixties, was the first *brahmacharini* (unmarried female) to join the movement. She was living in the Los Angeles temple and working as an illustrator for the BBT when Prabhupada died and the gurus took over. Like most devotees she was convinced that, since Krishna had appointed the new gurus through Prabhupada, they were infallible.

One of Prabhupada's disciples who had become disaffected since his death changed her mind about that. He read her transcripts of the tapes that were made when Prabhupada was on his deathbed and named his successors and explained the difference between a rtvik guru and an acharya.

Jadurani was enraged. The gurus were bogus; they had stolen Prabhupada's movement. She began preaching revolution, telling Los Angeles devotees that ISKCON's only hope was to excommunicate the gurus. Ramesvara quickly sent her into exile. She took a bus to Pittsburgh and joined up with Yuvati's mother, who was also trying to ignite an insurrection against the gurus. Jadurani went on welfare and started banging out pamphlets calling for a revolution to overthrow the gurus.

When Kirtanananda heard Jadurani was in Pittsburgh, he called and asked her to come down to New Vrindaban to paint some pictures for the Palace of Gold. Jadurani arrived and immediately began preaching revolution. She told devotees that Kirtanananda was bogus and that anyone who accepted him as Prabhupada's successor was a fool. Two female devotees, Parayani and Isani, ran to Kirtanananda and told him what Jadurani was saying.

"We think she should be beaten," Parayani said. "We think she should be made an example of what happens to someone who blasphemes a pure devotee."

"Sounds like a good idea, but I don't want to hear about it," Kirtanananda replied.

The two women went to Kanka, Susan Hebel, and asked her to help them beat up Jadurani.

"You've got to be kidding," Hebel said, "Jadurani's a tweety bird, she's no threat to anyone."

"She must be taught a lesson," Isani had said.

The next day the two women attacked Jadurani without warning behind the Temple of Understanding and knocked her down. They kicked her in the head, shattering her glasses. Then they jumped on her chest and beat her in the face with their fists.

Steven Hebel was walking past the temple when he heard screams. He ran around to the back and saw that two women were beating Jadurani, an old friend since their days together in the New York temple. He rushed over and pulled off the attackers. Blood was pouring down Jadurani's face, blinding her. Hebel was wiping the blood away with his sleeve when the two women once again attacked.

Hebel fought them off.

"We want her sari!" Isani screamed. "Tear it off her and give it to us!"

"What the hell do you want with that?" Hebel asked.

He looked at Jadurani and saw that her sari was streaked with blood and grime.

"We want to run it up the flagpole," Parayani said. "We want to show people what happens when you speak against Kirtanananda!"

Bryant had pulled out a pocket notebook and was furiously taking notes.

"That's an amazing story," he said when Yuvati finished. "How come I never heard it?"

"They keep you in the dark and feed you shit, just like mushrooms," Yuvati said. "That's one of the ways they control you. I probably never would have heard about it if my mother wasn't friends with Jadurani."

"What else? What else do you know about New Vrindaban?" Bryant asked eagerly.

"Well, you know about Advaita getting busted, right?" Yuvati asked.

"Advaita? Who's he?"

Yuvati groaned.

"Sulocana, you're so naïve," she said again. "You've always wanted to believe that the movement is pure. Do you remember when you went nuts just because one girl's bra strap slipped down her shoulder?"

Bryant blushed. But his curiosity was now inflamed. He quickly started quizzing Yuvati, and it was after midnight before he let her go and returned to his van.

Jane doesn't know any of this stuff about Kirtanananda, Bryant thought as he lay in bed formulating a plan. He decided to open Jane's eyes and prove Kirtanananda was in maya. That would force Kirtanananda to let Jane go.

Bryant decided to start with the guru's decision to initiate Jane. He knew Prabhupada's books were full of references to marriage. If he could get hold of Prabhupada's letters and track down the references, he would be able to show Jane that Kirtanananda had committed a grave error when he came between them.

Bryant was so excited, he couldn't sleep. He got out of bed and took a walk. He was going to do it. In the morning, he would leave for Los Angeles and get Prabhupada's letters from the BBT. Then he would look up every New Vrindaban refugee he could find and ask them about their experiences in the commune. He would write everything down and mail it to Jane.

"I'm going to expose him," Bryant said aloud. "I'm going to expose Kirtanananda."

A Messianic Mission

"Listen to this! Just listen to this! You're not gonna believe it!"

Steve Bryant was sitting at the table in his van surrounded by piles of paper. His friend Yuvati was standing behind him, looking over his shoulder at the mess. She playfully began rubbing his neck and running her hands through his thick blond hair.

"Come on, this is serious," Bryant said, shaking her off. "Go over there and sit down."

Bryant had driven down to Los Angeles and asked for a set of Prabhupada's letters at the Bhaktivedanta Book Trust. When the devotee in charge of the collection asked why he wanted to see them, Bryant, with a characteristic lack of finesse, had told him the truth. The next day, Ramesvara ordered Bryant banned from the BBT.

That's when he got lucky. A Los Angeles devotee who had photocopied a set of the letters to help Jadurani with her unsuccessful insurrection heard through the grapevine what Bryant was trying to do. The devotee had never bothered to read the letters, but thought they might be useful to Bryant and gave them to him.

"This is dynamite," Bryant almost shouted at Yuvati. "It's gonna blow Kirtanananda sky-high." He had found the letter Prabhupada wrote to Brahmananda after Kirtanananda had betrayed his spiritual master.

"Kirtanananda's a thief!" Bryant screamed after reading it to Yuvati. "He claims he's Prabhupada's only true successor and here's proof he tried to steal the movement right from under Prabhupada's nose. There's at least a dozen letters here that condemn him. Listen to this one:

" 'Sometimes there is a risk in the matter of direct

315

service. For example, Kirtanananda was giving me direct service by massaging me, cooking for me, and so many other things. He became puffed up, so much so that he thought his Spiritual Master a common man, and was existing only on account of his service. This mentality at once pushed him down.' "

"Wow! I didn't know about this," Yuvati said.

"I'll bet nine out of ten devotees don't know about it," Bryant said proudly.

"I wonder what would happen if the devotees who think he's God on earth read this?" Yuvati asked.

"He'd be history. But there's more. Kirtanananda's only half of it. Listen to this."

Bryant had always been manic, but Yuvati had never seen him like this. His right leg trembled under the table as if an electric current was stimulating it. His hands shook, and his voice had jumped an octave higher than normal.

"The gurus all claim they ascended to their high positions because Prabhupada had absolute faith in them, right?" Bryant asked.

"I suppose," Yuvati said. She had always considered the gurus like little kids playing "Let's pretend" and usually tried not to think about them.

"They claim Prabhupada had absolute confidence in them, right?" Bryant continued, pressing on.

" Right," Yuvati agreed.

"Lies! Lies! Lies!" Bryant shouted. "They're bogus! Listen to what Prabhupada said about his 'infallible' successors:

" 'I appointed GBC to give me relief from management, but on the contrary, complaints and counter-complaints are coming to me. How can my brain be peaceful?' It's all in this letter he wrote to Jayatirtha in 1975.

"And listen to this letter he wrote to Pusta Krsna. 'This fighting spirit will destroy everything, but what can I do? You American and European boys are trained up in this fighting attitude. Now put it aside and simply work cooperatively for spreading this movement all over the world.'

"Prabhupada considered the GBC more of a problem than a solution!" Bryant exulted. "He wrote Ramesvara in 1975 saying, 'If Tamal Krishna flies ten thousand miles to lodge some complaint against Jayatirtha, what can I do? If you leaders cannot work together, then how can you expect the others to cooperate with you?' And look at this letter to Karandhara: "I think it best if the GBC members always travel. In this way, they will avoid the propensity to sit down and plot and scheme.' Prabhupada foresaw all the current problems fifteen years ago. He wrote Gurudas telling him not to install telexes, because the GBC will only use them to gossip more!"

Yuvati was amazed.

"Sulocana, this is really incredible," she said. "I never knew Prabhupada had all these troubles."

"Nobody knows," Bryant said. "They tried to hide these letters. That obviously is why Ramesvara banned me from the BBT."

"What are you gonna do with all this stuff?" Yuvati asked.

"I'm not sure yet," Bryant said. "I've been too busy to think much about it."

That night Bryant read until his eyes were so tired that the words blurred. He put down the letters and went outside. He locked his van and walked up the dirt road that led into Bhaktivedanta Village. There were more stars in the sky than he could remember seeing.

He was walking along, thinking about Prabhupada, when the revelation hit him. All at once, his life made sense. Why had he joined the movement? Why had he never risen to a responsible position in ISKCON? Why had he married a woman whose brain was made of silly putty? Why had Kirtanananda come between them? Why was Jane divorcing him?

Because Krishna had given him a mission. Krishna wanted him to save the movement. It was all Krishna's plan. All meant to be.

"Kuladri? Sulocana here."

"Yes?" Kuladri asked dully.

"Have you talked to Kirtanananda? Has he agreed to

debate me?" Bryant's questions came rapid-fire. He was calling from the small apartment he had rented on Kittredge Street in Berkeley..

"He's been very busy. I haven't had a chance to ask him," Kuladri said. "As a matter of fact, he isn't even here now. He's traveling."

"Well, that's it, then," Bryant said. "I'm going to go public."

"Go public?" Kuladri asked.

"That's right," Bryant said. "I'm going to take everything I've found to the press and blow New Vrindaban off the map. Too bad. I was hoping we could resolve this internally."

"I'll speak to him about it when he gets back," Kuladri said.

"I'm sure you will," Bryant said angrily. "And I'm sure he won't do a damn thing. I've been calling for weeks, and he still hasn't answered my challenge to a debate. That's why I'm going public."

"Threats will get you nowhere," Kuladri said.

"They're not threats," Bryant said. "They're promises."

Kuladri hung up.

Bryant walked over to the sink to get a glass of water. For the past six months, he had been living in Berkeley, banging out an exposé called "The Guru Business." He was writing it in the van, where he had installed a $495 Commodore Pet computer and a small printer. He was sleeping in the van, too. The apartment wasn't secure enough. Every night he drove around Berkeley looking for a new place to park. He tried to make sure he never spent two nights on the same street, or even in the same neighborhood.

The first thing he had done when he arrived in Berkeley from Three Rivers was look up his old friend Jerome Greene, who was selling cheap oil paintings in shopping malls. Greene was beside himself with excitement when he read Prabhupada's letters. He plugged Bryant into a network of renegade Krishnas who were living in the Bay Area. After they read the letters, they agreed to join Bryant's campaign to overthrow the gurus.

One by one, the renegades had deserted Bryant and

his war. Bryant considered himself Krishna's divinely appointed instrument of retribution and was as autocratic as his archenemy, Kirtanananda. He treated the renegades as his devotees. They wanted to help write "The Guru Business"; he insisted on writing it alone. They wanted him to finish the book and get it printed. They then planned to mail copies to devotees in temples all over the world. They set up a Devotee Access Service using a mailbox in the Berkeley Post Office. When devotees read the revelations in the book, they would be able to get in touch with the revolutionaries and join the crusade.

But Bryant ignored their plans. He couldn't wait to finish the book. As soon as he collected new inflammatory information about New Vrindaban or Kirtanananda, he reacted like a kid with a secret. He'd call Kuladri, tell him everything and threaten to go public. Then he'd print out letters to temple presidents all over the world. He'd ramble on about his latest discovery and declare that the solution to the guru problem was to kill them all.

"The penalty of false preaching is death," he wrote in almost every letter.

The renegades got tired of Bryant's kamikaze tactics and tried to rein him in. Bryant called them gutless. Shouting matches followed. One by one, the renegades stopped visiting the van and withdrew from his war. Bryant didn't seem to notice.

"I'm going to show up with an army and take over the commune," Bryant threatened Kuladri. It was self-delusion. The truth was that even his best friend, Jerome Greene, had quit working with him.

That didn't bother Bryant. Krishna had given him a mission and had provided the perfect opportunity. In less than two weeks, starting on September 16, 1985, the GBC would be holding a big meeting in New Vrindaban. The only problem was how could he get back to West Virginia without getting himself killed? He picked up the phone and dialed 304-555-1212. When the operator answered, he asked for the Marshall County Sheriff's Department.

"I'm leading a campaign to overthrow Kirtanananda

and the rest of the bogus gurus," Bryant told Donald
Bordenkircher, the surprised sheriff. "There's all kinds
of criminal activities going on in New Vrindaban. I want
to come out there and expose them, but I can't unless I
get police protection."

"You really believe that once you enter this county
your life is in danger without police protection?" Bordenkircher asked, after turning on his tape recorder.

"Without a doubt," Bryant said, pride ringing in his
voice. "Keith Ham would kill me in a second if he caught
me. They beat up a girl named Jadurani who was doing
nothing compared to what I'm doing. She was just challenging his authority philosophically. I've been assassinating
his character. I've literally destroyed his reputation within
the society."

"So what you're telling me is, I could have a holy war
on my hands," the sheriff said.

"That's exactly right!" Bryant replied, even prouder.
"That's it."

The sheriff agreed to place Bryant in protective custody if he came to Moundsville. Early the next morning,
Bryant bought a bus ticket to Wheeling, West Virginia.
He wasn't about to take the van. The van was far too
easy a target.

"Could you help me with this thing? I'm not sure how
it goes on."

Tom Westfall helped the New Vrindaban security guard
fit the Second Chance bulletproof vest over his shoulders. It was September 20, 1985, the last day of the big
meeting at New Vrindaban. Westfall was on duty at the
main entrance to the commune, taking pictures for his
files. He had seen a lot of strange sights in his years as
the Krishna cop. But this was one of the strangest.

The New Vrindaban security guards were evidently
scared to death. Their faces were as white as the wispy
layer of clouds that covered the sky. The hands of one of
them shook visibly. They stopped every car and searched
every package, no matter how small.

"We've got information that somebody is going to
plant a bomb in the Palace of Gold," one of the guards

confided to Westfall. "We also hear an armed gang plans to show up to assassinate all our leaders."

The security guard was so plainly frightened that he convinced Westfall an attack really could occur at any minute. Westfall hurried to his squad car, opened his camera bag, and loaded it with extra ammunition.

Could Steve Bryant, the guy locked in protective custody down in the county jail, be the cause of all this? Westfall wondered as he walked back to the main entrance. Or was something else going on?

"I'd sure like to know what's happening in those meetings," Westfall told one of the deputies. "I'd feel a whole lot better if I did."

"I thought you had all kinds of contacts out here," the deputy said.

"I do, but none of them are attending the meetings," Westfall said. "The only people allowed in are temple presidents, members of the GBC, and gurus."

Inside the lodge that Steve Bryant had once hoped to manage, Ravindra Svarupa, the president of the Philadelphia temple, was feeling better about the movement than he had at any time since Prabhupada's death. His spirits picked up every time he looked around the room. Everybody, even the most senior gurus, was sitting on two rows of mattresses along the walls. The vyasasanas were gone. Everyone was on the same level.

Steve Bryant was down in the county jail telling every reporter who would listen that the New Vrindaban meeting had been called to deal with his charges. In fact, the meeting was the result of Ravindra's reform movement.

When Prabhupada died and the gurus took over, Ravindra had sunk into a long, deep depression. He eventually developed a mysterious stomach disease that whittled down his weight and sapped his vitality.

He had begun to snap out of it after the North American temple presidents held a meeting in September 1984, in Towaco, New Jersey, a small town near the Newark Airport. The routine meeting about sankirtan problems had turned into an intense discussion about why and how ISKCON had gone wrong.

The answer, everyone agreed, was the gurus.

The presidents had gone back to their temples and taken a survey of their devotees. A few months later, they returned to Towaco for another meeting. The first order of business was to review the survey's findings.

Question: Are there fundamental and compelling problems with the guru system as it presently exists?

An astounding 94 percent answered yes.

Question: In general, are you satisfied that our ISKCON gurus are exemplifying a spiritual standard expected of a *vaishnava* acharya?

This time 94 percent answered no.

Question: Are many of the gurus displaying an arrogance that is totally inconsistent with the example set by Prabhupada?

Ninety-one percent answered yes.

Ravindra, who had a Ph.D. in religion from Temple University, knew a call to arms when he heard one; he also knew how to write. He began crafting a series of well-reasoned attacks on the gurus—"Ending the Fratricidal War," "Under My Order—Reflections on the Guru in ISKCON," and "Serving Srila Prabhupada's Will." He circulated the papers through the movement. Soon his phone was ringing off the hook.

Kirtanananda denounced the papers as heresy. Bhagavan, the European Sun King, was furious. Ramesvara, the Los Angeles guru, called to scream at Ravindra.

Devotees, on the other hand, were ecstatic. The day after Ramesvara called, Ravindra received a card that said "Good job! Thank You! At last, some hope!" It was signed "Members of Ramesvara's women's sankirtan team."

Devotees also called to warn Ravindra that he was now in danger. Atreya Rishi, the GBC member who was locked in a struggle with Hansadutta and Kirtanananda for control of the Berkeley temple, called to commiserate and warn Ravindra about the gurus' tactics. Rishi said he was getting death threats. "Beware, you are messing with a pure devotee," a voice would say when he answered the phone.

"You've got a wife and kids. You're crazy to get involved in this," Rishi told Ravindra.

One afternoon a few days later, Ravindra got a call from a man who identified himself as a "detective from New Jersey."

"What's your name? Where are you from?" Ravindra asked.

"That's not important," the man said quickly. "I'm calling to tell you that we've heard you're organizing another big meeting in Towaco. We have information that leads us to believe that the organizer of that meeting could be in danger."

Ravindra told his wife about the call and asked if she thought he should quit the reform movement.

"Don't be ridiculous!" she said. "If you buy that stuff about threats to your wife and kids, everybody will be intimidated. We can't let Kirtanananda and a few thugs take over ISKCON."

Sitting on his mattress, Ravindra recalled his wife's courage and smiled to himself. The hard work, the countless telephone calls, and the fear were paying off. For three days, the meetings had crackled with energy. One devotee after another had entered the room, stepped up to the microphone, and borne witness to how the gurus' autocratic behavior had crippled the movement.

Even the GBC had been swept along by the antiguru sentiment. After a few minutes' debate, it had passed a number of resolutions designed to rid the movement of what Ravindra and his supporters called DAD—the "Dreaded Acharya Disease." The meeting had agreed to do away with the gurus' exclusive vyasasanas. And puga, guru worship. And to dilute the gurus' power, it planned to increase the number of gurus to fifty. But best of all, the meeting had passed a resolution to remove the underlying cause of the internecine war that was devouring the movement—the idea that each devotee serves only his guru. It agreed to give any devotee who obtained written permission from three GBC members the power to initiate.

Finally, the meeting had also taken care of one other important piece of business. Steve Bryant, Sulocana, had been excommunicated for issuing death threats in "abhorrent, blasphemous language."

This last day of the meeting was especially exciting because there were rumors that Kirtanananda was going to make an appearance. Kirtanananda had boycotted the conference, even though gurus had come from around the world to attend. He had instructed his followers to treat the visitors as if they were legionnaires, not fellow devotees. He considered the meetings anarchy, beneath the notice of a true acharya. Now, however, it appeared he had changed his mind and would address the convention.

Early in the afternoon, the doors swung open and Kirtanananda's disciples flooded the meeting room. When they were all packed in, two devotees carried in Kirtanananda's vyasasana.

"The language of furniture," Ravindra remarked to Bahudaka, Peter Chatterton, president of the Vancouver temple and his closest ally in the reform wing.

A few moments later, Kirtanananda entered and sat down on the vyasasana.

"Kirtanananda, we love you!" a devotee shouted from the back of the room.

"Be quiet," Kirtanananda snapped. "They won't let you say that here."

"So that's what we're doing here, destroying people's love," Ravindra whispered sarcastically to Bahudaka.

Kirtanananda looked down at the other gurus. Then he began reading a paper as if he were delivering tablets from on high. Kirtanananda's message was simple: Kirtanananda was the true acharya. There would be no peace until everyone recognized that.

"Why did you steal devotees from the Toronto temple?" someone yelled from the back when Kirtanananda finished delivering his message.

"Why do your devotees steal from other temples? Why do your sankirtan teams go wherever they please?" someone else asked.

Kirtanananda didn't deign to offer a response. He stood up and strode out of the room, his followers obediently trailing in his wake.

"It appears the only true acharya thinks free speech is not for the rabble," Bahudaka said to Ravindra.

"I think he just made a big mistake," Ravindra said.

Steve Bryant leaned on the counter in the Marshall County Jail, signing his release forms and waiting for a deputy to return his valuables. Sheriff Bordenkircher, a lean man with a gray pompadour, light blue eyes, a lantern jaw, and a foul tongue, was on the other side of the counter, looking through a pile of arrest reports.

The sheriff had spent hours talking to Bryant and was disgusted with him. Bryant had told him long tales of murder and cover-ups, of drug smuggling and drug dealing, of women being beaten and children abused. The sheriff had pressed for details.

"Steven, give me names," Bordenkircher had asked repeatedly. "Give me something to go on. Get me people who will sign complaints."

Bryant had backed off.

"I can't do that, Sheriff," he kept saying. "I really want to, but these people are afraid for their lives, and I've given my word."

When Bryant wasn't talking to the sheriff, he was on the pay phone in the jail's exercise room, calling every newspaper and television station in the area. A few papers and TV stations had done minor stories—"Devotee Claims Guru Stole His Wife," "Devotee is Excommunicated from Krishnas"—but that was all. Like the sheriff, most reporters had concluded that Bryant was a kook.

"I'll be back," Bryant promised Bordenkircher. "I'm gonna overthrow Keith Ham if it's the last thing I do."

"Steven, will you get the fuck out of here?" Bordenkircher said. "I'm too busy to play games with a goddamn martyr."

Bryant looked at the sheriff. A smile slowly formed on his lips.

"I think you're starting to understand, Sheriff. I really do," he said.

Kirtanananda stood under the floodlights, overseeing the guru kula boys who were laying brick over the dirt road that led to the Palace of Gold. It was Sunday,

October 27, 1985, five weeks after the end of the New Vrindaban meetings. The days were getting shorter and colder, and people in the Moundsville area were talking about the big season the John Marshall High School football team was having.

But in the commune, the focus was on completing the road before winter swept over the mountains and snow buried McCreary's Ridge. For three hours after prasadam every evening, the boys gathered for what devotees called a "brick marathon." And every night, Kirtanananda personally supervised. That night Michael Shockman, Triyogi, was also watching.

Shockman was at the edge of the parking lot, out of the glare of the floodlights. The son of a state senator from LaMoure, North Dakota, Shockman had come to New Vrindaban from the Detroit temple a few weeks earlier. Immediately known as a weirdo, Shockman had lofty ambitions. He asked Kirtanananda to give him sannyasa. Kirtanananda refused, and Shockman had ended up working in the kitchen and picking up litter around the palace. Shockman resented the humiliation and went around the commune muttering to himself. At times he would stop, his eyes fixed on an ill-defined spot somewhere in the distance. He would stare at it in silence, sometimes for minutes and sometimes for hours.

While the boys laid brick, Shockman waited quietly, forgotten in the shadows. When Kirtanananda turned his back, Shockman picked up a three-foot-long steel spike, a bricklayer's tool weighing twenty pounds. He raced up behind the guru. Raising the spike above his head like a club, he brought it crashing down onto Kirtanananda's skull. Drops of blood showered the guru kula boys, as if a watermelon had splattered on concrete.

Kirtanananda hit the bricks face-first. The guru kula boys screamed. Shockman raised the spike and hit the guru twice more on the base of the skull. Then he ran across the parking lot.

Kuladri chased him. Shockman turned and swung the spike at his head. Kuladri ducked under the bar and tackled Shockman. Several guru kula kids ran up and piled on, pinning Shockman to the ground.

"Call an ambulance! We've got to get Kirtanananda to a hospital," Kuladri yelled. He ran over and looked at the guru.

He was deep in a coma.

An ambulance arrived from Moundsville and, with sirens screaming, rushed Kirtanananda to the Ohio Valley Medical Center in Wheeling. Kuladri rode in the back. He refused to leave Kirtanananda, just as Kirtanananda had refused to leave Prabhupada after his stroke during the 1967 Memorial Day weekend. Three days later, a Medivac helicopter airlifted Kirtanananda to Allegheny General Hospital in Pittsburgh, where a team of Hindu doctors took over the case. The swami spent twenty-six days in Allegheny General and underwent two operations to remove hematomas and drain the cerebrospinal fluid that had collected at the base of his skull.

Kirtanananda survived. When he returned to the commune, he needed a walker to get around. Later, he used two canes. One of his first decisions after he again took charge of New Vrindaban was to buy two specially trained German shepherd attack dogs, who never left his side, night or day.

"How are you, Swami?" Tom Westfall asked when they passed each other near the Temple of Understanding one morning.

"Not well, not well at all," Kirtanananda said. "I have severe headaches, bouts of dizziness, and double vision."

"That's really too bad," Westfall said.

"It is," Kirtanananda said. "Right now I'm seeing two of you, and that's two too many."

Then he turned and hobbled away.

On December 4, 1985, two weeks after he got out of the hospital, Kirtanananda called a press conference at New Vrindaban. In a quivering voice, he charged that the attack was all Steve Bryant's fault: he had influenced Michael Shockman.

Michael Shockman was immediately slapped behind bars in the Marshall County Jail. He was given fifteen months for assault.

Shortly after his sentencing, he received an unsigned letter postmarked Berkeley, California. The letter said,

> You will be spiritually rewarded for attacking Swami Kirtanananda. These gurus more or less have declared open season on themselves and they have no one to blame but themselves. It is only a matter of time before each 'guru' is dead or wishes he were. Their fate is sealed by their actions.

The desk officer and everybody else in the Marshall County Jail remembered Steve Bryant from the days he had spent there in protective custody. They were all convinced it was he who had written the letter.

It wasn't long after the letter arrived that Bryant called, asking to speak to Sheriff Bordenkircher.

"Is there a message for the sheriff?" the officer asked Bryant. "He's off duty."

"Yeah," Bryant said. "Tell him he shouldn't have Shockman in jail. Tell him he should give the man a medal."

Jonestown in Moundsville

"Take sannyasa. Unless you give up your family, you'll never reach Krishna."

"Kirtanananda, please don't do this to me," Kuladri pleaded. "I've got five kids. I can serve you and be a husband and a father, too."

"You must choose between your spiritual life and your mundane attachments to the material plane," Kirtanananda said.

"Please, Kirtanananda, don't make me give up my family."

"You're in maya," Kirtanananda hissed. He then turned and hobbled away on his two canes, flanked by his two guard dogs.

"It isn't right," Kuladri muttered as he watched Kirtanananda go. "I've been the temple president for almost ten years. I'm the one who got the palace built. And now he does this to me."

Kuladri walked into his office only to find Terry Sheldon, the president of the Cleveland temple, sitting behind his desk. Sheldon, Tapahpunja, had arrived in New Vrindaban the day after Shockman had brained Kirtanananda. A tall, strong man with a shaved head, broad nose, and big ears, Sheldon was the son of labor organizers who had tried to teach him that Joe Hill was right—God is a pie-in-the-sky fantasy created to oppress the people. Sheldon revolted. At fourteen, he was a hippie in the Haight, shoplifting to buy drugs. A few years later, he joined the Krishnas in Berkeley and eventually migrated to New Vrindaban.

"Something's happened to Kirtanananda," Kuladri said to Sheldon, shaking his head as he sat down in the chair opposite his own desk. "He's becoming more and more illogical. He flies into rages over nothing."

"Don't question him—not in my presence," Sheldon warned.

"I think it's the medication he's on," Kuladri continued, ignoring Sheldon. "I think that's what's doing it."

Sheldon slammed his fist on the desk. "What's the matter with you, man? Are you so damn dumb you can't see what's happening?"

"What are you talking about?" an alarmed Kuladri asked.

"He wants you out. You're finished. Done. Tell me how I can make it clearer and I will."

"But why? What did I do?" Kuladri asked.

"You didn't protect him," Sheldon said with hatred in his voice. "You let Shockman get to him. You're weak. With Steve Bryant on the loose, Kirtanananda needs people who can protect him."

In the first week of January 1986, Bryant drove to the Bay Area and asked Jerome Greene to sell the Ford van for him. On January 9, he flew to Detroit.

For over a week, Bryant stayed holed up in his old room at his parents' house. He was grinding out a paper called "Jonestown in Moundsville," an abridged version of "The Guru Business." Bryant planned to have the broadside professionally printed. Then he would place a copy under the windshield wiper of every car, and in every mailbox, in Moundsville.

"The devotees haven't done a damn thing," Bryant told his father. "They've been under the thumbs of the gurus so long, they've lost their spirit. That's why I'm taking this to the people of Moundsville. Those hillbillies down there can be mean. When I let them know what's going on in New Vrindaban, they'll force the authorities to shut the place down. And if the authorities don't do it, they'll storm the palace and do it themselves."

"Steven, I haven't told you what to do since you turned eighteen," Jack Bryant said very quietly. "And I'm not gonna start now. I'm gonna beg. Don't go down there.

Please. Let those crazies self-destruct if they want to, and go on with your life."

"I can't do that. It's my duty to Krishna."

Bryant paused for a moment.

"But I'll tell you what I will do: I'll have a beer with you."

Jack Bryant couldn't believe his ears.

"We haven't had a beer together since you joined the Krishnas," he said.

"I know. I figure it's about time we did," Bryant said.

"Jamuna? Sulocana here."

"Sulocana? Where are you?" Jane asked.

Jane's new husband, Ralph Seward, leaped off the couch and raced to the phone to listen in.

"You think I'd tell you where?" Bryant said. "What do you take me for, an idiot like that guy Kirtanananda had you marry?"

"What do you want?" Jane asked.

"To warn you," Bryant said.

"Why?" Jane asked. She had grown immune to Bryant's threats.

"Because I care about my sons, that's why," Bryant said indignantly. "Kirtanananda's a vindictive son of a bitch. I'm going to launch an attack on him and I don't want him to retaliate against Sarva and Nimai. I'm not asking you to come back to me—we're finished, I know. I'm asking you to leave the commune for your sons' sake."

"What kind of attack? Sulocana, what are you going to do?"

"You'll see," Bryant said.

Then he hung up.

"Hello, Mrs. Bryant. This is Jerome Greene calling."

"Jerome! It's so good to hear your voice. I haven't talked to you since, well, I can't remember when. How are you? How's Marianne?"

"We're fine. Still out here on the West Coast. I called to talk to Sulocana. I figured if he ever needed a friend, it's now."

"He's already left for West Virginia," Helga said.

"Gee, that was fast," Greene said.

"He bought another van. An old Dodge. He drove down there in that."

"Do you have a number where he is? I'd like to find out how he's doing."

"Wait a second and I'll get it. But whatever you do, don't give it to anybody else."

"Of course not, Mrs. Bryant."

"Randall, it's Tirtha."

"Tirtha! Where you calling from?" Randall Gorby asked. He had become used to calls from Tom Drescher.

"Detroit. I'm traveling with Tapahpunja, Terry Sheldon. I've got a telephone number in your area I'd like you to check out."

"Where is it?" Gorby asked.

"I'm not exactly sure," Drescher replied.

"No problem." Gorby said. "It won't take but an hour or so to check it."

"It's almost nine. I'll call again around ten. If you're not there, I'll keep trying till I get you."

Randall Gorby had been the Krishnas' best friend in West Virginia since he'd met Keith Ham and Howard Wheeler in the summer of 1968. In the early seventies, Gorby was the Krishna's straw man, buying property for them from farmers unwilling to sell to the sect. Married and the father of seven children, Gorby worked for thirty-three years for Wheeling Pittsburgh Steel before retiring in 1982. A genuine blue-collar intellectual who had often lectured at Bethany College, a small liberal-arts school in his home town, Gorby was a socialist and a labor activist who reflexively sided with the underdog. He also had an abiding interest in Eastern religions, which dated from World War II, when he was stationed in India, Burma, and China for two and one-half years. In India, Gorby became friendly with several Brahmins, who taught him the rudiments of Hinduism. He'd kept studying on his own.

One of Gorby's many Krishna friends had introduced him to Drescher during the summer of 1983, the very summer Drescher had killed St. Denis. The two became friendly, trading a trailer for a school bus and swapping wood stoves. Soon they developed a father-son relationship.

Gorby called the number Drescher gave him and found out it was the Scott Motel. He drove across the river to Saint Clairsville, Ohio, and saw that an old Dodge van was parked in front of the motel.

Drescher called shortly after Gorby got back home.

"Nice going, Randall," Drescher said after Gorby passed the information along.

"Where are you?" Gorby asked.

"Still in Detroit. We're heading your way."

Gorby went to bed. At 4:30 A.M. the phone woke him.

"Randall? It's Tirtha again. Did I wake you?"

"Yeah."

"Sorry," Drescher said.

"Where are you now?" Gorby said groggily.

"Steubenville, Ohio. Listen, I need your help."

"Where do you want me to meet you?"

"How about exit fourteen on I-Seventy in an hour. That's the Saint Clairsville exit. We'll take it from there."

"Hello, Mrs. Bryant. This is Jerome Greene calling from California."

"Jerome!" Two calls in two days. This really is something," Helga said.

"Two calls? Mrs. Bryant, I haven't talked to you in months."

Helga Bryant shuddered. Before leaving, Steve had left careful instructions about what to do if Jerome called him. ' 'Watch out for someone pretending to be Jerome," he had said several times. "New Vrindaban calls people all the time pretending to be someone else. Before you say anything, ask Jerome to name the city where we worked after we left London.

"Where did you and my son work after you left London?" Helga asked.

"Newcastle-upon-Tyre, why?"

"Oh, my God! Somebody called here yesterday claiming to be you, and I gave them the number of the motel where Steven is staying."

"It had to be somebody from New Vrindaban," Greene said quickly. "You'd better get word to Steve right away."

Helga hung up and immediately called the Scott Motel. There was no answer from her son's room.

Gorby and Drescher were sitting in Gorby's car, down the block from the Scott Motel. They had been waiting there since five-thirty in the morning. At nine-thirty, Bryant walked out to his van.

"There he goes," Drescher said. He ran back to his own car and the two of them followed Bryant.

Bryant drove through Saint Clairsville and headed east on I-70. He got off at the downtown Wheeling exit and drove around until he found a parking place. Then he walked into the Federal Court Building.

Drescher rejoind Gorby. "What the fuck is he gonna do in there?" he asked. "Is he gonna file suit to get his kids back, or something?"

"That would be a state case, not federal," Gorby said.

"Then what's he doing in there?" Drescher asked.

"My guess is, he's talking to the FBI. That's where their offices are."

Drescher was silent, staring hard at the people walking in and out of the building.

"You know, I'm going to have to kill that son of a bitch," he said quietly. "Just like I did St. Denis. I'm no virgin. Dan Reid and I killed him. But he died hard. He died like a wild boar hog."

Steve Bryant was lying in a sagging bed in a cheap rooming house five miles south of Moundsville, nipping on a bottle of vodka. He had just finished putting the final touches to "Jonestown in Moundsville."

Bryant had moved to the boarding house after his mother reached him and told him that she'd given his location to someone pretending to be Jerome Greene. He took another hit of the vodka and looked at the red label. He was breaking his vows, but it was the only way to steady his nerves. He'd quit when this was over.

There was a knock on the door. Bryant jumped. He

worked to calm himself, reached under the pillow, grabbed his .45, and moved to the side of the door.

"Who's there?" he asked tensely.

"Sheriff's deputies. Open up," a voice said.

Bryant relaxed slightly. He opened the door a few inches and saw two young deputies, Sam Elson and Mike Younger.

"Just a moment," he said.

He shut the door, removed the chain, and stepped aside.

"So, what's up?" Bryant asked as the two deputies entered. "The sheriff want to see me?"

Bryant had been talking to Sheriff Bordenkircher and his chief deputy, Joe Hummel, ever since he had arrived in the area. They knew where he was and why he was in Marshall County.

" 'Fraid not, Steven. You're under arrest," Elson said matter-of-factly.

"For *what?*" Bryant screamed.

"For threatening to commit a violent act. Your ex-wife's husband filed a complaint claiming you've been calling her and making threats."

"That's a lie and you know it. I only called once and that was to warn her." Bryant said.

"Sorry, Steven," Younger said and turned Bryant around to handcuff him. "I've got orders to take you in."

While he read Bryant his rights, Elson searched him.

"Jesus, what's this?" Elson said, jumping away from Bryant. He was holding the .45 that Bryant had tucked into his belt.

The deputies searched the room and found a couple of joints' worth of marijuana, a couple of tabs of LSD, and some codeine. They boxed up copies of "The Guru Business," "Jonestown in Moundsville," and transcripts of Bryant's interviews with dissident devotees. They found his address book and threw it on top of the other material. Then they hustled him to the squad car.

"Hey, Westfall, we've got a bunch of your buddies here," the desk officer said as Westfall walked into the sheriff's department.

"Buddies?" the sergeant asked.

"Yeah. There's a whole bunch of Kritters in the Chief Deputy's office."

"You're kidding. What the hell are they doing there?" Westfall asked.

"Damned if I know," the desk officer said.

Westfall went back to Hummel's office and knocked on the door. There was no answer. He opened it a crack and peeked into the room.

Bordenkircher's Chief Deputy Sheriff, Joe Hummel, wasn't there. Bryant's papers were spread out over Hummel's desk. A half-dozen Krishnas were going through them. One was dictating into a cassette tape recorder from the open address book.

Westfall was furious. In police departments across the country, evidence seized in the course of a search is turned over to custodians, who catalog and guard it until it is needed by the court. But that didn't happen here. The sheriff's office had kept all the evidence seized in Bryant's hotel room, including the .45, in Hummel's office.

Westfall had asked Hummel several times for permission to examine it.

Hummel had always refused.

Westfall closed the door and ran down to the sheriff's office. He knocked and entered without waiting for permission. Sheriff Bordenkircher was sitting at his desk, smoking a cigarette. A framed sash, studded with Boy Scout merit badges, hung on the wall behind him.

"Sheriff, what the hell is going on here?" Westfall demanded.

"What the fuck are you talking about?" the sheriff said.

"You got Krishnas down in Hummel's office going through Bryant's papers," Westfall said. "One of them has a tape recorder that he's using to take down the names and addresses."

"Calm down, Tom. I know all about it. I invited them in," Bordenkircher said.

"You *what?*" Westfall shouted, trying hard not to lose his composure.

"Tom, what we've got here is a crazy guy who shows

up with a fucking loaded gun. He says he wants to kill the fuckin' guru. He says he's got undercover people up there workin' with him."

"There's nobody up there working with him, I could have told you that," Westfall said.

The sheriff went on as if Westfall hadn't spoken.

"If he's got people up there working with him, we gotta know who they are. We gotta know what we're dealing with here, Tom. If a fucking holy war is gonna break out on the ridge, we gotta be prepared."

Westfall started to lash out at the sheriff, but stopped himself. The man was beneath contempt. Westfall turned and walked out of the office without saying a word.

Bordenkircher watched him go and shrugged. The sheriff had started his career in law enforcement as a guard at San Quentin. During the Vietnam War, he worked in the Office of Public Safety, a police agency that operated out of the State Department. It sent him to South Vietnam as the U.S. liaison to the director of prisons.

He came to Moundsville in 1973 to become warden at the West Virginia State Penitentiary. One of his first decisions was to install a snitch system. He quit to run for sheriff in 1984. Robert Lightner, his popular predecessor, had served two four-year terms and, under the law, could not succeed himself.

But Lightner, a local, had made clear his plans to run again in 1988. Since Lightner hated the Krishnas, and vice versa, Bordenkircher thought they just might be his key to success. If he could build some bridges to New Vrindaban, the Krishna vote might swing a close election his way.

Bordenkircher began by having long conversations with Kuladri about a new special-deputies program he wanted to start. The sheriff claimed the county needed more cops in case a riot broke out at the penitentiary. The special deputies would be issued ID cards, badges, and baseball-style hats with the department's insignia on the front and would ride along with regular deputies.

A secretary told Westfall about the program. He went through the applications and discovered several Krishnas had applied to be special deputies. Several of them had criminal records.

"But no criminal records in this state," the sheriff said when Westfall confronted him about the applications. "If they haven't done anything in West Virginia, I can appoint them and swear them in."

Westfall slowly shook his head, turned, and walked out of the room.

"I'm *what?*" David Gold said with complete incredulity.

"You're fired," Bryant repeated.

Bryant and his attorney were in an interview room in the Marshall County Jail, where Bryant had been locked up for over two months awaiting trial. Razor-tongued and aggressive to the point of being rude, David Gold was the lawyer to get if you had a beef with New Vrindaban. Gold had handled everything, from Richard Rose's suit to get his farm back, to the child-custody suit brought by Howard Wheeler's wife.

"But I won!" Gold said. "I got the 'intent to commit a violent act' charge dismissed. We can beat the weapons charge, too."

"You beat the charge on a technicality," Bryant said angrily. "You didn't even put me on the stand. I don't want you to do that with the second charge. That's why I'm firing you. I'm going to defend myself."

"You're firing me for doing my job?" Gold asked.

"I'm firing you because you didn't do what I wanted," Bryant said.

"And what you want is to turn the gun trial into the Krishna version of the Chicago Seven, right?" Gold asked.

"Right." Bryant said. "I'm gonna call every reporter I've ever talked to and make sure they're there."

"Suit yourself," Gold said, snapping his briefcase shut.

Bryant's trial on the gun charge began at ten o'clock on Thursday, April 3. It ended at five-thirty that afternoon. Bryant's defense took up most of the time.

He put his mother on the stand and had her testify about the phone call from somebody claiming to be Jerome Greene.

Then he took the stand.

"From what my mother has said, you can see why it was necessary for me to carry a gun," Bryant told the six-person jury. "To explain how this all started, I have to go back to the breakup of my marriage. To understand a Krishna-conscious marriage, you must understand a woman's role in traditional Hindu society.

"Now, . . . " he began.

Steve Bryant's father looked at the jury. They were bored out of their skulls. One middle-aged man kept nodding off and waking with a start. Jack couldn't blame him. He was bored stiff, too.

The jury took less than twenty minutes to convict Bryant. The judge didn't take much longer to sentence him to six months in the county jail.

Jack Bryant put up five thousand dollars in bond money. If Steven's appeal for a new trial was denied, he would have to surrender to the sheriff in ninety days.

It took eight days for the check and the paperwork to clear. As soon as Bryant was released, he jumped in his van and drove straight to his parents' house in suburban Detroit.

Tom Drescher followed. He waited outside the house. Late that night, after the Bryants had gone to bed and their home was dark, Drescher snuck up the driveway. He crouched behind the bumper of Bryant's van and attached a Snoopy sticker to the metal.

The next time Drescher saw the van, it was in Los Angeles.

Holy War

Monkey on a Stick

"When you got married the first time, did your husband propose?" Bryant asked Kathy Berry, the woman he had been seeing since he first came to Three Rivers, two years before.

"No," Kathy said. "The temple president in LA arranged the whole thing. It was the flower ceremony. You know the routine."

They were holding hands, sitting on a large rock in the middle of the Kaweah River, downstream from the town of Three Rivers. It was April 1986, and the sun was approaching summer intensity.

"OK, this time it's gonna be different. I'm not gonna get down on my knees, but I'm gonna propose: Do you want to get married?"

Berry couldn't believe her ears.

"What about your campaign against the gurus? You've always said that comes first."

"Not anymore. It's over. You and your kids come first now."

"Over?"

"Done. I'm finished with it. I've finally realized I can't save ISKCON if ISKCON doesn't want to be saved."

"When did you decide all this?" Berry asked.

"In jail, mostly. And on the trip back out here. When it took the karmis only twenty minutes to convict me, I figured the hell with it. They don't care; the devotees don't care; nobody cares. The whole time I was locked up, nobody called me. Nobody dropped a line. You and Yuvati were the only ones to write."

"Don't be so hard on yourself," Berry said. "You woke up a lot of people."

"The only one I woke up is me," Bryant said, smiling more to himself than at Berry. "I'm turning it all over to Krishna. I've even stopped carrying a gun."

They looked into a deep pool of swirling water and were silent for a while.

"Here's the deal," Bryant finally said. "I've thought it all through. You ready?"

"Ready," Berry said.

"I'm going to sell the jewelry business. I've been talking to three devotees. They've offered me ten thousand dollars for the whole thing. I'm going to LA to seal the deal. Then I'm going to use that money to start a business customizing campers. I've got a lot of ideas. There's an ex-devotee in Mount Shasta who's got a garage. I called him the other day, and he said I could use his place until I get the business going."

Bryant paused to look at the river.

"And I'm gonna get my kids back," he said. "I'm gonna hire David Gold."

"Who?" Kathy interrupted.

"David Gold, the lawyer I had in Moundsville. I pissed him off pretty bad, but I think I've patched it up. I called to apologize just before I left, and I think he'll take the case."

Bryant stopped talking. The only sound was the river rushing past the boulders.

"So, what do you say?" Bryant asked.

"Well, you've hit me with an awful lot," Berry said. "I'm going to have to think about it."

"Sure, take your time," Bryant said, trying but failing to mask the disappointment in his voice. "It's a big decision. There's no hurry."

They fell silent again.

"I just thought about it," Berry said, smiling.

"I want to marry you."

"It's 1986, for crying out loud! I've been out of the movement for over three years. How'd you find me?" Vladimir Vassilievich, Vipra, asked.

"They've got your address at the Berkeley temple," the devotee said.

Vassilievich, forty-seven years old, was living at home with his elderly Ukrainian mother in a beautiful two-story brick building in San Francisco's Sunset district. The two men were standing on the front porch, sheltered from the stiff April wind that was blowing bits of paper down the street.

"So, why'd you look me up?"

"Do you remember Sulocana, Steve Bryant?"

"Yeah, sure. He used to come through Berkeley all the time."

"They want to off this guy," the devotee told him.

"Who does?"

"The New Vrindaban hierarchy."

"Are you making me an offer?" Vassilievich asked.

"If you help us out, we'll see that you're treated right."

"You're crazy," Vassilievich shot back. "Bryant is harmless. Now get outta here. You're bringing back a lot of memories that I've spent a lot of energy trying to forget."

Steve Bryant stopped his van in front of the Village Store in Three Rivers.

"You stay here and watch the computer stuff," Bryant said to Kathy Berry. "I'll run in and get us something to drink."

Bryant went inside and Kathy got out and wandered over to a newspaper rack where an old dog was sleeping in the sun. She crouched down to pet him. When she looked up, she noticed that a man in a white truck parked across the lot was staring at her. She petted the dog again. When she looked up, the man was walking toward her.

"You got Michigan plates on your van. You from Michigan?" the guy asked.

"No, my friend is," Berry said.

The man nodded and smiled and walked back to his truck. As soon as he pulled away, Berry ran into the store, where Bryant was in the checkout line holding a quart of lemon-flavored mineral water.

"There's a guy out there who's following us," Berry told him anxiously. "He was looking at me and the van, and then he came up and asked if I was from Michigan."

"So? He's probably a Michigan tourist," Bryant said. "There's lots of them out here."

"Sulocana, I'm telling you, this guy is following you," Berry said. "He's creepy."

Bryant put the mineral water on the counter, put his arm around Berry, and kissed her.

"Just when I'm getting over being paranoid, it looks like you've caught the disease. It must be infectious," Bryant said with a grin. "Come on, forget it. Let's go swimming."

Steve Forbes, Nistrigunya, a part-time devotee, part-time carpenter, out-of-work actor, and an old friend of Steve Bryant, reached down and picked up a can of Coors Light that was on the floor beside him.

"Empty," Forbes said, dropping the can. "Let's have one more."

"No thanks, two's my limit," Bryant said.

"It's early," Forbes said.

"It's not. It's almost midnight," Bryant said.

"Come on, one more," Forbes said. ' 'I haven't seen you in months. And if you're going up to Mount Shasta, who knows when we'll get together again?"

Bryant smiled. "I told you, I've got to get some sleep. I'm meeting the devotees who are gonna buy my jewelry business first thing in the morning."

"So sleep here. I got a bed in the back room. It's got to be better than that old van of yours."

Bryant smiled again. "I'm trying to have more faith in Krishna," he said. "I'm trying not to be so paranoid. But there are people out there who want to kill me. If I stay here, I'm putting you in danger, and there's no sense doing that."

Forbes thought his old friend was being melodramatic.

"Anything you say, Sulocana. You've spent so damn much time in vans over the past few years, you probably have trouble sleeping in a house."

"You're right," Bryant laughed. "Anyway, thanks for dinner. It was great talking about old times. I expect I'll be in LA a few more days. Let's get together one more time."

"Sure, anytime. Call me when you know what you're doing. And congrats on your engagement. Send me an invite to the wedding."

"Be happy to," Bryant said.

Forbes watched Bryant walk to his rusted-out maroon van. Then he turned out the lights and went to bed.

Bryant drove a block and a half to the corner of Flint Avenue and Cardiff Street. He pulled over and was about to crawl in the back when he remembered he hadn't chanted his rounds. He was tired, but his head was clear—the two beers hadn't affected him at all. He was going to start a new life away from the movement, but he was determined to keep chanting and maintain his vows.

He began softly.

"Hare Krishna, Hare Krishna; Hare Rama, Rama Rama . . ."

Thomas Drescher approached the van from the back. He pulled out a .45, flattened his back against the side of the vehicle, and crept up to the driver's window. Then he took a step forward and turned a half circle. He extended his arms and used both hands to steady the heavy gun. It was aimed straight at Bryant's head.

Bryant saw something move out of the corner of his eye. He jerked his head around to look out the driver's window and saw Thomas Drescher's gun. It was too late.

Drescher fired. The bullet shattered the window and exploded into Bryant's cheek. It then went through his lower mandible and smashed into a carotid artery. Blood spurted. Drescher didn't wait to see the damage. He fired again. The second bullet also hit Bryant in the face.

He fell over onto the steering wheel, dead.

"Jerome? It's Helga Bryant. I'm calling with horrible news. They got Steven. He was shot in Los Angeles this morning."

Greene slumped into a couch. Bryant's mother was sobbing and trying to tell him about her son's murder. She mumbled a few sentences, but couldn't go on. She forced herself to give Greene the name and number of the Los Angeles police detective handling the case and begged him to call if he had any information that might help the investigation.

As soon as Jerome hung up, Marianne Greene came in from the kitchen, curious about who had called.

"What's wrong?" she said as soon as she glanced at her husband. "You look awful."

"Sulocana is dead. His mother just called. They killed him in Los Angeles."

Marianne gasped and put a hand over her mouth. Her legs turned weak. She tried to steady herself but sunk into a chair across from her husband.

"Who do you think did it?" she asked.

"Who do you think?" Jerome answered.

"But why now?" Marianne asked. "He wasn't fighting anybody anymore. He'd given up. They knew he'd settled down and was getting married. Why couldn't they just leave him in peace?"

"Because Sulocana is their monkey on a stick," Jerome said. Then he ran across the room, buried his face in his wife's lap, and began to cry.

The Executioner's Trail

Yuvati Matusow was exhausted. She'd been partying for five days straight, ever since she had driven to Los Angeles to visit her boyfriend. They were supposed to meet some friends and go out for a late dinner, but Yuvati had crashed. It would take a crane to get her up from her boyfriend's bed.

Yuvati laid there until nine, when she heard the front door open and her boyfriend greet two visitors. She recognized the voices as belonging to devotee friends from the Los Angeles temple. But she didn't pay any particular attention.

"Did you hear Sulocana was shot early this morning?" one of the devotees asked Yuvati's boyfriend. The question was like a shot of pure adrenaline. Yuvati jumped off the bed and ran into the front room, where her boyfriend and the two devotees were sitting.

"Sulocana's been shot?" she asked in a panic. "How is he? Where is he? What hospital is he in? I've got to go see him right away."

"You can't," one of the LA devotees said. "He's dead."

Yuvati shrieked. Yuvati seemed to be struck dumb. She stood and stared at the devotee. Then she shrieked again. Her boyfriend came over and put his arms around her. Yuvati shook him off and ran outside screaming. She raced up the sidewalk, howling like a coyote. She tried to stop herself by jamming her fist in her mouth. It only muffled the long shrieks. Her boyfriend caught up with her and pulled her hand out of her mouth. Yuvati screamed in his face.

Pictures of Bryant flashed through her mind. She could have saved him! He had called the day before to ask her

349

and her boyfriend to join him and Steve Forbes for dinner.

"We have other plans," Yuvati had told him.

"Oh," Bryant had said. "Stop by Steve's house later, if you can."

Yuvati had promised they would try. But when the time came, she'd been too tired. If only she'd gone to dinner, Sulocana might still be alive!

Steve Forbes lived only two blocks from Yuvati's boyfriend's house. She tore away from her boyfriend and sprinted all the way, her screams giving way to violent sobs. She raced through the front yard and burst into Forbes's house without knocking.

Forbes had just been fitted for braces and was sucking on an ice cube and talking on the phone when Yuvati stormed into his house. He hung up as soon as he saw her.

"How did it happen? Tell me how it happened!" she screamed.

"He insisted on sleeping in the van," Forbes said. "I turned off the lights and went to bed. I heard two shots, and I think I heard two cars tear away. I got up and walked out on the porch and listened. Everything was quiet, so I went back to bed. I guess I didn't want to face it, because I thought, Naw, it can't be, and went back to sleep."

"Have you talked to the cops?" Yuvati demanded.

"Sure. They called and I told them he'd been here. I told them about hearing two shots and two cars squealing away. They're supposed to interview me in a day or two."

"Did you tell them what Sulocana was doing?"

"You mean his campaign?" Forbes asked.

"What else?"

"No, they didn't get into that."

"We have to tell them right now. We're going to go right down to the police station and tell them now."

"Yuvati, it's too late," Forbes complained. "The detectives handling the case probably went home hours ago. We'll stop by tomorrow."

"Right now!" Yuvati shrieked.

Her boyfriend drove them to the police station in west Los Angeles. A night detective offered them coffee and led them into an interview room.

"We really don't have very much to go on," the detective acknowledged. "Do you know if your friend was involved in drugs? Was he having any serious domestic problems?"

"You do have something to go on," Yuvati said. "That's why we're here. You've got a religious assassination on your hands. Steve Bryant was a Hare Krishna. He was killed by a Hare Krishna from West Virginia."

The detective gave Yuvati a look of incredulity.

"This is going to be the most confusing case you've ever worked on," Yuvati continued. "The first thing you've gotta do is take a piece of paper and draw a line down the middle. Put Western names on one side and Krishna names on the other. That's the only way you'll be able to keep track of everybody."

The detective followed her directions. For the next half hour, Yuvati and Steve Forbes sketched out Bryant's crusade. They told the detective about Bryant's attempts to discredit and overthrow the gurus. They described the attack on Kirtanananda and how he blamed Bryant for the violence.

The detective's eyes began to glaze over.

"But do you have any idea who might have killed him?" he asked impatiently as the long list of names on his yellow legal pad grew.

"I *know* who killed him," Yuvati said. "Write this name down: Thomas Drescher, T-i-r-t-h-a."

"Yuvati, shut up!" Forbes interrupted. "Think about what you're saying. You don't have any proof that Drescher did it."

"He's the only one who's dumb enough and crazy enough to do it," Yuvati said.

The detective added the name to his list and thanked them for their cooperation. He then escorted Yuvati, her boyfriend, and Forbes out of the station. Yuvati and her boyfriend dropped off Forbes and returned to their small house in west LA. Early the next afternoon, two men knocked on the door. When Yuvati's boyfriend answered, they asked to see her. She had been up all night and didn't want to see anybody.

"You'd better talk to them," her boyfriend said. "They're cops."

"The department is taking your story about the Hare Krishnas being involved seriously, Miss Matusow," said the taller of the two homicide detectives, Leroy Orozco. "We want you to sit down and tell us everything you told the detective last night."

She did. And more. Yuvati spent three hours giving a crash course in the history of Krishna Consciousness to Orozco and his partner, Paul "The Stump" Tippin. Then she explained where Bryant fit in. When the cops finally left, she went back to bed and tried to get some sleep. The last time she had been this exhausted was after childbirth. But she still couldn't sleep. She couldn't stop thinking about Bryant and their last conversation. She had to fight an overwhelming desire to see his body. If she could just say good bye, she'd feel better.

She climbed out of bed, planning to go to the morgue. Instead, she picked up the phone and called her ex-husband, Paul Ferry, who was still living in New Vrindaban. Yuvati had split up with Ferry, the former treasurer of the commune, shortly after she had become pregnant with their first child. Ferry had wanted to stay in the commune with Kirtanananda; she had refused to raise a child there.

"So, you guys finally got around to killing Sulocana," Yuvati said sarcastically as soon as Ferry came on the line.

"Oh, Sulocana is dead?" Ferry asked. His voice didn't register any surprise.

"Yeah. Tirtha came out here and shot him twice in the head," Yuvati said.

"I saw Tirtha a couple of weeks ago on the farm, and he told me that he was going to do it," Ferry said. "He said he was going to go out to California and kill Sulocana. I thought he was just talking big and didn't pay any attention to him."

Yuvati hung up and ran across the room. She tore apart her purse looking for the card the homicide detectives had given her. When she found it, she ran back to the phone and called the number.

Detective Orozco answered.

"I was right about Tirtha!" she cried.

Randall Gorby was scared. He had refused to believe Tom Drescher when Drescher had said that he'd killed Charles St. Denis, or that he was going to kill Steve Bryant.

Gorby had often told his wife that Drescher was the king of the bullshitters. Drescher had been moved from orphanage to orphanage and kicked around so much as a kid that he needed to talk tough. But Gorby had believed that underneath the don't-fuck-with-me facade lurked a lovable guy who was as hungry for friends as an abandoned puppy.

The backwoods philosopher now realized he'd been dead wrong about Drescher. Beneath the tough-guy exterior lurked a cold-blooded killer. Gorby had read every story about Steve Bryant's murder in Los Angeles, frightened that he'd see Drescher's name. By helping Drescher track Bryant, Gorby could well be next on Drescher's list. If Drescher thought Gorby might go to the cops, the killer in Drescher would blow Gorby away just as he had blown away Chuck St. Denis and Steve Bryant.

Gorby thought about it for hours and realized he had no choice but to protect himself. One of his sons played in a bluegrass band with a state trooper named Bill Knight. That evening Gorby called Knight and told him what he knew. Knight talked to his superiors, who ordered a tap placed on Gorby's phone. The call they were waiting for came through on May 26, 1986, four days after Bryant's murder.

"You been reading the papers, Randall?" Drescher asked.

"I have, Tom. From what I can tell, you've been busy."

"I called to say good bye, Randall. Things are really hot. I'm going to India."

"When?" Gorby asked.

"Soon. The sooner the better," Drescher said.

"Where are you now?" Gorby asked.

"Over here in Kent, Ohio, at a restaurant with Terry Sheldon, my wife, and her kid. Randall, I really got to go. I just wanted to say good bye. You're the closest thing I ever had to a father."

The state police, who had monitored the call, radioed the information to the Kent police, who put out an all-points bulletin.

"He's traveling in a white Isuzu Trooper II," Ronald Piatt, a Kent detective, told the two uniformed officers riding with him in an unmarked squad car. "When last heard from, he was in a restaurant. I thought we'd check the places around campus first."

They cruised past Kent State University, paying special attention to the places favored by students. Piatt figured Drescher and his group would have split as soon as he hung up the receiver.

"There it is, up there," Piatt said. He could barely believe what he was seeing.

He drove by the Isuzu to make sure. Then he radioed for backup help and pulled over. Piatt and the uniformed cops got out of their cruiser, fanned out, and moved toward the truck. They drew their guns and crouched into position behind other vehicles in the restaurant's parking lot.

Drescher, his wife, his four-year-old stepson, and Sheldon came out of the restaurant a few minutes later and stopped to chat by the door. Every once in a while, Sheldon looked around nervously. But not Drescher. He looked for all the world like a clerk on his lunch break.

Finally, the group walked across the parking lot and piled into the Isuzu Trooper. The cops waited until Drescher put the key in the ignition. Then they swarmed around the truck.

"Freeze!" one screamed. "Police! Let's see your hands!"

Sheldon was too stunned to move.

"Get those hands up! Grab the ceiling!"

Sheldon followed orders. Drescher's four-year-old stepson began whimpering and clung to his mother. Her face remained absolutely expressionless. Drescher gave the cops his usual smug smirk, as if they'd pulled him over for nothing more serious than running a stop sign.

The cops handcuffed their prisoners, took them to the Portage County Jail, and began taking inventory of the Isuzu's contents. It took a long time. Every nook and cranny in the Trooper was crammed with clothing, kitchen utensils, camping gear, and food.

Police at the station searched Drescher and found a diary, which listed the make and license number of Steve Bryant's van, his addresses in Royal Oak, Michigan, and Berkeley, California, as well as detailed descriptions of Bryant's activities during his last five days alive. Drescher also was carrying four thousand dollars in cash. He told the cops that he'd got the money by selling his truck to the Krishnas.

Terry Sheldon was carrying articles about Steve Bryant's murder clipped from newspapers in Moundsville, Wheeling, and Pittsburgh. But the cops were particularly intrigued by a letter they found in his pocket. It ordered Sheldon to hide Drescher from the police. If the cops came looking for him, the unsigned letter instructed, Sheldon was to take Drescher to the New York City temple and then put him on a plane bound for India.

Drescher's common-law wife, Suzanne Bleudeu was carrying three Social Security cards, each with a different name and number.

The police released Bleudeu, but charged Sheldon with carrying a concealed weapon, a hooked-blade linoleum knife. The charge was an excuse to jail him until prosecutors could develop a case against him. They never did. He was released after three days and immediately disappeared.

The day after Drescher's arrest, Don Shade, an investigator for the West Virginia State Police, called Tom Westfall and asked if he had any information on Drescher.

"I've got a file on him thicker than a cut of prime rib," Westfall said eagerly. "He's the number-one suspect in the murder of a Krishna marijuana dealer named Chuck St. Denis."

Westfall took Shade through the St. Denis case. Shade talked it over with his department supervisors. The next day, the state police charged Drescher with the murder of Chuck St. Denis. Drescher was taken to the Marshall County Jail.

Sergeant Tom Westfall, dressed in his best blue suit, was as nervous as a kid about to pick up his prom date. Don Shade, the state police investigator, had called a week after the Bryant murder and asked him to come up to the Federal Building in Wheeling. The feds wanted to interview him.

Westfall waited in the fourth-floor corridor of the old stone building in Wheeling. He was looking through some of the Krishna files he had brought along, when Shade appeared.

"We're ready for you now," he told Westfall.

Westfall followed Shade into the room and was directed to a seat facing four men.

"You know Bob Cunningham," Shade said. Westfall nodded. Every cop in the state knew Cunningham, a six-foot-five, 270-pound state police investigator. In state police circles, Cunningham and Shade were considered the two best cops in West Virginia.

"This is Jeff Banwell, an FBI special agent based in Wheeling," Shade added. Westfall nodded at Banwell, who looked like the Marine officer he once was.

"And this is Bruce Smith, an assistant U.S. attorney who gets all the tough cases," Shade said. Smith, a brown-haired Nebraskan, smiled.

"We've got some names we'd like to ask you about," Smith said. Let's start with this fellow at the top of the list here. Who is this Kuladri?"

"Arthur Villa, the temple president," Westfall began. He continued without consulting his notes. "Went to Shady Side Academy, an exclusive school in Pittsburgh. Joined the movement after his second year at the University of Pittsburgh. He's power-hungry and loves lording his power over other devotees. But I'm convinced he's got a conscience. He's probably the only person out there who will stand up to the swami and tell him he's wrong."

"Tell us what you know about Thomas Drescher," Smith said.

The questioning went on for over two hours. Westfall's years of preparation were all paying off. He talked freely about sankirtan, the abuse of women, drugs, guns, and the dangerous conditions in the children's nursery.

"Does anybody else know who these people are?" Smith finally asked, turning to the three other cops sitting at the conference table.

Shade and Cunningham both shook their heads no.

"We've never worked a Krishna case," Cunningham said.

"Would you mind stepping outside for a moment?" Smith asked Westfall.

Westfall went back into the corridor and spent an anxious half hour watching the pedestrians four stories below. Then he was summoned back to the conference room.

"Would you have a problem if we contacted the sheriff about having you work with us while we investigate the Krishnas?" Smith asked.

"That would be great!" Westfall said, perhaps a shade too eagerly.

"There is one snag," Smith quickly added. "We've got a problem with your sheriff."

"I've got a lot of problems with my sheriff," Westfall replied.

"We don't want the sheriff to have any part of this," Smith said. "We don't want you to share any information with him that you develop. Is that clear?"

"It is," Westfall said. "But what do I say if he asks me about the case?"

"You don't," Smith said. "From now on, you report exclusively to the United States attorney for the Northern District of West Virginia."

On May 28, two days after Drescher's arrest in Kent, Ohio, Randall Gorby woke up in his second-story bedroom. A chain-smoker, Gorby yawned and stretched and immediately reached for a cigarette. He popped it in his mouth and struck a match.

The house exploded.

Gorby was rocketed straight up as if he had been shot

out of a cannon. He flew through a hole in the roof, watching it happen as if in slow motion. Splinters of lumber and shards of glass sailed by.

It seemed like he was in the air forever. He wasn't aware of the exact moment when he stopped traveling up and started going down. He fell back into the hole in the roof and crashed through the second floor. A heavy beam landed a few inches above his chest, protecting him from the falling debris. A flash fire burnt off his pajamas and scorched his flesh. It branded his wrist with the outline of his watch and tattooed strange and awful burn patterns on his skin.

But Randall Gorby survived. He was rushed to the Ohio Valley Medical Center in Wheeling and for several weeks occupied a room near where Kirtanananda was taken after Shockman brained him. Gorby was in critical condition—and incredible pain—for weeks with second- and third-degree burns over much of his body.

The state police called in the FBI, which concluded that the explosion was caused by a leak in Gorby's gas lines. Someone, the bureau found, had unscrewed a valve, allowing gas to seep into the house.

But the FBI never found out who had loosened the valve. Kirtanananda's spokesmen denied any involvement by New Vrindaban devotees. The explosion, they said, could only be blamed on Gorby, who, they claimed, had been trying to bypass the gas meter and cheat the gas company.

Revenge
from the Grave

"Prithu, look at this. Isn't this the new devotee who calls himself Gangamaya?"

Prithu, Peter Brinkmann, the president of the small Krishna temple in Belfast, Northern Ireland, looked at his wife's copy of the *ISKCON World Review,* the Krishna newspaper. There was a picture of a tall man with a shaved head, big ears, and a broad nose standing in front of a van. A sign on the van said "Palace Charities, Give Us This Day Our Daily Bread, Food Relief/Hot Meals Delivered To Your Door." The man and a small boy standing beside him were holding trays loaded with Styrofoam containers.

The caption identified the tall devotee as Tapahpunja, Terry Sheldon.

"It's him, it's the same person. Why is he calling himself Gangamaya?" Prithu asked his wife.

"Don't ask me," Martha Brinkmann said. "Ask him."

Prithu was waiting when the mysterious devotee came to afternoon prasadam.

"Look at this picture I have here," Prithu said. "Is this not you?"

The tall devotee glanced at the newspaper.

"Yeah, that's me," he admitted.

"Why aren't you using your real name?" Prithu asked. Sheldon didn't answer.

"This must have something to do with the killing of Sulocana," Prithu said.

"It does," Sheldon said.

"Did you kill him?"

"No."

"Then what did you do?"

"I engineered it," Sheldon said.

"Why?" Prithu asked.

"It was authorized."

"By whom?"

"It was authorized," Sheldon repeated.

"How could you do such a thing?" Prithu asked.

"He was an offender," Sheldon said.

"And what gives you guys in New Vrindaban the right to take the law into your own hands?"

"It was Vedic." Sheldon said.

"You'd better get out of here," Prithu said. "I don't want this temple connected in any way with New Vrindaban."

Sheldon had traveled to Northern Ireland by way of England, where he'd spent a month working in the kitchen of Govinda's, the Krishna restaurant in London. He left the Belfast temple hours after his conversation with Prithu and returned to London. From there, he flew to Bombay, India. Kirtanananda's Bombay Temple was said to be supported in large part by donations from an Indian industrialist named Nathaji, one of the wealthiest men in India.

Sheldon moved into Nathaji's house. A few months later, in November 1986, he received a special visitor: Kirtanananda.

The trial that was never supposed to take place was now set to begin. White had never wanted to prosecute Drescher. He'd only presented the St. Denis case to a grand jury because the Los Angeles police were slow in filing extradition papers for Drescher. It was the only way they could hold Drescher. Somehow the grand jury had returned an indictment, forcing White to try the case. He was livid because he thought he had a better chance of winning the lottery than a conviction.

The more he thought about it, the angrier White got. He figured he was probably going to lose his job along with the case. There was no way the good people of Marshall County were going to reelect the prosecutor who blew a Krishna murder case. White knew he had no choice but to face the jury.

The courtroom was less than half full when Debra

Gere was sworn in to testify about the long-running feud between Drescher and St. Denis over Drescher's house. She recounted in detail how St. Denis had finally got Drescher off his land, and told the jury she was convinced Drescher had killed her common-law husband. Howard Fawley, the former New Vrindaban treasurer, testified that Drescher had told him how St. Denis "died hard." Paul Ferry, Yuvati Matusow's ex-husband, testified that Drescher had described killing St. Denis and had questioned him about muriatic acid. Dr. Nick Tsacrios testified that Drescher had told him he had killed St. Denis. So did Randall Gorby.

In and out of the courtroom, the defense attorney, Robert McWilliams, claimed they were all lying. He charged that the prosecutors were conspiring against his client. Hadn't they bargained with Drescher's friend Dan Reid to testify against his client? They'd offered to reduce the charges against Reid, but Reid had refused. So they had made a better offer—limited immunity. He'd refused that. They'd finally made Reid an offer he couldn't refuse if he and Drescher *had* murdered St. Denis—total immunity. Reid had even declined that offer.

Over and over again, McWilliams hammered at the prosecution's failure to produce a body. He noted that the police had searched and searched for the mysterious corpse. They'd dug up half the commune, but hadn't found a shred of evidence. St. Denis could be alive and well and living in Florida. He could have taken a sudden and unannounced trip, as he'd done several times in the past. Perhaps he was on a drug run. He could return at any moment and walk into the courtroom.

The trial took four days; the jury took four hours. In a lightning-fast verdict, it found Drescher guilty of first-degree murder. On December 15, 1986, Judge Robert Halbritter sentenced Drescher to life imprisonment without mercy in the state penitentiary. "Without mercy" meaning no chance of parole.

It had taken more than three years. But Tom Westfall had finally fulfilled part of his promise to Debra Gere: He'd gotten one of her husband's killers.

Tom Westfall stayed home the day after the verdict was returned. He was in his den trying to fix his four-year-old son's Hot Wheels tricycle. He just about had the rear wheel back on when the phone rang. He picked up the receiver with one hand and cradled it under his ear while he went back to work.

It was Tom White.

"Get down here right away," he said. "Reid just pleaded guilty. He's going to lead us to St. Denis's body."

The nine-passenger, four-wheel-drive Chevy Suburban was slipping and sliding on the dirt track. Heavy November rains had turned it into a river of mud cutting across the crest of New Vrindaban.

The van was loaded with eight cops, but only two of them, Tom Westfall and Bob Cunningham, the state police investigator, looked like police officers. The others had beards like the guitarists in ZZ Top, long dirty hair, and ratty clothes. They were undercover narcotics agents recruited by Cunningham after Sheriff Bordenkircher had thrown Westfall a curve earlier that morning.

When Westfall had started working for the feds and had stopped sharing information with Bordenkircher, the sheriff had become suspicious. And uncooperative. And now obstreperous. The previous day Westfall had asked the sheriff to loan him some help. Bordenkircher had promised to lend him six deputies and a couple of the department's brand-new, four-wheel-drive Broncos. But when Westfall and Cunningham arrived at the sheriff's office, Bordenkircher said he was sorry, he couldn't spare the men. He couldn't spare the Broncos, either. Westfall had pleaded. The sheriff had remained firm.

Cunningham had stepped into the breach. He'd gotten on the phone and told a state police supervisor he needed six men right away.

They'd arrived an hour later.

"So this is the land of the living dead," one of the undercover officers said as the Chevy Suburban ground its way through the mud. "I keep expecting to see bodies rising out of the earth."

The narc wasn't far from wrong. Bodies were cropping

up almost regularly. First, the cops had exhumed St. Denis's grisly corpse from its watery grave. A few days later, a backhoe operator trenching a water line had dug up two corpses buried in cheap pine boxes only thirty inches under the ground. It took days to positively identify the heavily decomposed bodies—both devotees. One was Michael Neuman, who had asphyxiated in Kentucky when a kerosene stove malfunctioned in his sankirtan van. The other was Sylvia Walker, a mother of five, who had died of heart failure.

And then Westfall got a call from Walt Parry, the former temple commander, who had left the movement and was now living in Rhode Island. Parry said that he had buried a body on the commune in 1977 on Kirtanananda's orders. He gave Westfall a description of the site. Westfall obtained a warrant, and now he, Cunningham, and the narcs were on their way to dig it up.

Parry said it was buried in a deep ravine between the Palace of Gold and the house where Kirtanananda lived with the guru kula boys. In the early days of the commune, when the temple was little more than a vision, devotees had built a cable car to avoid the long hike across the ravine. But it had been torn down long ago. Parry said the body was near a tree that once had been used to anchor one end of the cable.

Westfall was telling the story to the other cops in the van when he saw a Landcruiser sliding toward them through the mud.

"That's the swami," he said, pointing to the mud-splattered Toyota.

Cunningham stopped the Suburban and waited for Kirtanananda. When the swami arrived, Westfall stepped down from the van and immediately sunk into the mud up to his ankles. He slogged over to the Landcruiser. Kirtanananda watched him approach and rolled down his window.

"What are you doing out here?" he demanded.

Westfall handed him a search warrant.

"We're looking for a body," he said.

"Whose body?" Kirtanananda asked.

"Read the warrant, Swami," Westfall said before returning to his van.

The Suburban ground its way up the hill, and the motley collection of cops got out and started to look around. They quickly found the tree that had been used to anchor the cable. Despite the heavy rain, the ground around it was all rocks and roots. It would take an air hammer to bury a body there. So the troupe began searching the area.

Westfall spotted a log. It was in the middle of the field, hundreds of feet from the nearest tree. He pointed it out to the other cops and suggested they start digging there.

"You think something's under it?" one of the narcs grumbled.

"It's not a bad guess," Westfall said. "If you're afraid an animal might dig up a body, you've got to cover it. There are only two things you can use, a pile of rocks or a big log."

They had just started digging when the cold November rain resumed. Within minutes, the group was soaked. It seemed pointless. The hole filled with water and mud almost as fast as they could dig. After four hours, they'd excavated less than four feet and worn out their patience. They were used to sitting in warm bars stinging drug deals, not digging like convicts on a chain gang.

"There's nothing buried here," one of the ZZ Top narcs complained for the umpteenth time.

"Just a little more," Cunningham patiently urged. "You never know."

"It's got to be here," Westfall added.

"All right," the narc said. "One last scoop. But that's it."

The narc sunk his shovel into the ground, pulled it up, and screamed.

"Oh, shit!" he wailed. "Oh, shit!"

The five other cops turned to look at him. He was holding his shovel at arm's length, gazing in horror at a human arm draped across the metal blade. The finger bones were broken. In places the flesh still clung to them, hanging like globs of gelatin.

The cops were transfixed. The rain streamed down

their faces, streaking their cheeks. Cunningham recovered first. He went to the Suburban and put in a call for the state medical examiner. Ten minutes later, the dispatcher reported that the medical examiner was tied up on another case and would not be able to get there until the next morning.

"It'll be dark in half an hour," Westfall said. "We can't leave the body up here alone all night."

"I'll get some troopers sent up to spend the night," Cunningham said. "Let's go down to that little store on the highway and use the phone. Everybody out here has got a scanner. If we use the radio, the whole county will know we've found a body."

Cunningham and Westfall got into the Suburban, leaving the four narcs to guard their find. They were driving down the hill when they spotted Kirtanananda's Landcruiser racing toward them through the mud. They stopped. The swami pulled up, halted on Westfall's side of the van, and rolled down his window.

"I read the search warrant and I don't understand it," Kirtanananda said, handing it through the window to Westfall.

"What don't you understand, Swami?" Westfall asked in his most obsequious voice.

"What are you looking for?" Kirtanananda asked.

"A body," Westfall said, pointing to the relevant paragraph in the warrant. "See, it says right here, 'a body.' "

"What kind of a body?" Kirtanananda asked without looking.

"Human," Westfall said.

Kirtanananda lost his temper.

"I asked what kind of body," he shouted. "Young, old, man, woman?"

"Swami," Westfall asked, "what have you got available?"

Cunningham started laughing. Kirtanananda threw the Toyota into reverse and stomped on the gas to turn around. The jeep lurched over the incline and into a ditch. The swami jammed it into first gear, but the wheels only spun. Finally, he got on his CB radio and summoned help.

Cunningham and Westfall continued downhill to Ma

Eddy's, where Cunningham put in a call for a couple of troopers. Then Westfall called Sheriff Bordenkircher's office and reported that they had found another body at New Vrindaban.

"It's gonna be pretty lonely for whoever has to spend the night up here," Cunningham observed on the way back to the grave site.

It was dark before they arrived at the grave. While they waited for the relief crew, the whole group piled into the Suburban to keep warm. Half an hour later, they spotted two sets of headlights down in the valley, winding their way up to the ravine.

"That must be our guy," Cunningham said. "Looks like he brought somebody with him."

He picked up the microphone and radioed their location to the trooper. The trooper radioed back that he was still on Highway 250, five miles from the commune.

"It's Krishnas!" one of the narcs shouted. "This could be an attack!"

The cops jumped out of the Suburban, unholstered their guns, and took cover.

Five minutes later, two Broncos pulled up to the grave site. Chief Hummel jumped out of the lead vehicle; a news team from WTRF, Channel Seven in Wheeling, piled out of the other.

The narcotics officers spotted the camera, dove back into the Suburban, and ducked under the seats. If they appeared on camera, their cover would be blown. While the narcs hid, Hummel led the news team to the grave and volunteered to do a stand-up. In the interview, he took credit for discovering the body.

"The sheriff didn't have a Bronco to spare when I needed one, but you've got a couple for the television crew," Westfall sneered at Hummel after he finished the interview.

"The sheriff is the one who's pushing this whole investigation, Tom," Hummel responded without a trace of irony. "If he hadn't loaned you to the feds, you never would have found this body."

The rest of the decomposed remains were dug up the next day and taken to the medical examiner. He was unable to identify them. Even Westfall, with all his sources, came up empty. Kirtanananda's spokesmen said the body was "Joe," one of the mentally disturbed devotees who came to New Vrindaban in the 1970s. Joe used to wander around the commune asking other devotees, "Is birdshit Krishna?"

New Vrindaban says Joe was trying to cross the cable hand over hand when he slipped and fell 150 feet to his death. Miraculously, the fall didn't break any of his bones. His only injury was to the back of his skull, which was crushed.

The discovery of one more body didn't change the routine at the commune.

A couple of weeks later, on Sunday morning, November 23, the New Vrindaban brats—as commune members called the packs of small children that scampered across the commune—were roaming the grounds of the palace. They were playing tag, darting in and out of buildings and amusing themselves as children do the world over. Three-year-old Nimai Bryant and a five-year-old friend were playing along the shore of the commune's man-made lake. They trotted onto the pier that ends in a white gazebo far from the nearest shore.

"I'll bet I can climb that thing to the top," Nimai's friend said.

"I'll bet I can, too," Nimai said, taking up the challenge.

The boys raced to the end of the pier. There was no gate to stop them. Nor were there any adults to warn them.

Nimai was halfway up the gazebo when he slipped and fell into ten feet of dirty brown water. He quickly disappeared beneath the opaque surface. His friend ran for help.

Too late. Nimai drowned.

Jane called Steve Bryant's parents a few hours later. They desperately wanted to be part of their grandsons' lives and had done their best to maintain cordial relations with Steve's ex-wife. They had, in fact, returned from a visit to New Vrindaban only ten days earlier.

"How are you, Jane?" Jack Bryant asked pleasantly when he heard her voice. "It's nice to hear from you."

"I'm not good, Mr. Bryant," Jane said. "Nimai drowned today."

Jack Bryant felt suddenly weak. He dropped into a chair at the kitchen table.

"Nimai what?" he asked quietly.

"He drowned today," Jane said. "It's heavy, isn't it. But he's in a better world."

The circumstances seemed suspicious, but there was no evidence that Nimai's death was anything but an accident.

Jack Bryant combed the newspapers for information about the death. Two days after Nimai's drowning, he found an Associated Press account of the incident. He read it and reread it, over and over again. Each time, he stopped at a quote from Kirtanananda.

Should I tell Helga? he asked himself again and again.

Nimai's death had devastated Helga. She was in bad shape, but Jack finally decided she had to know about this. He got up and walked down to the den, where his wife was sitting alone.

"There's an Associated Press story in the paper about Nimai," Jack said.

"Oh," she said dully.

"Listen to what Kirtanananda says: 'The devotees are very sorry about the drowning, but from a philosophical point of view, we could say there was some bad karma in that family. I'm very sorry, but we didn't create that karma.'"

Jack and Helga stared at each other, speechless.

"It's *our* fault Steven was killed?" Helga finally cried. "It's *our* fault Nimai drowned? All because there's bad karma in our family?"

"The son of a bitch is gloating. He's gloating over Nimai's death," Jack said.

Ghosts

Sex Is Sex

Susan Hebel's patience had run out.

This is it, she thought as she headed toward Kirtan-ananda's office. This is finally it. I'm going to make him deal with this.

Susan, Kanka, had tolerated many things during her eight years in New Vrindaban. She had tolerated them because she believed deeply that God had anointed Prabhupada as his messenger and sent him to America to bring the only true religion to the people of the United States; because she believed the Palace of Gold was there to deliver that message.

Susan had justified a lot of things: Advaita and the drugs, Dharmatma's cruelty toward women, the sankirtan scams, even Thomas Drescher's murdering Chuck St. Denis. She had tolerated Kirtanananda forcing her to become engaged to one of the commune's teachers, even though she was still married to Steven Hebel.

"Look, I'm not telling you you're not married to Steven," he'd said when she complained. "You can have two or three husbands. Draupadi, one of the Pandava princesses, had five."

Susan had let Kirtanananda bully her into marrying Danny Walker, a widower and the father of five small children. His previous wife, Sylvia, had died of heart problems. She had been buried like so much garbage and forgotten—until the backhoe operator had uncovered her body while digging a trench.

Susan had even tolerated Walker. He demanded sex all the time. When she objected or refused, he threw her against the walls and beat her. Like many other abused

371

women at New Vrindaban, Susan had turned to Kirtanananda and pleaded for help.

"Just tolerate it," he ordered.

Susan had justified so much. But not this. There was
no way she could tolerate what her thirteen-year-old son,
Scott, told her on a windy night in November, 1986. She
stormed into Kirtanananda's office and slammed the door
behind her. Kirtanananda looked up and frowned.

"I spent most of last night talking to Scott," Susan told
the guru. "He told me that for the last three years, he
and other boys in the guru kula have been *sexually molested*
by Sri Galima and his assistant."

When she verbalized the accusation, her rage dissolved
into grief. She stood speechless in front of the swami for
several moments and then began to sob. Tears rolled
down her cheeks. Kirtanananda sat back and watched.

"I feel so betrayed," she finally blubbered. "All these
years, I've given up my children. I sent them to the guru
kula when they turned five, trusting that they would be
loved and taken care of and would become devotees. I
never imagined that anyone would molest them."

"You stupid woman," Kirtanananda interrupted. "You
don't have any right to say that. Sex is sex. How much
sex have *you* had?"

His anger stopped Susan short. She struggled to
continue.

"Kirtanananda, you can't equate sex between a husband and wife and teachers molesting defenseless little
boys," Susan said.

"Sex is sex," Kirtanananda said once again. "Besides,
Sri Galima has rectified himself. He got married."

"You've got to get him out of the guru kula," Susan
said. "Sri Galima is sick. He needs help."

"He's staying right where he is, whether you like it or
not!" Kirtanananda screamed.

He then ordered her to leave.

Walking back to her tiny apartment, Susan was more
amazed than angry. She began looking at her service in a
new way. All these years he's been my spiritual master
and he never cared about me, she thought. He doesn't
care about Scott or the other boys in the guru kula. He

doesn't care about anything except making people do whatever he wants them to do. Kirtanananda isn't a guru. He's a fascist, a dictator.

All afternoon, she kept herself from crying because Scott was with her. She hid her pain, not wanting him to feel he'd done something wrong. He finally went out while she made dinner. Immediately, Susan picked the phone and told the story to her sister, who was living in Marin County, California.

"You've got to get out of there now," her sister said.

"It's hard. I've been here so long. I've been so dedicated to this project," Susan said.

"No, it's not; it's easy—just go," her sister ordered. "You don't have a choice. Just go."

"But how *can* I?" Susan said. She could no longer hold back her tears.

"Susan, do you want me to come out there and get you?" her sister asked. "Is that what you want?"

"No," Susan said immediately. "I'll do it. I'll do it on my own."

Susan spent the rest of the week planning her escape. When she had worked out a plan, she confided in her closest girlfriend. Neither of them said a word to anyone else. They knew that if word leaked out, the commune would trap her by holding her children hostage.

Susan went out on sankirtan as usual that weekend and didn't return to New Vrindaban until late Sunday night, after Dharmatma had gone to bed. Instead of immediately turning over the money she had collected, she kept it. Her girlfriend helped her load her things into a sankirtan van. Susan then woke up Scott and told him they were leaving. They drove up to the guru kula, snuck in, and woke up Susan's two young sons. They bundled them up and rushed them out to the van. Susan then drove nonstop to the Pittsburgh airport. After her plane was called, she dropped a coin in the public phone and called Dharmatma.

"I've got my kids and I'm leaving," she told him. "In five minutes, I'm getting on a plane to Los Angeles. Here, write this number down. It's the space in the parking lot where I left the van I borrowed."

*   *   *

Susan and her kids moved into a cozy little cabin in Bhaktivedanta Village in Three Rivers. She did not miss West Virginia. She did not even want to talk about the place with the other refugees who had fled from New Vrindaban to Three Rivers. She wouldn't even let herself think about her long years in Kirtanananda's service.

Susan kept silent and tried to rebuild her life. She didn't tell anybody about Scott's abuse except for her ex-husband, Steven Hebel. He and his second wife, Cynthia, shared a house with another devotee a couple of miles away. He had welcomed her to Bhaktivedanta, helping her get settled and finding a therapist for Scott through the Tulare County Children's Protective Services.

The therapist had told them that Scott's problems were severe because the molestations had occurred frequently, over a long period of time. But outwardly at least, Scott seemed as healthy and happy as any other kid. Steven bought him a trail bike, and he spent hours zipping along the village's dirt roads.

Susan supported the family the same way many devotees who leave the movement support themselves. On weekends, she'd drive a few hundred miles to Santa Barbara or Los Angeles or San Diego and use her only skill—the sankirtan scams she had perfected over so many years. But instead of handing over the money, she would keep it for groceries, clothing, and rent. She budgeted carefully, putting aside a little money every week. It took weeks, but eventually, she saved enough to rescue Tina.

Tina was her unofficially adopted daughter. The girl's parents had all but abandoned her to the New Vrindaban nursery. Susan saw her there one day, immediately fell in love, and took her home. For seven years Susan had cared for the child as one of her own. But when she had fled Kirtanananda and New Vrindaban, she'd had no choice but to leave Tina behind: there wasn't enough money for one more plane ticket.

As soon as Susan had enough for the plane fair, she called Kirtanananda and asked him to have Tina taken to the Pittsburgh airport.

"Why should I put Tina on a plane?" Kirtanananda snarled.

"Because she misses me and I miss her," Susan said. "She should be out here with me."

"OK, we'll make a deal," Kirtanananda said. "You send me Scott and I'll send you Tina."

"*What?*" Susan screamed. "So you can go on taking care of him the way you did before? So he can be molested for another three years?"

She hung up before Kirtanananda could answer.

Then she ran and told Steven about the call. They talked to Scott's counselor, who told them to file charges.

The next day, Susan called Tom Westfall.

Susan Hebel's call finally confirmed the second-hand stories and rumors about the sexual abuse of children in the guru kula. Tom Westfall began an aggressive investigation. He cruised up to New Vrindaban with two arrest warrants lying on the seat beside him. His unhurried pace belied his fury. He was on a mission. He wanted these two guys even more than he had wanted St. Denis's killers. Every time Westfall thought about the stories, he was sickened.

The boys were ordered to come to the front of the class and sit on Sri Galima's lap. Sri Galima then anally raped them, right in front of the class. Other boys were ordered to stay after class. Sri Galima tied their hands to their desks with duct tape and then assaulted them in the same way.

At night, Fredrick DeFrancisco, Sri Galima's assistant, crept into the boys' sleeping bags and performed oral sex on them.

When Westfall returned to West Virginia, he called other New Vrindaban parents. He cajoled and pleaded, but most of all he listened. Eventually, a few admitted that their children also had been molested by the commune's teachers. He finally had assembled enough evidence to obtain the warrants.

"I've got warrants for two people," Westfall said to Dick Dezio, the commune's spokesman, as soon as he arrived at New Vrindaban.

Dezio, who was working on a doctorate in economics, glanced at the warrants.

"DeFrancisco's no problem. Afraid I can't help you with Sri Galima," he said matter-of-factly.

"Why not?" Westfall demanded.

"He's gone."

"Where to?" Westfall asked.

"India."

"When?" Westfall said.

"He was sent a couple of weeks ago," Dezio said.

Dawn crept across the hills on the morning of January 5, 1987, as a caravan of more than fifty state police officers accompanied by FBI and IRS agents pulled up to the entrance of New Vrindaban. Westfall was in the lead; three empty tractor-trailers were at the rear.

The caravan stopped outside the main complex. The cops broke into small task forces and fanned out. One group kicked in the doors of the treasury; another smashed into the warehouse. In the treasury, which had steel-barred tellers' cages and looked like a bank out of an old western, the cops seized mounds of neatly stacked cash, filing cabinets loaded with financial records, and a computer used for bookkeeping. In the warehouse, they found mountains of material used during sankirtan scams.

There were thousands of round stickers with pictures of Pope John Paul II; hundreds of cases of stickers that showed Snoopy holding a beer mug next to clichés like Are We Having Fun Yet? There were bumperstickers, hats, buttons, and T-shirts with the insignia of every major-league baseball team, every team in the National Football League, and most major college football teams. There were even hats with a pink Styrofoam breast and a red nipple over the sign Boob Inspector.

Like citizens fighting a fire with a bucket brigade, the cops formed a line to load the material into the three semitrailers. It took twenty-five cops working all day to do the job. When the trucks arrived in Wheeling, it took five people three working days just to inventory it.

But the biggest catch was the computer. It took most of a week for FBI technicians to milk its information. Westfall waited anxiously. A week after the raid, he drove up to Wheeling and met with Bruce Smith, the assistant United States attorney in charge of the Krishna investigation.

"What did we learn from the books?" Westfall immediately asked Smith.

"That they take in five to six million dollars a year working the sankirtan scams," Smith said.

Westfall whistled.

"Where does it all go, Tom?" Smith asked. "The palace was finished years ago. What are they doing with all that money?"

"I honestly don't know," Westfall said. "I know the swami's got a safe in his house. I've heard he keeps up to a hundred grand there. I've also heard it might be in a Swiss bank or scattered around the country in private accounts. A devotee once told me that Keith Ham might have accounts in banks in Peekskill, New York."

Westfall paused to think a moment.

"I've also heard there might be treasure buried on the commune. Some years ago, they supposedly buried an old car up behind the swami's house. There's supposed to be a safe full of money in the trunk of the car."

On a sunny day three months later, Kirtanananda and an entourage of six devotees approached the main entrance of the West Virginia State Penitentiary. The nineteenth-century gray stone prison resembled a medieval fort. And, at least from a distance, the visiting Krishnas looked like penitent monks. They wore dhotis and sandals. Only Kirtanananda's profile did not fit: he wore dark sunglasses and walked with a black cane.

The guard nodded to the Krishnas and pointed to the visitor's registration forms. They didn't need any instruction on how to fill them out. The entourage knew the routine nearly as well as the guards. For weeks, a small group of Krishnas had been coming to the prison every Wednesday to visit Thomas Drescher and to stage a kirtan in the prison chapel.

Drescher's lawyers had appealed to the West Virginia Supreme Court the extradition order that would send their client to California to stand trial for the murder of

Steven Bryant. Drescher had passed the year awaiting the outcome of his appeal preaching Krishna Consciousness to other inmates. He was proving to be an able minister; he had made four new devotees.

All four were serving long prison terms.

Kirtanananda and his troupe quietly waited for the new devotees in the prison's small chapel. The silence was broken by a short buzzing. Then an electronic door opened and Drescher and a half-dozen inmates walked into the room. They spotted Kirtanananda and immediately dropped to their knees to offer obeisances. One of the inmates, his arms and chest bulging with muscles developed in the prison weight room, offered Kirtanananda a garland made from flowers picked in the prison garden. Kirtanananda inclined his head and allowed the devotee to hang the necklace around his neck. Then the swami waited while another prisoner covered a metal chair with a clean white sheet.

Finally, he sat down and the kirtan began. One devotee played the harmonium, another hit the mridanga drum, the rest kept the kartal cymbals chinging. The kirtan quickly reached a furious pace. The players played louder than usual and the dancers danced harder. It was by far the best service the Krishnas had staged in the prison. That was only right. This was the most important day in Thomas Drescher's life. On this day, he was to become a swami.

Umapati, Wally Sheffy, one of the first eleven devotees Prabhupada had initiated in New York, performed the ancient ritual. When it was over, Thomas Drescher, convicted murderer, convicted drug dealer, was reborn as Swami Tirtha, a master of the mind and senses.

Expecting
the Barbarians

Early on the morning of March 16, 1987, Ravindra Svarupa walked into the GBC room in one of the temples in Mayapur, India. Ceiling fans were whirling silently; the room was large, dark, and cool. Fifteen members of the GBC were sitting in large, overstuffed chairs.

"Hare Krishna," Ravrindra said softly as he took a seat.

Ravindra was the only non-GBC member to be invited to this meeting, but that was not the reason why his hands were trembling and he kept curling and uncurling his toes. He was on edge because what happened in the next few hours would determine the future of ISKCON.

The meeting was called to decide the fate of one of the first—and certainly the most important—of Prabhupada's original American disciples: Kirtanananda Swami Bhaktipada.

"I hear Kirtanananda's coming today," said Tamal Krishna, guru for the southwestern United States. "I hear he arrived in Calcutta yesterday and will be here later this morning."

"I hope he does come," said Satsvarupa, guru for the northeastern United States and author of a six-volume biography of Srila Prabhupada. "It would be better to deal with him face-to-face."

Ravindra, a well-read Ph.D., remembered a poem by Cavafy called "Expecting the Barbarians." Each day, there were new reports that Kirtanananda was coming. Each day, members of the reform movement Ravindra was spearheading tensed for the big confrontation. And each day, just like Cavafy's barbarians, Kirtanananda failed to appear.

"I wonder how many video cameras he'll bring this time," Ravindra said to his friend Satsvarupa, who allowed himself a small grin.

A year earlier, Kirtanananda and Ravindra had met to discuss the reform movement. Kirtanananda had arrived at the Philadelphia temple with his entourage, including two devotees carrying video cameras. The tapes they made were craftily edited and shown to devotees back in New Vrindaban, who watched their spiritual master defeat yet another foe.

"For something this important, he's liable to show up with ten cameras and Steven Spielberg," Ravindra joked.

"He may have enough money to afford Spielberg," Satsvarupa replied.

When Ravindra had arrived in Mayapur, he was expecting a battle. Several of the most reactionary gurus had banded together to fight the changes the reform movement was determined to make. But a month had gone by, and things were better than he had dared to hope. The reactionary gurus had lost their steam.

Ramesvara, the Los Angeles guru and Bhaktivedanta Book Trust president, was supposed to lead the gurus' counterattack. Ramesvara had evolved into an imperious, Machiavellian figure, much detested by the temple presidents who formed the core of the reform movement.

Before Ramesvara could get the counterattack rolling, devotees spotted him in the Santa Monica Mall with a fourteen-year-old girl. Instead of the saffron robe of a sannyasi celibate, Ramesvara sported a short-sleeve designer sweatshirt that exposed his recently developed muscles. He had on pleated trousers and expensive looking white shoes.

Pressured by the reform group, the GBC investigated and found that Ramesvara had been spotted out on the town with the teenage girl on several occasions. Ramesvara was warned, but he kept dating her. Rumor had it that they had an affair going. In the end, however, the girl was not Ramesvara's downfall. The GBC ousted him from his position as a guru because they felt that he had mismanaged the BBT, and they were tired of the way he mistreated people.

Then there was Bhavananda, Charles Backus, the Australian guru. Before he joined ISKCON, Backus had hung around Andy Warhol's Factory and was one of the girls in the movie *Chelsea Girls*. For years, rumors had been circulating that Bhavananda was a practicing homosexual. Several of his former devotees had even published a lurid broadside detailing the guru's homosexual encounters with a Calcutta cabdriver, a devotee in the Atlanta temple, and with devotees in Australia and Mayapur, where Bhavananda had been in charge of building the temple.

The GBC had placed Bhavananda on probation and had sent investigators to Australia. They discovered the Bhavananda had ignored his suspension and was continuing to initiate disciples. His devotees worshiped him like a god, and Bhavananda lived like a king, adorning himself with thousands of dollars' worth of gold and diamond-studded jewelry, and jetting off to soak up the sun on exotic tropical beaches.

The Bhavananda case was reopened at the Mayapur meetings. This time, the probation was not continued. Bhavananda was removed as a guru.

Finally, there was Bhagavan, William Ehrlichman, the European guru, ISKCON's equivalent of Louis XIV, the Sun King. His cruelty to devotees, his incessant demands for money and extravagances like his gold drinking goblet, the gold fixtures in his bathroom, and the BMW that was reserved for his use when he visited England had been ignored—until now.

When Bhagavan discovered the reformers were interviewing devotees who had left him in disgust, he denounced the reformers as anarchists and dragged up the tired old argument that spiritual progress could be made only after a devotee surrendered to one of Prabhupada's hand-picked successors. Bhagavan worked behind the scenes against the reformers, trying to convince gurus like Tamal Krishna to join him in a fight to keep the movement "the way Prabhupada would want it kept."

Bhagavan's devotees had all pledged to stand behind

their guru in his righteous battle against the usurpers. Then, one day in September 1986, they woke up to find that Bhagavan was gone. He left behind a turgid letter explaining that he had been having an affair with a devotee in the South African temple—one of Bhagavan's zones.

". . . By powers that are beyond me I am not able to remove the sentiments which have developed between myself and the concerned party, [sentiments] which are certainly out of place for a sannyasi . . ." Bhagavan wrote to his disciples.

The main topic of debate about Bhagavan at Mayapur was not whether or not to remove him. That decision was easy; nobody tried to defend the former Sun King. But GBC members spent a lot of time trying to determine how much money Bhagavan had stashed away to cushion his transition to life as a karmi.

And now it was Kirtanananda's turn.

So much had been accomplished. But it would matter very little if the GBC did not deal firmly with Kirtanananda. A mere slap on the wrist would send a devastating message to devotees who had been energized by the reform movement. They would know the GBC was still a gutless wonder. They would know there was no hope for the movement.

Harikesha, the guru for Eastern Europe, opened the meeting. "We can't throw Kirtanananda out," he said. "That's too extreme. We've got to draw a line. If he steps over it, then we'll act.

"You've been drawing lines and Kirtanananda's been stepping over them for years," Ravindra replied, leaning forward in his chair.

"But if we expel him, he's dangerous to us," Harikesha countered. "There's no telling what he'll do. If we keep him in ISKCON, we can at least keep some control over him."

"You've never been able to control him and you never will," Ravindra replied. "He's much more dangerous in the movement than out of it. He represents the worst abuses of the guru system. By voting to expel him, you are voting to expel those abuses from your hearts."

The discussion went on and on until finally, the GBC

members agreed to take a secret ballot. Kirtanananda was expelled from ISKCON. The tally was eleven in favor, one opposed, two abstaining.

Kirtanananda never did turn up in Mayapur. In a press release issued in New Vrindaban, he denounced the GBC's decision as "purely political" and refused to resign.

It had taken two decades, and neither the moment nor the forum was of his choosing. But Kirtanananda had finally done it: he was officially the leader of his very own cult.

Going Fishing

Tom Westfall was in his unmarked cruiser, rolling out of Moundsville on his way home. He had been working twelve- and fourteen-hour days six and seven days a week ever since the U.S. Attorney had hired him to investigate the Krishnas two years before. Today, Westfall was going fishing.

It was two in the afternoon on April 4, 1988. The sun was shining, and Westfall planned on picking up Tommy, his six-year-old son, and taking him to their special place on Big Wheeling Creek.

There was a ton of work to be done. The feds were busy preparing the trademark-violations case, which looked like it was going to be the biggest case of its kind in U.S. history. Drescher was still in the penitentiary in Moundsville, awaiting extradition to California, and Westfall was investigating whether there was a conspiracy to murder Steve Bryant.

But it looked like the murders, the bodies dug out of the ground in New Vrindaban, the drug dealing, the abuse of women and children, were all in the past. For one thing, the commune had shrunk from a high of around 600 devotees to about 135—every time Westfall went out there, he noticed more empty apartments. The guru kula was closed; Krishna children were now attending public schools in Moundsville and in the little community of Limestone.

Westfall's efforts to clean up New Vrindaban had been successful. He had made a case against Keith Weber, the commune's chief armorer. Todd Schenker, Weber's assistant, would be his next target.

Weber and Schenker were gun freaks, soldiers of for-

tune who, if they hadn't joined Kirtanananda, would be
spending their weekends in camouflage, playing war games
in the pine woods of Alabama or the redwood forests in
northern California.

Kirtanananda had articulated Weber and Schenker's
paranoid visions. In recent months, the swami had begun
sounding more and more like his old buddy, Hansadutta.
The world, he preached, would be destroyed in a nuclear
war. But, he claimed, he had anticipated this and located
New Vrindaban in the West Virginia hills; the winds
would blow radiation away from the commune. The devotees needed to arm themselves in order to fight off the
surviving karmis, who surely would come for Krishna
food and Krishna women.

Westfall figured that if he could nail the armorers, he
could eventually nail the commune's weapons. He had
arrested Weber for purchasing nine-millimeters, .45s, and
AR-15s in Ohio and for illegally bringing them into West
Virginia. Weber had appeared in court, pleaded guilty,
and been sentenced to three years in a federal prison.
But Weber was still hanging on in New Vrindaban, waiting to see if an appeal his attorney had filed would be
heard.

"Sergeant Westfall."

The dispatcher's voice crackled over the radio and
ended Westfall's reverie. The sergeant sighed and picked
up the microphone.

"Do you know where Todd Schenker's house is?" the
dispatcher asked.

"I do," Westfall said, marveling at the coincidence.
The house was only a few hundred feet downstream from
where Westfall and Tommy were going to fish.

"There's been a death there," the dispatcher said. "It
doesn't appear to be natural. We've sent out a uniformed
officer to protect the scene until you arrive."

"Is the body in the house?" Westfall asked.

"The body is *by* the house," the dispatcher replied.
"The report we received says it has been burned."

Westfall made a fast U-turn and headed up Route 250
to New Vrindaban. As he screamed around corners he
knew by heart, Westfall shook his head in amazement. It

was like the movie *Carrie*. Just when you think the horror is over, the hand comes out of the grave. He raced on, wondering if the body was Todd Schenker's, and if the death had anything to do with his investigations.

Westfall stopped in front of one of the two houses on the Schenker property, and jumped out of his car.

A new Honda and a new Datsun pickup truck stood in the driveway. A carefully cultivated garden bordered the nearest house, where Todd Schenker lived. Judy Schenker and their seven children lived in the other place.

"Where is it?" Westfall asked Denise Hart, the deputy who had already arrived at the scene.

"Over there," Hart said.

Westfall and Hart walked down a path that led to a small dump behind Schenker's house. Something that resembled a charred log was resting in front of a mound of garbage. Westfall went closer and saw it was a human body. The head seemed to be grinning—the lips had been burned away, exposing the teeth.

Westfall moved closer and knelt next to the body. The arms and legs were gone. The rib cage was there, but it was empty: the heart, lungs, stomach—everything was gone. Pieces of flesh that looked like a stringy, over-cooked roast hung off the ribs.

"Look at these things," deputy Hart said. "They're all over. I can't figure out what they are."

Westfall stood up and walked over to her. She pointed to something lying on the ground that was about six inches long and looked like a strip of leather. Westfall glanced to his left and to his right. Other strips were scattered within twenty feet of the body.

"Get some tape and start marking off a crime scene," Westfall told the deputy. "I'm going to call the medical examiner."

Westfall was walking past the house when he stopped in his tracks. Suddenly, he knew what had happened to the arms and legs. And why the entrails had disappeared.

Behind Schenker's house was a large cage. Inside, two pit bulls pressed their noses hard against the cyclone fence and eyed the intruder. Those strips of leather, Westfall thought, are *strips of human flesh*.

Westfall shuddered as he approached the other house, where Judith Schenker and her seven children lived. He knocked on the door and Judith answered. An intelligent, soft-spoken woman who had spent much of her youth training to be a concert pianist, Judith was stunned, almost catatonic.

Todd had been missing for five days, she told Westfall. She had discovered the charred body only a few hours earlier, when she carried some garbage back to the makeshift dump.

Westfall asked Judith for permission to search Todd's house. She said fine and he went through Todd's residence, looking for signs of a struggle or a shooting. There were none. He climbed into an attic the afternoon sun had made hot as a boiler room. When he opened the sliding door of a closet, a cold chill ran down his back.

The closet held a small arsenal. There were a mini-fourteen, a riot shotgun with a magazine extender, a number of assault rifles with folding stocks, and large quantities of ammunition. These weren't target rifles; they were man killers.

Westfall awoke and had the phone off the hook before it rang twice. He glanced at the clock radio next to his sleeping wife and saw that it was 12:15 A.M. The windows were open but the curtains hung still. Instead of long, soaking rains, April 1988 had brought heat and drought to West Virginia.

"Uh-huh," Westfall grunted into the receiver. It was the way he always answered the phone at night. The implication was: you call at this hour, you do the talking.

"What are the devotees telling you about Tapo's death?" a voice asked. Tapo was Tapomurti, Todd Schenker's Krishna name.

Westfall recognized the voice of a devotee who had given him good information in the past, but who never had identified himself. He heard a truck go by and figured the devotee was calling from the pay phone outside of Ma Eddy's General Store on Route 250.

"The ones who will talk say it's a suicide," Westfall said.

"Do you believe that?" the devotee asked.

"Do I believe that a man could shoot himself, burn himself, and then arrange to be eaten by his dogs? No, I can't say I believe that," Westfall replied.

"Okay, here's the story," the devotee said. "Judith is a golden cow. She gives money, not milk. I hear she inherited a couple of million, and most of the income goes to the community."

"Uh-huh," Westfall said.

"Todd made loans to devotees and was charging lots of interest," the devotee said.

"Loansharking," Westfall said.

"Right," the devotee said. "There's some talk that that's why he was killed. But there's something else that's probably more important."

"What's that?" Westfall asked.

"Todd told some people he was fed up with New Vrindaban," the devotee said. "He said he was leaving and taking his wife and kids with him."

"So if Todd left, a considerable amount of money would be leaving with him?"

"Right again," the devotee said.

"Maybe somebody wanted to stop him," Westfall suggested.

"Could be," the devotee said. "Listen, it's late and I've got to get back home. Good luck on this one. You're gonna need it."

The medical examiner's report was on Westfall's desk the next morning. Right on time as usual, Westfall thought, as he sat down to read it. He had the highest admiration for Dr. Irwin Sopher, head of the West Virginia Medical Examiners' Office. The doctor was incredibly precise and didn't miss a thing.

Westfall had read some grisly reports over the years, but none like this one. Pieces of bone and human flesh had been found all over the Schenker property. A well-gnawed femur was found in the pit bull cage.

Dr. Sopher concluded that the .22 round fired through the right temple had been instantly fatal. The fire that had charred the body had not been hot enough to melt metal; Sopher had found the bullet intact. The cops had picked through every piece of rotting garbage in the dump, but had not found a gun to match that bullet. In fact, they hadn't found a gun in the area, period. No gun, no suicide. Schenker's death was definitely a homicide.

An uneasy feeling came over Westfall as he read further into the report. The only identifiable feature remaining was the teeth. The hands were gone, so there were no fingerprints. The face was so badly burned, its features could not be reconstructed. What if the body wasn't Schenker's? What if someone had planned the murder so that the body *could not* be identified? But why would anyone do that?

An hour later, Westfall and detective Tom Grimm started calling all the dentists in the Moundsville-Wheeling area; then they called dentists in the Canton, Ohio area, where both Judith and Todd had grown up. In Moundsville, they found a dentist who had worked on Judith and the kids, but not on Todd. In Canton, they found a dentist who had purchased the practice of a deceased dentist who had once worked on Todd. The office still had Todd Schenker's name on the patient list, but that was all. The files on inactive patients had been destroyed.

Despite the rumors that Judith Schenker was wealthy, when Westfall subpoenaed Judith's bank records he discovered her account had only fifteen dollars in it. Since the late 1970s, she had been turning almost every penny over to Kirtanananda.

Westfall had also talked to members of Judith's family, who promised to send him a copy of a letter they had recently received from Todd. Anxiously, Westfall waited for it to arrive.

The letter came on May 10, 1988. It was dated March 12, 1988.

"I'm not Kirtanananda's man," Schenker wrote to his in-laws. "I'm no longer his follower. I can leave the commune anytime I want."

*   *   *

Westfall walked out of his office, on his way to lunch at a pizza joint half a mile up the road from downtown Moundsville. It was a hot day in June 1988—and so hot he had no interest in pizza. He was going to hit the salad bar.

There he was again, the guy was sitting beside the fountain outside the Marshall County Courthouse, facing the entrance to the sheriff's office. It was the third time in one week. The man was definitely following him.

Westfall walked up to the small, slightly built man who appeared to be in his late thirties. "You want something from me?" he asked.

The man introduced himself as a friend of Todd Schenker's. "You're looking for me, aren't you?" the man said.

Westfall hadn't been looking for him. He had recognized the name and knew the guy wasn't a Krishna, but that was about all he knew.

"Yeah, I've been looking for you," Westfall said, going into his tough cop act. "I just haven't been in any particular hurry. Come on, we can talk in my office."

They went back to Westfall's basement office and the fellow sat down in a beat-up folding chair.

"I think I may be in trouble," he said.

"How?" Westfall asked.

"I may be part of a conspiracy," he replied. "I thought maybe if I helped you, you could help me."

"I can't make any deals, but I can tell you that as long as you do what's right, I'll do what's right by you."

Schenker's friend took a long, hard look at Westfall and thought for a moment. "I don't want anyone to know about this," he said.

"No one will," Westfall replied. "For the time being, this is between us." He took one of his cards out of a desk drawer and wrote his home phone number on it. "Call me at either of these two numbers. Don't leave your real name. Make one up and we'll use that."

Schenker's friend smiled. "How about Max? I always wanted to be called Max."

"Max it is," Westfall said. "Now, what about this conspiracy?"

"That body you found? It isn't Todd's," Max said.

"Okay," Westfall said, noncommittally.

"Todd staged it. He faked his own death," Max continued. "He planned the whole thing. He even counted on you to be the one to do the investigation."

"Me?" Westfall asked, his eyelids rising involuntarily.

"Yeah," Max said, rushing along, "he said you were like a back injury. Some days are better than others, but the pain never really goes away."

"Why'd he do it?" Westfall asked.

"Money," Max replied. "Judith's money."

The way Max described it, Schenker didn't think one hundred thousand dollars a year was enough to live on in the karmi world. He wanted the two to three million that was locked up in Judith's trust funds. Her family would never turn the estate over to Judith, not while Todd was around. But if he was dead, maybe then the family would let Judith manage her estate.

"Is Judith in on this?" Westfall asked.

"No," the guy said. "They don't get along, that's why they live in different houses. Todd's plan was to wait until she got the money and then show up out of the blue."

"The body," Westfall pressed on, "whose is it? Who got shot in the head and doused with kerosene."

"I don't know," Max said.

"Any ideas?" Westfall asked. Max's upper lip began to quiver. "Well?"

"If I were you, I think I'd check death certificates. Find out who died a few days before Todd disappeared. Then start checking graves."

Max left and Westfall spent a half hour writing up notes. When he finished, he stuffed them into the Schenker file, went outside, and sat down by the fountain. It was the coolest place he knew.

He started thinking through the Schenker case. Was Max telling the truth? If he was, who had been killed, and who had pulled the trigger? Had Schenker done it? Had somebody helped? And if Schenker was alive, where was he? And who would be next—after Schenker?

Those questions inevitably led him back to the big

question, the one Westfall had been turning over in his mind for fifteen years, ever since his first encounter with New Vrindaban. How had people who had set out to make peace and love ended up molesting children, running drugs, committing murder?

He thought about that for a while, as he watched the water swirl in the fountain's basin. The need for something to believe in—for absolutes—had led tens of thousands of young people to the Krishnas. "Simple living, high thinking," the police sergeant muttered, rattling off the tenet the old swami had brought to the streets of New York twenty-two years earlier. "Maybe I'll figure it out some day." Right now, Westfall wanted to go home to his family.

Epilogue

Although no more than five hundred of the four thousand American devotees Prabhupada initiated remain in ISKCON, the movement has stopped losing members. A few temples, like the one in Philadelphia, are gaining devotees.

What follows is an update on some of the people in this book whose lives have been shaped or deeply affected by the movement Prabhupada brought to the West in 1965. They are listed in order of appearance in the story.

Dan Reid is in prison in West Virginia for the murder of Chuck St. Denis.

Debra Gere and **Nick Tsacrios** are happily married and living in Tolavan, in the small house that Thomas Drescher started and Chuck St. Denis finished. Nick is the commune's medic. Debra is working as a nurse in a long-term care hospital in Wheeling.

One of the last times Tom Westfall talked to Debra was during the winter of 1987, when he was investigating the arson fire that destroyed the house Debra and Chuck St. Denis had lived in. Westfall admired the ornamental kale that was growing in front of Debra and Nick's house. Debra asked if he wanted some; Westfall said sure and offered to pay her. "Sergeant Westfall, don't be ridiculous," Debra said, turning down the money. "You and I have been investigating crimes together for four years."

Shortly before he was kicked out of ISKCON, **Kirtanananda** went on a nationwide "First Amendment Freedom Tour." He appeared on "Larry King Live," "Sally Jesse Raphael," and many other lesser-known talk shows. Kirtanananda claimed the government's investigation into New Vrindaban was an attack on Hindus and Hinduism. He has consistently denied involvement in or knowledge of any of the criminal activities associated with New Vrindaban.

New Vrindaban published a full-page ad in the *India Tribune* to ask for donations and to charge that "Right now, today, everyone who belongs to the Indian community in the United States is facing a dangerous crisis! In the last twelve months, it has become obvious that New Vrindaban is being attacked by local, state, and federal officials who have no knowledge of Indian religion and tradition. They are blatantly trying to stop the pious activities of New Vrindaban, by legal means or otherwise."

Kirtanananda took his case all the way to the White House. On Wednesday, March 18, 1987, he had a forty-five minute meeting in the Old Executive Office Building in Washington, D.C. with Rudy Beserra, an assistant director of the Office of Public Liaison. Beserra said he met with Kirtanananda because the guru had been referred by Achamma Chandler, president of the Indian American Forum, a nonprofit lobby concerned with Indian-American relations.

Two days after the meeting, Ms. Chandler released a letter charging that Kirtanananda had "abused" her organization to serve his "ulterior motives."

Kirtanananda is doing some of the things he tried to get Prabhupada to do twenty years ago. His male disciples have abandoned dhotis to wear robes similar to those worn by Christian monks. There is a pipe organ in the Temple of Understanding. And New Vrindaban devotees sing a hymn called "Onward Krishna Soldiers."

During the summer of 1987, Kirtanananda shook up people living near Allentown, Pennsylvania and Lawrence Township, New Jersey. He swooped into those areas to announce that he was looking for land to buy so that he could build a walled city that would house twelve thousand people. The plan appears more closely based on the book of Revelations than the *Srimad-Bhagavatam*.

Basically, the belief is that the apocalypse is coming. The world will be destroyed by nuclear holocaust, AIDS, and a terrible depression. Only the residents of the self-sustaining walled city will survive.

Thomas Drescher is serving a life sentence without possibility of parole for the murder of Chuck St. Denis. He is in the West Virginia State Penitentiary, awaiting extradition to California for trial on murder-for-hire charges in the death of Steve Bryant. Authorities now say he may not stand trial until 1990, four years after it happened.

Tom Westfall is spending most of his time working on the Schenker case, and preparing for the upcoming trademark infringement case, which is scheduled to go to trial in the winter of 1989. He spends his free time fishing and coaching his children's—Tommy and Sarah's—baseball teams.

Kuladri, Arthur Villa, is living in Tucson, Arizona, and is selling office furnishings. Tom Westfall is convinced that Kuladri left due to his fears concerning the Steve Bryant murder. Kuladri expects to be called to testify before a grand jury.

Keith Weber pleaded guilty to firearms violations and was sentenced to three years in a federal penitentiary.

Suzanne Bleudeu, Drescher's common-law wife, is living in New Vrindaban.

Howard Wheeler, Hayagriva, is living outside of Jacksonville, Florida. He and Kirtanananda stay in close touch.

Hansadutta, Hans Kary, is running a trailer court in Cloverdale, a small town on Highway 101 in northern California.

Mukunda, Michael Grant, is ISKCON's director of media relations and the executive editor of the *ISKCON World Review*, the Krishna newspaper. He recently has been active in organizing demonstrations against the imprisonment of Krishna devotees in the Soviet Union.

George Harrison still chants Hare Krishna. "I spent some time at George's house during the summer of 1986," says Mukunda, Michael Grant. "He told me his beads aren't shiny, but he still rubs them."

Richard Rose is living in Benwood, West Virginia. During the summer, he runs an informal commune for people in search of "the truth" on the property he calls the "goat farm."

During the summer of '87, Rose and Kirtanananda happened to meet on a road that separates Rose's land from New Vrindaban's. Rose took a long look at the guru and said, "You know, we've grown old together."

Ravindra Svarupa was elected chairman of the GBC at the 1988 meeting in Mayapur, India. His efforts to purge the criminal elements from ISKCON—there are serious problems in Mayapur—and get ISKCON back on its feet continue.

Walt Parry, the former New Vrindaban temple commander, is living with his wife and children in a public campground in Rhode Island.

Bhagaan, the former Sun King, has married and is living in Berkeley, California.

Ramevara, Robert Grant, is working for his father, selling commercial real estate and doing condo conversions in New York City. He is engaged to be married.

Balimardan, the New York temple president who had the Bower of Bliss, occasionally shows up to chant in the Los Angeles temple. Natasha Toyota also lives in Los Angeles and occasionally visits the LA temple.

Jack and Helga Bryant are living in Royal Oak, Michigan. They are currently pursuing their case to obtain custody of their surviving grandson, Sarva.

Jane Seward, Jamuna, Bryant's former wife, is still living in New Vrindaban, still a loyal follower of Kirtanananda Swami.

Kathy Berry, the woman Bryant was going to marry, is living with her children in Three Rivers, California.

Jerome and Marianne Green, Bryant's best friends, are living on the West Coast. Jerome sells oil paintings in shopping malls.

Sheriff Donald Bordenkircher was defeated in his bid for reelection by Robert Lightner, his predecessor. Lightner won by six hundred votes in a five-thousand-vote election.

Dharmatma, Dennis Gorrick, has been removed as head of the women's sankirtan team but is still living in New Vrindaban. Gorrick owns jewelry stores in San Antonio, Texas; New Orleans; and Norfolk, Virginia.
One of his ex-wives filed suit for custody of their children. A judge ruled in Gorrick's favor.

Sharon Wilson is now an executive secretary in Texas and a member of a Baptist church. She was recently married. "I've never felt closer to God," she says.

At last report, **Guru Kripa,** Gregory Martin Gottfried, was living in a van parked outside the ISKCON temple in Honolulu, Hawaii.

Roy Richard, the former Laguna Beach temple president who set up the hash oil smuggling ring, lives in Los Angeles and occasionally visits the temple there. Joe Davis, his confederate, died of a heroin overdose a week after he was released from prison in 1984.

Tamal Krishna is guru for the American Southwest and the island of Fiji. Fiji's population is 50 percent Hindu, and Tamal is trying to convert them so that the island will become "the world's first Krishna-conscious nation." Tamal plans to build a large Krishna temple in Fiji.

The whereabouts of Hansadutta's right-hand man, **Michael Ralph Pugliese,** aka Dino Bandhu, aka Lance Presley, are unknown.

Joe Sanchez is a patrolman in the Berkeley Police Department.

Vladimir Vassilievich is still living at home with his elderly Ukrainian mother in San Francisco's Sunset district. Over the bed in his room is a big poster of racing Ferraris. On the other three walls are black-and-white pictures of San Francisco street scenes. Vassilievich now spends his days roaming San Francisco with a Leica. His portraits are quite good, disturbing and revealing in an Arbus/Avedon kind of way.

Vassilievich voluntarily took the rap for the guns found in Hansadutta's car but beat the charges on a legal technicality—the police did not have a search warrant. He left the movement immediately after the trial.

One of the first things Vassilievich did when he returned to "the real world" was go to Sears Point, a race course north of San Francisco. There was a classic car race that night, and it was won by Vassilievich's Ferrari, the car he gave to the movement when he joined, the car that is now worth $650,000.

"The guy pulled away from the pack," he said, sitting on his bed as he gave us the account. "You can't imagine how painful that was, standing there and seeing that. It took me three or four years to get over my [second] wife, but I finally got over her. I'll never get over that car."

Vassilievich was quiet for a few moments. Then he pointed to the black-and-white portraits on the wall and said, "One good thing did come out of it. I'd never have taken these pictures if I hadn't joined the Krishnas. When I got out, I had to do something to get another Ferrari and a high-school chick. I'm forty-seven. Think I've still got a chance for the chick?"

Bill Benedict, the devotee whose briefcase was stolen by Hansadutta's disciples in Berkeley, is running Balarams, the Krishna incense and scented oils company, in Visalia, California.

Steven and Cynthia Hebel have spent the 1980s drifting between drugs and Krishna Consciousness. In the spring of 1987, they settled in San Jose. In December, the couple entered a methadone maintenance program.

Cynthia got a job cleaning houses. A former devotee who had put a software company together hired Steven. The ex-devotee taught him how to use software that puts financial transactions on a spreadsheet. Steven is now going from one doctor's office to the next, training office workers to use the software.

Susan Hebel and her children left Three Rivers, California and moved to Susan's sister's town. They are thinking of opening a health food restaurant. In the spring of 1988, Susan went out on a date for the first time since the late sixties. She now has a steady boyfriend.

Yuvati Matusow, Steve Bryant's friend, gave birth to her fourth child in April 1987. When last heard from, she was living on welfare in Three Rivers, California.

Advaita, Emile Sofsky, is a fugitive from the Drug Enforcement Administration. There are rumors that in the winter, Sofsky sells scarves on the streets of New York.

Jadurani, Judy Koslofsky, the artist who was beaten in New Vrindaban for questioning Kirtanananda, made a separate peace with ISKCON and is living in the Miami temple.

Terry Sheldon, the former Cleveland temple president, is believed to be in Malaysia.

Randall Gorby spent weeks in the Ohio Valley Medical Center in Wheeling, West Virginia, undergoing numerous skin grafts. He was placed in a witness-protection program when he got out of the hospital. Gorby testified in the St. Denis murder case and the St. Denis arson trial. When Drescher goes on trial for the murder of Steve Bryant in Los Angeles, Gorby is expected to testify.

Sri Galima, Larry Gardner, who fled before he could be arrested on child molestation charges, is believed to be in India.

Fredrick DeFrancisco, Sri Galima's assistant at the guru kula, is serving a two-year sentence in West Virginia for child molestation.

Bhavananda, Charles Backus, the former Australian guru, is planning to open a health-food restaurant in Los Angeles.

On Tuesday, June 28, 1988, the American Rose Society awarded New Vrindaban its highest honor. The Associated Press commented:

> The Krishnas' roses showed no signs of disease or insects. . . . The judges were impressed with the garden's unusual backdrop, a gold India-style palace. Krishna devotees pamper the roses with hand watering but like most gardeners use pesticides, despite the Hindu doctrine of respect for all forms of life.

Notes

Page   The Planting Party

3: When they are initiated, ISKCON devotees are given Hindu names that symbolize their rebirth as loving followers of Krishna.

3–5: The dialogue between Dan Reid and Chuck St. Denis is reconstructed from author interviews with Debra Gere Tsacrios and Police Sergeant Tom Westfall, as well as from Dan Reid and Howard Fawley's testimony, in the St. Denis murder trial (December 2–5, 1986), and Reid's testimony in the trial (December 7–15, 1987) for the arson fire that destroyed the old farmhouse on the corner of Routes 88 and 250.

5–6: The account of Dan Reid's relationship with his wife, Brenda, is from interviews with several devotees, in particular, Susan and Steven Hebel. It was at their kitchen table that Brenda cried. Debra Gere Tsacrios also described their relationship, as did Dan Reid, at the arson trial.

6–7: The account of Debra Gere's inheritance is based on author and police interviews with her and on her testimony in the St. Denis murder trial.

8–11: The account of St. Denis's childhood is based on several long author interviews with his sister, Chrislyn, and on a short telephone interview conducted by the authors with his brother, Michael, who was in a drug rehabilitation program at the time. Chrislyn discussed St. Denis's use of drugs and the marijuana dealing he did for New Vrindaban.

11–13: The decision to open the nursery was described in interviews with Debra Gere Tsacrios; in her testimony in the St. Denis murder trial; and in former New Vrindaban treasurer Howard Fawley's testimony in the St. Denis murder trial.

11: The deal that St. Denis and Gere worked out to purchase the land from the commune was described at the St.
Denis murder trial by Howard Fawley, New Vrindaban
treasurer at the time.

12: The account of the trip to Garberville to buy high-
powered marijuana is from interviews with Steven Hebel.
Hebel was the connection who introduced St. Denis to the
growers.

13: The incident at the Georgia-Florida border is reconstructed from an author interview with Dr. Nick Tsacrios.

13–14: Dan Reid insisted during the farmhouse arson trial
that St. Denis did indeed rape his wife. He testifed that
Brenda had told him that St. Denis had raped her. He has
stuck to the charge through repeated police interviews.

13–14: Kirtanananda's role in the St. Denis matter is according to Dan Reid's testimony in the farmhouse arson trial.
Under cross-examination from James B. Lees, who was
representing Kirtanananda, Reid testified, "I was ready to
go out and do it on the spot and then I sought counsel
from Bhaktipada [Kirtanananda], who told me to seek out
Thomas Drescher, and at that point it was under Thomas
Drescher's direction." Later in the cross-examination, Attorney Lees asked Reid, "Okay, now what information
did you discuss with the swami at that time prior to the
swami's decision to refer you to Mr. Drescher?" Reid
answered, "I told him that I found out St. Denis raped my
wife and I wanted to kill him, and he said, 'So, who's
gonna care? Maybe you should go talk to Drescher about
this.' "

Norman Hewlett, a former president of the ISKCON
temple in Cleveland, one of New Vrindaban's satellite
temples, told the authors, "The real reason they were mad
at St. Denis was, he had received an inheritance. Anyone
who gets an inheritance, they're supposed to turn it over
to Bhaktipada [Kirtanananda], but this guy [St. Denis]
didn't."

14–15: Drescher's response to Reid's request to take care of
Chuck St. Denis is taken from Reid's testimony in the
farmhouse arson trial.

15: Background information on Thomas Drescher is derived
from a three-hour telephone interview with the authors,
conducted while Drescher was in the Marshall County Jail
waiting to go on trial for murdering Chuck St. Denis.

Sergeant Tom Westfall also spent hours interviewing Drescher about his past, particularly his time in the military. The bus incident was related by a former New Vrindaban devotee who contacted the authors after their story "Dial Om for Murder" appeared in *Rolling Stone,* April 9, 1987. She does not want her name used as she fears retaliation. 14–15: The account of Reid and Drescher planning St. Denis's murder is taken from Reid's testimony in the farmhouse arson trial.

17: The descriptions of the planting party, of Reid briefly meeting St. Denis and Debra Gere after the party, and of Reid's phone call to St. Denis come from an interview with Debra Gere Tsacrios, her testimony in the St. Denis murder trial, and Reid's testimony in the farmhouse arson trial.

18–21: The account of the St. Denis murder comes from Dan Reid's testimony in the farmhouse arson trial; from testimony by Howard Fawley—the former New Vrindaban treasurer—at both the St. Denis murder trial and the farmhouse arson trial; from Paul Ferry's testimony in the St. Denis murder trial; and from interviews with Tom White—the Marshall County Prosecutor—and from Dr. Nick Tsacrios. Drescher told Tsacrios that he learned in Vietnam that killing didn't bother him. Drescher has also recounted the murder to Sergeant Tom Westfall.

Dig a Hole

25–26: The account of the battle between St. Denis and Drescher over the house is taken from author interviews with Debra Gere Tsacrios, Dr. Nick Tsacrios, and Thomas Drescher.

27–28: Drescher's confession to Dr. Nick Tsacrios is taken from Tsacrios's testimony in the St. Denis murder case and from author interviews with Dr. Tsacrios.

28–29: Information about the marijuana dealer "Big John," or "John from Athens," comes from Howard Fawley's testimony in both the St. Denis murder case and in the farmhouse arson case; from Dan Reid's testimony in the farmhouse arson case; and from interviews with Debra Gere Tsacrios.

29–30: Kuladri's (Arthur Villa's) description of Sergeant Westfall comes from interviews with Debra Gere Tsacrios.

33: Kuladri's warning to New Vrindaban devotees not to cooperate with police investigating the murder of Chuck St. Denis is taken from Steven Bryant's unpublished exposé, "The Guru Business," page 9. Bryant writes that he was there when Kuladri made the announcement.

34–35: The account of the deaths of the two children, Radheya and Rohini, is based on interviews with Debra Gere Tsacrios; Gail Conger, a former New Vrindaban devotee; Don McAdams (Narendra), the stained-glass artist who designed and built the windows in the Palace of Gold; and Dan Reid's testimony in the farmhouse arson trial.

35: The account of Debra Gere discovering the welts and bruises on Jayadeva comes from an author interview with her.

36–38: The account of the arson comes from testimony in the trial, particularly that of Howard Fawley and Dan Reid. Howard Fawley, the former New Vrindaban treasurer, testified that after Debra Gere moved out of the old farm house, Kirtanananda "mentioned that it seemed like an opportune time to possibly have the building burned." Dan Reid testified that he approached Kirtanananda about burning down the farmhouse. "I told him [Kirtanananda], 'Howard said he had spoke to you about burning down the house and he wanted to know if you wanted it done, because Drescher was willing to do it.' And he [Kirtanananda] nodded that yes [he wanted it done]. And I asked him again, I said, 'So you want it done,' and he verbalized a yes answer."

Arthur Villa and Howard Fawley pleaded guilty to mail fraud for letters they wrote to the insurance company. Dan Reid pleaded guilty to conspiracy to commit arson. Thomas Drescher pleaded not guilty to setting the fire but was convicted and received a ten-year sentence. Kirtanananda Swami was indicted, tried, and found not guilty.

40–41: The description of Drescher pouring acid into Chuck St. Denis's grave comes from an interview with Dr. Nick Tsacrios; from Dan Reid's testimony in the farmhouse arson trial—Reid testified that he was there when Drescher did it; and from Paul Ferry's testimony in the St. Denis murder trial.

41–44: The account of the incident in the laundromat, and of the state police deciding that Dr. Nick Tsacrios was an unreliable witness, comes from an author interview with

Tsacrios. Tsacrios says that after Steve Bryant was murdered and the St. Denis case was re-opened, he saw "Unreliable Witness" scrawled at the top of a transcript of his original interview with the West Virginia State Police.

The Messiah and the Mott Street Gang

47–49: The description of the meeting between Howard Wheeler and Prabhupada in the Bowery comes from Wheeler's (Hayagriva's) book, *The Hare Krishna Explosion: The Birth of Krishna Consciousness in America, 1966–1969* (Palace Press, 1985), pp. 1–3; and from *Srila Prabhupada-lilamrta*, a six-volume biography of Prabhupada by Satsvarupa dasa Goswami (The Bhaktivedanta Book Trust, 1982). The account of the early days in the Bowery is in Vol. 2, *Planting the Seed*, pp. 67–104.

49–50: The description of the Mott Street Gang is taken from Hayagriva's *The Hare Krishna Explosion*, p. 3, and from interviews with early devotees in the New York temple, particularly Tarun Krishna, Hansadutta (Hans Kary), Mukunda (Michael Grant), and Swarup (Steven Hebel). The description of Kirtanananda's personality at the time comes from interviews with him and early devotees, particularly Nara Naranayana (Nathan Zakheim), Tarun Krishna, Hansadutta, and Mukunda.

49–51: The account of Prabhupada's class comes from hours of videotapes of his meetings with devotees, from lectures, from sacred Hindu texts, and from descriptions that occur throughout Hayagriva's *The Hare Krishna Explosion* and Satsvarupa's six-volume biography, *Srila Prabhupada-lilamrta*.

52–56: The account of Hans Kary's metamorphosis into Hansadutta is drawn from interviews with Kary. The list of rules Prabhupada taped to the temple window is reproduced in Hayagriva's *The Hare Krishna Explosion*, p. 71.

57–60: The account of Kirtanananda's background and hospitalization in Bellevue is drawn from an author interview with Kirtanananda. Kirtanananda dismissed the episode as "the result of a welfare scam." Hayagriva has an account of the episode in *The Hare Krishna Explosion*, pp. 52–54, 76–77. Nathan Zakheim also shed light on the incident in an interview.

58–59: The role Allen Ginsberg played in the early days of the movement is recounted in *The Hare Krishna Explosion,* pp. 26–28, 106–108 and in *Planting the Seed,* Vol. 2 of Satsvarupa's biography of Praphupada, pp. 195–197.

60–62: The parts of Prabhupada's *Easy Journey to Other Planets* that affected Hans Kary so deeply deal with karma and the *atman.* Karma is a law of moral cause and effect that says our actions effect us not just in this lifetime, but in future lives. As long as we keep collecting karma, we will keep being reborn to work it off.

The way to break out of the birth-death-karma cycle is to awaken the atman, the Hindu equivalent of the soul, the part of every living being that is divine. The atman is Hinduism's answer to the eternal question Who am I?

"You were never born; you will never die," Krishna tells Arjuna in the *Gita.* "You have never changed; you can never change. Unborn, eternal, immutable, immemorial, you do not die when the body dies. . . . Death is inevitable for the living; birth is inevitable for the dead."

62–63: The account of Kirtanananda's quick wit in dealing with "the Jesus guy" comes from an interview with Steven Hebel.

63: The account of Hansadutta's introduction of materialism into the movement by blowing the conch horn and asking for donations is taken from author interviews with Hansadutta.

64–65: The account of Kirtanananda and Hansadutta opening a temple in Montreal is based on an author interview with Hansadutta.

Drop Out, Fall In, Sing Out

66–68: The description of the Krishnas in San Francisco during the early flower power days is based on interviews with devotees who were there, particularly Mukunda, Michael Grant. This period is also well covered in *Only He Could Lead Them,* Vol. 3 of Satsvarupa's biography of Prabhupada, pp. 1–51.

66–68: Between 150 and 200 people joined ISKCON during the Summer of Love. Looked at from an eighties MBA point of view, the movement cleaned up because it offered a superior product at a time when San Francisco was packed with people in the market for new forms of spirituality.

Krishna was easy to sell to hippies. Most of them had rejected Christianity when they rejected their parents, and antiwar types were wearing "Kill a Commie for Christ" T-shirts on Haight Street. Besides, Christ died on a cross. Hippies did not want to hear about death, even Christ's death. Death was a bummer.

Most of the hippies who had heard of Buddha pictured an old man with a big belly, sitting under a tree. Krishna, on the other hand, was cool. He played the flute and hung out with beautiful girls. He wore flowers and feathers and went barefoot. Krishna was eternally young, and more than anything else, hippies wanted to be forever young.

68–72: The account of Prabhupada's stroke on Memorial Day is drawn from Hayagriva's *The Hare Krishna Explosion,* pp. 187–198, and *Only He Could Lead Them,*

Vol. 3 of Satsvarupa's biography, pp. 121–152. Mukunda, Michael Grant, and Swarup, Steven Hebel, also discussed the stroke during interviews.

72–77: "Beth Ann" is a composite character combining the experiences of two female devotees in the early days of the movement. Identifying details have been changed to protect the privacy of both women. One of the devotees contacted the authors after reading "Dial Om For Murder," a story published in *Rolling Stone* on April 9, 1987. "Dasher" is a pseudonym.

76–77: Compared to a conservative Hindu male, Prabhupada was rather enlightened about women. But from a contemporary American feminist perspective, he was a male chauvinist.

Prabhupada believed that women are controlled by their senses. They are "fire," men are "butter." Women's lust melts men.

Since women have no more control over passion than children do over tempers, they must be protected from their sensate natures and from marauding males who would take advantage of them. Their fathers protect them when they are girls, their husbands when they are wives, their sons when they are old.

To be controlled, a woman must be submissive. She obeys her husband, cooks, cleans house, bears Krishna-conscious children, and, traditionally, churns butter.

"By churning butter, they develop good bodies," Prabhupada is quoted as saying humorously in *The Hare Krishna Explosion.*

Prabhupada was the Carrie Nation of sex. He believed sex was maya, illusion, because it made people think happiness was possible through sensual gratification, when true happiness was only possible by loving God. Prabhupada allowed devotees to have sex only once a month, and only for the production of Krishna-conscious children. Sex for any other purpose was sense indulgence that tied people to the material world and threw more dirt on the spirit-soul, the atman.

"Prabhupada was wonderful," one of the devotees on whom Beth Ann is based says. "He had such strength. He used to say we should be humble as a blade of grass and have the patience of a tree. That's the way he was. He was completely without pretense."

This devotee's fondest memories of the sixteen years she spent in ISKCON are of her first few months in the Haight-Ashbury temple.

"The whole woman-subservient thing didn't bother me because we were treated with such love," she says. "We were so loose, so loose, it was good to have to clean up our act." The ISKCON men weren't into a macho trip. We were all equal, all trying to be good devotees. I was twenty and the men called me *mataji,* mother. I liked it because it was their way of relating to women in a way that wasn't sexual. We all traded jobs, cooking, cleaning, decorating the deities. It was fun, a lot more fun than being a hippie."

77–78: Hansadutta's moment in the spotlight in San Francisco International Airport comes from an interview with Hansadutta himself.

78–80 George Harrison's trip to San Francisco is described in *In Every Town and Village,* Vol. 4 of Satsvarupa's six-volume biography of Prabhupada, pp. 29–30.

Additional information came from author interviews with Mukunda, Michael Grant.

Ambitions Pupil

81–88: The conversation on the airplane is a dramatization intended to present Prabhupada's biography. Kirtanananda's eagerness to elicit his life story is derived from Kirtanananda's subsequent attempts to Westernize ISKCON and package it for the media. Much of the Prabhupada-Kirtanananda relationship as described here is based on Prabhupada's letters to Brahmananda, Hayagriva, Gargamuni, and Satsvarupa—all written while he was in India.

Prabhupada's trip to India is covered in *The Hare Krishna Explosion*, pp. 209–223, and *Only He Could Lead Them*, Vol. 3 of Satsvarupa's six-volume biography, pp. 175–218. Both works offer incomplete accounts in that neither mentions Kirtanananda's betrayal. The account of Prabhupada's life is condensed from Satsvarupa's biography and from a film produced by ISKCON called *Your Ever Well Wisher*.

83: Bhaktisiddhanta, Prabhupada's guru, traced his spirititual lineage back to Lord Chaitanya Mahaprabhu (1486–1533), the founder of bhakti yoga. Chaitanya was an arrogant young schoolteacher in Bengal before he became a devotee of Krishna early in the sixteenth century. Bengal at that time was under Turkish rule. Islam was the state religion; Hinduism and its practitioners were considered inferior.

Chaitanya was so mad with love for Krishna that he lost all his students and had to close his school. He rarely bathed and insisted on wearing the simplest clothes, eating the simplest food, and living with the fewest possible creature comforts. His love for Radha and Krishna was altogether spiritual, and Chaitanya carefully avoided women lest he be reminded of carnal love.

Chaitanya's way of expressing his divine love was to lead his devotees into villages to perform sankirtans. Hands raised above his head, leaping up and down while drums played and cymbals chinged, Chaitanya danced and chanted Krishna's names and often collapsed in the dirt in ecstatic exhaustion.

Chaitanya and his devotees also staged *yatras*, outdoor plays based on Krishna's pastimes with the gopis in Vrindaban. People who came to watch the sankirtans and yatras gave small donations of food and money. After a day or two, the devotees moved on to the next village and did it all over again.

Chaitanya eventually revitalized Hinduism in Bengal. He broke with Hindu tradition by initiating people from all castes. Caste was irrelevant because all people were equal spiritually. His movement grew so large, the Muslim governor in Bengal finally ordered the sankirtans stopped. Chaitanya immediately staged a huge sankirtan in front of the governor's house.

The governor had Chaitanya dragged into his house. If he did not stop the demonstration at once, the governor told Chaitanya, he would throw him in jail and throw away the key. Chaitanya began explaining what the sankirtan was all about. The governor listened and not only let the sankirtans continue, he eventually became a devotee.

Chaitanya left Bengal for Puri, a small town in Orissa, in northeast India. The king of Orissa gave him the money and support he needed to establish a center for his movement, but Chaitanya refused to meet him. The king represented money and power; he was too much a part of this world. Chaitanya allowed nothing to take his mind off Krishna and the world of eternal love.

Toward the end of his life, Chaitanya made a pilgrimage to Vrindaban, the small town near Delhi where Krishna appeared as a cowherd boy. Each time he saw something that reminded him of Krishna, he went into a fit of rapture. When he heard a flute playing, he went into a trance. When he first saw the sacred Jamuna River, he ran in and had to be pulled out.

Historians know that Chaitanya died in 1534, but they are not sure how. He may have drowned while in a trance or died of a fever. Devotees believe he disappeared into the deities in his temple in Puri.

84–85: The description of Kirtanananda's revolt is drawn primarily from Prabhupada's letters. A sampler of extracts follows:

> Kirtanananda Swami prearranged with you to reach on the 24th instant, but he arranged with me that he would stop in London and I gave him one important introduction letter. *Although he had in his mind not to stop in London* and yet promised before me that he would go, for which I gave him extra $20. I cannot understand why *he played with me* like this. If he had no desire to go to London he would have plainly told me like that. It has certainly *given me a great shock.* . . . It is all my misfortune. [Letter to Hayagriva, 9–27–67]

> *He was so much frenzied to see & meet his old friends* that he forgot the order of Krishna and indulged in a sort of sense gratification. *It is certainly a shocking incident* which I never expected from a disciple like Kirtanananda. [Letter to Satsvarupa, 10–3–67]

> He is too much puffed up nonsensically therefore you should copy this letter and forward to all centers that Kirtanananda has no right to dictate anything to the society in this way. I am very sorry that he is exploiting his present position as a sannyasi in this way. [Letter to Brahmananda, 10–4–67]

> My dear Kirtanananda, Why are you disturbing the whole situation in my absence? Please therefore do not misrepresent me. You have been given sannyasa to follow my principles and not to disturb me. If you do not agree with my philosophy you can work independent and not within the walls of ISKCON. You have not understood Krishna properly. Hope you are well. [Letter to Kirtanananda, 10–16–67]

> Kirtanananda was giving me direct service by massaging, cooking for me, and so many other things but later on by dictation of Maya, he became puffed up, so much so that he thought his Spiritual master a common man, and was existing only on account of his service. This mentality at once pushed him down. [Letter to Madhusudana, 12–28–67]

An author interview with Nathan Zakheim explored Kirtanananda's motivation, as did a long series of interviews with Ravindra Svarupa.

A Guru Defects, the Beatles Enlist

95–99: Kirtanananda's return to the New York temple and his subsequent ouster by Brahmananda are dramatizations derived from Prabhupada's letters (one of which is quoted in the text) and interviews with Nathan Zakheim, Tarun Krishna, and Ravindra Svarupa. Kirtanananda's dress, preaching, and Mayavadi philosophy, as well as his final confrontation with Brahmananda, his ouster from the temple, and the spitting incident were described in these letters and interviews.

Howard Wheeler and Keith Ham in their apartment is a dramatization. Their alleged homosexual relationship before joining the movement comes from Steven Hebel, Don McAdams, Yuvati Matusow, and Gail Conger.

"Kirtanananda came back from India and got back together with Hayagriva [Howard Wheeler]. I'm quite sure they were together as homosexuals," Nathan Zakheim says. "Kirtanananda was intensely envious of Prabhupada. Envy, greed, antiauthoritarianism, and messianic delusions fueled Kirtanananda and Hayagriva's revolt. They thought they were in total command of the next stage of the Aquarian movement."

Nathan Zakheim discussed the theft of Prabhupada's *Gita* manuscript: "Hayagriva [Wheeler] was editing Prabhupada's translation of the *Gita* for Macmillan. He and Kirtanananda stole it from Prabhupada and tried to publish it under their names. They weren't successful because no one would believe they had translated it. It took Prabhupada a long time to get his manuscript back."

Prabhupada's letters describe his efforts to get the manuscript back. Steve Bryant also describes the theft in "The Guru Business."

100–103: Richard Rose described his meeting with Ham and Wheeler in an interview in his home in McMechan, West Virginia. Hayagriva has an account of the meeting with Rose (and the shootout that followed) in *The Hare Krishna Explosion*, pp. 231–243. He calls Rose "Mr. Foster."

103–111: There is a complete account of the opening of the London temple and the devotees' experiences with George Harrison, John Lennon, and Yoko Ono in *In Every Town and Village*, Vol. 4 of Satsvarupa's biography of Prabhupada. A Bhaktivedanta Book Trust title, *Chant and Be Happy* (1982), also covers the relationship of George, John, Paul, and Yoko Ono with the Krishnas. Information was also obtained from interviews with Mukunda, Michael Grant.

George Harrison's description of Prabhupada appears in *In Every Town and Village:*

"He never said, 'I am the greatest' and 'I am God,' and all that. With him, it was only in the context of being a servant, and I liked that a lot. I think it's part of the spiritual thing. The more they know, then the more they actually know that they are the servant. And the less they know, the more they think are actually God's gift to mankind."

The Pretender's Throne

112–115: The account of Keith Ham and Howard Wheeler's decision to return to ISKCON and Prabhupada's decision to accept them back is a dramatization based on Prabhupada's letters and author interviews with devotees; in particular, Nathan Zakheim and Ravindra Svarupa. The sentiments attributed to Govinda das are typical of those expressed by rank and file devotees.

116–120: The account of Richard Rose's relationship with Ham and Wheeler and the shoot-out at his farm is based on an interview with Rose and on Hayagriva's *The Hare Krishna Explosion*, pp. 231–243. The charges against Rose for shooting the seventeen-year-old were later dropped.

120–124: The description of New Vrindaban in its early days comes from interviews with Nathan Zakheim, who was there.

"The atmosphere was grisly in that ratty old farmhouse. The kitchen was absolutely filthy," Zakheim recalls. "I'd talk to Kirtanananda about cleaning things up, but he wouldn't hear of it. Cleanliness meant nothing to him. He never shaved; he dressed in rags; he was missing teeth. The place looked like it was out of the Ozarks, except that everybody was worshiping Krishna.

"I've always thought of Kirtanananda as a strange mixture of extreme purity and extreme filth, of honey and manure," Zakheim continues. "He has a very deep and penetrating mind. He has great leadership ability. He can make people identify with his goals. But then, so could Hitler.

"There were heavy homosexual overtones between him and Hayagriva [Howard Wheeler]," Zakheim goes on. "Hayagriva would call 'Haaammmm' in a high, woman's voice, and Kirtanananda would answer, 'Yeeessssss, Mr. Wheeler?' in a voice that was full of double entendre.

Hayagriva was a very weak, emotional person, who was very upsetting to be around. If we were out of firewood, he'd bitch on and on, 'Oh, my God, we're out of wood, what are we going to do?' without ever doing a thing. Our VW broke down while he was driving and he sat there for hours, complaining like Elmer Fudd, totally unable to do anything. He was completely paranoid about bodily functions. He'd come out of the bathroom and go on for hours, trying to calculate whether or not he had taken a good shit.

"There was a hysterical side to Hayagriva, too. We built a dormer on the barn together. We made a pact not to sleep until it was finished, but I went off and fell asleep. When I came back, Hayagriva was incensed. He picked up a crowbar and came after me with it. He's a big, manly guy. I was lucky to escape."

120–123: Prabhupada's first visit to New Vrindaban is described in his letters, and in Hayagriva's *The Hare Krishna Explosion*, pp. 261–278. The account of Kirtanananda's exploitation of his relationship with Prabhupada is based on interviews with devotees, particularly Ravindra Svarupa and Sudhir Goswami, Philip Murphy.

"Kirtanananda was so dependent on personal association with Prabhupada," recalls Murphy, former president of the Los Angeles ISKCON temple and now, as Sudhir Goswami, the head of a temple in San Jose, California, that has split with ISKCON. "Kirtanananda was always whining, 'Oh, Prabhupada, you have to come to my temple soon. We'll make it so nice for you, you'll never leave.' There's an old Bengali proverb: Too much devotion is the sign of a thief."

123–124: The cookie ceremony was described in an interview with Steven Hebel. Why did devotees submit to Kirtanananda and the rigors of New Vrindaban? For a number of reasons: Some who thought they were surrendering to Krishna were, in fact, waging an endless battle with their parents. Kirtanananda appealed to that kind of devotee because living in the hills without running water was the ultimate "In your face!" to comfortably surburban parents. Staying at New Vrindaban was also a way for devotees to prove that their faith was pure. It had to be; otherwise, why would they be living in an unheated room above a barn that did not have a toilet?

Other devotees entered the movement seeking refuge from the world. For any number of reasons—character deficiencies, a spoiled or unhappy childhood—they were unable to make decisions and take responsibility for themselves. New Vrindaban was a perfect hiding place for that kind of devotee. Kirtanananda made every decision, from when to get up to whom to marry. If you did what he said, you were not only given room and board, you were given the illusion you were living a pure life that was superior to that of the karmis who were fighting it out in the nine-to-five world.

"A lot of devotees are afraid of the world," says Don McAdams, Narendra, the ex-devotee who designed and built the stained-glass windows in the Palace of Gold. "They're very insecure people who didn't fit in anywhere. You don't have to face your individuality in the Krishna movement. You can hide and become totally lost in a somewhat secure situation. You know you're going to eat and have a place to stay, and you know you don't have to be out there in the world, taking care of business.

"That's what it did for me. I'm not competitive. It was a place where I could live the spiritual life and do art and not have to worry about supporting myself. It was kind of like being a professional graduate student."

123–124: The description of "Joe" comes from an interview with Walt Parry, a former New Vrindaban temple commander. Parry later helped bury Joe.

124–127: Kirtanananda's sectarianism in Philadelphia (combining a number of incidents) was described in a series of interviews with Ravindra Svarupa.

Prabhupada knew what Kirtanananda was up to. Ravindra wrote to tell him New Vrindaban devotees had raided his temple. So did temple presidents in Chicago, Miami, St. Louis, and many other temples.

A devotee named Upendra wrote Prabhupada to tell him that Kirtanananda was pressuring people to go to New Vrindaban. Prabhupada wrote back, "I send herewith instructions to all of you that for the present, there is no necessity of going there. And in the future, nobody shall go there without getting my permission."

Brahmananda, president of the New York temple, wrote to complain that as a sannyasi, Kirtanananda was claiming a position in the movement second only to Prabhupada's.

The guru wrote Brahmananda, "In our society everyone
. . . who has dedicated his life and soul to this movement
are all on the same level as sannyasis. Nobody can claim
an extra honor from his godbrothers. I do not know why
Kirtanananda says that his authority overrides yours. At
the present moment, everyone is working under my authority. Similarly, Kirtanananda also should work under
my authority."

Prabhupada also wrote Kirtanananda a number of letters, most telling him to curtail his tactics and to "stop any
more influx into New Vrandavana [New Vrindaban] until
the place is self-dependent." The spiritual master figured
it would be a long time before the community would be
self-sufficient because no one there knew anything about
farming.

Prabhupada's attitude toward Kirtanananda was no different from his attitude toward any other devotee. His
fiercely held belief was that Krishna Consciousness was
like a hospital for the sprit. Krishna rejected no one who
was attracted to him. Thus, Prabhupada felt his job as
acharya was not to root out people who caused problems,
like Kirtanananda, but to find ways to engage them in
Krishna's service. Prabhupada was convinced that no matter how many problems a person had, as long as he
chanted sixteen rounds of the maha-mantra every day and
followed the regulative principles, Krishna would eventually transform him into an instrument of his mercy.

Clouds of Change

128–136: The description of the "motorcycle gang attack" at
New Vrindaban is reconstructed from author interviews
with Sergeant Tom Westfall. The Krishnas denied that
Elmore's daughter was ever in New Vrindaban, but Westfall
eventually discovered that she was.

"I found out later that she was there," Westfall says. "It
took me a long, long time to learn that, but eventually the
devotees admitted she was there. They ran her up into the
woods and hid her. After her father left, they took her up
to the Pittsburgh temple.

"That was a standard thing back then," Westfall continues. "Families would come to look for their children, and

the Krishnas would hide them in the woods. They had gotten pretty used to being threatened, so they didn't pay much attention to Elmore."

Kirtanananda's version of the attack was told in the *Philadelphia Inquirer* article, "Krishnas in West Virginia: Gold, Guns," December 31, 1978. "I think the only thing the Krishnas regretted," Kirtanananda told reporter Linda S. Herskowitz, "was that they didn't give up their lives to protect the deity from the demons."

Thirteen years after it happened, Kirtanananda was still milking the attack to gain public sympathy. In a 1986 letter appealing to "1,000 friends" to send $108 to "help us in our struggles," Kirtanananda wrote, "We called the police, who responded to our urgent call two hours later, after the assailants had safely gotten away. We did some investigation on our own, found the men, charged them, and brought them before a grand jury. Thirty people identified the men as being the attackers. Were they guilty? Not on your life. They were not even indicted."

136–138: The conversation between Walt Parry and Thomas Drescher on the firing range at New Vrindaban is reconstructed from interviews with Parry.

By his early teens, Parry, the product of a broken home in Philadelphia, was stealing cars and shooting methamphetamine to stay up all night. At sixteen, he was arrested for possession of a handgun and marijuana. At seventeen, he was riding with the Warlocks, a Philadelphia-area motorcycle gang that practices black magic.

"The biker's attitude is, 'You're paying money to a government that is ripping you off, that is going to blow you up, so why go the white man's nine-to-five route?' "

Parry says. "That made sense to me. We [the Warlocks] were on a run in Florida, sitting in a Denny's in Cocoa Beach. I looked across the street and the Krishnas were chanting. I asked this biker, 'Who are they?' He said, 'Don't go near them, they've got strong magic.'

"I got to thinking, if bikers were afraid of them, then the Krishnas must have stronger magic than they had. I started thinking that maybe it was white magic, and that maybe I wanted it."

137: Information about Keith Weber and Todd Schenker— the commune's armorers—comes from interviews with Sergeant Tom Westfall.

138–146: "Gary Dienstel" is a pseudonym for a devotee who
was kidnapped and deprogrammed in another state. The
kidnapping of Gary reflects changes in American culture
that were taking place in the early 1970s. Estimates of the
number of devotees Prabhupada initiated in the United
States and Canada range from four thousand to nine thousand. ISKCON is very sensitive about how many devotees
and how much money it has, and has never released exact
numbers. However, Dr. J. Stillson Judah, a religious scholar
and professor emeritus at the University of California,
Berkeley and the Graduate Theological Union, and author of *Hare Krishna and the Counterculture* (Books Demand UMI, 1980), believes that five thousand is as good
an estimate as any.

Whatever the exact figure, one thing is certain: Prabhupada initiated the vast majority of his devotees before 1974.
By 1974, the counterculture had all but vanished. Disco replaced blues-based rock and roll; cocaine replaced marijuana
and LSD; and the immediate and tangible—careers, cars,
clothes, and sex—replaced a long search for that ultimate
intangible, spirituality. By 1974, ISKCON was no longer
considered "far out"; it was under attack by deprogrammers.

"Dienstel" spoke to the authors only on the condition
that he not be identified. He left the movement, has
married, and now works as an accountant. He has left
ISKCON far behind and remembers his time in the movement with pain. "I was lucky; I got out before the 'guru
horrors' began," he says.

In later years, deprogrammers became more sophisti-
cated and it became more difficult for devotees to convince them that they had rejected their beliefs.

Frank Sterns is a composite who represents hundreds of
people across the country, maintaining a close relationship
with the temples, coming to eat prasadam, but not being
initiated.

Stocking God's Treasury

149–150: The description of Prabhupada's problems with married devotees is taken from his letters and from interviews
with Ravindra Svarupa. Prabhupada performed marriages
in a very cavalier fashion. Basically, it amounted to pointing at a man and a woman and saying, "You and you."

It was not that Prabhupada was insensitive to the importance of marriage. He simply assumed that because a man and a woman were both devotees of Krishna, there was no question but that they would be happy. Krishna Consciousness was a far stronger foundation on which to build a relationship than romantic love, which, like everything else in the material world was subject to vicissitude, and conflicts arising from family ties, money, and property. A Krishna-conscious husband and wife may argue, but it will be thunder without lightning. There is no danger they will harm each other or their relationship, because at all times they will remember the love Radha had for Krishna and will do their best to saturate their marriage with that spirit.

When the marriages didn't work out, Prabhupada fell back on tradition. Krishna's movement had been run by celibate males in India for over four hundred years. It was best that ISKCON be run by sannyasis, too.

"People began taking sannyasa for power, prestige, institutional advancement—for all the wrong reasons," says Ravindra Svarupa. "Sannyasa was the first rung of the ladder that led to the GBC and being named a successor to Prabhupada. Sannyasis were waited on hand and foot. Whenever they arrived at a temple, they were treated like royalty because they were 'holy men.' "

"Homosexuals used sannyasa to establish a superiority in the movement," adds Nathan Zakheim. "When a homosexual takes sannyasa, he can truthfully say he has no attraction to women. Homosexual sannyasis would say, 'You guys are attached to women, women are your attachment to the material world.' Of course, from a spiritual point of view, attachment to men is no better, but it is easier to hide. A lot of homosexual sannyasis lived with boys in an ashram and relished the closeness."

The rise of the sannyasis led to the fall of women in ISKCON. Instead of just being considered subservient, women were now regarded as inferior. They were bound to the material world by everything, from their libidinous nature to their menstrual cycle.

In the New York temple, a sannyasi named Gargamuni spit on a woman. In the Los Angeles temple, a balcony was built above the deities. Women were no longer allowed to chant and dance with men; they watched men dance and chant from the balcony. In the Berkeley temple, Beth Ann, the ex-hippie who joined in Haight-Ashbury, arrived early one evening for a Prabhupada lecture so she could get a seat near the front. A sannyasi came into the room and saw where she was sitting.

"He came running up to me and screamed, 'Woman! Harlot! Get back! Get back! All women sit in the back!' " Beth Ann recalls.

In all temples, women were banned from teaching *Srimad Bhagavatam* classes. Their spiritual lives were routinely neglected. Women were sent out to chant and sell magazines. When they returned, they cooked and cleaned and were forgotten. Being inferior, women were not going to advance very far spiritually, so what did it matter?

Worse yet, married men began verbally abusing and, in some cases, beating their wives.

"You had to show you were a together householder by neglecting or mistreating your wife," says Ravindra Svarupa. "You had to show you weren't attached to her, that you weren't a puppet in the hands of your wife.

"A lot of people who were made sannyasis shouldn't have been," Ravindra concludes. "They were sexually frustrated. Lust leads to anger, and they took out their anger on women."

150–152: Prabhupada's speeches are based closely on his letters, which treat the formation of the GBC, and Satsvarupa's description in his *In Every Town and Village,* Vol. 4 of his biography of Prabhupada.

When Prabhupada set up the GBC, he established a second power structure in the movement. The first was made up of the temple presidents, who were almost all married men. The GBC was made up of men who had taken vows of sannyasa. That the GBC sannyasis declared war on the married temple presidents suggests that spiritual eminence does not bring political wisdom.

From the time ISKCON took off in America, Prabhupada was ambivalent about his power. He delegated authority over ISKCON's temples to temple presidents and then to members of the GBC, so he could spend his time translating and writing. He was waiting to see what would happen when he gave his devotees responsibility.

At the same time, Prabhupada was the spiritual master. In a Western religion, such as Catholic or Lutheran Christianity, revelation is embodied in the church hierarchy. In an Eastern religion, revelation is embodied in the individual, the spiritual master who has reached samadhi. Prabhupada was, therefore, the authority on every subject. Devotees with problems appealed to Prabhupada. Temple presidents and GBC members with problems wrote to Prabhupada. Every decision, great and small, had to be cleared through him.

151: The account of Prabhupada's decision not to name Kirtanananda to the original GBC comes from interviews with Atreya Rishi, a former member of the GBC.

"Kirtanananda was the last person Prabhupada named to the GBC," says Rishi, an Iranian who graduated from Harvard Business School in 1965. Rishi was head of the Arthur Young accounting firm's Tehran office from the early seventies until the Khomeini revolution. He joined the movement in the late sixties and was named to the GBC in the midseventies.

"In those days [1975–77] I thought Kirtanananda was a great devotee," Rishi continues. "I was always asking Prabhupada, 'Why don't you name him to the GBC? He's doing great service.' Prabhupada would just look at me, or he would go on with what he was doing like he hadn't heard. Only at the end [of his life] when Prabhupada was an ocean of compassion, did he name Kirtanananda to the GBC."

152–155: Hansadutta described his sankirtan techniques at some length in an author interview. He also discussed his encounters with the German police in interviews. An article about the arrests, "Like a Movie Script," was published in *Der Spiegel* in December 1977. Although the Krishnas were arrested in 1974, they were not sentenced until 1978, when they were ordered to pay stiff fines. The German prosecutor claimed that although they had collected $1.1 million in seven months "to feed starving children in India," only $6,900 went to India—none of it to starving children.

156–158: Prabhupada's state of mind is based on his letters from this period. Prabhupada's conversation with Ramesvara is intended to summarize the major problems the movement faced at this time. Ramesvara's relationship with Prabhupada was described by many Los Angeles devotees; in particular, Sudhir Goswami, Philip Murphy, who was the

Los Angeles temple president under Ramesvara. Corroborating information came from Nathan Zakheim, Charlie Kirkland, Susan Kirkland, and Steven Hebel. Part of the dialogue was reconstructed from "The Pyramid Tapes," which are transcripts of conversations between several of ISKCON's leaders (including Sudhir, Hansadutta, Ramesvara). The conversations took place in a house in Topanga Canyon in Los Angeles on December 3, 1980. They are famous within ISKCON for their remarkable candor about the movement's problems.

158–163: Prabhupada's confrontation with Balimardan and his wife, Natasha Toyota, re-created here is one of the most frequently told stories in ISKCON. The devotees who gave the most detailed accounts of what took place were Sanatani, Susan Kirkland, and Ravindra Svarupa.

"The way Prabhupada handled the problem in New York was typical of the way he managed," Ravindra recalls. "He knew what was going on, but basically he took a hands-off attitude. He wanted each temple to be independent. He wanted devotees to deal with problems themselves. He only stepped in when they didn't."

Marriage and Murder Made in Godhead

167–172: "Jerome and Marianne Greene" are not the real names of Bryant's best friends. The couple have received death threats and live in fear. They have asked that their real names not be used here, and details about their lives have been changed. The material in these pages comes from long author interviews with them, primarily with Jerome.

168–170: Steve Bryant's background is described from interviews with his parents, Jack and Helga Bryant.

Helga Bryant on Steve after he joined the Krishnas: "He became a totally different person, it was an amazing turn-around. Before, we couldn't get him to read a book. Now he reads all the time. At dinner, we used to try to get him to talk about what was happening in the world. We couldn't even get him into an argument on Vietnam! Now he wanted to argue with us all the time. He went on and on about Krishna Consciousness until my ears were rattling. Everything was Krishna. If I said something about the weather, he'd say, 'Krishna makes it rain.' Finally I told him, 'You know what, Steve? You're boring.' He was no company at all."

170–171: The incident in which a devotee's bra strap "distracted" Bryant was described by Yuvati Matusow, a friend of Bryant's who was in the London temple at the time.

171–173: The description of Jane Rangeley's background and her marriage to Bryant comes from interviews with Jane; John Morgan, the father of her first child; Jerome Greene; and Jack and Helga Bryant.

John Morgan on Jane: "We went to concerts. We saw great bands, like the Allman Brothers and John McLaughlin and the Mahavishnu Orchestra. That's how we got together, around 1974. We lived together for quite a long time. Jane is one of the most beautiful people I've ever met. She's very open, very spiritual, and a bit naïve. She was always susceptible to worshiping somebody.

"I thought Bryant was pretty fucked-up," Morgan continues. "He was always worried about me coming back into the scene. Jane and I used to meet outside the temple. She was afraid to talk inside the temple. She didn't like him from the start. The marriage was just a business arrangement for Krishna."

174–183: When Jayatirtha rolled on the floor, devotees thought he was seeing Krishna and was overwhelmed by the sight, just as Arjuna was in the eleventh chapter of the *Gita*, when Krishna reveals himself:

> He [Krishna] appeared with an infinite number of faces, ornamented by heavenly jewels, displaying unending miracles and the countless weapons of his power . . . . If a thousand suns were to rise in the heavens at the same time, the blaze of their light would resemble the splendor of that supreme spirit. . . . Filled with amazement, his hair standing on end in ecstasy, [Arjuna] bowed before the Lord. . . .

Information about Jayatirtha-Tirthapada comes from interviews with Atreya Rishi, a former member of the GBC who rented out a farm he owns near Philo, California, to Jayatirtha and the Peace Krishnas; from Jerome Greene; from John Morgan, Jane Rangeley's boyfriend, who knew the Peace Krishnas very well; and from Ravindra Svarupa.

Ravindra told the story of the devotee couple who black-mailed Jayatirtha with the photographs, as did two devotees in Los Angeles who asked not to be named. Information about the murder in Nepal came from ISKCON devotees, in particular, Kelly Smith (Kashava). Jayatirtha's grisly death was described by John Morgan and free-lance writers in England, who called the authors seeking information about the ex-ISKCON guru and quoted material from London newspapers. Mukunda, Michael Grant, relayed information about the murder that ISKCON picked up through its clipping service. The information was confirmed by a Vancouver reporter.

Jayatirtha's bizarre behavior triggered the first of ISKCON's many guru crises.The other gurus and members of the GBC had asked Sridhara Goswami, Prabhupada's blind, ninety-three-year-old godbrother, what they should do about Jayatirtha's antics in August, 1980. Sridhara replied that "crying is merely to get name and fame," and that if Prabhupada "did not manifest these symptoms in public, why is he [Jayatirtha] trying to go above your guru?"

Jayatirtha was stripped of his guruship for one year. The GBC also required him to take a vow of sannyasa. The belief was that Jayatirtha's "emotionalism" was caused by his relationship with his wife.

There was something contradictory about Jayatirtha-Tirthapada. People describe him as intelligent and very gentle. "He was a wonderful, saintly person," says Atreya Rishi, the Iranian GBC member who remained close to Jayatirtha after he was kicked out of ISKCON. "He was very quiet with quite a strong vibration," says John Morgan, who got to know Jayatirtha after he left ISKCON. "He was very pleasant to be around, and he attracted a lot of devotees. The man definitely had charisma."

"Actually, what Jayatirtha was into was as old as the hills," adds Ravindra Svarupa. "They're called *Sahajayas* in India. That's a Bengali word that means 'natural.' They are basically Tantrics who have expropriated a lot of stuff from Lord Chaitanya. They have sex, but it's not just having sex. It's 'I become Krishna, you become Radha, we become one with the divine.' It's cheap. It's taking material things and claiming they are spiritual ecstasies."

Conning for Krishna

185–196: "Sharon Wilson" is a pseudonym for one of Dharmatma's three wives. Much of the description of Dharmatma comes from author interviews with her. Additional information came from interviews with Sergeant Tom Westfall, Susan Kirkland, Sanatani; Walt Parry, the former New Vrindaban temple commander; Norman Hewlett, the former Cleveland temple president; Susan Hebel; and Cynthia Hebel (Chitta). Sergeant Westfall interviewed Mary St. John (Mother Mahara) about Dharmatma.

St. John, a legendary ISKCON sankirtan collector, estimated for Westfall that in her decade in the movement, she personally collected over $3 million. She also told Westfall that Dharmatma "used to tell us women to steal clothes. When they would get caught and be put in jail, he would say they were stupid idiots. He had sex with so many of the women. When I asked him about it, he said, 'Well, Bhaktipada told me I have to do it.' One time I told Dharmatma I couldn't go out, I was so sick. I was throwing up all the time and my body was bloated. And he told me I was a liar and I was in maya."

190–195: The events recounted in the passages describing the airport combine the experiences of a number of people over a period of time. They are rendered together here to convey the experience of a woman's sankirtan team. The account of Drescher's role in the Pittsburgh airport sankirtans operation was described in an interview with Walt Parry.

Obviously, there is little chance of converting anybody to Krishna Consciousness in an airport, where people are in a hurry and preoccupied with their flights. But, the devotees told themselves, if they could get one of Prabhupada's books into people's hands, they would read them when they had time. Prabhupada's books were so potent, they would bring thousands of people to the movement. So the important thing was no longer chanting and preaching; it was distributing books. And making money.

When ISKCON discovered airports, it also discovered that women were far better at collecting money than men. If they took off their saris, scrubbed off the *tilak,* and put on low-cut blouses and tight skirts, young, attractive females could work the change-up and collect for charities that did not exist.

Their tactics soon had airport officials up in arms all over America. Before filing suit alleging "fraudulent and deceptive" solicitation practices in 1976, officials of the Portland, Oregon, airport took a random sample of 154 passengers who had been approached by the female devotees. Fifty-two percent said they did not know the person they had just talked to represented a religious group. Eighty-nine percent said they did not know the person was affiliated with ISKCON.

Between 1975 and 1981, there were more than 150 cases in courts around the country challenging ISKCON's right to solicit in public places. A number of talented lawyers had become devotees over the years. Working under Barry Fischer, who was ISKCON's chief legal adviser, the movement's legal team came up with a strong First Amendment defense.

Basically, the movement's lawyers argued that distributing books was a form of sankirtan and sankirtan was a religious practice. They argued that people in America have always been assured a right to practice religious beliefs that are not mainstream. The U.S. Supreme Court had upheld that right in *Murdock* v. *Pennsylvania*, a 1942 case.

If the devotees had cleaned up their act, there is a good chance the movement's legal team might have won in the courtroom. Instead, ISKCON cut its own throat. Prosecutors were able to sidestep the First Amendment issue by proving that devotees were concealing their identity and using deceptive practices, like the old short-change routine.

The first legal blow fell in August 1980. Federal Judge Howard G. Munson issued a forty-two-page decision in Syracuse, New York, prohibiting the Krishnas from performing sankirtan at the New York State Fair. Judge Munson found the devotees had "engaged in a widespread and systematic scheme of accosting, deceit, misrepresentation and fraud on the public." The judge cited slurring the word "Krishna" to make it sound like "Christian"; short-changing donors; female devotees flirting with potential male donors; and devotees zeroing in on teenagers and retarded people.

The second legal blow came in the fall of 1981. In

Heffron v. *ISKCON,* the U.S. Supreme Court affirmed a lower court's decision that ISKCON did not have a legal right to distribute literature or solicit funds at the Minnesota State Fair. A state fair is, of course, a public place, and assistant district attorneys all over the country used the case to keep devotees out of the local airports and shopping malls.

The amounts of money devotees talked out of wallets and purses in exchange for books is staggering. In *Hare Krishna in America* (Rutgers University Press, 1985), pp. 172–173, sociologist E. Burke Rochford estimates that it cost ISKCON $2.50 to publish *Bhagavad-Gita As It Is* and Prabhupada's other hardcover books.

"If we take the conservative figure of four dollars received for each book," Rochford writes, "ISKCON grossed over 13 million dollars between 1974 and 1978, just on hardback books alone."

That is indeed a conservative figure, since it includes only the United States and Canada. It does not include Hansadutta's activities in Germany or activities in other countries around the world where ISKCON devotees were working the streets. Nor does it include the paperbacks and pamphlets the Bhaktivedanta Book Trust, the BBT, was churning out by the thousand (Rochford estimates that between 1974 and 1980, devotees distributed almost five hundred thousand paperback books and pamphlets.) Also, Rochford's estimate does not include money earned from selling tens of thousands of *Back to Godhead* magazines. And—and this is a big *and*—it does not include money from "entrepreneurial" ventures that had nothing to do with books.

196–205: Information about Guru Kripa, Gregory Martin Gottfried, comes from interviews with Susan Kirkland, Nathan Zakheim, Berkeley police officer Joe Sanchez, and Ravindra Svarupa (who remembered Guru Kripa's poem to Prabhupada). The description of the jewelry store theft is based on accounts by Ravindra Svarupa and others. Japanese police have told Joe Sanchez than Guru Kripa was wanted in Japan for criminal activities. The scene with Chief Head is a dramatization derived from the fact that Guru Kripa fenced stolen goods through a contact in India. Information was also obtained from "The Krishna File," a four-part investigative series that ran in the *Sacramento Bee* from June 22 to June 25, 1980. Other articles that contain information about Guru Kripa are "The Hare Krishnas: Drugs, Weapons and Wealth," *Hustler*, December 1980, and "Hare Krishna, Hare Krishna, Guns 'n Ammo, Guns 'n Ammo," in *High Times* in January 1981.

Ravindra Svarupa on Prabhupada's relationship with Guru Kripa: "Prabhupada really wanted to see things done. He was pleased by achievement, by temples being built and books distributed. He wanted to get those books out like crazy. He felt that whatever happened, they could never stop this movement because the 'brainwashing' books were out. That required money. There is nothing in Krishna Consciousness that rejects money. It is all Krishna's energy.

"Prabhupada saw what people like Guru Kripa were doing and he preached and preached against it," Ravindra continues. "He once said that sixty percent of the leaders were not practicing Krishna Consciousness. He was absolutely certain that if people followed the four principles and chanted their sixteen rounds, they would be pure."

The Japanese police and the Japanese press eventually caught up with Guru Kripa and his band of twenty to twenty-five devotees. The police tracked the devotees down and arrested them, one and two at a time. After an investigation in 1975, the Japanese Ministry of Justice took away ISKCON's missionary status, exiled the few devotees still in the country, and banned new devotees from entering the country. In its report, the Justice Ministry cited cases ranging from extorting money from a child to slapping an old lady who had criticized the devotees.

204: The Food For Life program run by ISKCON is still going on, notably in Philadelphia, where devotees operate a mission on South Street and feed dozens of street people everyday.

Krishna's Mules

206–215: Information about the drug ring operating out of the temple in Laguna Beach comes from interviews with Walt Parry, who was there at the time, and from Steven Hebel, whose friend was a runner. The Davis-Richard conversations in India are dramatizations based on information on the origins of the smuggling ring and the characters of the

two ringleaders. The briefing of the devotees is taken
from the account of Hebel's friend, the runner. The ac-
count of the Kulik kidnapping is a dramatization based on
newspaper accounts and interviews with Steven Hebel.
Information also came from "Two Found Guilty in 1977
Bovan Slaying," *Orange Country Register,* March 31, 1979;
"Kidnapping Role," *Orange County Register,* May 5, 1979;
"The Krishna File," a four-part series that ran between
June 22 and June 25, 1980 in the *Sacramento Bee;*
"Krishnas: A Kingdom in Disarray," *Los Angeles Times,*
February 15, 1981.

Alexander Kulik was sentenced to nine years in prison
for possession of heroin. Some of the mobsters Kulik
recruited were soldiers in the New York/New Jersey Mafia
who had testified in mob cases and, in return, had been
placed in the federal witness-protection program and given
new names and new identities.

Jerry Peter Fiori, triggerman in the Bovan killing, re-
ceived a nine-year prison term for second-degree murder.
His accomplices, Raymond Resco and Anthony Marone,
Jr., received five years each.

Roy Richard, Joe Davis, and five other Krishna devotees who worked for Prasadam Distributing International
(PDI) received prison terms for their roles in the drug
trafficking operation.

A week after Davis was released from prison in 1984,
he died of a heroin overdose.

The Chosen

216–219: The account of Prabhupada's death is drawn from
interviews with devotees, and the ISKCON film *Your
Ever Well Wisher.*

218: Two "succession" tapes were actually made, in May
and July of 1977.

It is easy to understand why scores of the devotees
Prabhupada initiated left ISKCON in the late seventies
and early eighties. It is harder to understand why so many
stayed. According to *Hinduism Today,* an independent
newspaper published in Hawaii, approximately five hundred of the more than four thousand devotees Prabhupada
initiated still remain in ISKCON.

"People who had a lot of association with Prabhupada

thought the [new] gurus were flakes. But a lot of them stayed in the movement as long as they possibly could, even though they thought the gurus were total idiots," says Yuvati Matusow, who grew up in ISKCON. Her mother, Beatrice Wolfe, joined the movement in 1967, when Yuvati was five.

"People stayed because the movement was their lives," Yuvati continues. "It was all anybody had, all anybody knew. Your identity, your purpose, your livelihood all came from the movement. Just try applying for a job and putting 'Hare Krishna devotee, 1967 to 1985' on an application. It doesn't look so hot."

Plundering the Legacy

223–225: The description of the Bryants' marriage comes from interviews with Jane, Jerome Greene, and Jack and Helga Bryant.

224–225: The description of Bryant's jewelry business comes from interviews with Jerome Greene, Nathan Zakheim, and Jack and Helga Bryant.

226–230: The description of the gurus' meeting in Mayapur is a dramatization of the most discussed event in the movement's history—the division of ISKCON. The information comes from a number of sources: a series of letters by Ravindra Svarupa written as he was emerging as the leader of the reform movement deal with this; Hansadutta outlined the general nature of the discussion in author interviews; Philip Murphy, the Los Angeles temple president, and other Los Angeles devotees discussed Ramesvara's views about guru worship, also in author interviews. "The Pyramid Tapes" reveal the guru's disagreements on the numerous issues that preoccupied the movement after Prabhupada's death. The division of ISKCON resulting from the meeting was as specified here. Further insight into the relationships and conflicts among the gurus is found in E. Burke Rochford's *Hare Krishna in America*.

Krishna Consciousness, like all Eastern religions where enlightenment is embodied in the individual and not in an institution, is extremely autocratic. Devotees submit to the spiritual master, wives submit to husbands, and so on. An autocracy cannot work if there is more than one autocrat. Two or more will inevitably issue conflicting orders and cause chaos.

Prabhupada knew that better than anyone. If he had intended to choose a new acharya to rule ISKCON, he would have chosen one, not eleven rtviks.

"The word *acharya* indicates 'the spiritual head of an institution,' " a devotee named Pradyumna, who later left the movement in despair, pointed out in a letter he wrote to Satsvarupa in August 1978. "This meaning is very specific. It does not mean just anyone. It means only one who has been specifically declared by the previous acharya to be his successor above all others. . . . He alone, among all of his godbrothers, is given a raised seat and special honor. . . . He [alone] is the authority in all spiritual and material matters."

Prabhupada used to lament that Krishna had never sent him any first-class men, only second- and third-class men. He was not referring strictly to character, although he could have been. He was referring to the caste system.

In the *varnashrama,* the Vedic social system, people and occupations are divided into four basic types: the brahmana—priests, artists, intellectuals, and spiritually advanced leaders; the *kshatriya*—the administrators who implement the teachings of the brahmana and the warriors who defend the social order; *vaishya*—craftsmen, merchants, and farmers; *sudra*—unskilled laborers who lack intelligence and will, but are capable of productive work under supervision.

If Prabhupada had chosen an acharya to succeed him, it surely would have been someone the spiritual master considered a brahmin. Since there were no brahmins in the movement, Prabhupada chose eleven of his leading administrators and business men, kshatriyas and vaishyas, to be rtvik gurus.

"When they [ISKCON] made the gurus gods on earth, they made a tremendous mistake," says Professor J. Stillson Judah, author of *Hare Krishna and the Counterculture.* "Each [guru] could do no wrong, so each could do whatever he wanted to do. Each was free to define what was right.

"That's called antinomianism," Judah continues. "A religious figure believes he is empowered by God, so he believes he is above the law. He cannot be criticized, because he is a representative of God on earth."

The gurus did their best to promote the myth they were all infallible, but infighting soon turned their collective We-have-transcended-the-material-plane mentality into low farce. The first to act on his belief was Tamal Krishna, the guru of Bombay, the southwest United States, and Fiji. In the spring of 1980, Tamal began proclaiming himself Prabhupada's successor. He stopped teaching the purports Prabhupada had written to interpret the *Gita* and started teaching his own. Prabhupada's purports were full of errors, Tamal claimed. Tamal not only wanted obeisances from his disciples (people he had initiated) and from his godbrothers and godsisters (devotees initiated by Prabhupada), he wanted the other ten gurus to bow before him, too.

Most other gurus responded, "How can Tamal behave this way when it is *I* who should be the new acharya?" They warned Tamal to tone down, and when he did not, the other gurus hauled him in front of the GBC. Tamal was stripped of his guruship for a period of one year.

"When we got the gurus, we got eleven different ISKCONs," says Ravindra Svarupa. "There were some real unfriendly tensions between the gurus right from the start. They [the gurus] propped each other up because if the power of one guru was threatened, they all felt threatened. But when somebody finally fell, they turned on him and destroyed him.

"Tamal was an extremely elevated, autocratic guru, extremely dictatorial," Ravindra continues. "When they [the GBC] put him on ice, Bhagavan went into Tamal's zones and did everything he could to destroy Tamal's stature. He preached against Tamal and tried to take his devotees and generally just flattened Tamal like a steamroller."

Jayathirtha was expelled in 1982 and Hansadutta in 1985.

Hansadutta: Secretary for God

231–234: The account of Hansadutta's arrival in the San Francisco airport comes from an interview with Hansadutta and from "Secretary to God," an article published in the *San Francisco Chronicle*, August 12, 1978.

234–236: Hansadutta described his confrontation with Jiva, James Patrick Underwood, in an author interview. Additional information about Jiva came from interviews with

Berkeley police officer Joe Sanchez and former Hansadutta disciples Vladimir Vassilievich, Vern Davan, and Bill Costello.

236–238: The description of the radio scam comes from an interview with Hansadutta, and with Bramaha, Bill Costello, a former Hansadutta devotee who worked the scam all over the country.

238–239: The description of Hansadutta's relationship with "Sandy" and other women in the Berkeley temple comes from interviews with Hansadutta, who talked at length about Sandy, blaming her for his spiritual downfall, and from interviews with Berkeley police officer Joe Sanchez and former Hansadutta devotees Vladimir Vassilievich and Vern Davan. "Sandy" is a pseudonym and "Elaine" is a composite included to personify the other women who had sexual relations with Hansadutta.

239–241: The recording session is a combination of a number of such sessions described in an author interview by Hansadutta. The character of Eddie "Fast Fingers" Dawson represents the studio musicians who found Hansadutta "egocentric." The lyrics to Hansadutta's songs are taken from copies given to the authors by the former guru.

242–243: Hansadutta's problems with drugs and alcohol were described in detail by Atreya Rishi in several author interviews. The account of Hansadutta's trip to Asia and India was given in interviews with Hansadutta and Berkeley police officer Joe Sanchez. Hansadutta explained how the song "Guru-Guru" was pirated in the Philippines. The account Michael Pugliese reads on the airplane comes from a Berkeley temple press release.

243–247: The account of Hansadutta running amok on the Pan Am flight is re-created from author interviews with Hansadutta and Bill Costello, one of Hansadutta's devotees. Costello was in the airport waiting for Hansadutta to arrive. He was also one of the devotees who bailed the guru out of jail the next day. He and Vern Davan also described Hansadutta on occasions when he was under the influence of drugs and alcohol. Pugliese appears because he usually traveled with Hansadutta.

Krishna's Arsenal

248–251: Berkeley police officer Joe Sanchez described the lack of cooperation he received from federal agencies like the FBI and the IRS in an author interview. The stopping of Pugliese is an illustration of Sanchez's relationship with the Berkeley temple. These names were actually used by Pugliese, and such name-changing was rampant in the Berkeley temple at this time.

251–253: The account of Hansadutta's sermon in Mount Kailasa was given in interviews with Hansadutta, Joe Sanchez, Vladimir Vassilievich, Vern Davan, and Bill Costello. Information also came from the article "Swami Allegedly Urged Members to Arm," in the *Sacramento Bee*, June 13, 1980.

254–255: The account of the wounding of the five-year-old boy at Mount Kailasa comes from interviews with Joe Sanchez and Vladimir Vassilievich. In an interview, Hansadutta denied he shot the boy in the hand and blamed it on "a bozo devotee who was cleaning a gun."

"Spencer Lynn Joy, the acting president of Mount Kailasa, came forward and said the shooting was his fault," Sanchez says. "But when I talked to him, I was told by Mr. Joy it was Hansadutta who shot the boy. If I could find Mr. Joy, I believe he'd tell me again who fired the round at the child. I have been looking for Mr. Joy for three years. He has disappeared. He has not been in contact with family or friends."

255–261: The accounts of the theft from Bill Benedict's car and the subsequent police raids are taken from the Affidavit for Search Warrant prepared by Charles E. Crane, an inspector in the Berkeley Police Department, and interviews with Joe Sanchez and Vladimir Vassilievich. "The Krishna File," a four-part series that ran in the *Sacramento Bee* from June 22 to June 25, 1980, also provided information, as did "Krishna Arms Caches Draw Police Scrutiny in California," in the *New York Times*, June 9, 1980, and "Locker Rented by Krishna Member Yields Weapons," the *Sacramento Bee*, June 20, 1980.

262–263: The accounts of Hansadutta asking Vladimir Vassilievich to build a silenced, automatic machine gun, the plan to rob the Fort Ord payroll, and Vassilievich's thinking about going to the police come from an author interview with Vladimir Vassilievich. Joe Sanchez described the police discovery of the weapons in Hansadutta's car, as well as the death of Jiva.

266–268: The account of Hansadutta's shooting up Berkeley is from author interviews with Hansadutta and Joe Sanchez, and from "Guru Held in Shooting Spree," an article that appeared in the *Berkeley Voice*, September 4, 1984.

268: The description of Hansadutta and Kirtanananda joining forces to take control of the Berkeley temple is a dramatization based on interviews with Hansadutta and Atreya Rishi; on a letter Kirtanananda wrote Atreya Rishi dated June 6, 1986; on numerous motions and complaints filed in the court case; and on "Unrest among Krishnas," a UPI story filed on July 18, 1986.

Hansadutta and a core of diehard disciples moved to New Vrindaban in December 1985. The plan he and Kirtanananda hatched to take over the Berkeley temple went like this: Hansadutta's devotees, several of whom were still officially on the Berkeley temple board of directors, would declare themselves loyal to Kirtanananda. Kirtanananda's new followers would next declare that they represented a majority of the devotees in the Berkeley temple, and that they wanted Kirtanananda, not Atreya Rishi, to run the temple. When Rishi was removed, Kirtanananda would appoint Hansadutta president of the Berkeley temple, and the fallen guru would be back in power.

In January 1986, fifteen men loyal to Hansadutta and Kirtanananda stripped the Mount Kailasa farm. According to documents filed in the U.S. district court, they took a Chevy station wagon, two Dodge vans, 23,200 books, and fifteen thousand dollars in cash. The total estimated value was one hundred twenty-nine thousand dollars.

Atreya Rishi went screaming to the GBC. The GBC did nothing. Six months later, on June 6, 1986, Rishi got a letter from Kirtanananda demanding he turn over the temple.

I am writing to you concerning the Berkeley temple. Some of the devotees who have resided there, including some of the present directors of ISKCON of the Bay Area, Inc., have asked me to take personal responsibility for that particular center. If you

would be so inclined, we can make arrangements
for a smooth turnover. Hope this meets you in good
health.

"I took the 'smooth turnover' sentence as a veiled threat,"
Rishi says. "The implication was, 'You'd better get out, or
it won't be smooth. Twenty people will be arriving at your
doorstep.' I had been getting threatening phone calls. A
voice would say, 'You're messing around with a pure
devotee, you'd better be careful,' and hang up. I saw
there was no end to their aggressiveness, and I filed a
lawsuit to stop them."

Rishi won the case in the spring of 1987. New Vrindaban
agreed to pay the Berkeley temple forty thousand dollars
in damages and to leave the temple alone.

Sex, Pigs, and Husbands

269–270: The description of Howard Wheeler's homosexuality and drinking was discussed with Nathan Zakheim,
Ravindra Svarupa, Walt Parry, Steven Hebel, and New
Vrindaban devotees who asked not to be named. His
bringing Mexican boys to New Vrindaban and his apparent sexual relationships with them were described in interviews with Walt Parry and Beth Ann. The scene between
Wheeler and Kirtanananda is a dramatization based on
these sources.

"Hayagriva married a New Vrindaban devotee in Goa
[in West India, on the Arabian Sea]," Ravindra Svarupa
recalls. "A few weeks after the wedding, she was calling
the Bombay temple bitterly complaining about his [Haya-
griva's] pederasty with street boys. At the time, he was
writing a book about how to renounce sex. The joke in
the movement was, 'Yeah, have it everyday.' "

270: The description of Kirtanananda's relationship with
Samba—Devin Wheeler—and other boys in New Vrindaban, was discussed in interviews with dozens of former
New Vrindaban devotees. In particular, they include Walt
Parry, who said, "Kirtanananda liked to tickle the kid
[Samba]. I would see him touch him [Samba] in places you
don't touch anybody in public. He was a kid. If a man
touches a woman in that area, he wants one thing. If you
don't want to be considered fruity, don't touch a person

there." Information also came from Gail Conger; Don McAdams (for the quote on fish night); Richard Rose; and Yuvati Matusow. "Kirtanananda is horrible, ruthless, disgusting," Matusow says. "Hitler had Eva Braun. He had Samba. I guess Samba was really the only soft spot he had." Steve Bryant's "The Guru Business" is also full of charges about Kirtanananda's homosexuality.

Additional information came from interviews with devotees who asked that their names not be used; from "The Hare Krishnas Have Taken My Son," a letter from Cheryl Wheeler to the *Wheeling Intelligencer*, May 7, 1979; and from "Devin: Krishna Hearing Called Farce," an article in the *Wheeling Intelligencer*, May 15, 1979.

Mukunda, Michael Grant, said, in an interview, "ISKCON officials are working with law enforcement authorities to investigate reports that have developed in the last year [1988] that Kirtanananda has had sexual relations with minors."

270–271: The description of Kirtanananda's conception of women is from interviews and information from dozens of devotees; in particular, former New Vrindaban devotees Susan Hebel, Steven Hebel, Gail Conger, Mary St. John, Yuvati Matusow, Don McAdams, and Nathan Zakheim. Steve Bryant covered this ground in his exposé, "The Guru Business." McAdams recalled that at men's darshans, Kirtanananda was fond of saying, "Three things become better when you beat them: a drum, your dog, your wife." Kirtanananda made the analogy between a dog and a wife in an interview for CBS's "West 57th Street."

Kirtanananda's low regard for women is also evident in some of the commune's publications and press releases. Here, for example, is a passage from "Deep in the Well, or, Confessions of a Brahmacari-grhasta," which he published in *Brijabasi Spirit*, the New Vrindaban magazine:

Karmi women were gross. Even if they were well endowed with attractive features and personalities, he [the author] could see that their hearts were like razors. Krishna das knew that all they wanted was to be the center of attention, to be adored, loved, served and worshipped like God. He painfully observed how men were controlled by their wives and girlfriends. They sold their souls in return for sense gratification, but were actually as frustrated as the ass who gets kicked in the face by his mate.

271–273: The account of Kirtananda's relationship with Jane Bryant comes from an interview with Jane; from recordings of phone conversations Steve Bryant made with Jane; and from interviews with Jack and Helga Bryant.

273–275: The description of the children's nursery comes from interviews with former New Vrindaban devotees; in particular, Steven Hebel, Gail Conger, and Don McAdams. It is also confirmed in West Virginia Department of Health documents.

New Vrindaban has been plagued by health problems from its inception. The children's nursery is the most egregious example. But Kirtananda has never shown much concern for cleanliness or sanitation of any kind, and as in everything, the community follows his lead.

In January 1976, there was a hepatitis outbreak at the commune. A college professor named Dr. Plummer, who had taken a class to visit New Vrindaban, was infected with the disease there, as was one of his students. The professor died. Four cases of hepatitis in New York were traced back to the commune. The West Virginia Department of Health placed a quarantine on the commune and carried out an in-depth inspection. Some of the findings were recorded as follows:

Toilets at the farmhouse: Toilet seats not provided. The toilet room walls are filthy. Sewage from the toilets drains into an open septic tank. The drain line from the septic tank discharges onto the surface of the ground.

Dairy Facilities: Cows' flanks, etc., have caked manure on them. The milk cans, pails, and milkers are dirty. Some of the milk cans are badly corroded.

Food Preparation Facilities: Solid waste containers are dirty and not covered. Floor is dirty. Handwashing facilities are not provided. Outer openings are not protected against entry of rodents and insects. Utensils are dirty and cannot be sanitized. Pooled water around premises. Trash is stored in cardboard boxes. Toilet facilities are inadequate and unsanitary. Dogs observed in food preparation area.

Madhuvana Temple Farm (ten people reside at this site): Sewage from the house is running onto ground surface. Human excrement at one privy is being caught in a pail. Human excrement is on the floor and walls of the privy. A riser and seat are not provided. Refuse and rubbish are scattered on the ground of the farm.

The commune installed a new sewage system after the report, but living conditions remained deplorable. The nursery, in particular, remained as bad as it had always been.

"I remember walking by the nursery and seeing a ten-year-old girl outside with a whole bunch of toddlers in forty-degree weather," recalls Gail Conger, a former New Vrindaban devotee. "None of them had coats or shoes.

"Some of the women did try to change things, but they ran into stone walls," Conger continues. "Kuladri and Bhaktipada [Kirtanananda] said they would do something, but they never did. Getting the palace built was all that mattered. Everyone was pushed to the max to work to build the material community for Bhaktipada. You didn't dare balk or criticize. Everybody was all wrapped up in [attaining] spiritual perfection."

Between June and December of 1985, the Marshall County Health Department ran lab tests on more than one hundred New Vrindaban children under the age of twelve. When the tests came back, they showed the children were infected with parasites usually found in underdeveloped countries, where human feces are not properly disposed of. The most common disease was giardiasis, a parasitic infection that causes diarrhea, intestinal pain, and lethargy. There were also cases of pinworms, whipworms, round worms, fish tapeworms and entamoeba infestation.

The deaths of several children were clearly the result of neglect, and in one case, child abuse may have occurred. On April 4, 1974, two-year-old Derek Burtchell was dead on arrival at the Reynolds Memorial Hospital emergency room in Glen Dale, the town next to Moundsville. The boy's body was covered with hematomas. An autopsy revealed that he had died of peritonitis caused by a blow to the abdomen. The boy had received the blow approximately twenty-four hours before he arrived at the hospital. If he had been brought to the hospital soon after being struck, he almost certainly would have survived. Devotees claimed the child had been injured when he fell off a porch. The medical examiner, Dr. Manuel Villaverde, determined that the boy's injuries were not consistent with a fall and asked the West Virginia State Police to investigate. The case was not investigated and no charges were ever brought.

275–281: The material in this section is drawn from author interviews with Steven Hebel. Supplementary information was given by Cynthia and Susan Hebel.

281–282: The account of Thomas Meyers's beating of Mary St. John is from an interview with St. John carried out by Sergeant Tom Westfall. From the interview: "Bhaktipada used to tell him [Taru] to beat me up. Bahktipada told all the men to beat their wives. All the women were getting beat." Taru's disappearance was covered in interviews with Gail Conger and Don McAdams, who both heard Kirtanananda describe his dream; Sergeant Tom Westfall; and a New Vrindaban devotee who asked not to be named.

283–288: The account of Dharmatma's sexual exploits and attitude toward women, as well as his beating of Sharon Wilson comes from an interview with Wilson. She described her Sankirtan career in the same graphic detail. She also related the events to Sergeant Tom Westfall. Dharmatma's treatment of women was confirmed by Mary St. John, in an interview with Tom Westfall and in author interviews; Susan Hebel; Norman Hewlett; Don McAdams; and Susan Kirkland.

Black and Blue

291–294: The account of Steve Bryant's unhappiness in New Vrindaban is from his writings and author interviews with Jerome Greene, Bryant's ex-wife, Jane, and his parents, Jack and Helga.

293–294: The description of the fringie scene in New Vrindaban is drawn from interviews with Don McAdams, Debra Gere Tsacrios, Dr. Nick Tsacrios, and Sergeant Tom Westfall.

294–295: The description of Advaita handing Kirtanananda the suitcase stacked with money comes from an interview with Walt Parry, who witnessed the scene and saw the bills in the suitcase.

295–298: Steven Hebel's career as a drug dealer and the bust of the Quaalude lab in Columbus were described in long interviews with Hebel. Tom Drescher confirmed his arrest for making Quaaludes in an author interview. The authors have a photocopy of the letter Drescher's wife wrote to the Buffalo devotee.

299–301: The description of Cynthia Hebel's rape in New Orleans comes from interviews with Cynthia. John Hubner, one of the authors, published an account of this rape in *West* magazine, *San Jose Mercury News*, June 28, 1987.

A Fork in the Path

302–309: The account of Steve Bryant's infatuation with guns and right-wing politics comes from interviews with his ex-wife, Jane, and his parents, Jack and Helga Bryant. The description of Bryant grabbing his two boys and making a run for it comes from interviews with his ex-wife Jane, his parents Jack and Helga, and his friends, Yuvati Matusow and Gail Conger.

310: Bryant recorded his phone call to Kirtanananda from Dallas. The authors have a transcript of the call.

311–314: Jadurani's revolt against the ISKCON gurus and her beating was discussed in interviews with Nathan Zakheim, Steven Hebel, Susan Hebel, Yuvati Matusow (Jadurani was living at Yuvati's mother's house in Pittsburgh before she left for New Vrindaban), and in Steve Bryant's description of the event in "The Guru Business," pp. 79–80. The beating was reported in the *Los Angeles Times,* February 15, 1981. Kirtanananda's response to the female devotees was quoted by them to Yuvati.

A Messianic Mission

315–317: The description of Bryant in his van comes from author interviews with Yuvati Matusow and Jerome Greene.

317–318: Bryant recorded his phone call to Kuladri. The authors have tapes of the calls Bryant made during his campaign against the Krishnas.

319–320: Sheriff Bordenkircher recorded Bryant's call and provided the authors with a copy of the tape.

320–325: There were two GBC meetings at New Vrindaban in 1985, in August and September. A description of the two meetings obtained in interviews with GBC member Ravindra Svarupa has been rendered here as one meeting. Kirtanananda's behavior is as reported by Rivindra Svarupa.

325: The description of Steve Bryant in the Marshall County Jail is from interviews with Sheriff Bordenkircher.

325–327: The description of the braining of Kirtanananda by Michael Shockman is from interviews with Sergeant Westfall and Sheriff Bordenkircher. A New Vrindaban press release about the attack, undated and unsigned but issued under Kuladri's name, describes the incident in detail.

327: Kirtanananda's press conference was described in "Swami: Assailant Influenced?", an article in the *Wheeling Intelligencer,* December 5, 1985.

328: Steve Bryant's letter and his phone call to Sheriff Bordenkircher were discussed in interviews with the sheriff.

Jonestown in Moundsville

329–330: Kirtanananda's urging Kuladri to take sannyasa and Kuladri's misgivings about Kirtanananda are taken from a phone interview with Kuladri and interviews with Kuladri conducted by Sergeant Tom Westfall. The portrayal of Sheldon's attitude is based on Westfall's interviews with Kuladri and other New Vrindaban devotees.

331: Bryant recorded his phone call to Jane.

331–332: The description of the phone call Helga Bryant received from someone posing as Jerome Greene comes from an interview with Mrs. Bryant.

332–334: The description of Randall Gorby's friendship with Thomas Drescher and his role in following Steve Bryant is taken from Gorby's testimony in the St. Denis murder case. Although Gorby did not identify Bryant in his testimony, Bryant's identity was established in several bench conferences that interrupted his testimony. The conversation between Drescher and Gorby in Wheeling is re-created: the fact that Bryant was visiting the FBI is taken from Bryant's diary and confirmed by the FBI; Drescher's threat to kill Bryant was brought up and discussed by both the prosecutor and the defense attorney in the bench conferences, although Gorby was not allowed to testify to it directly. He did testify to Drescher's description of his role in St. Denis's murder.

334–335: The account of Bryant's arrest in Moundsville and his subsequent incarceration is from author interviews with Sergeant Tom Westfall, and Bryant's lawyer, David Gold, and from entries in the diary Bryant kept while he was in custody.

335–338: The account of the Krishnas' access to Bryant's papers is re-created based on interviews with Sheriff Bordenkircher and Sergeant Tom Westfall and from "Sheriff's Office Feared Unwitting Murder Link," a UPI story in the *Wheeling Intelligencer,* April 7, 1987, and "Sheriff: Handling of Krishna Address Book Not Hidden," *Wheeling News-Register,* April 7, 1987. The confrontation between Westfall and Bordenkircher has been moved to an earlier point in time.

338–339: Steve Bryant's decision to defend himself in court was discussed in interviews with David Gold and Jack and Helga Bryant.

Monkey on a Stick

343–344: The description of Steve Bryant and Kathy Berry deciding to get married comes from author interviews with Kathy Berry.

343–344: Steve Bryant's decision to abandon his campaign was discussed in interviews with Jack and Helga Bryant, Yuvati Matusow, Kathy Berry, and Jerome Greene.

344–345: Vladimir Vassilievich on the devotee who approached him about murdering Steve Bryant: "He looked me up and told me that the New Vrindaban hierarchy wanted to off this guy [Bryant]. He was tailing Steve Bryant, recruiting the hit, and he sort of made me an offer. The insinuation was, 'Hey, we know you're a competent gunman. We want to get this guy real bad. We'll treat you right.'

"It didn't get beyond that because I didn't let it. I thought, Here's another one of those crazy assholes from New Vrindaban and forgot about it. I've expended a fair amount of energy over the years, trying to forget all about the Krishnas."

346–347: The description of Bryant's evening with Forbes comes from interviews with Jack and Helga Bryant and

Yuvati Matusow, who talked with Forbes shortly after the murder, in addition to Los Angeles devotees who asked not to be named and "Crimes Among the Krishnas," the *Philadelphia Inquirer Magazine*, April 5, 1987. The details of the murder are based on the autopsy report. Additional information came from "Maverick Krishna Silenced by a Mysterious Murder," *San Francisco Examiner*, July 6, 1986; "Furor among the Hare Krishnas, UPI wire, July 6, 1986; "Suspect held in death of ex-Hare Krishna," *Detroit Free Press*, June 6, 1986; "Murder among the Krishnas," *Akron Beacon Journal*, June 22, 1986; "Killing Sparks Federal Probe of Krishna Sect," *Los Angeles Times*, July 20, 1986; "Tempest in Temple," *Pittsburgh Post Gazette*, September 15, 1986.

The Executioner's Trail

349–353: The description of Yuvati Matusow's reaction to Steve Bryant's death and her role in the early investigation of Bryant's murder comes from interviews with Matusow.

353–356: The description of placing a tap on Gorby's phone, and Drescher's phone call to Gorby as well as his arrest, come from interviews with Sergeant Tom Westfall. Additional information comes from "Furor among the Hare Krishnas," UPI wire, July 6, 1986; "Murder among the Krishnas," *Akron Beacon Journal*, June 22, 1986; "Crimes Among the Krishnas," the *Philadelphia Inquirer Magazine*, April 5, 1987.

356–357: The California trial of the Steve Bryant murder-for-hire charge has been prolonged by repeated appeals of Drescher's extradition.

The Los Angeles case is expected to include the eyewitness testimony of a devotee at the Los Angeles temple. The devotee admits he helped Drescher keep Bryant under surveillance. He has told devotees and police that if and when Drescher caught up with Bryant, Drescher would administer a beating. Even as early as Drescher's arrest, police in Kent, Ohio, where he was arrested, stated that there had been an eyewitness to the killing. *Pittsburgh Post Gazette*, September 15, 1986.

357–358: The description of the explosion at Gorby's house comes from interviews with Sergeant Tom Westfall and federal law enforcement officers. The incident was discussed at length during a long phone interview with Thomas Drescher. Additional information came from "Furor among the Hare Krishnas," UPI wire, July 6, 1986; "Maverick Krishna Silenced by a Mysterious Murder," *San Francisco Examiner,* July 6, 1986; "Murder among the Krishnas," *Akron Beacon Journal,* June 22, 1986; "Crimes Among the Krishnas," the *Philadelphia Inquirer Magazine,* April 5, 1987.

Revenge from the Grave

359–360: The description of Peter Brinkmann's conversation with Terry Sheldon comes from a phone interview with Brinkmann conducted by the authors.

360–362: The description of the St. Denis murder trial is from interviews with Sergeant Tom Westfall and Chrislyn St. Denis, who testified.

As evidence that the commune was not involved in a cover-up of the murder, Kirtanananda points to the fact that he told Howard Fawley to tell the authorities everything he knew. "If we were trying to cover up the murder, why would we have Fawley come forward?" asks Dick Dezio, a spokesman for the community.

But Fawley did not "come forward" until three years after the murder. Sergeant Tom Westfall believes that Fawley's testimony was provided only after prosecutors promised not to involve the commune's hierarchy in the case.

362–367: The description of the unearthing of the body of devotee "Joe" comes from author interviews with Walt Parry, who buried the body, and Tom Westfall, who helped dig it up.

367–368: The description of Nimai's drowning comes from interviews with Sheriff Donald Bordenkircher, Sergeant Tom Westfall, and Jack and Helga Bryant. The AP story, "Son of Murdered Krishna Drowns," was published in the *Detroit Free Press* on November 24, 1986.

Sex Is Sex

371–375: Susan Hebel's treatment by Walker, her flight from New Vrindaban, and the child molestation that occurred there are described from author interviews with Susan

Hebel and Steven Hebel, and Sergeant Tom Westfall's investigation of the charges the Hebels filed. Additional charges of child molestation at New Vrindaban have been leveled since DeFrancisco's conviction.

Child molestation and abuse has been a severe problem at ISKCON temples across America and in India. An LA devotee was sentenced to ninety-nine years in prison for molesting children he was supposed to be caring for in the temple's nursery. Other cases have been discovered in Denver and Dallas.

On July 10, 1987, Jagadisha Goswami, ISKCON's minister of education acknowledged the problem in a press release that said in part, ". . . more than several incidents have occurred in the history of ISKCON's guru kulas when a child or children have been sexually abused by adults or older children. This has also been a serious problem in society at large, and a considerable amount of time and energy has been spent studying the causes and effects. Because of several recent incidents and recent discoveries of older incidents in our guru kulas, I have been made aware of the many and serious (especially emotional) problems that abused children usually suffer from, the worst being that they become abusers themselves later on."

376–377: The description of the trademark-violation raid comes from interviews with federal authorities and Sergeant Tom Westfall. Additional information came from the article, "Troubled Paradise: Krishna Site Focus of Probes," the *Philadelphia Inquirer,* March 9, 1987.

377–378: The description of the ceremony making Thomas Drescher a swami comes from "New Swami is Convicted Killer," a UPI story published in the *Wheeling News Register,* August 24, 1987, and the article, "Hare Krishna Leader Goes to Prison," In *Brijabasi Spirit,* the New Vrindaban newsletter (no date). Kirtanananda preached to prisoners in the *Brijabasi Spirit* story: "Actually, you have a great opportunity for making spiritual advancement in here. You have the realization that you are locked up in a prison. But factually everyone in this material world is imprisoned—all locked up tightly. You know you are in a miserable condition, so you can become very serious [in your search for] a solution to the problem.

"Just like Tom [Drescher] here. He has become very serious and is making great spiritual advancement. I've never seen him so Krishna Conscious.

Expecting the Barbarians

379–383: The material in this chapter is based on interviews with Ravindra Svarupa, who was appointed to the GBC in 1987 and elected its president in March 1988; on devotee accounts of Ramesvara's relationship with the teenage girl; on the broadsides concerning Bhavananda's homosexuality; and on the letters written by Bhagavan to his disciples.

Going Fishing

384–392: The account of the Todd Schenker murder investigation is based on numerous author interviews with Sergeant Tom Westfall.

Acknowledgments

This book is to an unusual degree a team effort. It would not have been possible without a great number of people. Our captain was John Hubner, the principal writer.

We hope that this book gives some solace to Steve Bryant's family.

We wish to thank and recognize Sergeant Tom Westfall. He seeks justice for the sect's victims—usually Krishna members themselves—while other law-enforcement officers around the country were dismissing them as crackpots who deserved whatever they got. Long before anyone else appeared on the horizon, Tom Westfall had devoted his career to the painstaking gathering of crucial information.

We also want to acknowledge Berkeley police officer Joe Sanchez. Without him, a key piece of the puzzle would be missing—not only from this book, but also from investigations currently underway.

This book naturally focuses on the movement's dark side and the crimes committed in Krishna's name. But we do not want to overlook or forget the thousands of ISKCON devotees who have worshiped and worked honestly and faithfully to build the religious movement in the West. Most are unaware of their leaders' misdeeds. Many have struggled valiantly against the corrupt gurus, often at great personal risk. We want especially to thank Mukunda Goswami and Ravindra Svarupa, leaders who fought to clean up the sect and had the courage to admit its failings publicly, and Steven Hebel, Swarup, whose candor helped us understand how a religious movement became diverted into a criminal enterprise. We wish them a better future.

We owe a great debt to our editor, Marie Arana-Ward of Harcourt Brace Jovanovich. Marie transformed our work into a book. She led us without our knowing it. Her advice, suggestions, and support were invaluable. We would also like to thank assistant editor Jonathan Ezekiel, copyeditor Giles Townsend, attorney Kathleen Bursley, and editorial intern Michael Haggerty.

Without Philippa Brophy's vision, work, and help, this book would merely be an idea.

There were many other contributors. We couldn't have done without Jill Wolfson's vision, editing, and patience, or Jane Whitney's work, help, and love. We want to thank Robert Vare of *Rolling Stone,* who nurtured the idea and helped launch it; Jeffrey Klein, Bob Ingle, Charles Matthews, Carol Doup Muller, Bambi Nicklen, and Gary Parker of *West* magazine at the *San Jose Mercury News;* as well as Dan Lewis, Soma Golden, and David Jones of the National Desk at the *New York Times.*

We also want to acknowledge attorneys David Gold and Jon Turak, who quietly helped; Dr. Mark Juergensmeyer and Dr. J. Stillson Judah, for their scholarly insights; Nandini and Uddhava, for their help; Kathy Anderson, for her loving encouragement; Alexander Sam Hubner and Max Whitney, who taught us about love; Jonathan Krim, Marty Linsky, Darlene and Cleto Genelza, and Greg Otis, Tom Frail, Jan Schaffer, Martha Jablow, Sally Swift, John Motyka, Donna Dewey, Doug Vaughan, Michael Issikoff, Charlotte Lucas, Michael Margolis, Sam Singer, William K. Stevens, and Reilley's Arms.

JOHN HUBNER
LINDSEY GRUSON
May 1988

Index

Acharya, 216, 311
  death of Prabhupada and new,
    217–218
  Kirtanananda as, 324
  notes on, 431
  rtvik, 218
Advaita (Emile Sofsky aka John
    Jenkins), 313
  current status, 399
  drug smuggling by, 294–295, 441
Alcott, Bronson, 100
Allegheny General Hospital, 327
Amala-Das, 121–122
Ambudrara, see Gere, Debra
Antiguru movement, 321–323
Apple Records, 103–107
Arjuna, 48, 50, 68
Arranged marriages, 124, 149–150,
    159, 187, 343, 371,
    418–419
Arson, 36–38
Artist's Studio, 4, 16, 19
Associated Press, 368, 400
Atman, 406
Atreya Rishi:
  Berkeley temple and, 268,
    435–436
  on Kirtanananda and the GBC,
    421
  in notes, 423, 424, 433
  warning to Ravindra, 322–323
Avalon Ballroom, 66–68
Aziz, 208, 210

Back to Godhead, 125, 138, 198,
    427
Backus, Charles, see Bhavananda
Balarama's Enterprises, 256
Balimardan, 158–162, 422
  current status, 396
Banwell, Jeff, 356
Beatles, 78–80, 103–110
  notes on, 412–413
Bellevue Hospital, 58–59, 97, 123,
    405
Benedict, Bill, 256–259
  current status, 398–399
  theft from, 256–260, 434

Berkeley temple, 231–268
  Atreya Rishi and, 268, 435–436
  Ferrari donated to, 253–254, 398
  as haven for criminals, 251
  women's sankirtan team, 234–239
Berry, Kathy, 343–344, 345–346,
    443
  current status, 397
Beserra, Rudy, 394
"Beth Ann," 72–77
  New Vrindaban and, 114–116,
    121–122
  defection from, 124
  notes on, 407, 408, 420, 436
Bethany College, 332
Beth Israel Hospital, 71–72
Bhagavad-Gita As It Is (Prabhupada),
    32, 61, 108, 109
  described, 47–48
  fundamentalist interpretation of,
    51, 135
  selling, 153, 187–196, 197
  money from, 427
  translation of, 56, 58
  publication of, 99, 152, 412
Bhagavan (William Ehrlichman),
    154, 432
  current status, 396
  desire to be new acharya, 217
  as Krishna Sun King, 226–227,
    322, 381
  ouster as guru, 382
  as rtvik, 218, 226–229
Bhaktisiddhanta, 82, 83, 216, 409
Bhaktivedanta Book Trust (BBT),
    152, 155–156, 157, 277,
    311, 427
  Bryant and Prabhupada's letters
    from, 313–314, 315
  mismanagement of, 380–381
Bhaktivedanta Manor, 177
Bhaktivedanta Village, 310–311,
    317
  Kanka at, 374
Bhakti yoga, 50, 51, 139, 409
Bhavananda (Charles Backus), 226
  current status, 400
  ousted as guru, 381, 447

Big Brother and the Holding
  Company, 66, 67
Big John, 21, 28–29, 403
Bleudeu, Suzanne, 38
  attack on, 43
  child abuse by, 35
  current status, 395
  Drescher's arrest and, 354–355
Bloopers (devotees who left the
  movement), 179, 206,
  233–234, 280
  see also individuals
Blue Boy Nursery, 4, 11–13, 37
Bombay, India, 81–82
  new temple in, 151, 203, 360
Bordenkircher, Sheriff Donald, 335,
  445
  attempted murder of Kirtanananda
    and, 328, 442
  background of, 337
  Bryant in protective custody and,
    319–320, 321, 325, 442
  defeat in bid for reelection, 397
  evidence against Bryant and, 336
  exclusion of, from Drescher
    murder case, 357, 362, 366
Boston University, 276
Bovan, Steven, 211–214
  murder of, 213–214, 429
Braeger, Eugene, 16
Brahmacharini, 311
Brahmacharis, 134, 157, 158, 167
Brahman, 96
Brahmana, 431
Brahmananda, 315
  break with Kirtanananda, 95–98,
    411–412, 415–416
  Hebel and, 277, 278
  Prabhupada's stroke and, 69–70,
    71–72
Bramaha, 433, 434
Brijabasi Spirit, 281, 437, 446
Brinkmann, Martha, 359
Brinkmann, Peter, 359–360, 445
Bryant, Helga, 169–170, 307
  current status, 396
  Greene and, 333–334
    impersonation of, 331–332, 334,
      338, 442
    son's murder and, 347–348
  Nimai's drowning and, 367–368,
    445
  in notes, 422–423, 430, 438, 440,
    441, 443
Bryant, Jack, 168–169
  current status, 396
  Nimai's drowning and, 367–368,
    445
  in notes, 430, 438, 440, 441,
    443
  son's break with Krishnas and,
    307, 309, 330–331, 339

Bryant, Jane Rangely (Jamuna),
  171–173, 175, 223–226
  current status, 397
  Kirtanananda and, 271–273, 438
    initiation by, 272–273, 292, 309,
      313
  new husband of, 331
  in New Vrindaban nursery,
    274–275
  Nimai's drowning, 367–368
  refusal to leave New Vrindaban,
    302–309
    kidnapped children and,
      306–309, 441
  treatment by husband, 172–173,
    272–273, 292, 294, 430
Bryant, Nimai, 302, 331
  drowning of, 367–368
  kidnapping of, 306–309, 441
Bryant, Sarva Dharma, 292, 302,
  331, 396
  kidnapping of, 306–309
Bryant, Steve (Sulocana), 167–177,
  291–294
  arrest of, 335, 443
    Gold and, 338
    Krishnas' examination of
      evidence, 335–337, 443
    trial, 338–339, 443
  background of, 168–170, 422–423
  Berry and, 343–344, 345–346
  as brahmachari, 167
  desire to leave New Vrindaban,
    302–309, 440, 441
    kidnapping of children and,
      306–309, 441
  Kirtanananda and, 309–310, 440
  right-wing politics and, 305–306,
    441
  desire to marry, 167–168, 171
  Jayatirtha and, 175–177
  jewelry business of, 223–225, 272,
    292, 344, 346, 430
  Kirtanananda and, 291–293,
    302–347, 442
    break between, 313–314
    death penalty and, 319
    debate between, 317–318
    end of campaign against,
      343–344, 347, 443
    exposé of, 313–320, 324–325
    going public and, 318–320, 330,
      331
    Greene and, 318, 319, 331–332,
      333–334
    Jadurani story and, 311–313
    Jamuna and, 310
    Krishna's mission and, 317,
      319, 331
    Prabhupada's letters and,
      313–317, 318–319
    renegade Krishnas and, 318–319

Bryant, Steve (Sulocana) (cont.)
  Shockman's attempted murder
    of, 326–327, 442
    threats against, 331, 335
    Yuvati and, 311–317
  kirtans and, 174
  murder of, 347–348
    attempt to enlist Vassilievich
      in, 344–345, 443
    Greene on, 347–348
    notes on, 444
    Sheldon and, 359–360
    tracking prior to, 331–334,
      338–339, 442, 443, 444
  Prabhupada's death and, 225–226
  wife of, see Bryant, Jane
    Rangely
Burtchell, Derek, 439–440

Caste system, 431
Catholicism, 60, 100
Chaitanya Charitamrita, 90
Chaitanya Mahaprabhu, Lord, 84,
  90, 113, 135, 150, 216
  described, 51, 83
  notes on, 409–410, 424
Chakradara, see St. Denis, Chuck
Chandler, Achamma, 394
Chant and Be Happy, 412
Cheryl, 270, 437
Chief Head, 200–202, 427
Child abuse, 35–36, 439–440
Child molestation, 371–376, 437,
  445–446
Christianity, 76
Cleaver, Janet, 17, 43
  murder of St. Denis and, 22, 28
Cleaver, Kurt, 17, 293–294
  murder of St. Denis and, 22–23, 28
Clements, Buddy, 133–135
Cleveland State University, 281
Cocaine, 4, 16, 279, 281
Columbia University, 49, 51, 56
Conger, Gail, 404, 412, 437, 438,
  439, 440
Costello, Bill (Bramaha), 433, 434
Cox, Harvey, 91
Crane, Charles E., 260–261, 434
Cults, 141–142, 383
Cunningham, Bob, 356–357
  recovery of New Vrindaban
    bodies, 362–367

Dalldorf, Hartwig Heinrich, 259
Darpada, 260–261
Darshan, 270
Daruka, see Reid, Dan
"Dasher," 72–76, 407
Davan, Vern, 433, 434
Davis, Joe, 206–215, 279
  death of, 397
  notes on, 428–429

Dawson, Eddie "Fast Fingers,"
  239–241, 433
Deadwyler, William, see Ravindra
  Svarupa
DeFrancisco, Frederick, 375–376,
  446
  current status, 400
Delhi, India, 88–89
Deprogrammers, 138–146
  Bhagavan on, 147
  notes on, 418
Devin, 270, 436–437
Dezio, Dick, 375–376, 445
Dharmatma (Dennis Gorrick), 281,
  373
  current status, 397
  Cynthia and, 298–299, 300–301
  described, 189–190, 425
  Kirtanananda and, 189–190
  Pittsburgh Airport scam and,
    185–196
  sports paraphernalia scam, 286
  treatment of women, 188–190,
    425, 440
  Wilson and, 283–288, 425, 440
Dickmeyer, Elizabeth Reuter, 8,
  154
Dienstel, Gary, 138–146
  notes on, 418
"Dreaded Acharya Disease" (DAD),
  323
Drescher, Thomas (Tirtha), 124,
  384
  arson and, 36–38
  background of, 15
  child abuse by, 35–36
  as commune enforcer, 15, 32,
    136–138
  current status, 395
  feud with St. Denis, 12, 25–38
  leaves commune, 38
  murder of Bryant, 347
    accusations about, 351–353
    arrest for, 353–356, 444
    plan for, told to Ferry and
      Gorby, 352–353, 442–443
    tracking prior to, 331–334,
      338–339, 353, 355, 442,
      443, 444
  murder of St. Denis, 14–16, 19–21
    accusations about, 32, 33
    admissions of, 27–28, 38–39,
      334, 352–353, 361
    conviction for, 361
    in notes, 401–403, 404
    state police charge of, 355–356
    trial for, 360–361, 445
  ordained as swami, 378, 446
  Pittsburgh airport scam and,
    194–195
  Quaalude factory of, 296–297, 441

Drescher, Thomas (Tirtha) (*cont.*)
  returns to commune, 39
  Tsacrios and, *see* Tsacrios, Dr.
    Nick, Drescher and
Drug dealing, 294–297, 441
  as way of uniting with God,
    297–298
Drug Enforcement Administration
  (DEA), 297
Drugs, 4, 5, 122
  ban on, 5
  Bryant and, 335
  culture of, 79
  Hebel and, 280–281
  kirtans and, 174–177, 179–182
  St. Denis and, 9–10
  Tsacrios and, 24
Drug smuggling, 206–215, 279
  Advaita and, 294–296, 441
  Bovan and, 211–214
  Davis and, 206–215
  end of, 214–215
  Kulik and, 209–215
    kidnapping of, 212–213, 429
  money laundering and, 210–211
  notes on, 428–429
  organized crime and, 211
  Richard and, 206–210, 214–215
  theft from, 210–211
Drutaka, 132–133

East Village Other, The, 52
East Village Theater, 68
Easy Journey to Other Planets
  (Prabhupada), 60, 86, 406
Ehrlichman, William, *see* Bhagavan
"Elaine," 239, 433
Elmore, Charles, 133–135, 416
Elson, Sam, 335
E.M.I. Recording Studios, 106
"Ending the Fratricidal War," 322
"Expecting the Barbarians," 379

Fawley, Howard, 361
  arson and, 36–37, 38
  in notes, 401, 402, 403, 404, 445
Federal Bureau of Investigation
  (FBI), 251, 334, 356, 434,
    442
  Gorby explosion and, 358
Ferry, Paul, 352, 361
  in notes, 403, 404
Fiji, 227, 229–230, 397
Fiori, Jerry Peter, 429
Fischer, Barry, 426
Fischer, Lawrence, 154
Fischer Mansion, 154
Food for Life, 428
Forbes, Steve, *see* Nistrigunya
Ford, Alfred Brush, 8, 154
Ford, Henry, 8, 154
Fort Ord, plan to rob, 262, 434–435

Gandhi, Mohandas, K., 82, 83, 135
Gangamaya, 359–360
Gardner, Larry, *see* Sri Galima
Gargamuni, 157, 419
Gaudiya Math, 216
GBC, *see* Governing Body
  Commission
Genghis Khan, 253
Gere, Debra (Ambudrara), 3–4,
  17–18
  current status, 393
  as "fringie," 5–6
  inheritance of, 6–7, 11, 14
  murder of St. Denis and, 22–43
    attack on Bleudeu and, 43
    possible reasons for, 34–36
    reaction to, 39
    trial testimony, 360–361
  in notes, 401, 402, 404, 440
  Tsacrios and, 25, 38–39, 42–43
German temple, 152–155, 259, 278
Ginsberg, Allen, 58–59, 406
  in San Francisco, 66, 68
Gold, David, 338, 344
  in notes, 443
Golfer, 190–191, 193, 195
Gorby, Randall, 7
  background of, 332–333
  Bryant's murder and, 353–354,
    361, 442–443
  current status, 399–400
  Drescher's arrest and, 353–354,
    444
  gas explosion in home of,
    357–358, 444–445
  tracking Bryant, 333–334, 353,
    442
Gorrick, Dennis, *see* Dharmatma
Gottfried, Gregory Martin, *see*
  Guru Kripa
Govardhan, 198–200
Governing Body Commission
  (GBC), 151–152, 256
  cooperation, 152
  as a disaster, 156, 158, 316–317
  formation of, 151, 420
  Hansadutta and, 265–266
    excommunication of, 268
  homosexuality and, 157
  Jayatirtha and, 178, 179–180
    excommunication of, 179–180,
      432
  Kirtanananda and, 151, 157,
    216–217, 421
  Prabhupada's death and, 216–218
    aftermath of, 226–229
  Ravindra's reform movement and,
    see Hare Krishnas, reform
      movement in
  revolution against, 311–312
  Tamal Krishna and, 432
  war against maya and, 152

Govinda das, 113–115, 413
Govinda's Restaurants, 210, 211, 296, 360
Grant, Michael, *see* Mukunda
Grant, Robert, *see* Ramesvara
Grateful Dead, 66
"Greene, Jerome," 167–168, 171–172, 223, 224
  Bryant's exposé and, 318, 331–332, 333–334
  current status, 397
  impersonation of, 331–332, 333–334, 338, 442
  Jayatirtha and, 176–177
  murder of Bryant and, 347–348
  in notes, 422, 423, 440, 441, 442, 443
  Prabhupada's death, 225
"Greene, Marianne," 171, 172, 223, 224, 348, 397
  in notes, 422
  Prabhupada's death and, 225
Grihasthas, 86
Grimm, Tom, 389
"Guru Business, The," 318, 319, 330, 335
  in notes, 404, 412, 437, 441
"Guru, Guru, on the Wall," 240–241
  in the Philippines, 244, 433
Guru Kripa (Gregory Martin Gottfried), 196–205
  Chief Head and, 200–202
  current status, 397
  Prabhupada and, 201–205, 428
  scams of, in Tokyo, 198–200, 204, 427–428
Guru kula, 285, 325, 326, 372–376, 384, 446

Haight Ashbury Free Medical Clinic, 268
Hair, 106
Halbritter, Judge Robert, 361
Ham, Keith, *see* Kirtanananda Swami Bhaktipada
Ham, Reverend, 51, 59–60
Hansadutta (Hans Kary), 52–56, 231–247, 322
  alcohol and drugs, 234, 243–244, 252, 262, 265, 266, 268, 433
  alias of, 250
  arrests of, 246–247, 267–268
  as aspiring rock star, 239–242, 433
  in the Philippines, 243, 244–245, 433
  background of, 53–54
  contempt for everything, 265
  current status, 395
  depression of, 242–243
  desire to be new acharya, 217

  devotees of, 231–234, 242, 244–245, 246–247, 252–253, 265, 268
  excommunication of, 268, 435
  expulsion from Berkeley temple, 268, 435
  Ford Ord payroll and, 262, 434–435
  in Germany, 152–155, 421
  guns and, 251–255, 258–264, 267, 434–435
  Jiva and, 234–236, 262, 263, 264–265, 432–433
  Kirtanananda and, 56, 60–61, 112, 265, 268, 435
  mental breakdowns of, 245–247, 266–268, 433, 435
  in Montreal, 64–65
  in notes, 405, 406, 408, 430
  Prabhupada and, 52–53, 55, 61–62
  raising money and, 78, 152–154, 251
  Ramesvara and, 241, 242, 263–264
  as rtvik, 226–229
    return from Mayapur, 231–234, 432
  sankirtans and, 62–63, 77–78, 421
  as secretary for God, 234
  temple-hopping trip of, 243–247, 433
  theft from Benedict and, 258
  women and, 233–236, 238–239, 246, 265, 433
Hare, 51, 174
Hare Krishnas, xiii–xvi, 392
  arranged marriages of, 124, 149–150, 159, 187, 343, 371, 418–419
  Beatles and, 104–111
  demanding practices of, 5–6, 55–56
  deprogramming, 138–146, 147
  devotees, 8, 54–65, 152
    dress of, 95, 96
    initiation of, 61–62, 113–114, 146–147, 218, 323, 401
    Kirtanananda's initiation of, 272–273, 292, 309, 313
    loss of, 179, 206, 233–234, 280, 429–430
    number of, 418
    purity of, 148
    stealing, 158, 227, 324
  drug-induced kirtans, 174–177, 179–182
  early days of movement, 47–64
  excommunication from, 179–180, 268, 297
  expansion of movement, 63–65, 113
  fringies, 5–6, 17, 293–294, 303, 440

Hare Krishnas (*cont.*)
guns and, 16, 136–138, 251–255,
 258–264, 385, 387, 434–435
mantra of, 6, 50, 51–52, 58, 61,
 68, 69
 Beatles recording of, 106–107
puga and, 227–229, 323
reform movement in, 321–325,
 379–383
 Bhagavan and, 322, 381–382
 Bhavananda and, 381
 fight against, 380
 Kirtanananda and, 322, 324–325,
 379–380, 382–383
 Ramesvara and, 322, 380–381
renegades with Bryant, 318–319
sankirtans of, *see* Sankirtans
sannyasi, *see* Sannyasi
scams of, 31–32, 185–205, 425–428
 in Germany, 152–155, 421
 in Japan, 196–200, 204, 250,
 427, 428
 justification for, 121–122, 155,
 201, 207–208
 at Pittsburgh Airport, 185–196,
 425
 record selling, 237–238, 242,
 246
 trademark violation, 286, 384,
 446
 Wilson and, 285–287
statues of deities, 170, 203, 257
status competition, 154
theft by, 125–127, 198–201,
 256–260, 324, 415
Towaco, New Jersey, meetings of,
 321–325
"us against them" mentality,
 146–148
women and, 157, 173
Hare Krishna and the Counterculture
 (Judah), 418, 431
Hare Krishna Explosion, The
 (Hayagriva), 270, 405, 406,
 407, 408, 409, 412, 413, 414
Hare Krishna in America (Rochford),
 427, 430
Harikesha, 382
 as rtvik, 382
Harrison, George, 78–80, 104–109,
 177, 396
 notes on, 408, 412–413
Harrison, Patti, 78–80
Hart, Denise, 386
Harvard University, 91, 95
Hatha yoga, 230
Hayagriva, *see* Wheeler, Howard
Hebel, Cynthia (Chitta), 278–279,
 295–296, 374
 current status, 399
 drugs and, 280, 281
 husband's arrest and, 298, 299

 in notes, 425, 440
 rape of, 299–301, 441
 on sankirtan team, 298–299
Hebel, Scott:
 homosexual molestation of,
 372–375
 at New Vrindaban nursery,
 274–275, 281
Hebel, Steven (Swarup), 273–274,
 293–294, 374
 background of, 275–276
 current status, 399
 Cynthia and, 278–281, 295–296
 drug dealing and, 295–298, 441
 arrest for, 298
 Drescher and, 296–297
 drug use and, 279–281
 fascination with death, 276
 Jadurani beating and, 312–313
 Krishna Consciousness and, 277
 marriage of, 278–279
 New Vrindaban nursery and,
 273–275
 in notes, 401, 402, 405, 406, 407,
 412, 428–429, 436, 437,
 438, 440, 441, 445–446
 Ramesvara and, 280
Hebel, Susan O'Neal (Kanka), 312
 background of, 277–278
 current status, 399
 marriage of, 278–279
 at New Vrindaban, 279, 281
 escape from, 373
 homosexual molestation of
 child, 372–375, 445–446
 in notes, 401, 425, 437, 440, 441
 Tina and, 374–375
Heffron vs. *ISKCON*, 427
Hell's Angels, 67
Herskowitz, Linda S., 417
Herzog, Thomas, *see* Tamal Krishna
Hewlett, Norman, 402, 425, 440
Hill, Joe, 329
Hillyard, Roger, 67
Himavati (Helena Kary), 53–54,
 61–62
 divorce of, 230
Hinduism, 47–52, 83, 332
 fundamentalist, 51, 101, 135
 impersonalist, 96
 notes on, 406, 409–411
Hippies, 52, 53, 55, 329
 commune for, 102–103, 117–118
 notes on, 407
 in San Francisco, 66–68, 72–80
Homosexuality:
 Bhavananda and, 381, 447
 Ham and Wheeler and, 97,
 269–270, 412, 413, 436–437
 molestation of children, 372–376,
 437, 445–446
 sannyasis and, 157, 419–420

Hornick, Dr. Edward, 58–59
Hummel, Joe, 335, 336
  evidence against Bryant and, 336
  recovery of New Vrindaban
    bodies, 366

Immel, James, *see* Jayatirtha
India, 77, 81–91, 223
  Beatles in, 80, 104, 105, 109
  described, 88–91
Indian American Forum, 394
India Tribune, 394
Inland Mutual Insurance Company,
    38
Internal Revenue Service (IRS),
    251, 434
International Society for Krishna
    Consciousness (ISKCON),
    10, 141–142, 161, 170, 229,
    311, 343
  annual meeting of, 150–152,
    179–180, 206, 380–383
  divisions of, 8, 151, 226–230,
    430–432
  drug money for, 210
  Governing Body Commission, *see*
    Governing Body Commis-
    sion (GBC)
  Hansadutta's guns, 264
  Hebel, Steven (Swarup) and, 278,
    279
  income from sale of books and
    magazines, 426–427
  notes on, 409, 418, 419, 429–430
  reform of, 321–325, 379–383, 396
  women and, 419–420
ISKCON World Review, 359, 395
Islam, 51, 83, 409–410

Jadurani (Judy Koslofsky), 311–313,
    315, 320
  current status, 399
  notes on, 441
Jagadisha Goswami, 446
Jaladuta, 87, 225
Jamuna, *see* Bryant, Jane Rangely
Janaki, 64, 66, 103–104
Japa-mala beads, 61
Japan, 196–200, 204, 250
Jayadeva, 35, 404
Jayatirtha (James Immel)
    (Tirthapada), 174–184, 256,
    317
  drug-induced kirtans of, 176–177
  excommunication of, 179–180, 432
  GBC and, 178, 179–180
  murder of, 183–184
  murder of Nataipada and,
    182–183
  notes on, 423–424
  sexual escapades of, 177–179
Jefferson Airplane, 66

Jiva (James Patrick Underwood),
    262, 263
  death of, 264–265, 435
  Hansadutta and, 234–236, 262,
    263, 264–265, 432–433
  record scam and, 237–238, 246
  women and, 234–236, 237–238
Jnana yoga, 50
John Birch Society, 305–306
"Jonestown in Moundsville," 330,
    334, 335
Joplin, Janis, 66
Joy, Spencer Lynn, 255, 434
Judah, Dr. J. Stillson, 418, 431

Kali-yuga, age of, 252
Kanka, *see* Hebel, Susan O'Neal
Kanthi beads, 4
Karma, 60–61, 406
  justification of theft and, 123
  meat-eating and, 169
Karma yoga, 50
Karmi names, 30
Karmis, 252–253
Kary, Hans, *see* Hansadutta
Kary, Helena, *see* Himavati
Kaufmann, Peter, 259
Kennedy, John F., 53
Kent State University, 354
Kettershof Castle, 154
Kirkland, Charlie, 422
Kirkland, Susan (Sanatani), 422,
    425, 427, 440
Kirtanananda Swami Bhaktipada
    (Keith Ham):
  apocalyptic predictions of, 385,
    394–395
  arson and, 36–37, 404
  attempted murder of, 326–327, 442
  in Bellevue Hospital, 57–60, 405
  as "Black Keith," 96–97
  Bryant and, *see* Bryant, Steve,
    Kirtanananda and
  current status, 393–395
  devotees of, 7, 121–123, 136,
    414–415
  Dharmatma and, 189–190
  division of ISKCON and, 8
  Drescher and, 377–378, 446–447
  dress code and, 95, 96
  expulsion from ISKCON, 382–383
  expulsion from movement, 96–98,
    410–411
  father of, 51, 59–60
  Hansadutta and, 56, 60–61, 112,
    265, 268, 435
  homosexuality of, 97, 412,
    413–414, 436–437
  Kanka and, 371–373, 374–375
  as Mayavadi, 96
  money and, 7, 294–295, 377, 389,
    441

Kirtanananda Swami Bhaktipada
    (Keith Ham) *(cont.)*
  in Montreal, 64–65, 406
  New Vrindaban and, *see* New
      Vrindaban
  on Nimai's drowning, 368
  omission from GBC, 151, 157,
      216–217, 421
  Palace of Gold and, 8, 10–11, 14
  Prabhupada and, 415–416
    anointment as first American
        sannyasi by, 90, 96
    break between, 90–91, 95–99,
        315–316, 410–412
    comparison between, 112–113
    as cook for, 56
    as favorite disciple, 58, 77, 81
    GBC and, 151, 157, 216–217,
        316–317
    in India, 77, 81–91
    life story of, 81–88, 408–409
    at New Vrindaban, 120–122,
        414
    reconciliation between, 112–115,
        413
    stroke of, 68–72
    as successor to, 91, 157, 218
  on publicity, 232–233
  Ramesvara and, 157
  Ravindra and, 125–127, 415–416
    reform movement of, 322,
        324–325, 379–380, 382–383
  recovery of New Vrindaban
      bodies and, 363–367
  with Rose in West Virginia,
      100–103, 116–117
  as rtvik, 218, 227, 229
  St. Denis and, 13–15, 402
  Samba and, 270, 436–437
  sankirtan and, 62–63
  search for sannyasi, 48–52
  Sheldon and, 360
  split in New York temple over,
      95–98
  theft and, 125–127
  as true acharya, 324
  Wheeler and, *see* Wheeler,
      Howard, Kirtanananda
      and
  women and, 270–271, 371–372,
      437–438, 440
    Jamuna and, 271–273, 292,
        303–314, 438
Knight, Bill, 353
Koslofsky, Judy, *see* Jadurani
Krishna, 4, 8, 67–68
  acts done in service of, 122,
      126–127
  Bhagavad-Gita and, 50
    notes on, 407
  Prabhupada explaining, 50–51,
      109

  statues of, 170, 174, 203, 257
Krishna Consciousness, 7–8, 60, 64,
      66, 68, 146, 147, 163, 242,
      416
  Beatles and, 103–111
  goal of, 65, 297–298
  notes on, 430–431
  Prabhupada's early life and, 82–87
  three new temples of, 151, 203
  in Vrindaban, 89–90
  women and, 172–173
Krishna das (Rinnian Rangely), 302
  renaming of, 273
Kshatriya, 431
KSNA, 236–237, 239
Kuladri (Arthur Villa), 34, 38
  attempted murder of Kirtanananda
      and, 326–327, 329–330,
      441, 442
  Bryant and, 303, 317–319, 441,
      442
  current status, 395
  described, 356
  missing boys and, 34
  in notes, 403, 404
  special-deputies program and, 337
  urged to take sannyasa, 329, 442
  on Westfall, 31
Kulik, Alexander, 209–215
  kidnapping of, 211–213
  notes on, 429

Lakshmi, 123, 203–204
Leary, Timothy, 32–33, 52, 176
Ledger's Liquor Store, 267
Lees, James B., 402
Lennon, John, 80, 105, 107–110,
      412
Lightner, Robert, 337, 397
Loansharking, 388
Los Angeles Times, 429, 441, 444
LSD, 9, 67, 79
  -induced kirtans, 174–176, 179–182

McAdams, Don:
  Bryant and, 293–294
  on devotees, 415
  in notes, 404, 412, 437, 438, 440
McCartney, Linda, 106
McCartney, Paul, 80, 105, 106, 412
Machiavelli, 154
McWilliams, Robert, 361
Mahara, *see* St. John, Mary
Maharishi, 53, 55
  Beatles and, 80, 105, 109
Mangal-aratik, 6, 39
Mantra, 6, 50, 51–52, 58, 61, 68, 69
"Mantra Rock Dance," 66–68
Marijuana, 79
  cultivating, 12–13, 296
  smuggling, 10–11
Marone, Anthony, Jr., 429

Marshall County Health Department, 439
Marshall County Jail, 327, 328, 338, 356
  Bryant in protective custody in, 319–320, 321, 325, 442
  Shockman in, 327
Massage, 69, 70, 71, 150, 203
Matusow, Yuvati, 311, 441
  Bryant's murder and, 349–353
  current status, 399
  on Kirtanananda, 437
  in notes, 412, 423, 437, 441, 443–444
  Prabhupada's letters, 315–317
  on remaining in the movement, 437
  stories told by, 313
Maya, 135, 150, 266–267, 272
  attack by, 135, 152
  causes of, 167, 181, 245–246
  Kirtanananda and, 114
  war against, 146, 152
Mayapur, India, 135, 149–150, 201, 202–205
  ISKCON's annual meeting in, 150–152, 179–180, 206, 380–383
  new temple in, 151, 203, 226, 396
Mayavadi, 96
Meyers, Thomas (Taru), 281–282, 440
Molestation of children, homosexual, 372–376
"Monkey on a stick," 14, 348
Morarji, Mrs. Sumati, 86–87
Morgan, John, 171, 173
  in notes, 423–424
Morrison, Van, 240
Mott Street Gang, 47–52, 112, 405
Moundsville, West Virginia, 330
Mount Kailasa farm, 242, 251–255
  arsenal at, 252–254, 258–260
  notes on, 435
  shooting "accident" at, 254–255, 434
  theft to finance, 257–260
Mukunda (Michael Grant), 56
  Beatles and, 103, 108, 111
  current status, 395–396
  in notes, 405, 407, 424
  in San Francisco, 64, 66–68
Munson, Judge Howard G., 426
Murphy, Philip, 414, 421–422, 430

Naranayana, see Zakheim, Nathan
Narendra, see McAdams, Don
Nataipada, 180–183
Nathaji, 360
Navaniticara (John Tierney), 180
  murder of Jayatirtha, 183–184
Nepal, 180–183

Neuman, Michael, 363
New Vrindaban, 3–4, 120–124, 268–314
  as armed camp, 16, 136–138, 385, 387
  attack on, 128–135, 416–417
    reaction to, 135–136
  building of, 120–122, 126
  children at, 273–275, 281, 285, 287, 325–326, 384, 439–440
    homosexual molestation of, 371–376, 437, 445–446
  commune enforcer, 15, 32, 136–138
  current changes at, 394–395, 396
  defense force of, 308
  described, 7–8, 413, 438–439
  drug dealing and, 296–298
  FBI raid on, 376–377
  first winter at, 7, 120
  health problems at, 438–439
  naming of, 7
  nursery at, 273–275, 281, 287, 438, 439
  Palace of Gold, see Palace of Gold
  Prabhupada at, 120–122, 414
  purchase of land for, 7, 100–103, 116–117, 332
  raising money for, 157, 185–196
  recovery of bodies buried in, 362–367, 445
  recruiting for, 112, 120, 136
  resort complex at, 303
  rose garden at, 400
  security guards at, 320–321
  September 1985 meeting at, 320–321, 442
  smuggling drugs at, 10–11
New York, 278
New York Times, 434
New York University, 47, 49
Nice But Dead, 242
  in the Philippines, 244
Nistrigunya (Steve Forbes):
  Bryant's murder and, 350–351
  last meeting with Bryant, 346–347
  Yuvati and, 350–351
Northeastern University, 74

Ohio State University, 120, 296
Ohio Valley Medical Center, 327, 358
Ono, Yoko, 107–110, 412
Orozco, Leroy, 352–353

Palace of Gold, 217, 229, 275, 312, 371
  brick marathon for, 325–326
  described, 271, 291
  financing of, 8, 10–11, 14
  origin of, 7–8
  peacock windows of, 293

Parry, Walt, 136–138, 294
  body in New Vrindaban and, 363, 415, 445
  current status, 396
  on Kirtanananda and Samba, 436–437
  in notes, 417, 425, 428, 436, 441
Peace Kirshnas, 180–184, 423–424
Peace on Earth Crafts Store, 180
Philadelphia Inquirer, 417, 444, 445, 446
Piatt, Ronald, 354
Pittsburgh International Airport, 185–196
Pittsburgh Post Gazette, 444
Prabhupada, A. C. Bhaktivedanta Swami, 7–8, 32, 47–91
  abandoned family of, 83, 85
  arrival in New York, 87
  background of, 81–88, 408–409
  Beatles and, 108–111
  death of, 216–219, 429
    aftermath of, 225–230, 430–432
  drug money to, 215
  expansion of movement and, 63–64
  as fundamentalist, 51, 101, 135
  GBC and, 151–152, 157, 158, 420–421
  godbrother of, 265–266, 280, 424
  guru of, 82, 83, 216
  Guru Kripa and, 201–205, 428
  Hansadutta and, 52–53, 55, 61–62
  heart attack, 68–72, 77, 113, 407
  initiation ceremony of, 61–62, 114
  Kirtanananda and, *see* Kirtanananda, Prabhupada and
  on Krishna, 50–51, 109
  legacy of, 216–219
  letters from, 410–411, 416
    Bryant and, 313–317, 318
  misunderstanding of the Western mind, 91, 149–150
  Mott Street Gang and, 47–52
  newspapers on, 52, 66
  New Vrindaban and, 120–122, 414
    attack on, 135–136
  New York temple and, 158–163, 422
  notes on, 405, 412–413
  original names of, 82
  ostentatious demonstrations and, 175
  problems in America, 149–150, 155–163, 415–416, 418–420, 421–422
  Ramesvara and, 156–158, 421–422
  return to India, 78, 81–91
  in San Francisco, 66–68, 113–115
  successors to, 91, 156, 216–218, 265–266
  on women, 173, 407–408, 418–419

Pradyumna, 431
Prasadam Distributing International (PDI), 210–211, 429
Preston, Billy, 106
Prithu (Peter Brinkmann), 359–360
Puga, 227–229, 323
Pugliese, Michael Ralph, 234, 243–245, 259, 398
  aliases of, 250
  arrest of, 249–250
  in notes, 433, 434
Pusta Krsna, 316
"Pyramid Tapes, The," 422, 430

Quaalude factory, 296–297, 441

Radha, 180
  statues of, 170, 174, 203, 257
Radheya, 34, 404
Raharani, 85
Rama, 51
Ramesvara (Robert Grant), 311–312, 317, 430
  Bryant and, 315, 317
  current status, 396
  described, 157, 380
  desire to be new acharya, 217
  Hansadutta and, 241, 242, 263–264
  Hebel and, 280
  ousted as guru, 380–381, 447
  Prabhupada and, 156–158, 421–422
  raising money and, 188
  Ravindra's reform movement and, 322, 380–381
  as rtvik, 226–229
Rangely, Rinnian, *see* Krishna das
Rathayatra, 114
Ravindra Svarupa (William Deadwyler):
  current status, 396
  on ISKCON gurus, 432
  on Jayatirtha, 423–424
  in notes, 411, 413, 414, 422, 427, 436, 442
  on Prabhupada, 428
  reform movement of, 321–325, 379–383, 430, 447
  on sannyasis, 419, 420
  theft from temple of, 125–127, 415
Reid, Brenda, 3, 4, 5, 21
  alleged rape of, 3, 4, 13–14, 402
Reid, Dan (Daruka), 293–294
  arson and, 36–37, 38, 404
  current status, 393
  death of son, 34–35
  leaves commune, 38
  meeting with Kirtanananda, 13–14
  murder of St. Denis and, 13–21, 334, 401, 402, 403
  accusations about, 34, 35–36

Reid, Dan (Daruka) (*cont.*)
  attempted police deals over, 361
  guilty plea of, 362
  treatment of wife, 4
Resco, Raymond, 429
Reuther, Walter, 8, 154
Reynolds Memorial Hospital, 25, 439–440
Richard, Roy Christopher, 206–210, 214–215, 279
  current status, 397
  notes on, 428–429
Richardson, Dennis Lee, 261
Rochford, E. Burke, 427, 430
Rohini, 34, 404
Rolling Stone, 242, 403
Rolling Stones, 123
Rose, Richard, 338
  attack on home of, 118–120, 413
  current status of, 396
  disaffection with Krishnas, 116–117
  land lease form, 102–103, 116–117
  meets with Ham and Wheeler, 100–103, 412
  son of, 118–119
Rousseau, Jean-Jacques, 154
Rtviks:
  conflict among, 226–229
  Jadurani and, 311–312
  naming of, 218
  notes on, 431–432

Sacramento Bee, 428, 429, 434
Sahajayas, 424
St. Denis, Chrislyn, 9–11
St. Denis, Chuck (Chakradara):
  accusation of rape against, 3, 4, 13–14, 402
  background of, 8–11, 401
  as drug dealer, 10–11, 32, 296
  feud with Drescher, 12, 25–28
  as "fringie," 5–7
  Gere's inheritance and, 6–7, 11, 14
  as Krishna devotee, 9–10
  murder of, *see* Drescher, murder of St. Denis
  in notes, 401–403, 404, 445
  recovery of body, 363
St. Denis, Michael, 9, 401
St. John, Mary (Mahara), 191, 437
  beating of, 281–282, 440
  on Dharmatma, 425
Samadhi, 150, 180
Samba (Devin), 270
  notes on, 436–437
Sanatani, *see* Kirkland, Susan
Sanchez, Joe, 248–251, 398
  arrest of Richardson, 261
  Hansadutta's machine gun and, 263

  in notes, 427, 433, 434, 435
  picture of, 256
  theft from Benedict and, 256–261
  Westfall and, 250–251
"Sandy," 236–238, 433
  Hansadutta and, 238–239, 246
  record scam and, 237–238
San Francisco Chronicle, 66, 234, 432
San Francisco Examiner, 444, 445
San Francisco Oracle, 100, 118
San Jose Mercury News, 441
Sankirtans, 56, 83, 322
  Berkeley women's team, 236–239
  Hansadutta and, 77–78
  Kirtanananda and, 62–63
  legal attacks and, 426–427
  money from, 377, 427
  in New Orleans, 299–301
  New Vrindaban women's team, 38, 185–196, 281, 285–287, 298–301
  as the "pick," 285
  as a scam, 31–32, 204, 374, 376–377
Sannyasi, 47–48, 86
  first American, 90, 96
  on the GBC, 151, 157
  Hansadutta and, 230, 238–239
  homosexuality of, 157, 419
  Jiva and, 235, 238
  Kuladri and, 329
Satsvarupa, 217–218
  Ravindra's reform movement and, 379–380
  as rtvik, 218
Schenker, Judith, 386–391
Schenker, Todd, 16, 37, 138, 384–385, 417
  suspected murder of, 385–392, 395, 447
Scindia Steamship Company, 86
Scott Motel, 333–334
Sergeant Pepper's Lonely Hearts Club Band, 78
"Serving Srila Prabhupada's Will," 322
Seward, Ralph, 331
Sex-to-drugs-to-God philosophy, 180
Sgt. Pepper's Guns, 260
Shade, Don, 355–357
Shady Side Academy, 356
Shastri, Lal Bahadur, 86
Sheffy, Wally, 378
Sheldon, Terry (Tapahpunja), 332
  disappearance of, 355
  Drescher's arrest and, 354–355
  Kuladri and, 329–330, 442
  on the run, 359–360, 399, 445
Shockman, Michael (Triyogi), 326–328, 330, 442
Sinsemilla, 12, 296

Sixties movements, 32–33, 278, 418
Smith, Bruce, 356–357, 377
Smith, Kelly (Kashava), 424
Sofsky, Emile, *see* Advaita
Sopher, Dr. Irwin, 388–389
Spirit of Liberty Marketing, 180
Sridhara Goswami, 265–266, 280
  on Jayatirtha, 424
Sri Galima, 372, 375–376
  current status, 400
Srila Prabhupada-lilamrta
  (Satsvarupa), 379, 405, 407,
  408, 409, 412, 420
Srimad-Bhagavatam, 84, 85, 86, 89,
  128, 152
Stanley, Augustus Owsley, 67
Starr, Ringo, 80, 105
Sterns, Frank, 146–148, 418
Sudhir Goswami, 414, 421–422
Sullivan's Gunshop, 37
Sulocana, *see* Bryant, Steve
Swarup, *see* Hebel, Steven
Syamakunda, 295
Syamasundara, 104–108
Syracuse University, 24

Tamal Krishna (Thomas Herzog), 317
  desire to be new acharya,
    217–218, 432
  Fiji and, 227, 229–230, 397
  Ravindra's reform movement and,
    379, 381
  as rtvik, 218, 226–227
  stealing devotees, 157–158, 227
  suspension of, 265–266, 432
Tantrics, 424
Tapahpunja, *see* Sheldon, Terry
Taru, 281–282, 440
Tarun Krishna, 405, 411–412
Temple of Understanding, 291
Temple University, 125, 322
Tierney, John (Navaniticara), 180
  murder of Jayatirtha, 183–184
Tilaka, 57
Time, 78
Tippin, Paul "The Stump," 352
Tirtha, *see* Drescher, Thomas
Tirthapada, 180–182
  murder of, 183–184
  notes on, 423–424
Tittenhurst, 107–111
Tolavan, 36, 124, 281, 293, 303
Toyota, Natasha, 159–162, 422
  current status, 396
Trademark-violations case, 286–287,
  384, 446
"Travels and Preachings of His
  Divine Grace, Hansadutta
  Swami, The," 244
Trident Studios, 106
Triyogi (Michael Shockman), 326,
  327–328, 330, 442

Tsacrios, Dr. Nick, 13
  current status, 393
  described, 24
  Drescher and, 23–28
    admission of murder by, 27–28,
      38–39, 40–42
    fear of, 41–44
    threat to Tsacrios by, 43
    trial, 361
  Gere and, 25, 38–39, 42–43
  in notes, 401, 402, 403, 404–405,
    440
Tulane University, 24
Tulare County Children's Protective
  Services, 374

Umapati (Wally Sheffy), 378
"Under My Order—Reflections on
  the Guru in ISKCON,"
  322
Underwood, James Patrick, *see* Jiva
United Press International (UPI),
  443, 444, 445, 446
United States Attorney for the
  Northern District of West
  Virginia, 356–357, 384
University of Buffalo, 226
University of Florida, 24
University of Pittsburgh, 356

Vaishya, 431
Van Meter, Ben, 67
Varnashrama, 431
Vassilievich, Vladimir (Vipra):
  attempt at enlisting, to murder
    Bryant, 344–345, 443
  current status, 398
  as Mount Kailasa gunsmith,
    253–255
  in notes, 433, 434–435
  return of stolen property, 260
  special gun for Hansadutta,
    262–264, 434–435
    accepting blame, 264
Vedic, 360
  social system, 431
Villa, Arthur, *see* Kuladri
Villaverde, Dr. Manuel, 440
Vipra, *see* Vassilievich, Vladimir
Vrindaban, India, 77, 85–86
  described, 90
  new temple in, 151, 216

Walker, Danny, 371–372, 445–446
Walker, Sylvia, 363, 371
Walters, Ronald Roy (Darpada),
  260–261
Warhol, Andy, 381
Warlocks, 136, 417
Weber, Keith, 16, 137, 138,
  384–385, 417
  current status, 395

Westfall, Martha, 39–40, 129–136
Westfall, Sergeant Tom, 29–33, 393
  attack on New Vrindaban and,
    129–135, 416–417
    Clements and Ellmore and,
      133–135
    confusion over, 131–132
    Drutaka on, 132–133
    new devotees and, 136
  background of, 29–30
  Bordenkircher and, 336–337, 357,
    443
  Bryant and, 336–337
  current status, 395
  FBI raid on New Vrindaban and,
    376–377
  Kirtanananda and, 327
  as "Krishna cop," 30–33
  murder of St. Denis and, 33, 445
    inability to act on, 39–40, 42–44
    promise about, 40, 361
    state police charge of, 355–356
  in notes, 401, 403, 416–417, 425,
    440, 442, 443, 444–446,
    447
  recovery of New Vrindaban
    bodies, 362–367
  Sanchez and, 250–251
  Schenker and, 385–392, 447
  Sri Galima's homosexual abuse of
    children and, 375–376
  Taru and, 282
  testimony to U.S. attorney,
    356–357
West Liberty State College, 30
West Virginia Department of
  Health, 438–439
West Virginia Medical Examiner's
  Office, 388–389
West Virginia State Penitentiary,
  377–378
West Virginia State Police, 23, 29,
  355–356
  in notes, 404–405, 440
Wheeler, Cheryl, 270, 437
Wheeler, Devin (Samba), 270
  notes on, 436–437
Wheeler, Howard (Hayagriva),
  47–52, 56, 123, 338
  current status, 395
  described, 413–414

  on GBC, 151
  Kirtanananda and:
    in Bellevue, 58–59
    comparing Prabhupada with,
      112–113
    expulsion of, free movement,
      98–99, 411–412
    homosexuality, 97, 269–270,
      412, 413, 436–437
    at New Vrindaban, 269–270
    search for a sannyasi, 47–49
    in West Virginia, 99–103,
      116–117, 412, 413–414
  in notes, 405
  as teacher, 112, 120
  wives of, 270, 437
White, Tom, 39, 44
  St. Denis murder case, 362
"Wilson, Sharon," 185–196
  background of, 186–187
  current status, 397
  Dharmatma and, 283–285, 425,
    440
  Pittsburgh Airport scam and,
    190–196
Wolfe, Beatrice, 430
Women:
  in the Berkeley temple, 233–239
  Dharmatma and, 188–190, 283–288,
    425, 440
  Hansadutta and, 233–236, 238–239,
    246, 251, 265
  Kirtanananda and, 270–271,
    371–372, 437–438, 440
  Krishna-conscious, 172–173, 419
  Prabhupada and, 173, 407–408,
    418–419
  sankirtan teams, see Sankirtans
  sannyasis and, 157, 419
WTRF, 366

Younger, Mike, 335
Your Ever Well Wisher, 409,
  429
Yuvati, *see* Matusow, Yuvati

Zakheim, Nathan (Naranayana),
  115
  on homosexuals, 419
  in notes, 405, 411, 412, 413–414,
    422, 427, 436, 437, 441